FROM INQUIRY TO ACADEMIC WRITING

A Practical Guide

SECOND EDITION

Stuart Greene
University of Notre Dame

April Lidinsky
Indiana University South Bend

Bedford/St. Martin's   BOSTON ▪ NEW YORK

For Bedford/St. Martin's

Senior Executive Editor: Stephen A. Scipione
Production Editor: Katherine Caruana
Senior Production Supervisor: Jennifer Peterson
Senior Marketing Manager: Molly Parke
Associate Editor: Shannon Walsh
Editorial Assistant: Alyssa Demirjian
Copyeditor: Linda McLatchie
Indexer: Mary White
Photo Researcher: Kathleen Karcher
Permissions Manager: Kalina Ingham Hintz
Senior Art Director: Anna Palchik
Text Design: Jean Hammond
Cover Design: Marine Miller
Cover Art: Charles Biederman, *#24, Constable*, 1977–1979, painted aluminum,
    41-1/2 × 33-1/8 × 12". Collection of Frederick R. Weisman Art Museum at the
    University of Minnesota, Minneapolis. Biederman Archive, Weisman Art
    Museum, Gift of Charles J. Biederman. L1998.39.168.
Composition: Achorn International, Inc.
Printing and Binding: RR Donnelley and Sons

President: Joan E. Feinberg
Editorial Director: Denise B. Wydra
Editor in Chief: Karen S. Henry
Director of Marketing: Karen R. Soeltz
Director of Production: Susan W. Brown
Associate Director, Editorial Production: Elise S. Kaiser
Managing Editor: Elizabeth M. Schaaf

Library of Congress Control Number: 2011921334

Manufactured in the United States of America.

6   5   4   3   2   1
f   e   d   c   b   a

For information, write: Bedford/St. Martin's, 75 Arlington Street, Boston, MA
02116 (617-399-4000)

ISBN-13: 978-0-312-60140-9

Preface for Instructors

Academic writing is the challenging intellectual price of admission to college. Not only must students learn to write, they also must learn to read — and even to think — in complex new ways. That's where *From Inquiry to Academic Writing: A Practical Guide* comes in. As it acknowledges and explains the challenges of academic writing, it offers a clear, methodical approach to meeting those challenges. Our students, and many others, have told us that the approach demystifies academic thinking, reading, and writing, while helping them see that the rewards of learning such skills carry over to civic and life issues beyond their college years.

More specifically, *From Inquiry to Academic Writing* is a composition rhetoric that introduces students to college-level inquiry, analysis, and argument. It is based on a first-year composition course where we guide students to produce essays that use evidence and sources in increasingly complex ways. In this book as well as our classes, we present academic writing as a collaborative conversation, undertaken in the pursuit of new knowledge. We teach students to see that academic writing is a social act in which they are expected to work responsibly with the ideas of others. At the same time, we encourage students to see themselves as makers of knowledge who use sources to advance arguments about important academic and cultural issues.

▪ How the Book Is Organized

Broadly speaking, the chapters follow a path that begins with academic thinking and proceeds through academic reading and research, integrating academic writing throughout. Nevertheless, the chapters are freestanding enough to be taught in any order that suits your course. What unites them is our constant emphasis on the recursive and overlapping nature of these thinking, reading, and writing skills and the centrality of the writing process. Indeed, we assume students will be writing throughout the semester and so we punctuate every chapter with short readings and activities that ask students to pause and attempt the kinds of writing they will need to practice throughout the various stages of developing their papers. The readings range from scholarly writing (by, for example, Shirley Brice Heath, and Sidonie Smith and Julia Watson) to essays by scholars and public intellectuals (such as E. D. Hirsch, Jr., and Barbara Ehrenreich) to writing from popular newspapers and magazines (an editorial by Anna Quindlen, for example).

Chapter 1 presents an overview of academic writing as a process motivated by inquiry, and is followed by chapters that offer strategies for reading critically and working with other writers' ideas. Inevitably, reading and writing processes are intertwined. Thus in Chapter 2 we encourage students to practice "writerly" reading — reading texts as writers who can analyze critically the decisions other writers make — so that they can implement the most appropriate strategies given their own purpose for writing. While Chapters 2 through 5 address the nuts and bolts of getting started on writing, from how to mark a text to forming questions and developing a working thesis, we recognize that this process is rarely linear, and that it benefits from conversation with invested readers. Chapters 6 and 7 help students develop and support their theses by providing a range of strategies for finding and working with sources; for example showing students the ways they can use summary, paraphrase, and synthesis in the service of their purposes as writers. In Chapters 8 and 9 we link "writerly" reading with the ability to practice "readerly" writing, or writing that is self-conscious about the needs of real readers.

Chapter 10 presents revision in the context of peer groups. The responses of classmates can help students determine when they might need to read additional material before shaping more effective research questions, for example, or when a draft indicates that more evidence-gathering will be needed to support a student's argument. Our supporting materials for peer workshops foster productive group interaction at every stage of the peer review process. In Chapter 11, we provide students with strategies for conducting original research that build upon earlier chapters on using personal experience or writing a researched argument. Finally, an appendix introduces the basics of MLA and APA citation styles.

As we noted earlier, although the process of developing an academic argument can be messy and unruly, the structured step-by-step pedagogy in the rhetoric text should support students during each stage of the process. Most readings are followed by "Reading as a Writer" questions that send students back into the reading to respond to the rhetorical moves writers make. In every chapter, "Steps to" boxes summarize the major points about each stage of thinking, reading, and writing, offering quick references that bring key information into focus for student review and practice. "Practice Sequences" in each chapter ask students to try out and build on the strategies we have explained or demonstrated. We also provide templates, formulas, and worksheets that students may use to generate ideas or to organize information as they read and write. Your students should feel further supported and encouraged by seeing the abundance of student writing we use as examples in the rhetoric text, side by side with the examples of professional writing we include.

■ New to the Second Edition

We are gratified that the publisher's surveys showed that instructors who used the first edition found our approach to academic writing to be effective and popular with their students. However, while these instructors did not want us to tamper significantly with the rhetorical instruction in the book, they let us know that the range of readings we included could be more expansive and varied, and occasionally more attuned to their students' contemporary interests. Therefore, in comparison to the twenty sample readings in the first edition, the second edition includes thirty sample readings (including student essays). A few highlights:

- Chapter 1 on habits of academic writing now concludes with literacy narratives by Richard Rodriguez and Gerald Graff, writers who describe their initiation into academic habits of mind.

- Chapters 2 and 3 now include brief contemporary essays that enact academic conversation. In Chapter 2, Eugene Provenza Jr. responds to E. D. Hirsch Jr.'s classic manifesto on cultural literacy that precedes it in the chapter; in Chapter 3, two writers respond to the issue of grade inflation.

- Chapter 7 is no longer built around readings on the civil rights era, but around a sequence of short recent essays about whether online writing practices such as texting develop students' sense of audience better than more formal writing instruction.

- Throughout, more student essays have been added, and all of them have been annotated to call out the rhetorical moves the student writers perform in their model essays. For example, in Chapter 5 a student essay on texting and literacy is annotated to show how the student states and supports a thesis.

Finally, we have added a section on visual rhetoric to the end of Chapter 8's discussion of rhetorical appeals and logic. We know that students are fond of and adept at detecting the appeals of advertisements, but we have provided them with an overtly rhetorical method for performing such analysis, supported with a sample analysis and additional opportunities for practice.

▪ Available with an Anthology of Readings

From Inquiry to Academic Writing is available in an alternative version that appends an extensive collection of readings to its text chapters. The longer version, *From Inquiry to Academic Writing: A Text and Reader*, Second Edition, includes an additional fifty readings organized in chapters focusing on issues in the six fields of education, media studies, business, international relations, biology, and environmental studies. The anthology provides a rich sampling of the kinds of academic and cultural conversations that students should be prepared to enter in their college years, and beyond.

▪ Available as an E-Book

From Inquiry to Academic Writing: A Practical Guide, Second Edition, is available as an e-book in the CourseSmart PDF format. Please contact your Bedford/St. Martin's Press representative for more details.

▪ Additional Resources

We have prepared an instructor's manual, *Resources for Teaching From Inquiry to Academic Writing: A Practical Guide*, Second Edition. The manual addresses every step of the process of academic writing we set forth in the rhetoric text, with additional comments on the readings integrated in the text chapters. Not only do we discuss many of the issues involved in taking our rhetorical approach to academic argument—problems and questions students and instructors may have—we also suggest background readings on the research informing our approach.

The instructor's manual is available bound into the back of the Instructor's Edition, but can also be downloaded from the companion site, **bedfordstmartins.com/frominquiry**. Additional resources on the Web site include downloadable templates, worksheets, and summary boxes for students, AuthorLinks that supplement the readings in the book, and connections to the suite of online resources offered by Bedford/St.Martin's, including *Re:Writing*.

▪ Acknowledgments

We would first like to thank the many reviewers who commented on the proposal, the manuscript, and the first edition. Invariably their comments were useful, and frequently helpful and cheering as well. The list of reviewers includes Angela Adams, Loyola University–Chicago; Steve Adkison, Idaho State University; Teresa Fernandez Arab, University of Kansas; Yesho Atil, Asheville-Buncombe Technical Community College; Paula Bacon, Pace University–Pleasantville; Susan Bailor, Front Range Community College; Mary Ellen Bertolini, Middlebury College; Laurel Bollinger,

University of Alabama–Huntsville; Margaret Bonesteel, Syracuse University; James Brill, University of California, Chico; Laurie Britt-Smith, St. Louis University; William Brugger, Brigham Young University–Idaho; Lise Buranen, California State University–Los Angeles; Jeffrey Cebulski, Kennesaw State University; Marie Coffey, San Antonio College; Carolyn Cole, Oklahoma Baptist University; Tami Comstock-Peavy, Arapahoe Community College; Emily Cosper, Delgado Community College; Karen Cox, City College of San Francisco; Ryan Crider, Missouri State University; Calum Cunningham, Fanshawe College–London; J. Madison Davis, University of Oklahoma–Norman; Anne DeMarzio, University of Scranton; Erin Denney, Community College of San Francisco; Jason DePolo, North Carolina A&T State University; Brock Dethier, Utah State University; Eugenia C. Eberhart, Garden City Community College; Lisa Egan, Brown University; Ed Eleazer, Francis Marion University; Elaine Fredericksen, University of Texas–El Paso; Hannah Furrow, University of Michigan–Flint; Christine A. Geyer, Cazenovia University; Rhoda Greenstone, Long Beach City College; Rima Gulshan, George Mason University; Sinceree Gunn, University of Alabama–Huntsville; Juli E. Hale, King College; Jane Hammons, University of California, Berkeley; Amy Hankins, Blue River Community College; Ann Hartney, Fort Lewis College; Virginia Scott Hendrickson, Missouri State University; Zachery Hickman, University of Miami; Monica Hogan, Johnson County Community College; Jean Incampo, Gateway Community College; T. Christine Jespersen, Western State College of Colorado; Margaret Johnson, Idaho State University; Laura Katsaros, Monmouth University; Karen Keaton Jackson, North Carolina Central University; Therese Jones, Lewis University; Trevor Kearns, Greenfield Community College; Howard Kerner, Polk Community College; Lynn Kilpatrick, Salt Lake Community College; Jeff Klausman, Whatcom Community College; Tamara Kuzmenkov, Tacoma Community College; Erin Lebacqz, University of New Mexico; Lindsay Lewan, Arapahoe Community College; April Lewandowski, Front Range Community College–Westminster; Renee Major, Louisiana State University; Diane L. Maldonado, Point Park University; Loren Loving Marquez, Salisbury University; Mark McBeth, John Jay College; Timothy McGinn, Northwest Arkansas Community College; Amanda McGuire Rzicznek, Bowling Green State University; Erica Messenger, Bowling Green State University–Main; Alyce Miller, Indiana University; Lamata Mitchell, Rock Valley College; Whitney Myers, University of New Mexico; Teddy Norris, St. Charles Community College; Lolly J. Ockerstrom, Park University; Judy Olson, California Sate University, Los Angeles; Jill Onega, University of Alabama–Huntsville; Robert Peltier, Trinity College; Valeries L. Perry, Lewis University; Jeanette Pierce, San Antonio College; Mary Jo Reiff, University of Tennessee; Mary Roma, New York University; David Ryan, University of San Francisco; Daniel Schenker, University of Alabama–Huntsville; Roy Stamper, North Carolina State University; Scott Stevens, Western Washington University; Sarah Stone, University of California–Berkeley; Joseph Sullivan, Marietta College;

Gretchen Treadwell, Fort Lewis College; Raymond M. Vince, The University of Tampa; Charles Warren, Salem State College; Patricia Webb, Arizona State University; Susan Garrett Weiss, Goucher College; Worth Weller, Indiana University-Purdue University–Fort Wayne; and Jackie White, Lewis University.

We are also grateful to the many people at Bedford/St. Martin's, starting with president Joan E. Feinberg, editorial director Denise B. Wydra, and editor-in-chief Karen S. Henry. We would especially like to thank Leasa Burton, who believed in this project early on and told us to be prepared to revise. Revise a lot. (And we have!) Steve Scipione has been a terrific editor who read our work carefully and who offered sage advice every step of the way. We could not have completed this project without Steve and Leasa and their tireless assistants, Kate Mayhew, Shannon Walsh, and Allie Goldstein. In the marketing department we thank marketing director Karen R. Soeltz, market development manager Karita dos Santos, marketing manager Molly Parke, and her assistants Lindsay Talbot and Laura Horton. The talented production department conscientiously steered the manuscript through a demanding schedule to create the book you hold. We thank Susan W. Brown and Elise S. Kaiser, production manager Elizabeth M. Schaaf, assistant managing editor John Amburg, and especially Katherine Caruana, the book's patient and scrupulous production editor. Linda McLatchie provided exceptionally alert and constructive copyediting; Kalina Hintz and Kathleen Karcher negotiated the complicated process of permissions acquisition. Anna Palchik oversaw the design of the book; Donna Dennison and Marine Miller designed the cover.

Stuart Greene writes: I wish to thank the many students and faculty with whom I have worked over the years. Specifically, I would like to thank Kelly Kinney, Stephen Fox, Rebecca Nowacek, and Katherine Weese who served as my assistant directors in the past and who taught me a great deal about the teaching of writing. I would also like to thank Robert Kachur who contributed a great deal to our early iterations of this book. And I will always appreciate the many discussions I have had with John Duffy during these many years and with Connie Mick, a tireless and innovative teacher of writing. Susan Ohmer provided much insight into my understanding of media and student culture. A special thanks to Mike Palmquist with whom I taught writing as "conversation" over twenty years ago and who gave this book direction. Finally, I thank Denise Della Rossa, who has listened to me rehearse these ideas for years. I dedicate this book to her.

April Lidinsky writes: I am grateful for the superb pedagogical training I received from Lou Kelly at the University of Iowa, and Kurt Spellmeyer and Hugh English at Rutgers, the State University of New Jersey. My talented colleagues at Indiana University South Bend — particularly Rebecca Brittenham, Mike Keen, Bruce Spitzer, and Becky Torstrick — challenge me to expand my classroom practices in inventive and multi-disciplinary ways. Of course, no one shapes our pedagogy quite like our students, and I am gratified to have shared two decades' worth of classrooms with students whose names and writing projects have stuck with me and influenced my teaching in ways I am sure they cannot imagine. More personally, I am indebted to my parents, JoElla Hunter and Tom Lidinsky, for their model of lifelong reading and learning, and to Ken Smith for his talent for crafting sentences as well as a life of meaning. Our daughters, Grace and Miriam, are passionate thinkers, readers, and writers, and remind me that above all, learning should be joyful and always surprising.

Contents

8 From Ethos to Logos
Appealing to Your Readers 199

9 From Introductions to Conclusions

Drafting an Essay   247

Starting with Inquiry
Habits of Mind of Academic Writers

WHAT IS ACADEMIC WRITING?

In the strictest sense, *academic writing* is what scholars do to communicate with other scholars in their fields of study, their *disciplines*. It's the research report a biologist writes, the interpretive essay a literary scholar composes, the media analysis a film scholar produces. At the same time, *academic writing* is what you have to learn so that you can participate in the different disciplinary conversations that take place in your courses. You have to learn to *think* like an academic, *read* like an academic, *do research* like an academic, and *write* like an academic—even if you have no plans to continue your education and become a scholar yourself. Learning these skills is what this book is about.

Fair warning: It isn't easy. Initially you may be perplexed by the vocabulary and sentence structure of many of the academic essays you read. Scholars use specialized language to capture the complexity of an issue or to introduce specific ideas from their discipline. Every discipline has its own vocabulary. You probably can think of words and phrases that are not used every day but that are necessary, nevertheless, to express certain ideas precisely. For example, consider the terms *centrifugal force*, *Oedipus complex*, and *onomatopoeia*. These terms carry with them a history of study; when you learn to use them, you also are learning to use the ideas they represent. Such terms help us describe the world specifically rather than generally; they help us better understand how things work and how to make better decisions about what matters to us.

Sentence structure presents another challenge. The sentences in academic writing are often longer and more intricate than the sentences in popular magazines. Academics strive to go beyond what is quick, obvious, and general. They ask questions based on studying a subject from multiple points of view, to make surprising connections that would not occur to someone who has not studied the subject carefully. It follows that academic writers are accustomed to extensive reading that prepares them to examine an issue, knowledgeably, from many different perspectives, and to make interesting intellectual use of what they discover in their research. To become an adept academic writer, you have to learn these practices as well.

Academic writing will challenge you, no doubt. But hang in there. Any initial difficulty you have with academic writing will pay off when you discover new ways of looking at the world and of making sense of it. Moreover, the habits of mind and core skills of academic writing are highly valued in the world outside the academy.

Basically, academic writing entails making an **argument**—text crafted to persuade an audience—often in the service of changing people's minds and behaviors. When you write an academic essay, you have to

- define a situation that calls for some response in writing;
- demonstrate the timeliness of your argument;
- establish a personal investment;
- appeal to readers whose minds you want to change by understanding what they think, believe, and value;
- support your argument with good reasons;
- anticipate and address readers' reasons for disagreeing with you, while encouraging them to adopt your position.

Academic argument is not about shouting down an opponent. Instead, it is the careful expression of an idea or perspective based on reasoning and the insights garnered from a close examination of the arguments others have made on the issue.

The chapters in the first part of this book introduce you to the habits of mind and core skills of academic writing. By **habits of mind**, we mean the patterns of thought that lead you to question assumptions and opinions, explore alternative opinions, anticipate opposing arguments, compare one type of experience to another, and identify the causes and consequences of ideas and events. These forms of **critical thinking** demand an inquiring mind that welcomes complexities and seeks out and weighs many different points of view, a mind willing to enter complex conversations both in and out of the academy. We discuss academic habits of mind in the rest of Chapter 1 and refer to them throughout this book.

Such habits of mind are especially important today, when we are bombarded with appeals to buy this or that product and with information that may or may not be true. For example, in "106 Science Claims and a Truckful of Baloney" (*The Best American Science and Nature Writing*, 2005), William Speed Weed illustrates the extent to which the claims of science vie for our attention alongside the claims of advertising. He notes that advertisers often package their claims as science, but wonders whether a box of Cheerios really can reduce cholesterol.

As readers we have a responsibility to test the claims of both science and advertising in order to decide what to believe and act upon. Weed found that "very few of the 100 claims" he evaluated "proved completely true" and that "a good number were patently false." Testing the truth of claims—learning to consider information carefully and critically and to weigh competing points of view before making our own judgments—gives us power over our own lives.

The habits of mind and practices valued by academic writers are probably ones you already share. You are behaving "academically" when you comparison-shop, a process that entails learning about the product in magazines and on the Internet and then looking at the choices firsthand before you decide which one you will purchase. You employ these same habits of mind when you deliberate over casting a vote in an election. You inform yourself about the issues that are most pressing; you learn about the candidates' positions on these issues; you consider other arguments for and against both issues and candidates; and you weigh those arguments and your own understanding to determine which candidate you will support.

Fundamentally, academic habits of mind are *analytical*. When you consider a variety of factors—the quality and functionality of the item you plan to buy, how it meets your needs, how it compares to similar items before making a shopping choice—you are conducting an **analysis**. That is, you are pausing to examine the reasons why you should buy something, instead of simply handing over your cash and saying, "I want one of those."

To a certain extent, analysis involves breaking something down into its various parts and reflecting on how the parts do or don't work together. For example, when you deliberate over your vote, you may consult one of those charts that newspapers often run around election time: A list of candidates appears across the top of the chart, and a list of issues appears on the side. You can scan the columns to see where each candidate stands on the issues, and you can scan the rows to see how the candidates compare on a particular issue. The newspaper editors have performed a preliminary analysis for you. They've asked, "Who are the candidates?" "What are the issues?" and "Where does each candidate stand on the issues?"; and they have presented the answers to you in a format that can help you make your decision.

But you still have to perform your own analysis of the information before you cast your ballot. Suppose no candidate holds your position on every issue. Whom do you vote for? Which issues are most important to you? Or suppose two candidates hold your position on every issue. Which one do you vote for? What characteristics or experience are you looking for in an elected official? And you may want to investigate further by visiting the candidates' Web sites or by talking with your friends to gather their thoughts on the election.

As you can see, analysis involves more than simply disassembling or dissecting something. It is a process of continually asking questions and looking for answers. Analysis reflects, in the best sense of the word, a *skeptical* habit of mind, an unwillingness to settle for obvious answers in the quest to understand why things are the way they are and how they might be different.

This book will help you develop the questioning, evaluating, and conversational skills you already have into strategies that will improve your ability to make careful, informed judgments about the often conflicting and confusing information you are confronted with every day. With these strategies, you will be in a position to use your writing skills to create change where you feel it is most needed.

The first steps in developing these skills are to recognize the key academic habits of mind and then to refine your practice of them. We explore four key habits of mind in the rest of this chapter:

1. inquiring,
2. seeking and valuing complexity,
3. understanding that academic writing is a conversation, and
4. understanding that writing is a process.

ACADEMIC WRITERS MAKE INQUIRIES

Academic writers usually study a body of information so closely and from so many different perspectives that they can ask questions that may not occur to people who are just scanning the information. That is, academic writers learn to make **inquiries**. Every piece of academic writing begins with a question about the way the world works, and the best questions lead to rich, complex insights that others can learn from and build on.

You will find that the ability to ask good questions is equally valuable in your daily life. Asking thoughtful questions about politics, popular culture, work, or anything else—questions like What exactly did that candidate mean by "Family values are values for all of us," anyway? What is lost and gained by bringing Tolkien's *Lord of the Rings* trilogy to the screen? What does it take to move ahead in this company?—is the first step in understanding how the world works and how it can be changed.

Inquiry typically begins with **observation**, a careful noting of phenomena or behaviors that puzzle you or challenge your beliefs and values (in a text or in the real world). Observing phenomena prompts an attempt to understand them by **asking questions** (Why does this exist? Why is this happening? Do things have to be this way?) and **examining alternatives** (Maybe this doesn't need to exist. Maybe this could happen another way instead.).

For example, Mark Edmundson, a professor of English at the University of Virginia, *observes* that his students seem to prefer classes they consider "fun" over those that push them to work hard. This prompts him to *ask* how the consumer culture—especially the entertainment culture—has altered the college experience. In his essay "On the Uses of a Liberal Education," he wonders what it means that colleges increasingly see students as customers they need to please with Club Med–style exercise facilities that look "like a retirement spread for the young" more than as minds to be educated. He further *asks* what will happen if we don't change course—if entertaining students and making them feel good about themselves continue to be higher priorities than challenging students to stretch themselves with difficult ideas. Finally, he looks at alternatives to entertainment-style education and *examines those alternatives* to see what they would offer students.

In her reading on the American civil rights movement of the 1950s and 1960s, one of our students *observed* that the difficulties many immigrant groups experienced when they first arrived in the United States are not acknowledged as struggles for civil rights. This student of Asian descent *wondered why* the difficulties Asians faced in assimilating into American culture are not seen as analogous to the efforts of African Americans to gain civil rights (Why are things this way?). In doing so, she *asked* a number of relevant questions: What do we leave out when we tell stories about ourselves? Why reduce the struggle for civil rights to black-and-white terms? How can we represent the multiple struggles of people who have contributed to building our nation? Then she *examined alternatives*—different ways of presenting the history of a nation that prides itself on justice and the protection of its people's civil rights (Maybe this doesn't need to exist. Maybe this could happen another way.). The academic writing you will read—and write yourself—starts with questions and seeks to find rich answers.

Steps to Inquiry

1 **Observe.** Note phenomena or behaviors that puzzle you or challenge your beliefs and values.

2 **Ask questions.** Consider why things are the way they are.

3 **Examine alternatives.** Explore how things could be different.

A Practice Sequence: Inquiring

The activities below will help you practice the strategies of observing, asking questions, and examining alternatives.

1 Find an advertisement for a political campaign (you can find many political ads on the Internet), and write down anything about what you observe in the ad that puzzles you or that challenges your beliefs and values. Next, write down questions you might have (Do things have to be this way?). Finally, write down other ways you think the ad could persuade you to vote for this particular candidate (Maybe this could happen another way instead.).

2 Locate and analyze data about the students at your school. For example, you might research the available majors and determine which departments have the highest and lowest enrollments. (Some schools have fact books that can be accessed online; and typically the registrar maintains a database with this information.) Is there anything that puzzles you? Write down any questions you have (Why are things the way they are?). What alternative explanations can you provide to account for differences in the popularity of the subjects students major in?

ACADEMIC WRITERS SEEK AND VALUE COMPLEXITY

Seeking and valuing complexity are what inquiry is all about. As you read academic arguments (for example, about school choice), observe how the media work to influence your opinions (for example, in political ads), or analyze data (for example, about candidates in an election), you will explore reasons why things are the way they are and how they might be different. When you do so, we encourage you not to settle for simple either/or reasons. Instead, look for multiple explanations.

When we rely on **binary thinking**—imagining there are only two sides to an issue—we tend to ignore information that does not fall tidily into one side or the other. Think of the sound-bite assertions you hear bandied about on talk shows on the pretext of "discussing" a hot-button issue like stem-cell research or abortion: "It's just wrong/right because it is!" Real-world questions (How has the Internet changed our sense of what it means to be a writer? What are the global repercussions of fast food? How do we make sense of terrorism?) don't have easy for-or-against answers. Remember that an **issue** is a subject that can be explored and debated. Issue-based questions, then, need to be approached with a mind open to complex possibilities. (We say more about identifying issues and formulating issue-based questions in Chapter 4.)

If we take as an example the issue of terrorism, we would discover that scholars of religion, economics, ethics, and politics tend to ask very different questions about terrorism and to propose very different approaches for addressing this worldwide problem. This doesn't mean that one approach is right and the others are wrong; it means that complex issues are likely to have multiple explanations, rather than a simple choice between A and B.

In her attempt to explain the popularity of the Harry Potter books and movies, Elizabeth Teare, a professor of English, provides a window on the steps we can take to examine the complexity of a topic. She begins her essay "Harry Potter and the Technology of Magic" with the observations that author J. K. Rowling is one of the ten most influential people in publishing and that her books have "transformed both the technologies of reading and the way we understand those technologies." Motivated by a sense of curiosity, if not puzzlement, Teare formulates a guiding question: "What is it that makes these books—about a lonely boy whose first act on learning he is a wizard is to go shopping for a wand—not only an international phenomenon among children and parents and teachers but also a topic of compelling interest to literary, social, and cultural critics?" Notice that in doing so, she indicates that she will examine this question from the multiple perspectives of literary, social, and cultural critics. To find answers to this question, Teare explores a range of perspectives from a variety of sources, including publishers' Web sites, trade journals, academic studies, and works of fiction for young readers.

One of our students was curious about why a well-known musician, Eminem, was at once so widely popular and so bitterly reviled, a phenomenon he observed in discussions with friends and in reviews of Eminem's music. He set out to understand these conflicting responses by examining the differing perspectives of music critics, politicians, religious evangelists, and his peers; and then he formulated an issue-based question: "How can we explain Eminem's popularity given the ways people criticize Eminem personally and his music?" In looking at this issue, the student opened himself to complexity by resisting simple answers to his question about why Eminem and his music evoked such different and conflicting responses.

Steps to Seeking and Valuing Complexity

1 **Reflect on what you observe.** Clarify your initial interest in a phenomenon or behavior by focusing on its particular details. Then reflect on what is most interesting and least interesting to you about these details, and why.

2 **Examine issues from multiple points of view.** Imagine more than two sides to the issue, and recognize that there may well be other points of view too.

3 **Ask issue-based questions.** Try to put into words questions that will help you explore why things are the way they are.

A Practice Sequence: Seeking and Valuing Complexity

These activities build on the previous exercises we asked you to complete.

1 Look again at the political ad. Think about other perspectives that would complicate your understanding of how the ad might persuade voters.

2 Imagine other perspectives on the data you found on the students in your school. Let's say, for example, that you've looked at data on student majors. How did you explain the popularity of certain majors and the unpopularity of others? How do you think other students would explain these discrepancies? What explanations would faculty members offer?

ACADEMIC WRITERS SEE WRITING AS A CONVERSATION

Another habit of mind at the heart of academic writing is the understanding that ideas always build on and respond to other ideas, just as they do in the best kind of conversations. Of course, conversations in academic writing happen on the page; they are not spoken. Still, these conversations are quite similar to the conversations you have through e-mail and instant messaging: You are responding to something someone else has written (or said) and are writing back in anticipation of future responses.

Academic writing also places a high value on the belief that good, thoughtful ideas come from conversations with others, *many* others. As your exposure to other viewpoints increases, as you take more and different points of view into consideration and build on them, your own ideas will develop more fully and fairly. You already know that to get a full picture of something, often you have to ask for multiple perspectives. When you want to find out what "really" happened at an event when your friends are telling you different stories, you listen to all of them and then evaluate the evidence to draw conclusions you can stand behind—just as academic writers do.

Theologian Martin Marty starts a conversation about hospitality in his book *When Faiths Collide* (2004). *Hospitality* is a word he uses to describe a human behavior that has the potential to bring about real understanding among people who do not share a common faith or culture. As Marty points out, finding common ground is an especially important and timely concern "in a world where strangers meet strangers with gunfire, barrier walls, spiritually land-mined paths, and the spirit of revenge." He believes that people need opportunities to share their stories, their values, and their beliefs; in doing so, they feel less threatened by ideas they do not understand or identify with.

Yet Marty anticipates the possibility that the notion of hospitality will be met with skepticism or incomprehension by those who find the term "dainty." After all, he observes, that there are hospitality suites and hospitality industries suggests current usage of the term is different from historical usage, particularly in the Bible. To counter the incredulity or incomprehension of those who do not immediately understand his use of the term *hospitality*, Marty gives his readers entrée to a conversation with other scholars who understand the complexity and power of the kind of hospitality shown by people who welcome a stranger into their world. The stranger he has in mind may simply be the person who moves in next door; but that person could also be an immigrant, an exile, or a refugee.

Marty brings another scholar, Darrell Fasching, into the conversation to explain that hospitality entails welcoming "the stranger . . . [which] inevitably involves us in a sympathetic passing over into the other's life and stories" (cited in Marty, p. 132). And John Koenig, another scholar Marty cites, traces the biblical sources of the term in an effort to show the value of understanding those we fear. That understanding, Marty argues, might lead to peace among warring factions. The conversation Marty begins on the page helps us see that his views on bringing about peace have their source in other people's ideas. In turn, the fact that he draws on multiple sources gives strength to Marty's argument.

The characteristics that make for effective oral conversation are also in play in effective academic conversation: empathy, respect, and a willingness to exchange and revise ideas. **Empathy** is the ability to understand the perspectives that shape what people think, believe, and value. To express both empathy and respect for the positions of all people involved in the conversation, academic writers try to understand the conditions under which each opinion might be true and then to represent the strengths of that position accurately.

For example, imagine that your firm commitment to protecting the environment is challenged by those who see the value of developing land rich with oil and other resources. In challenging their position, it would serve you well to understand their motives, both economic (lower gas prices, new jobs that will create a demand for new houses) and political (less dependence on foreign oil). If you can demonstrate your knowledge of these factors, those committed to developing resources in protected areas will listen to you. To convey empathy and respect while presenting your own point of view, you might introduce your argument by saying:

> Although it is important to develop untapped resources in remote areas of the United States both to lower gas prices and create new jobs and to eliminate our dependence on other countries' resources, it is in everyone's interest to use alternative sources of power and protect our natural resources.

As you demonstrate your knowledge and a sense of shared values, you could also describe the conditions under which you might change your own position.

People engaging in productive conversation try to create change by listening and responding to one another rather than dominating one another. Instead of trying to win an argument, they focus on reaching a mutual understanding. This does not mean that effective communicators do not take strong positions; more often than not they do. However, they are more likely to achieve their goals by persuading others instead of ignoring them and their points of view. Similarly, writers come to every issue with an agenda. But they realize that they may have to compromise on certain points to carry those that mean the most to them. More important, they understand that their perceptions and opinions may be flawed or limited, and they are willing to revise them when valid new perspectives are introduced.

In an academic community, ideas develop through give-and-take, through a conversation that builds on what has come before and grows stronger from multiple perspectives. You will find this dynamic at work in your classes, when you discuss your ideas: You will build on other people's insights, and they will build on yours. As a habit of mind, paying attention to academic conversations can improve the thinking and writing you do in every class you take.

Steps to Joining an Academic Conversation

1 **Be receptive to the ideas of others.** Listen carefully and empathetically to what others have to say.

2 **Be respectful of the ideas of others.** When you refer to the opinions of others, represent them fairly and use an evenhanded tone. Avoid sounding scornful or dismissive.

3 **Engage with the ideas of others.** Try to understand how people have arrived at their feelings and beliefs.

4 **Be flexible in your thinking about the ideas of others.** Be willing to exchange ideas and to revise your own opinions.

A Practice Sequence: Joining an Academic Conversation

The following excerpt is taken from Thomas Patterson's *The Vanishing Voter* (2002), an examination of voter apathy. Read the excerpt and then complete the exercises that follow.

> Does a diminished appetite for voting affect the health of American politics? Is society harmed when the voting rate is low or in decline? As the *Chicago Tribune* said in an editorial, it may be "humiliating" that the United States, the oldest continuous democracy, has nearly the lowest voting rate in the world. But does it have any practical significance? . . .

The increasing number of nonvoters could be a danger to democracy. Although high participation by itself does not trigger radical change, a flood of new voters into the electorate could possibly do it. It's difficult to imagine a crisis big and divisive enough to prompt millions of new voters to suddenly flock to the polls, especially in light of Americans' aversion to political extremism. Nevertheless, citizens who are outside the electorate are less attached to the existing system. As the sociologist Seymour Martin Lipset observed, a society of nonvoters "is potentially more explosive than one in which most citizens are *regularly* involved in activities which give them some sense of participation in decisions which affect their lives."

Voting can strengthen citizenship in other ways, too. When people vote, they are more attentive to politics and are better informed about issues affecting them. Voting also deepens community involvement, as the philosopher John Stuart Mill theorized a century ago. Studies indicate that voters are more active in community affairs than nonvoters are. Of course, this association says more about the type of person who votes as opposed to the effect of voting. But recent evidence, as Harvard University's Robert Putnam notes, "suggests that the act of voting itself encourages volunteering and other forms of government citizenship."

1   In this excerpt, Patterson presents two arguments: that increasing voter apathy is a danger to democracy and that voting strengthens citizenship. With which of these arguments do you sympathize more? Why? Can you imagine reasons that another person might not agree with you? Write them down. Now do the same exercise with the argument you find less compelling.

2   Your instructor will divide the class into four groups and assign each group a position—pro or con—on one of Patterson's arguments. Brainstorm with the members of your group to come up with examples or reasons why your group's position is valid. Make a list of those examples or reasons, and be prepared to present them to the class.

3   Your instructor will now break up the groups into new groups, each with at least one representative of the original groups. In turn with the other members of your new group, take a few moments to articulate your position and the reasons for it. Remember to be civil and as persuasive as possible.

4   Finally, with the other members of your new group, talk about the merits of the various points of view. Try to find common ground ("I understand what you are saying; in fact, it's not unlike the point I was making about . . ."). The point of this discussion is not to pronounce a winner (who made the best case for his or her perspective) but to explore common ground, exchange and revise ideas, and imagine compromises.

ACADEMIC WRITERS UNDERSTAND THAT WRITING IS A PROCESS

Academic writing is a process of defining issues, formulating questions, and developing sound arguments. This view of writing counters a number of popular myths: that writing depends on inspiration, that writing should happen quickly, that learning to write in one context prepares you to write in other contexts, and that revision is the same as editing. The writing process addresses these myths. First, choosing an idea that matters to you is one way to make your writing matter. And there's a better chance that writing you care about will contribute in a meaningful way to the conversation going on about a given issue in the academic community. Second, writers who invest time in developing and revising their ideas will improve the quality of both their ideas and their language—their ability to be specific and express complexity.

There are three main stages to the writing process: collecting information, drafting, and revising. We introduce them here and expand on them throughout this book.

■ Collect Information and Material

Always begin the process of writing an essay by collecting *in writing* the material—the information, ideas, and evidence—from which you will shape your own argument. Once you have read and marked the pages of a text, you have begun the process of building your own argument. The important point here is that you start to put your ideas on paper. Good writing comes from returning to your ideas on your own and with your classmates, reconsidering them, and revising them as your thinking develops. This is not something you can do with any specificity unless you have written down your ideas. The box below shows the steps for gathering information from your reading, the first stage in the process of writing an academic essay. (In Chapter 2, these steps are illustrated and discussed in more detail.)

Steps to Collecting Information and Material

1 **Mark your texts as you read.** Note key terms; ask questions in the margins; indicate connections to other texts.

2 **List quotations you find interesting and provocative.** You might even write short notes to yourself about what you find significant about the quotes.

3 **List your own ideas in response to the reading or readings.** Include what you've observed about the way the author or authors make their arguments.

> **4** **Sketch out the similarities and differences among the authors whose work you plan to use in your essay.** Where would they agree or disagree? How would each respond to the others' arguments and evidence?

▪ Draft, and Draft Again

The next stage in the writing process begins when you are ready to think about your focus and how to arrange the ideas you have gathered in the collecting stage. Writers often find that writing a first draft is an act of discovery, that their ultimate focus emerges during this initial drafting process. Sometimes it is only at the end of a four-page draft that a writer says, "Aha! This is what I really want to talk about in this essay!" Later revisions of an essay, then, are not simply editing or cleaning up the grammar of a first draft. Instead, they truly involve *re*vision, seeing the first draft again to establish the clearest possible argument and the most persuasive evidence. This means that you do not have to stick with the way a draft turns out the first time. You can—and must!—be willing to rewrite a substantial amount of a first draft if the focus of the argument changes, or if in the process of writing new ideas emerge that enrich the essay. This is why it's important not to agonize over wording in a first draft: It's difficult to toss out a paragraph you've sweated over for hours. Use the first draft to get your ideas down on paper so that you and your peers can discuss what you see there, with the knowledge that you (like your peers) will need to stay open to the possibility of changing an aspect of your focus or argument.

Steps to Drafting

1 **Look through the materials** you have collected to see what interests you most and what you have the most to say about.

2 **Identify what is at issue,** what is open to dispute.

3 **Formulate a question** that your essay will respond to.

4 **Select the material you will include,** and decide what is outside your focus.

5 **Consider the types of readers** who might be most interested in what you have to say.

6 **Gather more material** once you've decided on your purpose—what you want to teach your readers.

7 **Formulate a working thesis** that conveys the point you want to make.

8 **Consider possible arguments** against your position and your response to them.

■ Revise Significantly

The final stage, revising, might involve several different drafts as you continue to sharpen your insights and the organization of what you have written. As we discuss in Chapter 10, you and your peers will be reading one another's drafts, offering feedback as you move from the larger issues to the smaller ones. It should be clear by now that academic writing is done in a community of thinkers: That is, people read other people's drafts and make suggestions for further clarification, further development of ideas, and sometimes further research. This is quite different from simply editing someone's writing for grammatical errors and typos. Instead, drafting and revising with real readers, as we discuss in Chapter 10, allow you to participate in the collaborative spirit of the academy, in which knowledge making is a group activity that comes out of the conversation of ideas. Importantly, this process approach to writing in the company of real readers mirrors the conversation of ideas carried on in the pages of academic books and journals.

Steps to Revising

1 Draft and revise the introduction and conclusion.

2 Clarify any obscure or confusing passages your peers have pointed out.

3 Provide details and textual evidence where your peers have asked for new or more information.

4 Check to be sure you have included opposing points of view and have addressed them fairly.

5 Consider reorganization.

6 Check to be sure that every paragraph contributes clearly to your thesis or main claim and that you have included signposts along the way, phrases that help a reader understand your purpose ("Here I turn to an example from current movies to show how this issue is alive and well in pop culture").

7 Consider using strategies you have found effective in other reading you have done for class (repeating words or phrases for effect, asking rhetorical questions, varying your sentence length).

The four academic habits of mind we have discussed throughout this chapter—making inquiries, seeking and valuing complexity, understanding writing as a conversation, and understanding writing as a process—are fundamental patterns of thought you will need to cultivate as an academic writer. The core skills we discuss through the rest of the book build on these habits of mind.

BECOMING ACADEMIC: TWO NARRATIVES

In the following passages, two writers describe their early experiences as readers. Trained as academic writers, Richard Rodriguez and Gerald Graff are well known outside the academy. In this excerpt from *Hunger of Memory*, Rodriguez describes what it was like growing up as a bookish bilingual "scholarship boy" in a Spanish-speaking household. In the other excerpt, from *Beyond the Culture Wars*, Graff narrates how he disliked reading books, especially literature and history books, well into his undergraduate years as an English major. Both of their narratives turn around moments of recognition triggered by exposure to the ideas of others. As you read the selections, consider these questions:

- Where are the turning points in each narrative? What are the most important things the writers seem to learn?
- What incidents or insights did you find most interesting in the narratives? Why?
- What seem to be the key ideas in each narrative? Do these ideas strike you as being potentially useful in your own work as a thinker and writer?
- Do you find that the writers exhibit academic habits of mind (making inquiries, seeking and valuing complexity, seeing writing as a kind of conversation)? If so, where?

RICHARD RODRIGUEZ

Scholarship Boy

Richard Rodriguez was born into a Mexican immigrant family in San Francisco, California, and spoke only Spanish until age six. He had a formidable education, receiving a BA from Stanford University and an MA from Columbia University; studying for a PhD at the University of California, Berkeley; and attending the Warburg Institute in London on a Fulbright fellowship. Instead of pursuing a career in academia, he became a journalist. He is perhaps best known for his contributions to PBS's *The NewsHour with Jim Lehrer* and for his controversial opposition to affirmative action and bilingual education. His books include *Hunger of Memory: The Education of Richard Rodriguez* (1981), *Mexico's Children* (1990), *Days of Obligation: An Argument with My Mexican Father* (1992), and *Brown: The Last Discovery of America* (2002).

■ ■ ■

I stand in the ghetto classroom—"the guest speaker"—attempting to lecture on the mystery of the sounds of our words to rows of diffident students. "Don't you hear it? Listen! The music of our words. *'Sumer is*   *1 i-cumen in. . . .'* And songs on the car radio. We need Aretha Franklin's voice to fill plain words with music—her life." In the face of their empty stares, I try to create an enthusiasm. But the girls in the back row turn to watch some boy passing outside. There are flutters of smiles, waves. And someone's mouth elongates heavy, silent words through the barrier of glass. Silent words—the lips straining to shape each voiceless syllable: *"Meet meee late errr."* By the door, the instructor smiles at me, apparently hoping that I will be able to spark some enthusiasm in the class. But only one student seems to be listening. A girl, maybe fourteen. In this gray room her eyes shine with ambition. She keeps nodding and nodding at all that I say; she even takes notes. And each time I ask a question, she jerks up and down in her desk like a marionette, while her hand waves over the bowed heads of her classmates. It is myself (as a boy) I see as she faces me now (a man in my thirties).

The boy who first entered a classroom barely able to speak English, twenty years later concluded his studies in the stately quiet of the reading room in the British Museum. Thus with one sentence I can summarize my academic career. It will be harder to summarize what sort of life connects the boy to the man.   *2*

With every award, each graduation from one level of education to the next, people I'd meet would congratulate me. Their refrain always the same: "Your parents must be very proud." Sometimes then they'd ask me how I managed it—my "success." (How?) After a while, I had several quick answers to give in reply. I'd admit, for one thing, that I went to an excellent grammar school. (My earliest teachers, the nuns, made my success their ambition.) And my brother and both my sisters were very good students. (They often brought home the shiny school trophies I came to want.) And my mother and father always encouraged me. (At every graduation they were behind the stunning flash of the camera when I turned to look at the crowd.)   *3*

As important as these factors were, however, they account inadequately for my academic advance. Nor do they suggest what an odd success I managed. For although I was a very good student, I was also a very bad student. I was a "scholarship boy," a certain kind of scholarship boy. Always successful, I was always unconfident. Exhilarated by my progress. Sad. I became the prized student—anxious and eager to learn. Too eager, too anxious—an imitative and unoriginal pupil. My brother and two sisters enjoyed the advantages I did, and they grew to be as successful as I, but none of them ever seemed so anxious about their schooling. A second-grade student, I was the one who came home and corrected the "simple" grammatical mistakes of our parents. ("Two negatives make a positive.") Proudly I announced—to my family's startled silence—that a teacher had said I was losing all trace of a Spanish accent. I was oddly annoyed when I was unable to get parental help with a homework assign-   *4* ment. The night my father tried to help me with an arithmetic exercise, he kept reading the instructions, each time more deliberately, until I pried the textbook out of his hands, saying, "I'll try to figure it out some more by myself."

When I reached the third grade, I outgrew such behavior. I became   5 more tactful, careful to keep separate the two very different worlds of my day. But then, with ever-increasing intensity, I devoted myself to my studies. I became bookish, puzzling to all my family. Ambition set me apart. When my brother saw me struggling home with stacks of library books, he would laugh, shouting: "Hey, Four Eyes!" My father opened a closet one day and was startled to find me inside, reading a novel. My mother would find me reading when I was supposed to be asleep or helping around the house or playing outside. In a voice angry or worried or just curious, she'd ask: "What do you see in your books?" It became the family's joke. When I was called and wouldn't reply, someone would say I must be hiding under my bed with a book.

(How did I manage my success?)   6

What I am about to say to you has taken me more than twenty years   7 to admit: *A primary reason for my success in the classroom was that I couldn't forget that schooling was changing me and separating me from the life I enjoyed before becoming a student.* That simple realization! For years I never spoke to anyone about it. Never mentioned a thing to my family or my teachers or classmates. From a very early age, I understood enough, just enough about my classroom experiences to keep what I knew repressed, hidden beneath layers of embarrassment. Not until my last months as a graduate student, nearly thirty years old, was it possible for me to think much about the reasons for my academic success. Only then. At the end of my schooling, I needed to determine how far I had moved from my past. The adult finally confronted, and now must publicly say, what the child shuddered from knowing and could never admit to himself or to those many faces that smiled at his every success. ("Your parents must be very proud. . . .")

At the end, in the British Museum (too distracted to finish my disserta-   8 tion) for weeks I read, speed-read, books by modern educational theorists, only to find infrequent and slight mention of students like me. (Much more is written about the more typical case, the lower-class student who barely is helped by his schooling.) Then one day, leafing through Richard Hoggart's *The Uses of Literacy*, I found, in his description of the scholarship boy, myself. For the first time I realized that there were other students like me, and so I was able to frame the meaning of my academic success, its consequent price—the loss.

Hoggart's description is distinguished, at least initially, by deep under-   9 standing. What he grasps very well is that the scholarship boy must move between environments, his home and the classroom, which are at cultural extremes, opposed. With his family, the boy has the intense plea-sure of intimacy, the family's consolation in feeling public alienation. Lavish emotions texture home life. *Then*, at school, the instruction bids him to trust lonely reason primarily. Immediate needs set the pace of his parents' lives. From his mother and father the boy learns to trust sponta-neity and nonrational ways of knowing. *Then*, at school, there is mental calm. Teachers emphasize the value of a reflectiveness that opens a space between thinking and immediate action.

Years of schooling must pass before the boy will be able to sketch the cultural differences in his day as abstractly as this. But he senses those differences early. Perhaps as early as the night he brings home an assign-ment from school and finds the house too noisy for study.   *10*

> He has to be more and more alone, if he is going to "get on." He will have, probably unconsciously, to oppose the ethos of the hearth, the intense gre-gariousness of the working-class family group. Since everything centres upon the living-room, there is unlikely to be a room of his own; the bed-rooms are cold and inhospitable, and to warm them or the front room, if there is one, would not only be expensive, but would require an imaginative leap—out of the tradition—which most families are not capable of making. There is a corner of the living-room table. On the other side Mother is iron-ing, the wireless is on, someone is singing a snatch of song or Father says intermittently whatever comes into his head. The boy has to cut himself off mentally, so as to do his homework, as well as he can.[1]

The next day, the lesson is as apparent at school. There are even rows of desks. Discussion is ordered. The boy must rehearse his thoughts and raise his hand before speaking out in a loud voice to an audience of class-mates. And there is time enough, and silence, to think about ideas (big ideas) never considered at home by his parents.

Not for the working-class child alone is adjustment to the classroom difficult. Good schooling requires that any student alter early child-hood habits. But the working-class child is usually least prepared for the change. And, unlike many middle-class children, he goes home and sees in his parents a way of life not only different but starkly opposed to that of the classroom. (He enters the house and hears his parents talking in ways his teachers discourage.)   *11*

Without extraordinary determination and the great assistance of oth-ers—at home and at school—there is little chance for success. Typically most working-class children are barely changed by the classroom. The exception succeeds. The relative few become scholarship students. Of these, Richard Hoggart estimates, most manage a fairly graceful tran-sition. Somehow they learn to live in the two very different worlds of   *12*

[1] All quotations in this selection are from Richard Hoggart, *The Uses of Literacy* (London: Chatto and Windus, 1957), chapter 10.

their day. There are some others, however, those Hoggart pejoratively terms "scholarship boys," for whom success comes with special anxiety. Scholarship boy: good student, troubled son. The child is "moderately endowed," intellectually mediocre, Hoggart supposes—though it may be more pertinent to note the special qualities of temperament in the child. High-strung child. Brooding. Sensitive. Haunted by the knowledge that one *chooses* to become a student. (Education is not an inevitable or natural step in growing up.) Here is a child who cannot forget that his academic success distances him from a life he loved, even from his own memory of himself.

Initially, he wavers, balances allegiance. ("The boy is himself [until he   13
reaches, say, the upper forms] very much of *both* the worlds of home and school. He is enormously obedient to the dictates of the world of school, but emotionally still strongly wants to continue as part of the family circle.") Gradually, necessarily, the balance is lost. The boy needs to spend more and more time studying, each night enclosing himself in the silence permitted and required by intense concentration. He takes his first step toward academic success, away from his family.

From the very first days, through the years following, it will be with   14
his parents—the figures of lost authority, the persons toward whom he feels deepest love—that the change will be most powerfully measured. A separation will unravel between them. Advancing in his studies, the boy notices that his mother and father have not changed as much as he. Rather, when he sees them, they often remind him of the person he once was and the life he earlier shared with them. He realizes what some Romantics also know when they praise the working class for the capacity for human closeness, qualities of passion and spontaneity, that the rest of us experience in like measure only in the earliest part of our youth. For the Romantic, this doesn't make working-class life childish. Working-class life challenges precisely because it is an *adult* way of life.

The scholarship boy reaches a different conclusion. He cannot afford   15
to admire his parents. (How could he and still pursue such a contrary life?) He permits himself embarrassment at their lack of education. And to evade nostalgia for the life he has lost, he concentrates on the benefits education will bestow upon him. He becomes especially ambitious. Without the support of old certainties and consolations, almost mechanically, he assumes the procedures and doctrines of the classroom. The kind of allegiance the young student might have given his mother and father only days earlier, he transfers to the teacher, the new figure of authority. "[The scholarship boy] tends to make a father-figure of his form-master," Hoggart observes.

But Hoggart's calm prose only makes me recall the urgency with which   16
I came to idolize my grammar school teachers. I began by imitating their accents, using their diction, trusting their every direction. The very first facts they dispensed, I grasped with awe. Any book they told me to read,

I read—then waited for them to tell me which books I enjoyed. Their every casual opinion I came to adopt and to trumpet when I returned home. I stayed after school "to help"—to get my teacher's undivided attention. It was the nun's encouragement that mattered most to me. (She understood exactly what—my parents never seemed to appraise so well—all my achievements entailed.) Memory gently caressed each word of praise bestowed in the classroom so that compliments teachers paid me years ago come quickly to mind even today.

The enthusiasm I felt in second-grade classes I flaunted before both   17
my parents. The docile, obedient student came home a shrill and precocious son who insisted on correcting and teaching his parents with the remark: "My teacher told us. . . ."

I intended to hurt my mother and father. I was still angry at them for   18
having encouraged me toward classroom English. But gradually this anger was exhausted, replaced by guilt as school grew more and more attractive to me. I grew increasingly successful, a talkative student. My hand was raised in the classroom; I yearned to answer any question. At home, life was less noisy than it had been. (I spoke to classmates and teachers more often each day than to family members.) Quiet at home, I sat with my papers for hours each night. I never forgot that schooling had irretrievably changed my family's life. That knowledge, however, did not weaken ambition. Instead, it strengthened resolve. Those times I remembered the loss of my past with regret, I quickly reminded myself of all the things my teachers could give me. (They could make me an educated man.) I tightened my grip on pencil and books. I evaded nostalgia. Tried hard to forget. But one does not forget by trying to forget. One only remembers. I remembered too well that education had changed my family's life. I would not have become a scholarship boy had I not so often remembered.

Once she was sure that her children knew English, my mother would   19
tell us, "You should keep up your Spanish." Voices playfully groaned in response. "¡Pochos!" my mother would tease. I listened silently.

After a while, I grew more calm at home. I developed tact. A fourth-   20
grade student, I was no longer the show-off in front of my parents. I became a conventionally dutiful son, politely affectionate, cheerful enough, even—for reasons beyond choosing—my father's favorite. And much about my family life was easy then, comfortable, happy in the rhythm of our living together: hearing my father getting ready for work; eating the breakfast my mother had made me; looking up from a novel to hear my brother or one of my sisters playing with friends in the backyard; in winter, coming upon the house all lighted up after dark.

But withheld from my mother and father was any mention of what   21
most mattered to me: the extraordinary experience of first-learning. Late afternoon: In the midst of preparing dinner, my mother would come up behind me while I was trying to read. Her head just over mine, her breath

warmly scented with food. "What are you reading?" Or, "Tell me all about your new courses." I would barely respond, "Just the usual things, nothing special." (A half smile, then silence. Her head moving back in the silence. Silence! Instead of the flood of intimate sounds that had once flowed smoothly between us, there was this silence.) After dinner, I would rush to a bedroom with papers and books. As often as possible, I resisted parental pleas to "save lights" by coming to the kitchen to work. I kept so much, so often, to myself. Sad. Enthusiastic. Troubled by the excitement of coming upon new ideas. Eager. Fascinated by the promising texture of a brand-new book. I hoarded the pleasures of learning. Alone for hours. Enthralled. Nervous. I rarely looked away from my books—or back on my memories. Nights when relatives visited and the front rooms were warmed by Spanish sounds, I slipped quietly out of the house.

It mattered that education was changing me. It never ceased to matter. My brother and sisters would giggle at our mother's mispronounced words. They'd correct her gently. My mother laughed girlishly one night, trying not to pronounce *sheep* as *ship*. From a distance I listened sullenly. From that distance, pretending not to notice on another occasion, I saw my father looking at the title pages of my library books. That was the scene on my mind when I walked home with a fourth-grade companion and heard him say that his parents read to him every night. (A strange-sounding book—*Winnie the Pooh*.) Immediately, I wanted to know, "What is it like?" My companion, however, thought I wanted to know about the plot of the book. Another day, my mother surprised me by asking for a "nice" book to read. "Something not too hard you think I might like." Carefully I chose one, Willa Cather's *My Ántonia*. But when, several weeks later, I happened to see it next to her bed unread except for the first few pages, I was furious and suddenly wanted to cry. I grabbed up the book and took it back to my room and placed it in its place, alphabetically on my shelf.

"Your parents must be very proud of you." People began to say that to me about the time I was in sixth grade. To answer affirmatively, I'd smile. Shyly I'd smile, never betraying my sense of the irony: I was not proud of my mother and father. I was embarrassed by their lack of education. It was not that I ever thought they were stupid, though stupidly I took for granted their enormous native intelligence. Simply, what mattered to me was that they were not like my teachers.

But, "Why didn't you tell us about the award?" my mother demanded, her frown weakened by pride. At the grammar school ceremony several weeks after, her eyes were brighter than the trophy I'd won. Pushing back the hair from my forehead, she whispered that I had "shown" the *gringos*. A few minutes later, I heard my father speak to my teacher and felt ashamed of his labored, accented words. Then guilty for the shame. I felt such contrary feelings. (There is no simple roadmap through the heart of the scholarship boy.) My teacher was so soft-spoken and her words were edged sharp and clean. I admired her until it seemed to me that she spoke too carefully. Sensing that she was condescending to them, I became nervous. Resentful. Protective. I tried to move my parents away. "You both must be very proud of Richard," the nun said. They responded quickly. (They were proud.) "We are proud of all our children." Then this afterthought: "They sure didn't get their brains from us." They all laughed. I smiled.

GERALD GRAFF

Disliking Books

Gerald Graff received his BA in English from the University of Chicago and his PhD in English and American literature from Stanford University. In his distinguished academic career, he has taught at numerous universities and is currently a professor of English and education at the University of Illinois at Chicago. He is probably best known for his pedagogical theories, especially "teaching the controversies," an approach he argues for most famously in his book *Beyond the Culture Wars: How Teaching the Conflicts Can Revitalize American Education* (1993), from which this excerpt is taken. His other well-known books include *Literature Against Itself: Literary Ideas in Modern Society* (1979), *Professing Literature: An Institutional History* (1987), and *Clueless in Academe: How Schooling Obscures the Life of the Mind* (2003).

■   ■   ■

I like to think I have a certain advantage as a teacher of literature because when I was growing up I disliked and feared books. My youthful aversion to books showed a fine impartiality, extending across the whole spectrum of literature, history, philosophy, science, and what by then (the late 1940s) had come to be called social studies. But had I been forced to choose, I would have singled out literature and history as the reading I disliked most. Science at least had some discernible practical use, and you could have fun solving the problems in the textbooks with their clear-cut answers. Literature and history had no apparent application to my experience, and any boy in my school who had cultivated them—I can't recall one who did—would have marked himself as a sissy.

As a middle-class Jew growing up in an ethnically mixed Chicago neighborhood, I was already in danger of being beaten up daily by rougher working-class boys. Becoming a bookworm would have only given them a decisive reason for beating me up. Reading and studying were more permissible for girls, but they, too, had to be careful not to get too intellectual, lest they acquire the stigma of being "stuck up."

In *Lives on the Boundary*, a remarkable autobiography of the making   *3*
of an English teacher, Mike Rose describes how the "pain and confusion"
of his working-class youth made "school and knowledge" seem a saving
alternative. Rose writes of feeling "freed, as if I were untying fetters," by
his encounters with certain college teachers, who helped him recognize
that "an engagement with ideas could foster competence and lead me
out into the world."[1] Coming at things from my middle-class perspective, however, I took for granted a freedom that school, knowledge, and
engagement with ideas seemed only to threaten.

My father, a literate man, was frustrated by my refusal to read any-   *4*
thing besides comic books, sports magazines, and the John R. Tunis and
Clair Bee sports novels. I recall his once confining me to my room until I
finished a book on the voyages of Magellan, but try as I might, I could do
no better than stare bleakly at the pages. I could not, as we would later
say, "relate to" Magellan or to any of the other books my father brought
home—detective stories, tales of war and heroism, adventure stories with
adolescent heroes (the *Hardy Boys*, *Hans Brinker, or The Silver Skates*),
stories of scientific discovery (Paul de Kruif's *Microbe Hunters*), books on
current events. Nothing worked.

It was understood, however, that boys of my background would go to   *5*
college and that once there we would get serious and buckle down. For
some, "getting serious" meant prelaw, premed, or a major in business to
prepare for taking over the family business. My family did not own a business, and law and medicine did not interest me, so I drifted by default into
the nebulous but conveniently noncommittal territory of the liberal arts.
I majored in English.

At this point the fear of being beaten up if I were caught having any-   *6*
thing to do with books was replaced by the fear of flunking out of college
if I did not learn to deal with them. But though I dutifully did my homework and made good grades (first at the University of Illinois, Chicago
branch, then at the University of Chicago, from which I graduated in
1959), I continued to find "serious" reading painfully difficult and alien. My
most vivid recollections of college reading are of assigned classics I failed
to finish: *The Iliad* (in the Richmond Lattimore translation); *The Autobiography of Benvenuto Cellini*, a major disappointment after the paperback jacket's promise of "a lusty classic of Renaissance ribaldry"; E. M.
Forster's *Passage to India*, sixty agonizing pages of which I managed to
slog through before giving up. Even Hemingway, Steinbeck, and Fitzgerald, whose contemporary world was said to be "close to my own experience," left me cold. I saw little there that did resemble my experience.

---

[1] Mike Rose, *Lives on the Boundary* (New York: Free Press, 1989), pp. 46–47.

Even when I had done the assigned reading, I was often tongue-tied   7
and embarrassed when called on. What was unclear to me was what I
was supposed to *say* about literary works, and why. Had I been born a
decade or two earlier, I might have come to college with the rudiments
of a literate vocabulary for talking about culture that some people older
than I acquired through family, high school, or church. As it was, "cul-
tured" phrases seemed effete and sterile to me. When I was able to produce the kind of talk that was required in class, the intellectualism of it
came out sounding stilted and hollow in my mouth. If *Cliffs Notes* and
other such crib sheets for the distressed had yet come into existence, with
their ready-to-copy summaries of widely taught literary works, I would
have been an excellent customer. (As it was, I did avail myself of the prim-
itive version then in existence called *Masterplots*.)

What first made literature, history, and other intellectual pursuits   8
seem attractive to me was exposure to critical debates. There was no
single conversion experience, but a gradual transformation over several
years, extending into my first teaching positions, at the University of New
Mexico and then Northwestern University. But one of the first sparks I
remember was a controversy over *The Adventures of Huckleberry Finn*
that arose in a course during my junior year in college. On first attempt,
Twain's novel was just another assigned classic that I was too bored to
finish. I could see little connection between my Chicago upbringing and
Huck's pre–Civil War adventures with a runaway slave on a raft up the
Mississippi.

My interest was aroused, however, when our instructor mentioned   9
that the critics had disagreed over the merits of the last part of the novel.
He quoted Ernest Hemingway's remark that "if you read [the novel] you
must stop where the nigger Jim is stolen by the boys. This is the real end.
The rest is cheating." According to this school of thought, the remainder
of the book trivializes the quest for Jim's freedom that has motivated the
story up to that point. This happens first when Jim becomes an object
of Tom Sawyer's slapstick humor, then when it is revealed that unbe-
knownst to Huck, the reader, and himself, Jim has already been freed by
his benevolent owner, so that the risk we have assumed Jim and Huck to
be under all along has been really no risk at all.

Like the critics, our class divided over the question: Did Twain's ending   10
vitiate the book's profound critique of racism, as Hemingway's charge of
cheating implied? Cheating in my experience up to then was something
students did, an unthinkable act for a famous author. It was a revelation
to me that famous authors were capable not only of mistakes but of ones
that even lowly undergraduates might be able to point out. When I chose
to write my term paper on the dispute over the ending, my instructor
suggested I look at several critics on the opposing sides, T. S. Eliot and
Lionel Trilling, who defended the ending, and Leo Marx, who sided with
Hemingway.

Reading the critics was like picking up where the class discussion had   *11*
left off, and I gained confidence from recognizing that my classmates and
I had had thoughts that, however stumbling our expression of them, were
not too far from the thoughts of famous published critics. I went back
to the novel again and to my surprise found myself rereading it with an
excitement I had never felt before with a serious book. Having the controversy over the ending in mind, I now had some issues *to watch out for*
as I read, issues that reshaped the way I read the earlier chapters as well
as the later ones and focused my attention. And having issues to watch
out for made it possible not only to concentrate, as I had not been able to
do earlier, but to put myself in the text—to read with a sense of personal
engagement that I had not felt before. Reading the novel with the voices
of the critics running through my mind, I found myself thinking of things
that I might say about what I was reading, things that may have belonged
partly to the critics but also now belonged to me. It was as if having a
stock of things to look for and to say about a literary work had somehow
made it possible for me to read one.

One of the critics had argued that what was at issue in the debate   *12*
over *Huckleberry Finn* was not just the novel's value but its cultural significance: If *Huckleberry Finn* was contradictory or confused in its attitude toward race, then what did that say about the culture that had
received the novel as one of its representative cultural documents and
had made Twain a folk hero? This critic had also made the intriguing
observation—I found out only later it was a critical commonplace at that
time—that judgments about the novel's aesthetic value could not be separated from judgments about its moral substance. I recall taking in both
this critic's arguments and the cadence of the phrases in which they were
couched; perhaps it would not be so bad after all to become the sort of
person who talked about "cultural contradictions" and the "inseparabil-
ity of form and content." Perhaps even mere literary-critical talk could
give you a certain power in the real world. As the possibility dawned on
me that reading and intellectual discussion might actually have something to do with my real life, I became less embarrassed about using the
intellectual formulas.

The Standard Story

It was through exposure to such critical reading and discussion over a   *13*
period of time that I came to catch the literary bug, eventually choosing
the vocation of teaching. This was not the way it is supposed to happen.
In the standard story of academic vocation that we like to tell ourselves,
the germ is first planted by an early experience of literature itself. The
future teacher is initially inspired by some primary experience of a great
book and only subsequently acquires the secondary, derivative skills of

critical discussion. A teacher may be involved in instilling this inspiration, but a teacher who seemingly effaces himself or herself before the text. Any premature or excessive acquaintance with secondary critical discourse, and certainly with its sectarian debates, is thought to be a corrupting danger, causing one to lose touch with the primary passion for literature. . . .

The standard story ascribes innocence to the primary experience of literature and sees the secondary experience of professional criticism as corrupting. In my case, however, things had evidently worked the other way around: I had to be corrupted first in order to experience innocence. It was only when I was introduced to a critical debate about *Huckleberry Finn* that my helplessness in the face of the novel abated and I could experience a personal reaction to it. Getting into immediate contact with the text was for me a curiously triangular business; I could not do it directly but needed a conversation of other readers to give me the issues and terms that made it possible to respond. *14*

As I think back on it now, it was as if the critical conversation I needed had up to then been withheld from me, on the ground that it could only interfere with my direct access to literature itself. The assumption was that leaving me alone with literary texts themselves, uncontaminated by the interpretations and theories of professional critics, would enable me to get on the closest possible terms with those texts. But being alone with the texts only left me feeling bored and helpless, since I had no language with which to make them mine. On the one hand, I was being asked to speak a foreign language—literary criticism—while on the other hand, I was being protected from that language, presumably for my own safety. *15*

The moral I draw from this experience is that our ability to read well depends more than we think on our ability to *talk well* about what we read. Our assumptions about what is "primary" and "secondary" in the reading process blind us to what actually goes on. Many literate people learned certain ways of talking about books so long ago that they have forgotten they ever had to learn them. These people therefore fail to understand the reading problems of the struggling students who have still not acquired a critical vocabulary. *16*

How typical my case was is hard to say, but many of the students I teach seem to have grown up as the same sort of nonintellectual, nonbookish person I was, and they seem to view literature with some of the same aversions, fears, and anxieties. That is why I like to think it is an advantage for a teacher to know what it feels like to grow up being indifferent to literature and intimidated by criticism and what it feels like to overcome a resistance to talking like an intellectual. *17*

A Practice Sequence: Composing a Literacy Narrative

Rodriguez and Graff have written autobiographical *literacy narratives*—their own stories of dealing with some aspects of how they became literate and their relationship with reading. Rodriguez's narrative is part of *Hunger of Memory: The Education of Richard Rodriguez*, a memoir that also explores the politics of language in American culture. Graff's narrative is embedded in his *Beyond the Culture Wars: How Teaching the Conflicts Can Revitalize American Education*, which, as the subtitle suggests, presents arguments and proposals for altering educational practices.

We would like you to write your own literacy narrative. The following practice sequence suggests some strategies for doing so.

1 Reflect on your experiences as a reader. Spend some time jotting down answers to these questions (not necessarily in this order) or to other related questions that occur to you as you write.

- Can you recall the time when you first began to read?
- What are the main types of reading you do? Why?
- How would you describe or characterize yourself as a reader?
- Is there one moment or event that encapsulates who you are as a reader?
- What are your favorite books, authors, and types of books? Why are they favorites?
- In what ways has reading changed you for the better? For the worse?
- What is the most important thing you've learned from reading?
- Have you ever learned something important from reading, only to discover later that it wasn't true, or sufficient? Explain.

2 Write your literacy narrative, focusing on at least one turning point, at least one moment of recognition or lesson learned. Write no fewer than two pages but no more than five pages. See where your story arc takes you. What do you conclude about your own "growing into literacy"?

3 Then start a conversation about literacy. Talk with some other people about their experiences. You might talk with some classmates—and not necessarily those in your writing class—about their memories of becoming literate. You might interview some people you grew up with—a parent, a sibling, a best friend—about their memories of you as a reader and writer and about their own

memories of becoming literate. Compare their memories to your own. Did you all have similar experiences? How were they different? Do you see things the same way? Then write down your impressions and what you think you may have learned.

4 Recast your literacy narrative, incorporating some of the insights you gathered from other people. How does your original narrative change? What new things now have to be accounted for?

5 Like Graff, who takes his own experience as a starting point for proposing new educational policies, can you imagine your insights having larger implications? Explain. Do you think what you've learned from reading Graff's and Rodriguez's literacy narratives has implications for the ways reading is taught in school?

From Reading as a Writer to Writing as a Reader

Reading for class and then writing an essay might seem to be separate tasks, but reading is the first step in the writing process. In this chapter we present methods that will help you read more effectively and move from reading to writing your own college essays. These methods will lead you to understand a writer's purpose in responding to a situation, the motivation for asserting a claim in an essay and entering a particular conversation with a particular audience.

READING AS AN ACT OF COMPOSING: ANNOTATING

Leaving your mark on the page—**annotating**—is your first act of composing. When you mark the pages of a text, you are reading critically, engaging with the ideas of others, questioning and testing those ideas, and inquiring into their significance. **Critical reading** is sometimes called *active reading* to distinguish it from memorization, when you just read for the main idea so that you can "spit it back out on a test." When you read actively and critically, you bring your knowledge, experiences, and interests to a text, so that you can respond to the writer, continuing the conversation the writer has begun.

Experienced college readers don't try to memorize a text or assume they must understand it completely before they respond to it. Instead they read strategically, looking for the writer's claims, for the writer's key ideas and terms, and for connections with key ideas and terms in other texts. They also read to discern what conversation the writer has entered, and how the writer's argument is connected to those he or she makes reference to.

When you annotate a text, your notes in the margins might address the following questions:

- What arguments is this author responding to?
- Is the issue relevant or significant?
- How do I know that what the author says is true?
- Is the author's evidence legitimate? Sufficient?
- Can I think of an exception to the author's argument?
- What would the counterarguments be?

Good readers ask the same kinds of questions of every text they read, considering not just *what* a writer says (the content), but *how* he or she says it given the writer's purpose and audience.

The marks you leave on a page might indicate your own ideas and questions, patterns you see emerging, links to other texts, even your gut response to the writer's argument—agreement, dismay, enthusiasm, confusion. They reveal your own thought processes as you read and signal that you are entering the conversation. In effect, they are traces of your own responding voice.

Developing your own system of marking or annotating pages can help you feel confident when you sit down with a new reading for your classes. Based on our students' experiences, we offer this practical tip: Although wide-tipped highlighters have their place in some classes, it is more useful to read with a pen or pencil in your hand, so that you can do more than draw a bar of color through words or sentences you find important. Experienced readers write their responses to a text in the margins, using personal codes (boxing key words, for example), writing out definitions of words they have looked up, drawing lines to connect ideas on facing pages, or writing notes to themselves ("Connect this to Edmundson on consumer culture"; "Hirsch would disagree big time—see his ideas on memorization in primary grades"; "You call THIS evidence?!"). These notes help you get started on your own writing assignments, and you cannot make them with a highlighter.

Annotating your readings benefits you twice. First, it is easier to participate in class discussions if you have already marked passages that are important, confusing, or linked to specific passages in other texts you have read. It's a sure way to avoid that sinking feeling you get when you return to pages you read the night before but now can't remember at all. Second, by marking key ideas in a text, noting your ideas about them, and making connections to key ideas in other texts, you have begun the process of writing an essay. When you start writing the first draft of your essay, you can quote the passages you have already marked and explain what you find significant about them based on the notes you have already made to yourself. You can make the connections to other texts in the paragraphs of your own essay that you have already begun to make on the pages of your textbook. If you mark your texts effectively, you'll never be at a loss when you sit down to write the first draft of an essay.

Let's take a look at how one of our students marked several paragraphs of Douglas Massey and Nancy Denton's *American Apartheid: Segregation and the Making of the Underclass* (1993). In the excerpt below, the student underlines what she believes is important information and begins to create an outline of the authors' main points.

1. racist attitudes

2. private behaviors

3. & institutional practices
lead to ghettos (authors' claim?)

Ghetto = multistory, high-density housing projects.
Post-1950

I remember this happening where I grew up, but I didn't know the government was responsible. Is this what happened in There Are No Children Here?

The spatial isolation of black Americans was achieved by a conjunction of <u>racist attitudes</u>, <u>private behaviors</u>, and <u>institutional practices</u> that disenfranchised blacks from urban housing markets and led to the creation of the <u>ghetto</u>. Discrimination in employment exacerbated black poverty and limited the economic potential for integration, and black residential mobility was systematically blocked by pervasive discrimination and white avoidance of neighborhoods containing blacks. <u>The walls of the ghetto were buttressed after 1950</u> by government programs that promoted slum clearance and <u>relocated displaced ghetto residents into multi-story, high-density housing projects</u>.   *1*

In theory, this self-reinforcing cycle of prejudice, discrimination, and segregation was broken during the 1960s by a growing rejection of racist sentiments by whites and a series of court decisions and federal laws that banned discrimination in public life. (1) <u>The Civil Rights Act of 1964 outlawed racial discrimination in employment</u>, (2) the <u>Fair Housing Act of 1968 banned discrimination in housing</u>, and   *2*

Authors say situation of "spatial isolation" remains despite court decisions. Does it?

(3) the <u>*Gautreaux* and *Shannon* court decisions prohibited public authorities from placing housing projects</u> exclusively in black neighborhoods. Despite these changes, however, the <u>nation's largest black communities remained as segregated as ever in 1980</u>. Indeed, many urban areas displayed a pattern of intense racial isolation that could only be described as <u>hypersegregation</u>.

Although the racial climate of the United States improved outwardly during the 1970s, <u>racism still restricted the residential freedom of black Americans</u>; it just did so in   *3*

Subtler racism, not on public record.

less blatant ways. In the aftermath of the civil rights revolution, few whites voiced openly racist sentiments; realtors no longer refused outright to rent or sell to blacks; and few

Lack of enforcement of Civil Rights Act? Fair Housing Act? Gautreaux and Shannon? Why? Why not?

local governments went on record to oppose public housing projects because they would contain blacks. This lack of overt racism, however, did not mean that prejudice and discrimination had ended.

Notice how the student underlines information that helps her understand the argument the authors make.

1. She numbers the three key factors (racist attitudes, private behaviors, and institutional practices) that influenced the formation of ghettos in the United States.

2. She identifies the situation that motivates the authors' analysis: the extent to which "the spatial isolation of black Americans" still exists despite laws and court decisions designed to end residential segregation.

3. She makes connections to her own experience and to another book she has read.

By understanding the authors' arguments and making these connections, the student begins the writing process. She also sets the stage for her own research, for examining the authors' claim that residential segregation still exists.

READING AS A WRITER: ANALYZING A TEXT RHETORICALLY

When you study how writers influence readers through language, you are analyzing the **rhetoric** (available means of persuasion) of what you read. When you identify a writer's purpose for responding to a situation by composing an essay that puts forth claims meant to sway a particular audience, you are performing **rhetorical analysis** — separating out the parts of an argument to better understand how the argument works as a whole. We discuss each of these elements — *situation*, *purpose*, *claims*, and *audience* — as we analyze the following preface from E. D. Hirsch's book *Cultural Literacy: What Every American Needs to Know* (1987). Formerly a professor of English, Hirsch has long been interested in educational reform. That interest developed from his (and others') perception that today's students do not know as much as students did in the past. Although Hirsch wrote the book more than twenty years ago, many observers still believe that the contemporary problems of illiteracy and poverty can be traced to a lack of cultural literacy.

Read the preface. You may want to mark it with your own questions and responses, and then consider them in light of our analysis (following the preface) of Hirsch's rhetorical situation, purpose, claims, and audience.

E. D. HIRSCH JR.

Preface to *Cultural Literacy*

E. D. Hirsch Jr., a retired English professor, is the author of many acclaimed books, including *The Schools We Need and Why We Don't Have Them* (1996) and *The Knowledge Deficit* (2006). His book *Cultural Literacy* was a best seller in 1987 and had a profound effect on the focus of education in the late 1980s and 1990s.

■ ■ ■

Rousseau points out the facility with which children lend themselves to our false methods: . . ."The apparent ease with which children learn is their ruin."
— JOHN DEWEY

There is no matter what children should learn first, any more than what leg you should put into your breeches first. Sir, you may stand disputing which is best to put in first, but in the meantime your backside is bare. Sir, while you stand considering which of two things you should teach your child first, another boy has learn't 'em both.
— SAMUEL JOHNSON

To be culturally literate is to possess the basic information needed to thrive in the modern world. The breadth of that information is great, extending over the major domains of human activity from sports to science. It is by no means confined to "culture" narrowly understood as an acquaintance with the arts. Nor is it confined to one social class. Quite the contrary. Cultural literacy constitutes the only sure avenue of opportunity for disadvantaged children, the only reliable way of combating the social determinism that now condemns them to remain in the same social and educational condition as their parents. That children from poor and illiterate homes tend to remain poor and illiterate is an unacceptable failure of our schools, one which has occurred not because our teachers are inept but chiefly because they are compelled to teach a fragmented curriculum based on faulty educational theories. Some say that our schools by themselves are powerless to change the cycle of poverty and illiteracy. I do not agree. They *can* break the cycle, but only if they themselves break fundamentally with some of the theories and practices that education professors and school administrators have followed over the past fifty years. [1]

Although the chief beneficiaries of the educational reforms advocated in this book will be disadvantaged children, these same reforms will also enhance the literacy of children from middle-class homes. The educational goal advocated is that of mature literacy for *all* our citizens. [2]

The connection between mature literacy and cultural literacy may already be familiar to those who have closely followed recent discussions [3] of education. Shortly after the publication of my essay "Cultural Literacy," Dr. William Bennett, then chairman of the National Endowment for the Humanities and subsequently secretary of education in President Ronald Reagan's second administration, championed its ideas. This endorsement from an influential person of conservative views gave my ideas some currency, but such an endorsement was not likely to recommend the concept to liberal thinkers, and in fact the idea of cultural literacy has been attacked by some liberals on the assumption that I must be advocating a list of great books that every child in the land should be forced to read.

But those who examine the Appendix to this book will be able to judge   4
for themselves how thoroughly mistaken such an assumption is. Very few specific titles appear on the list, and they usually appear as words, not works, because they represent writings that culturally literate people have read about but haven't read. *Das Kapital* is a good example. Cultural literacy is represented not by a *prescriptive* list of books but rather by a *descriptive* list of the information actually possessed by literate Americans. My aim in this book is to contribute to making that information the possession of all Americans.

The importance of such widely shared information can best be under-   5
stood if I explain briefly how the idea of cultural literacy relates to currently prevailing theories of education. The theories that have dominated American education for the past fifty years stem ultimately from Jean Jacques Rousseau, who believed that we should encourage the natural development of young children and not impose adult ideas upon them before they can truly understand them. Rousseau's conception of education as a process of natural development was an abstract generalization meant to apply to all children in any time or place: to French children of the eighteenth century or to Japanese or American children of the twentieth century. He thought that a child's intellectual and social skills would develop naturally without regard to the specific content of education. His content-neutral conception of educational development has long been triumphant in American schools of education and has long dominated the "developmental," content-neutral curricula of our elementary schools.

In the first decades of this century, Rousseau's ideas powerfully influ-   6
enced the educational conceptions of John Dewey, the writer who has the most deeply affected modern American educational theory and practice. Dewey's clearest and, in his time, most widely read book on education, *Schools of Tomorrow*, acknowledges Rousseau as the chief source of his educational principles. The first chapter of Dewey's book carries the telling title "Education as Natural Development" and is sprinkled with quotations from Rousseau. In it Dewey strongly seconds Rousseau's opposition to the mere accumulation of information.

Development emphasizes the need of intimate and extensive personal acquaintance with a small number of typical situations with a view to mastering the way of dealing with the problems of experience, not the piling up of information.

Believing that a few direct experiences would suffice to develop the skills that children require, Dewey assumed that early education need not be tied to specific content. He mistook a half-truth for the whole. He placed too much faith in children's ability to learn general skills from a few typical experiences and too hastily rejected "the piling up of information." Only by piling up specific, communally shared information can children learn to participate in complex cooperative activities with other members of their community.

7

This old truth, recently rediscovered, requires a countervailing theory of education that once again stresses the importance of specific information in early and late schooling. The corrective theory might be described as an anthropological theory of education, because it is based on the anthropological observation that all human communities are founded upon specific shared information. Americans are different from Germans, who in turn are different from Japanese, because each group possesses specifically different cultural knowledge. In an anthropological perspective, the basic goal of education in a human community is acculturation, the transmission to children of the specific information shared by the adults of the group or polis.

8

Plato, that other great educational theorist, believed that the specific contents transmitted to children are by far the most important elements of education. In *The Republic* he makes Socrates ask rhetorically, "Shall we carelessly allow children to hear any casual tales which may be devised by casual persons, and to receive into their minds ideas for the most part the very opposite of those which we shall wish them to have when they are grown up?" Plato offered good reasons for being concerned with the specific contents of schooling, one of them ethical: "For great is the issue at stake, greater than appears—whether a person is to be good or bad."

9

Time has shown that there is much truth in the durable educational theories of both Rousseau and Plato. But even the greatest thinkers, being human, see mainly in one direction at a time, and no thinkers, however profound, can foresee the future implications of their ideas when they are translated into social policy. The great test of social ideas is the crucible of history, which, after a time, usually discloses a one-sidedness in the best of human generalizations. History, not superior wisdom, shows us that neither the content-neutral curriculum of Rousseau and Dewey nor the narrowly specified curriculum of Plato is adequate to the needs of a modern nation.

10

Plato rightly believed that it is natural for children to learn an adult culture, but too confidently assumed that philosophy could devise the one best culture. (Nonetheless, we should concede to Plato that within our culture we have an obligation to choose and promote our best traditions.) On the other side, Rousseau and Dewey wrongly believed that adult culture

11

is "unnatural" to young children. Rousseau, Dewey, and their present-day disciples have not shown an adequate appreciation of the need for transmission of specific cultural information.

In contrast to the theories of Plato and Rousseau, an anthropological   *12* theory of education accepts the naturalness as well as the relativity of human cultures. It deems it neither wrong nor unnatural to teach young children adult information before they fully understand it. The anthropological view stresses the universal fact that a human group must have effective communications to function effectively, that effective communications require shared culture, and that shared culture requires transmission of specific information to children. Literacy, an essential aim of education in the modern world, is no autonomous, empty skill but depends upon literate culture. Like any other aspect of acculturation, literacy requires the early and continued transmission of specific information. Dewey was deeply mistaken to disdain "accumulating information in the form of symbols." Only by accumulating shared symbols, and the shared information that the symbols represent, can we learn to communicate effectively with one another in our national community.

Now let's take a look at the steps to rhetorical analysis.

■ Identify the Situation

The **situation** is what moves a writer to write. To understand what motivated Hirsch to write, we need look no further than the situation he identifies in the first paragraph of the preface: "the social determinism that now condemns [disadvantaged children] to remain in the same social and educational condition as their parents." Hirsch wants to make sure his readers are aware of the problem so that they will be motivated to read his argument (and take action). He presents as an urgent problem the situation of disadvantaged children, an indication of what is at stake for the writer and for the readers of the argument. For Hirsch, this situation needs to change.

The urgency of a writer's argument is not always triggered by a single situation; often it is multifaceted. Again in the first paragraph, Hirsch identifies a second concern when he states that poverty and illiteracy reflect "an unacceptable failure of our schools, one which has occurred not because our teachers are inept but chiefly because they are compelled to teach a fragmented curriculum based on faulty educational theories." When he introduces a second problem, Hirsch helps us see the interconnected and complex nature of the situations authors confront in academic writing.

■ Identify the Writer's Purpose

The **purpose** for writing an essay may be to respond to a particular situation; it also can be what a writer is trying to accomplish. Specifically, what does the writer want readers to do? Does the writer want us to think about an issue, to change our opinions? Does the writer want to make us aware of a problem that we may not have recognized? Does the writer advocate for some type of change? Or is some combination of all three at work?

Hirsch's main purpose is to promote educational reforms that will produce a higher degree of literacy for all citizens. He begins his argument with a broad statement about the importance of cultural literacy: "Cultural literacy constitutes the only sure avenue of opportunity for disadvantaged children, the only reliable way of combating the social determinism that now condemns them to remain in the same social and educational condition as their parents" (para. 1). As his argument unfolds, his purpose continues to unfold as well. He identifies the schools as a source of the problem and suggests how they must change to promote literacy:

> Some say that our schools by themselves are powerless to change the cycle of poverty and illiteracy. I do not agree. They *can* break the cycle, but only if they themselves break fundamentally with some of the theories and practices that education professors and school administrators have followed over the past fifty years. (para. 1)

The "educational goal," Hirsch declares at the end of paragraph 2, is "mature literacy for *all* our citizens." To reach that goal, he insists, education must break with the past. In paragraphs 5 through 11, he cites the influence of Jean-Jacques Rousseau, John Dewey, and Plato, tracing what he sees as the educational legacies of the past. Finally, in the last paragraph of the excerpt, Hirsch describes an "anthropological view, . . . the universal fact that a human group must have effective communications to function effectively, that effective communications require shared culture, and that shared culture requires transmission of specific information to children." It is here, Hirsch argues, in the "transmission of specific information to children," that schools must do a better job.

▪ Identify the Writer's Claims

Claims are assertions that authors must justify and support with evidence and good reasons. The **thesis**, or **main claim**, is the controlling idea that crystallizes a writer's main point, helping readers track the idea as it develops throughout the essay. A writer's purpose clearly influences the way he or she crafts the main claim of an argument, the way he or she presents all assertions and evidence.

Hirsch's main claim is that "cultural literacy constitutes the only sure avenue of opportunity for disadvantaged children, the only reliable way of combating the social determinism that now condemns them to remain in the same social and educational condition as their parents" (para. 1). Notice that his thesis also points to a solution: making cultural literacy the core of public school curricula. Here we distinguish the main claim, or thesis, from the other claims or assertions that Hirsch makes. For example, at the very outset, Hirsch states that "to be culturally literate is to possess the basic information needed to thrive in the modern world." Although this is an assertion that requires support, it is a **minor claim**; it does not shape what Hirsch writes in the remainder of his essay. His main claim, or thesis, is really his call for reform.

▪ Identify the Writer's Audience

A writer's language can help us identify his or her **audience**, the readers whose opinions and actions the writer hopes to influence or change. In Hirsch's text, words and phrases like *social determinism*, *cycle of poverty and illiteracy*, *educational reforms*, *prescriptive*, and *anthropological* indicate that Hirsch believes his audience is well educated. References to Plato, Socrates, Rousseau, and Dewey also indicate the level of knowledge Hirsch expects of his readers.

Finally, the way the preface unfolds suggests that Hirsch is writing for an audience that is familiar with a certain **genre**, or type, of writing: the formal argument. Notice how the author begins with a statement of the situation and then asserts his position. The very fact that he includes a preface speaks to the formality of his argument. Hirsch's language, his references, and the structure of the document all suggest that he is very much in conversation with people who are experienced and well-educated readers.

More specifically, the audience Hirsch invokes is made up of people who are concerned about illiteracy in the United States and the kind of social determinism that appears to condemn the educationally disadvantaged to poverty. Hirsch also acknowledges directly "those who have closely followed recent discussions of education," including the conservative William Bennett and liberal thinkers who might be provoked by Bennett's advocacy of Hirsch's ideas (para. 3). Moreover, Hirsch appears to assume that his readers have achieved "mature literacy," even if they are not actually "culturally literate." He is writing for an audience that not only is well educated but also is deeply interested in issues of education as they relate to social policy.

Steps to Analyzing a Text Rhetorically

1 **Identify the situation.** What motivates the writer to write?

2 **Identify the writer's purpose.** What does the writer want readers to do or think about?

3 **Identify the writer's claims.** What is the writer's main claim? What minor claims does he or she make?

4 **Identify the writer's audience.** What do you know about the writer's audience? What does the writer's language imply about the readers? What about the writer's references? The structure of the essay?

Hirsch's writings on cultural literacy have inspired and provoked many responses to the conversation he initiated more than twenty years ago. Eugene F. Provenzo's book *Critical Literacy: What Every American Needs to Know*, published in 2005, is a fairly recent one. Provenzo examines the source of Hirsch's ideas, his critiques of scholars like John Dewey, the extent to which Hirsch's argument is based on sound research, and the implications of Hirsch's notion of cultural literacy for teaching and learning. Despite the passage of time, Hirsch's book remains relevant in discussions about the purpose of education, demonstrating how certain works become touchstones and the ways academic and cultural conversations can be sustained over time.

A Practice Sequence: Analyzing a Text Rhetorically

To practice the strategies of rhetorical analysis, we would like you to read "Hirsch's Desire for a National Curriculum," an excerpt from Eugene F. Provenzo's book, using these questions as a guide:

- What motivates Provenzo as a writer?
- What does he want readers to think about?
- What is Provenzo's main point?
- Given the language Provenzo uses, who do you think his main audience is?

EUGENE F. PROVENZO JR.

Hirsch's Desire for a National Curriculum

Eugene F. Provenzo Jr. is a professor in the Department of Teaching and Learning in the School of Education at the University of Miami in Coral Gables, Florida. His career as a researcher has been interdisciplinary in nature. Throughout his work, his primary focus has been on education as a social and cultural phenomenon. One of his prime concerns has been the role of the teacher in American society. He is also interested in the impact of computers on contemporary children, education, and culture. He is author or co-author of numerous books, including *Teaching, Learning, and Schooling: A Twenty-first Century Perspective* (2001); *Internet and Online Research for Teachers* (Third Edition, 2004); and *Observing in Schools: A Guide for Students in Teacher Education* (2005).

■ ■ ■

To a large extent, Hirsch, in his efforts as an educational reformer, wants to establish a national curriculum.   *1*

> Our elementary schools are not only dominated by the content-neutral ideas of Rousseau and Dewey, they are also governed by approximately sixteen thousand independent school districts. We have viewed this dispersion of educational authority as an insurmountable obstacle to altering the fragmentation of the school curriculum even when we have questioned that fragmentation. We have permitted school policies that have shrunk the body of information that Americans share and these policies have caused our national literacy to decline.

This is an interesting argument when interpreted in a conservative political context. While calling for greater local control, Hirsch and other conservatives call for a curriculum that is controlled not at the state and local level, but at the national level by the federal government.

Putting contradictions like this aside, the question arises as to whether or not Hirsch even has a viable curriculum. In an early review of Hirsch's *Cultural Literacy*, Hazel Whitman Hertzberg criticized the book and its list of 5,000 things every American needs to know for its fragmentation. As she explained:

> Hirsch's remedy for curricular fragmentation looks suspiciously like more fragmentation. Outside of the dubious claim that his list represents what literate people know, there is nothing that holds it together besides its arrangement in alphabetical order. Subject-matter organization is ignored. It is not hard to imagine how Hirsch's proposal would have been greeted by educational neoconservatives had it been made by one of those professors of education who he charges are responsible for the current state of cultural illiteracy.

Hertzberg wonders what Hirsch's "hodgepodge of miscellaneous, arbitrary, and often trivial information" would look like if it were put into a coherent curriculum.

In 1988 Hirsch did in fact establish the Core Knowledge Foundation, which had as its purpose the design of a national curriculum. Called the "Core Knowledge Sequence," the sequence offered a curriculum in six content areas: history, geography, mathematics, science, language arts, and fine arts. Hirsch's curriculum was intended to represent approximately half of the total curriculum for K–6 schools. Subsequent curriculum revisions include a curriculum for grades seven and eight as well as one at the preschool level.

Several hundred schools across the United States currently use Hirsch's model. A national conference is held each year, which draws several thousand people. In books like *What Your First Grader Needs to Know* (1991) as well *A First Dictionary of Cultural Literacy: What Our Children Need to Know* (1989) and *The Dictionary of Cultural Literacy* (1993), along with the Core Knowledge Sequence, one finds a fairly conservative but generally useful curriculum that conforms to much of the content already found in local school systems around the country.

Hirsch seems not to recognize that there indeed is a national curriculum, one whose standards are set by local communities through their acceptance and rejection of textbooks and by national accreditation groups ranging from the National Council of Teachers of Mathematics to the National Council for Social Studies Teachers and the National Council of Teachers of English. One need only look at standards in different subject areas in school districts across the country to realize the extent to which there is indeed a national curriculum.   *5*

Whether the current curriculum in use in the schools across the country is adequate is of course open to debate. Creating any curriculum is by definition a deeply political act, and is, or should be, subject to considerable negotiation and discussion at any level. But to act as though there is not a de facto national curriculum is simply inaccurate. First graders in most school districts across the country learn about the weather and the seasons, along with more basic skills like adding and subtracting. Students do not learn to divide before they learn how to add or multiply. Local and state history is almost universally introduced for the first time in either third or fourth grade. It is reintroduced in most states at the seventh or eighth grade levels. Algebra is typically taught in the ninth grade. Traditions, developmental patterns of students, textbook content, and national subject standards combine to create a fairly uniform national curriculum.   *6*

Hirsch's complaint that there is no national curriculum is not motivated by a desire to establish one but rather a desire to establish a curriculum that reflects his cultural and ideological orientation. It is a sophisticated assault on more inclusive and diverse models of curriculum and culture—one that represents a major battle in the culture wars of the last twenty years in the United States.   *7*

WRITING AS A READER: COMPOSING A RHETORICAL ANALYSIS

One of our favorite exercises is to ask our students to choose a single paragraph from a text they have read and to write a rhetorical analysis of it. Once you are able to identify *how* writers make their arguments, you are better able to make use of their strategies in your own writing. You may be amazed by how much you can say or write about a single paragraph in an essay once you begin to consider such factors as purpose and audience.

For example, one of our students wrote a rhetorical analysis of a paragraph from Sidonie Smith and Julia Watson's *Reading Autobiography: A Guide for Interpreting Life Narratives* (2001). In the following passage from

Smith and Watson's book, they discuss the concept of *agency*. Scholars in fields such as sociology have sought to explain the relationship between individuals and the institutions that influence their everyday lives—education, capitalism, and politics. Scholars recognize that the values, beliefs, and linguistic practices of a community can exert pressures on and even limit the ways individuals make decisions and take action—that is, the ways they assert a sense of agency. How do individuals create, innovate, and make choices apart from the communities they inhabit or the institutions that have such a significant impact on them? Smith and Watson draw on scholarship in literary criticism to think about what it means to act with a sense of agency in writing autobiography, a form of life narrative.

Note that in the passage, Smith and Watson cite numerous other writers and works, sometimes generally (Catherine Belsey on subject construction) and sometimes very specifically (a direct quotation from an argument by Elizabeth Wingrove). For reasons of space—and because they don't bear on the assignment—the full list of works cited for the passage has been omitted.

▪ Write a Rhetorical Analysis of a Paragraph

Read this passage, making notes on its rhetorical situation, purpose, main claim, and audience. You may want to underline passages where the writers make the following points explicit:

- the situation to which they are responding
- the purpose of their analysis and argument
- their main claim or thesis
- who they believe their audience is

SIDONIE SMITH AND JULIA WATSON

Agency

Sidonie Smith is the Martha Guernsey Colby Collegiate Professor of English and Women's Studies at the University of Michigan. Her fields of specialization include autobiography studies, narrative and human rights, feminist theories, and women's studies in literature. She has additional interests in travel narratives, literature and memory, and postcolonial literatures and theory.

Julia Watson is associate dean in arts and humanities and professor of comparative studies at the Ohio State University. Her interests include life narrative and theory of autobiography, feminist theory and women's writing, twentieth-century postcolonial and multicultural autobiography, and visual autobiography and film.

We like to think of human beings as agents of or actors in their own lives, rather than passive pawns in social games or unconscious transmitters of cultural scripts and models of identity. Consequently, we tend to read autobiographical narratives as proofs of human agency, relating actions in which people exercise free choice over the interpretation of their lives and express their true selves. In fact, traditional autobiography has been read as a narrative of agency, evidence that subjects can live freely. But we must recognize that the issue of how subjects claim, exercise, and narrate agency is far more complicated.

We have noted that discursive systems emergent in social structures shape the operations of memory, experience, identity, and embodiment. People tell stories of their lives through the cultural scripts available to them, and they are governed by cultural strictures about self-presentation in public. If individuals are constituted through discursive practices, how, then, can they be said to control the stories they tell about themselves? Some contemporary investigations of agency are helpful in addressing this question.

Theories of Agency

Analysts of agency have found the theorist Louis Althusser helpful in thinking through these issues. Althusser argued that the subject is a subject of ideology—not in the narrow sense of propaganda but in the broad sense of the pervasive cultural formations of the dominant class. Althusser recognized the power of coercive state institutions to conform subjects to particular behaviors, beliefs, and identities—institutions such as the military and the police. He also recognized that there are less overtly coercive institutions—social services, educational institutions, the family, literary and artistic institutions—that "hail" subjects who enter them. By "hailing" Althusser meant the process through which subjects become interpellated, become what institutional discourses and practices make of them. They are "subjected." Most important, individuals understand themselves to be "naturally" self-produced because the power of ideology to hail the subject is hidden, obscured by the very practices of the institution. In this way, people are invested in and mystified by their own production as subjects, by their own "subjection." That is, they have "false consciousness": they collude in their own lack of agency by believing that they have it. It is not enough, then, to say that people exercise free will. The concept of "free will" is itself embedded in a discourse about the Enlightenment individual, a historically specific discourse through which subjects understand themselves as intellectually mature and free to make their own choices. To claim that all humans have something called "free will" in this way is to misunderstand an ideological concept as a "natural" aspect of existence.

Other theorists have taken this challenge to agency as a starting point from which to rethink its possibility. Political theorist Elizabeth Wingrove,

1

2

3

4

in rereading Althusser, argues that "agents change, and change their world, by virtue of the systemic operation of multiple ideologies." The key here is the multiplicity of ideologies through which the subject is hailed. These multiple ideologies "expose both the subject and the system to perpetual reconfiguration" (871). In that reconfiguration new possibilities emerge for knowing oneself as a subject and for understanding a system. (See also Catherine Belsey on subject construction.)

French sociologist and theorist Michel de Certeau locates agency in   5
what he terms "transverse tactics." Individuals and groups deploy such tactics to manipulate the spaces in which they are constrained, such as the workplace or the housing project. For instance, a factory worker may superimpose another system (of language or culture) onto the system imposed on him in the factory. Combining systems, he can create "a space in which he can find ways of using the constraining order of the place or of the language" to establish "a degree of plurality and creativity." Such modes of "re-use," then, are interventions that open a space of agency within constrained systems (29–30). For the French theorist Jean-François Lyotard the flexible and uncontrollable networks of language, through which people construct their worlds, spawn unexpected moves and countermoves. As a result language itself holds strategic potential for the formation of new sociopolitical subjects.

For postcolonial theorist Arjun Appadurai, agency in this particular   6
historical moment of global capitalism resides in imagination mobilized as "an organized field of social practices" (327). Imagination negotiates between "sites of agency," namely, the imagined communities in which we participate, and "globally defined fields of possibility" (327). Situated amid multiple forms of imagined worlds, individuals as sites of agency deploy their imaginations as a social fact and a kind of work to navigate the disjunctures of global flows that create radically different self-understandings.

Feminist philosopher Judith Butler situates agency in what she calls the   7
"performativity" of subjectivity. According to Butler, identity is enacted daily through socially enforced norms that surround us. Thus it is through our reenactment of the norms of, say, masculinity or femininity that we know ourselves to be "a heterosexual man" or "a woman." But this enforcement of norms cannot be totally effective since individuals fail to conform fully to them because of the multiplicity of norms we are called to reenact in our everyday lives. The failure to conform signals the "possibility of a variation" of "the rules that govern intelligible identity." And with failure come reconfigurations or changes of identities (*Gender Trouble*, 145).

Like Butler, feminist theorist Teresa de Lauretis defines the unconscious   8
as a potential source of agency. The unconscious is a psychic domain of disidentification ("Eccentric Subjects," 125–27), a repository of all the experiences and desires that have to be repressed in order for the subject to conform to socially enforced norms. As such, it lies at the intersection of the psychic and the social. A repository of the repressed, the unconscious

is also a potential site of agency; its excess is a source of resistance to socially enforced calls to fixed identities. And the anthropologist Sherry B. Ortner situates agency in the ability with which people play the "games" of culture—with their rules and structures—with wit and intelligence. For Ortner, sociocultural structures are always partial rather than total. And thus here is always the possibility of changing the rules—although not of escaping rules altogether.

We have briefly noted several theorizings of agency as multiple: ideologies; transverse tactics and modes of disuse; the flexible network of language; the navigation of imagined communities; performativity; psychic disidentification; the games of culture. These concepts offer critical frameworks for considering how people, in the act of narrating their lives, might change the stories they tell, might gain access to other cultural scripts, might come to understand themselves differently, might, that is, exercise agency.

9

Now read our student's rhetorical analysis of paragraph 3 from Smith and Watson's piece on agency; we have annotated her analysis to point out the moves she is making in her own writing.

The student states what she believes is the authors' purpose.

The particular paragraph that I chose in *Reading Autobiography: A Guide for Interpreting Life Narratives* begins a discussion on the various theories of agency. Its purpose is to investigate the concept of agency in order to determine how individuals can be said to control the stories they tell about themselves.

1

The student identifies the audience based on the kind of information the authors provide. She also states their purpose: the context that prompts their discussion.

The authors assume that the audience has very little or no background about how the concept of agency has been approached in various theories and scholarly interpretations. This is evidenced by the fact that the paragraph essentially introduces and explains a popular theory. By explaining the theory, Smith and Watson are attempting to establish the various contexts in which autobiography is interpreted and understood.

2

She underscores the writers' style and method of argument, which makes use of others' ideas. Their use of evidence affects their tone.

In order to further their own ideas about agency and provide further guides to the study of autobiography, the authors refer to existing analyses and theories. By citing the theorist Louis Althusser, Smith and Watson provide evidence to support and solidify their own claims and develop their own methods. In presenting Althusser's ideas, they are rather objective and matter-of-fact in their style or tone. It is also important to note that this particular paragraph is placed within a larger section that compares and contrasts several theories of agency.

3

Finally, the student explains how she would employ a similar tactic in writing her own argument.

Overall, the paragraph I selected uses other scholarly arguments as evidence and presents an interesting and important theory of agency in the study of autobiography. Smith and Watson's use of another's arguments to support and strengthen their own is an effective strategy, and I would certainly use it for similar reasons.   4

A Practice Sequence: Writing a Rhetorical Analysis of a Paragraph

1 Review your annotations and write a paragraph in which you describe Sidonie Smith and Julia Watson's rhetorical situation, their purpose, their main claim, and their audience.

2 Now write an analysis of a paragraph from Sidonie Smith and Julia Watson's *Reading Autobiography: A Guide for Interpreting Life Narratives*. Choose a substantial paragraph (not paragraph 3!) that you find especially interesting, either for what the authors write or for how they write it. Using quotations from the text, compose one page in which you consider the situation they respond to, their purpose as writers, or their audience.

■ Write a Rhetorical Analysis of an Essay

By now you should be developing a strong sense of what is involved in analyzing a paragraph rhetorically. You should be ready to take the next steps: performing a rhetorical analysis of a complete text and then sharing your analysis and the strategies you've learned with your classmates.

Read the next text, "Cultural Baggage" by Barbara Ehrenreich, annotating it to help you identify her situation, purpose, thesis, and audience. As you read, also make a separate set of annotations—possibly with a different color pen or pencil, circled, or keyed with asterisks—in which you comment on or evaluate the effectiveness of her essay. What do you like or dislike about it? Why? Does Ehrenreich persuade you to accept her point of view? What impressions do you have of her as a person? Would you like to be in a conversation with her?

BARBARA EHRENREICH

Cultural Baggage

Barbara Ehrenreich is a social critic, activist, and political essayist. Her book *Nickel and Dimed: On (Not) Getting By in America* (2001) describes her attempt to live on low-wage jobs; it became a national best seller in the United States. Her book, *Bait and Switch: The (Futile) Pursuit of the American Dream* (2005), explores the shadowy world of the white-collar unemployed. Recent books of cultural analysis by Ehrenreich include

Bright-Sided: How the Relentless Promotion of Positive Thinking Is Undermining America and *This Land Is Their Land: Reports from a Divided Nation* (both published in 2009). Ehrenreich has also written for *Mother Jones, The Atlantic, Ms., The New Republic, In These Times*, Salon.com, and other publications. "Cultural Baggage" was originally published in the *New York Times Magazine* in 1992.

■ ■ ■

An acquaintance was telling me about the joys of rediscovering her ethnic and religious heritage. "I know exactly what my ancestors were doing 2,000 years ago," she said, eyes gleaming with enthusiasm, "and *I can do the same things now.*" Then she leaned forward and inquired politely, "And what is your ethnic background, if I may ask?"   *1*

"None," I said, that being the first word in line to get out of my mouth.   *2* Well, not "none," I backtracked. Scottish, English, Irish—that was something, I supposed. Too much Irish to qualify as a WASP; too much of the hated English to warrant a "Kiss Me, I'm Irish" button; plus there are a number of dead ends in the family tree due to adoptions, missing records, failing memories, and the like. I was blushing by this time. Did "none" mean I was rejecting my heritage out of Anglo-Celtic self-hate? Or was I revealing a hidden ethnic chauvinism in which the Britannically derived serve as a kind of neutral standard compared with the ethnic "others"?

Throughout the 1960s and 70s, I watched one group after another—   *3* African Americans, Latinos, Native Americans—stand up and proudly reclaim their roots while I just sank back ever deeper into my seat. All this excitement over ethnicity stemmed, I uneasily sensed, from a past in which *their* ancestors had been trampled upon by *my* ancestors, or at least by people who looked very much like them. In addition, it had begun to seem almost un-American not to have some sort of hyphen at hand, linking one to more venerable times and locales.

But the truth is, I was raised with none. We'd eaten ethnic foods in my   *4* childhood home, but these were all borrowed, like the pasties, or Cornish meat pies, my father had picked up from his fellow miners in Butte, Montana. If my mother had one rule, it was militant ecumenism in all manners of food and experience. "Try new things," she would say, meaning anything from sweetbreads to clams, with an emphasis on the "new."

As a child, I briefly nourished a craving for tradition and roots. I im-   *5* mersed myself in the works of Sir Walter Scott. I pretended to believe that the bagpipe was a musical instrument. I was fascinated to learn from a grandmother that we were descended from certain Highland clans and longed for a pleated skirt in one of their distinctive tartans.

But in *Ivanhoe*, it was the dark-eyed "Jewess" Rebecca I identified   *6* with, not the flaxen-haired bimbo Rowena. As for clans: Why not call them "tribes," those bands of half-clad peasants and warriors whose idea of cuisine was stuffed sheep gut washed down with whiskey? And then there was the sting of Disraeli's remark—which I came across in my early teens—to the effect that his ancestors had been leading orderly, literate lives when my ancestors were still rampaging through the Highlands daubing themselves with blue paint.

Motherhood put the screws on me, ethnicity-wise. I had hoped that by marrying a man of Eastern European Jewish ancestry I would acquire for my descendants the ethnic genes that my own forebears so sadly lacked. At one point, I even subjected the children to a seder of my own design, including a little talk about the flight from Egypt and its relevance to modern social issues. But the kids insisted on buttering their matzos and snickering through my talk. "Give me a break, Mom," the older one said. "You don't even believe in God."

After the tiny pagans had been put to bed, I sat down to brood over Elijah's wine. What had I been thinking? The kids knew that their Jewish grandparents were secular folks who didn't hold seders themselves. And if ethnicity eluded me, how could I expect it to take root in my children, who are not only Scottish English Irish, but Hungarian Polish Russian to boot?

But, then, on the fumes of Manischewitz, a great insight took form in my mind. It was true, as the kids said, that I didn't "believe in God." But this could be taken as something very different from an accusation—a reminder of a genuine heritage. My parents had not believed in God either, nor had my grandparents or any other progenitors going back to the great-great level. They had become disillusioned with Christianity generations ago—just as, on the in-law side, my children's other ancestors had shaken their Orthodox Judaism. This insight did not exactly furnish me with an "identity," but it was at least something to work with: We are the kind of people, I realized—whatever our distant ancestors' religions—who do *not* believe, who do not carry on traditions, who do not do things just because someone has done them before.

The epiphany went on: I recalled that my mother never introduced a procedure for cooking or cleaning by telling me, "Grandma did it this way." What did Grandma know, living in the days before vacuum cleaners and disposable toilet mops? In my parents' general view, new things were better than old, and the very fact that some ritual had been performed in the past was a good reason for abandoning it now. Because what was the past, as our forebears knew it? Nothing but poverty, superstition, and grief. "Think for yourself," Dad used to say. "Always ask why."

In fact, this may have been the ideal cultural heritage for my particular ethnic strain—bounced as it was from the Highlands of Scotland across the sea, out to the Rockies, down into the mines, and finally spewed out into high-tech, suburban America. What better philosophy, for a race of migrants, than "Think for yourself"? What better maxim, for a people whose whole world was rudely inverted every thirty years or so, than "Try new things"?

The more tradition-minded, the newly enthusiastic celebrants of Purim and Kwanzaa and Solstice, may see little point to survival if the survivors carry no cultural freight—religion, for example, or ethnic tradition. To which I would say that skepticism, curiosity, and wide-eyed ecumenical tolerance are also worthy elements of the human tradition and are at least as old as such notions as "Serbian" or "Croatian," "Scottish" or "Jewish." I make no claims for my personal line of progenitors except that they remained loyal to the values that may have induced all of our ancestors, long, long ago, to climb down from the trees and make their way into the open plains.

A few weeks ago, I cleared my throat and asked the children, now 13 mostly grown and fearsomely smart, whether they felt any stirrings of ethnic or religious identity, etc., which might have been, ahem, insufficiently nourished at home. "None," they said, adding firmly, "and the world would be a better place if nobody else did, either." My chest swelled with pride, as would my mother's, to know that the race of "none" marches on.

A Practice Sequence: Writing a Rhetorical Analysis of an Essay

1 Write a brief rhetorical analysis of Barbara Ehrenreich's essay, referring to your notes and citing passages where she indicates her situation, purpose, main claim, and audience.

2 An option for group work: As a class, divide into three or more groups. Each group should answer the following questions in response to their reading of Ehrenreich's essay "Cultural Baggage":

Group 1: Identify the situation(s) motivating Ehrenreich to write. Then evaluate: How well does her argument function as a conversation with other authors who have written on the same topic?

Group 2: Analyze the audience's identity, perspectives, and conventional expectations. Then evaluate: How well does the argument function as a conversation with the audience?

Group 3: Analyze the writer's purpose. Then evaluate: Do you believe Ehrenreich achieves her purpose in this essay? Why or why not?

Then, as a class, share your observations:

- To what extent does the author's ability as a conversationalist—that is, her ability to enter into a conversation with other authors and her audience—affect your evaluation of whether she achieves her purpose in this essay?

- If you were to meet this writer, what suggestions or advice would you give her for making her argument more persuasive?

Much if not all of the writing you do in college will be based on what you have read. This is the case, for example, when you summarize a philosopher's theory, analyze the significance of an experiment in psychology, or, perhaps, synthesize different and conflicting points of view in making an argument about race and academic achievement in sociology.

As we maintain throughout this book, writing and reading are inextricably linked to each other. Good academic writers are also good critical readers: They leave their mark on what they read, identifying issues, making judgments about the truth of what writers tell them, and evaluating the adequacy of the evidence in support of an argument. This is where writing and inquiry begin: understanding our own position relative to the scholarly conversations that we want to enter. Moreover, critical readers try to understand the strategies that writers use to persuade readers to agree with them. At times, these are strategies that we can adapt in advancing our arguments. In the next chapter, we provide some strategies for identifying and evaluating the adequacy of a writer's claims.

From Identifying Claims to Analyzing Arguments

A **claim** is an assertion of fact or belief that needs to be supported with **evidence** — the information that backs up a claim. A main claim, or **thesis**, summarizes the writer's position on a situation and answers the question(s) the writer addresses. It also encompasses all of the minor claims, along with their supporting evidence, that the writer makes throughout the argument.

As readers, we need to identify a writer's main claim, or thesis, because it helps us organize our own understanding of the writer's argument. It acts as a signpost that tells us, "This is what the essay is about," "This is what I want you to pay attention to," and "This is how I want you to think, change, or act."

When you evaluate a claim, whether it is an argument's main claim or a minor claim, it is helpful to identify the type of claim it is: a claim of fact, a claim of value, or a claim of policy. You also need to evaluate the reasons for and the evidence that supports the claim. Because academic argument should acknowledge multiple points of view, you also should be prepared to identify what, if any, concessions a writer offers his or her readers, and what counterarguments he or she anticipates from others in the conversation.

IDENTIFYING TYPES OF CLAIMS

To illustrate how to identify a writer's claims, let's take a look at a text by educators Myra and David Sadker that examines gender bias in schools. The text is followed by our analyses of the types of claims (fact, value, and policy) and then, in the next section, of the nature of the arguments (use of evidence, concessions, and counterarguments) the authors present.

MYRA SADKER AND DAVID SADKER

Hidden Lessons

Myra Sadker was a professor of education at American University until 1995, the year she died. Dr. Sadker coauthored *Sexism in School and Society*, the first book on gender bias in America's schools, in 1973 and became a leading advocate for equal educational opportunities.

David Sadker is a professor at American University and has taught at the elementary, middle school, and high school levels. David Sadker and his late wife earned a national reputation for their groundbreaking work in confronting gender bias and sexual harassment. "Hidden Lessons" is an excerpt from their book *Failing at Fairness: How Our Schools Cheat Girls* (1994).

■ ■ ■

Sitting in the same classroom, reading the same textbook, listening to the same teacher, boys and girls receive very different educations. From grade school through graduate school female students are more likely to be invisible members of classrooms. Teachers interact with males more frequently, ask them better questions, and give them more precise and helpful feedback. Over the course of years the uneven distribution of teacher time, energy, attention, and talent, with boys getting the lion's share, takes its toll on girls. Since gender bias is not a noisy problem, most people are unaware of the secret sexist lessons and the quiet losses they engender.

Girls are the majority of our nation's schoolchildren, yet they are second-class educational citizens. The problems they face—loss of self-esteem, decline in achievement, and elimination of career options—are at the heart of the educational process. Until educational sexism is eradicated, more than half our children will be shortchanged and their gifts lost to society.

Award-winning author Susan Faludi discovered that backlash "is most powerful when it goes private, when it lodges inside a woman's mind and turns her vision inward, until she imagines the pressure is all in her head, until she begins to enforce the backlash too—on herself."[1] Psychological backlash internalized by adult women is a frightening concept, but what is even more terrifying is a curriculum of sexist school lessons becoming

---

[1] Editor's note: Journalist Susan Faludi's book *Backlash: The Undeclared War Against American Women* (1991) was a response to the antifeminist backlash against the women's movement.

secret mind games played against female children, our daughters, and to-morrow's women.

After almost two decades of research grants and thousands of hours of classroom observation, we remain amazed at the stubborn persistence of these hidden sexist lessons. When we began our investigation of gender bias, we looked first in the classrooms of one of Washington, D.C.'s elite and expensive private schools. Uncertain of exactly what to look for, we wrote nothing down; we just observed. The classroom was a whirlwind of activity so fast paced we could easily miss the quick but vital phrase or gesture, the insidious incident, the tiny inequity that held a world of meaning. As we watched, we had to push ourselves beyond the blind spots of socialization and gradually focus on the nature of the interaction between teacher and student. On the second day we saw our first example of sexism, a quick, jarring flash within the hectic pace of the school day:

> Two second-graders are kneeling beside a large box. They whisper excit-edly to each other as they pull out wooden blocks, colored balls, counting sticks. So absorbed are these two small children in examining and sorting the materials, they are visibly startled by the teacher's impatient voice as she hovers over them. "Ann! Julia! Get your cottonpickin' hands out of the math box. Move over so the boys can get in there and do their work."

Isolated here on the page of a book, this incident is not difficult to inter-pret. It becomes even more disturbing if you think of it with the teacher making a racial distinction. Picture Ann and Julia as African-American children moved away so white children can gain access to the math mate-rials. If Ann and Julia's parents had observed this exchange, they might justifiably wonder whether their tuition dollars were well spent. But few parents actually watch teachers in action, and fewer still have learned to interpret the meaning behind fast-paced classroom events.

The incident unsettles, but it must be considered within the context of numerous interactions this harried teacher had that day. While she talked to the two girls, she was also keeping a wary eye on fourteen other active children. Unless you actually shadowed the teacher, stood right next to her as we did, you might not have seen or heard the event. After all, it lasted only a few seconds.

It took us almost a year to develop an observation system that would register the hundreds of daily classroom interactions, teasing out the gen-der bias embedded in them. Trained raters coded classrooms in math, reading, English, and social studies. They observed students from differ-ent racial and ethnic backgrounds. They saw lessons taught by women and by men, by teachers of different races. In short, they analyzed Amer-ica's classrooms. By the end of the year we had thousands of observation sheets, and after another year of statistical analysis, we discovered a syn-tax of sexism so elusive that most teachers and students were completely unaware of its influence.

Recently a producer of NBC's *Dateline* contacted us to learn more   8
about our discovery that girls don't receive their fair share of education. Jane Pauley, the show's anchorwoman, wanted to visit classrooms, capture these covert sexist lessons on videotape, and expose them before a television audience. The task was to extricate sound bites of sexism from a fifth-grade classroom where the teacher, chosen to be the subject of the exposé, was aware she was being scrutinized for sex bias.

Dateline had been taping in her class for two days when we received   9
a concerned phone call. "This is a fair teacher," the producer said. "How can we show sexism on our show when there's no gender bias in this teacher's class?" We drove to the NBC studio in Washington, D.C., and found two *Dateline* staffers, intelligent women concerned about fair treatment in school, sitting on the floor in a darkened room staring at the videotape of a fifth-grade class. "We've been playing this over and over. The teacher is terrific. There's no bias in her teaching. Come watch."

After about twenty minutes of viewing, we realized it was a case of   10
déjà vu: The episodal sexist themes and recurring incidents were all too familiar. The teacher was terrific, but she was more effective for half of the students than she was for the other. She was, in fact, a classic example of the hundreds of skillful well-intentioned professionals we have seen who inadvertently teach boys better than girls.

We had forgotten how difficult it was to recognize subtle sexism before   11
you learn how to look. It was as if the *Dateline* staff members were wearing blinders. We halted the tape, pointed out the sexist behaviors, related them to incidents in our research, and played the tape again. There is a classic "aha!" effect in education when people finally "get it." Once the hidden lessons of unconscious bias are understood, classrooms never look the same again to the trained observer.

Much of the unintentional gender bias in that fifth-grade class could   12
not be shown in the short time allowed by television, but the sound bites of sexism were also there. *Dateline* chose to show a segregated math group: boys sitting on the teacher's right side and girls on her left. After giving the math book to a girl to hold open at the page of examples, the teacher turned her back to the girls and focused on the boys, teaching them actively and directly. Occasionally she turned to the girls' side, but only to read the examples in the book. This teacher, although aware that she was being observed for sexism, had unwittingly transformed the girls into passive spectators, an audience for the boys. All but one, that is: The girl holding the math book had become a prop.

Dateline also showed a lively discussion in the school library. With both   13
girls' hands and boys' hands waving for attention, the librarian chose boy after boy to speak. In one interaction she peered through the forest of girls' hands waving directly in front of her to acknowledge the raised hand of a boy in the back of the room. Startled by the teacher's attention, the boy muttered, "I was just stretching."

The next day we discussed the show with future teachers, our students *14* at The American University. They were bewildered. "Those teachers really were sexist. They didn't mean to be, but they were. How could that happen—with the cameras and everyone watching?" When we took those students into classrooms to discover the hidden lessons for themselves, they began to understand. It is difficult to detect sexism unless you know precisely how to observe. And if a lifetime of socialization makes it difficult to spot gender bias even when you're looking for it, how much harder it is to avoid the traps when you are the one doing the teaching.

Now let's consider the types of claims in the Sadkers' argument.

▪ Identify Claims of Fact

Claims of fact are assertions (or arguments) *that a problem or condition has existed, exists, or will exist.* Claims of fact are made by individuals who believe that something is true; but claims are never simply facts, and some claims are more objective, and so easier to verify, than others.

For example, "It's raining in Portland today" is a "factual" claim of fact; it's easily verified. But consider the argument some make that the steel and automotive industries in the United States have depleted our natural resources and left us at a crisis point. This is an assertion that a condition exists. A careful reader must examine the basis for this kind of claim: Are we truly facing a crisis? And if so, are the steel and automotive industries truly responsible? A number of politicians counter this claim of fact by insisting that if the government were to harness the vast natural resources in Alaska, there would be no "crisis." This is also a claim of fact, in this case an assertion that a condition will exist in the future. Again, it is based on evidence, evidence gathered from various sources that indicates sufficient resources in Alaska to keep up with our increasing demands for resources and to allay a potential crisis.

Our point is that most claims of fact are debatable. They may be based on factual information, but they are not necessarily true. Most claims of fact present **interpretations** of evidence derived from **inferences**. That is, a writer will examine evidence (for example, about the quantity of natural resources in Alaska and the rate that industries harness those resources and process them into goods), draw a conclusion based on reasoning (an inference), and offer an explanation based on that conclusion (an interpretation).

So, for example, an academic writer will study the evidence on the quantity of natural resources in Alaska and the rate that industries harness those resources and process them into goods; only after the writer makes an informed decision on whether Alaska's resources are sufficient to keep pace with the demand for them will he or she take a position on the issue.

In the first paragraph of their essay, the Sadkers make the claims of fact that female students are "more likely to be invisible members of classrooms" and that teachers interact differently with female students than they do with male students. The careful reader will want to see how the Sadkers support these claims of fact throughout the essay. Can they convincingly present their argument about "the secret sexist lessons and the quiet losses they engender" in the paragraphs that follow?

■ Identify Claims of Value

A claim of fact is different from a **claim of value**, which *expresses an evaluation of a problem or condition that has existed, exists, or will exist*. Is a condition good or bad? Is it important or inconsequential?

For example, an argument that developing the wilderness in Alaska would irreversibly mar the beauty of the land indicates that the writer values the beauty of the land over the possible benefits of development. A claim of value presents a judgment, which is sometimes signaled by a value-laden word like *ugly, beautiful,* or *immoral,* but may also be conveyed more subtly by the writer's tone and attitude.

Sadker and Sadker make a claim of value when they suggest that a "majority of our nation's schoolchildren" have become "second-class educational citizens" and point out that the consequences of treating girls differently from boys in school has resulted in a "loss of self-esteem, decline in achievement, and elimination of career options" for girls (para. 2). Of course, the critical reader's task is to question these evaluations: Does gender bias in the classroom affect self-esteem, achievement, and career options? Both of these statements are minor claims, but they make assertions that require support. After all, how do the Sadkers know these things? Whether or not readers are persuaded by these claims depends on the evidence or reasons that the authors use to support them. We discuss the nature of evidence and what constitutes "good reasons" later in this chapter.

■ Identify Claims of Policy

A **claim of policy** is an argument for what should be the case, *that a condition should exist*. It is a call for change.

Two recent controversies on college campuses center on claims of policy. One has activists arguing that universities and colleges should have a policy that all workers on campus earn a living wage. The other has activists arguing that universities and colleges should have a policy that prevents them from investing in countries where the government ignores human rights.

Claims of policy are often signaled by words like *should* and *must*: "For public universities to live up to their democratic mission, they *must* provide all their workers with a living wage." Myra and David Sadker make a claim of policy when they assert that "educational sexism" must be eradicated; otherwise, they point out, "more than half our children will be shortchanged and their gifts lost to society" (para. 2).

Not all writers make their claims as explicitly as the Sadkers do; nor does every argument include all three types of claims. But you should be able to identify the three different types of claims. Moreover, you should keep in mind what the situation is and what kind of argument can best address what you see as a problem. Ask yourself: Does the situation involve a question of fact? Does the situation involve a question of value? Does the situation require a change in policy? Or is some combination at work?

Steps to Identifying Claims

1 **Ask:** Does the argument assert that a problem or condition has existed, exists, or will exist? If so, it's a claim of fact.

2 **Ask:** Does the argument express an evaluation of a problem or condition that has existed, exists, or will exist? If so, it's a claim of value.

3 **Ask:** Does the argument call for change, and is it directed at some future action? If so, it's a claim of policy.

A Practice Sequence: Identifying Claims

What follows is a series of claims. Identify each one as a claim of fact, value, or policy. Be prepared to justify your categorizations.

1 Taxing the use of fossil fuels will end the energy crisis.

2 We should reform the welfare system to ensure that people who receive support from the government also work.

3 Images of violence in the media create a culture of violence in schools.

4 The increase in homelessness is a deplorable situation that contradicts the whole idea of democracy.

5 Distributing property taxes is the one sure way to end poverty and illiteracy.

6 Individual votes don't really count.

7 Despite the 20 percent increase in the number of females in the workforce over the past forty years, women are still not treated equitably.

8 Affirmative action is a policy that has outlived its usefulness.

9 There are a disproportionate number of black males in American prisons.

10 The media are biased, which means we cannot count on newspapers or television news for the truth.

ANALYZING ARGUMENTS

Analyzing an argument involves identifying the writer's main and minor claims and then examining (1) the reasons and evidence given in support of each claim, (2) the writer's concessions, and (3) the writer's attempts to handle counterarguments.

■ Analyze the Reasons Used to Support a Claim

Stating a claim is one thing; supporting that claim is another. As a critical reader, you need to evaluate whether a writer has provided *good reasons* to support his or her position. Specifically, you will need to decide whether the support for a claim is recent, relevant, reliable, and accurate. As a writer, you will need to use the same criteria when you support your claims.

Is the source recent?   Knowledgeable readers of your written arguments not only will be aware of classic studies that you should cite as "intellectual touchstones"; they will also expect you to cite recent evidence, evidence published within five years of when you are writing.

Of course, older research can be valuable. For example, in a paper about molecular biology, you might very well cite James Watson and Francis Crick's groundbreaking 1953 study in which they describe the structure of DNA. That study is an intellectual touchstone that changed the life sciences in a fundamental way.

Or if you were writing about educational reform, you might very well mention E. D. Hirsch's 1987 book *Cultural Literacy*. Hirsch's book did not change the way people think about curricular reform as profoundly as Watson and Crick's study changed the way scientists think about biology, but his term *cultural literacy* continues to serve as useful shorthand for a particular way of thinking about curricular reform that remains influential to this day.

Although citing Hirsch is an effective way to suggest you have studied the history of an educational problem, it will not convince your readers that there is a crisis in education today. To establish that, you would need to use as evidence studies published over the past few years to show, for example, that there has been a steady decline in test scores since Hirsch wrote his book. And you would need to support your claim that curricular reform is the one sure way to bring an end to illiteracy and poverty with data that are much more current than those available to Hirsch in the 1980s. No one would accept the judgment that our schools are in crisis if your most recent citation is more than twenty years old.

Is the source relevant?   Evidence that is relevant must have real bearing on your issue. It also depends greatly on what your readers expect. For example, suppose two of your friends complain that they were unable to sell their condominiums for the price they asked. You can claim there is a crisis in the housing market, but your argument won't convince most readers if your only evidence is personal anecdote.

Such *anecdotal evidence* may alert you to a possible topic and help you connect with your readers, but you will need to test the **relevance** of your friends' experience—Is it pertinent? Is it typical of a larger situation or condition?—if you want your readers to take your argument seriously. For example, you might scan real estate listings to see what the asking prices are for properties comparable to your friends' properties. By comparing listings, you are defining the grounds for your argument. If your friends are disappointed that their one-bedroom condominiums sold for less than a three-bedroom condominium with deeded parking in the same neighborhood, it may well be that their expectations were too high.

In other words, if you aren't comparing like things, your argument is going to be seriously flawed. If your friends' definition of what constitutes a "reasonable price" differs dramatically from everyone else's, their experience is probably irrelevant to the larger question of whether the local housing market is depressed.

Is the source reliable?   You also need to evaluate whether the data you use to support your argument are reliable. After all, some researchers present findings based on a very small sample of people that can also be rather selective.

For example, a researcher might argue that 67 percent of the people he cited believe that school and residential integration are important concerns. But how many people did this person interview? More important, who responded to the researcher's questions? A reliable claim cannot be based on a few of the researcher's friends.

Let's return to the real estate example. You have confirmed that your friends listed their condominiums at prices that were not out of line with the market. Now what? You need to seek out reliable sources to continue testing your argument. For example, you might search the real estate or business section of your local newspaper to see if there are any recent stories about a softening of the market; and you might talk with several local real estate agents to get their opinions on the subject.

In consulting local newspapers and local agents, you are looking for **authoritative sources** against which to test your anecdotal evidence—the confirmation of experts who report on, study, evaluate, and have an informed opinion on local real estate. Local real estate agents are a source of **expert testimony**, firsthand confirmation of the information you have discovered. You would probably not want to rely on the testimony of a single real estate agent, who may have a bias; instead, talk with several agents to see if a consensus emerges.

Is the source accurate?   To determine the accuracy of a study that you want to use to support your argument, you have to do a little digging to find out who else has made a similar claim. For instance, if you want to cite authoritative research that compares the dropout rate for white students with the rate for students of color, you could look at research conducted by the Civil Rights Project. Of course, you don't need to stop your search there. You could also check the resources available through the National Center for Education Statistics. You want to show your readers that you have done a relatively thorough search to make your argument as persuasive as possible.

The accuracy of **statistics**—factual information presented numerically or graphically (for example, in a pie or bar chart)—is difficult to verify. To a certain extent, then, their veracity has to be taken on faith. Often the best you can do is assure yourself that the source of your statistical information is authoritative and reliable—government and major research universities generally are "safe" sources—and that whoever is interpreting the statistical information is not distorting it.

Returning again to our real estate example, let's say you've read a newspaper article that cites statistical information about the condition of the local real estate market (for example, the average price of property and volume of sales this year in comparison to last year). Presumably the author of the article is an expert, but he or she may be interpreting rather than simply reporting on the statistics.

To reassure yourself one way or the other, you may want to check the sources of the author's statistics—go right to your source's sources—which a responsible author will cite. That will allow you to look over the raw data and come to your own conclusions. A further step you could take would be to discuss the article with other experts—local real estate agents—to find out what they think of the article and the information it presents.

Now, let's go back to Myra and David Sadker's essay. How do they develop their assertion that girls are treated differently from boys in classrooms from "grade school through graduate school"? First, they tell us (in paragraph 4) that they have been conducting research continuously for "almost two decades" and that they have accumulated "thousands of hours of classroom observation." This information suggests that their research is both recent and relevant.

But are their studies reliable and accurate? That their research meets the reliability criterion is confirmed by the grants they received over the years: Granting institutions (experts) have assessed their work and determined that it deserved to be funded. Grants confer authority on research. In addition, the Sadkers explain that they observed and refined their analyses over time to achieve accuracy: "As we watched, we had to push ourselves beyond the blind spots of socialization and gradually focus on the nature of the interaction between teacher and student."

In paragraph 7, the authors provide more evidence that the observations that support their claim are accurate. Not only have they observed many instances of gender bias in classrooms; so have trained "raters." The raters add objectivity to the findings because they did not share the Sadkers' interest in drawing a specific conclusion about whether gender bias exists in classrooms. Also the raters observed a wide cross section of students and teachers from "different racial and ethnic backgrounds." At the end of their study, the Sadkers had collected thousands of pieces of data and could feel quite confident about their conclusion—that they had "discovered a syntax of sexism so elusive that most teachers and students were completely unaware of its influence."

Steps to Evaluating Support for a Claim

Ask yourself:

1 **Is the source recent?** Has it been published in the past few years? How have things changed since then? If the source was not published recently, is it still an important part of the conversation worth acknowledging?

2 **Is the source relevant?** Does the evidence have real bearing on the claim? Is it pertinent? Is it typical of a larger situation or condition?

3 **Is the source reliable?** Does the evidence come from recognized experts and authoritative institutions?

4 **Is the source accurate?** Are the data presented in the source sufficient? Have they been gathered, interpreted, and reported responsibly? How do they compare with other data you have found?

■ Identify Concessions

Part of the strategy of developing a main claim supported with good reasons is to offer a **concession**, an acknowledgment that readers may not agree with every point the writer is making. A concession is a writer's way of saying, "Okay, I can see that there may be another way of looking at the issue or another way to interpret the evidence used to support the argument I am making."

For instance, you may not want your energy costs to go up, but after examining the reasons why it may be necessary to increase taxes on gasoline—to lower usage and conserve fossil fuels—you might concede that a tax increase on gasoline could be useful. The willingness to make concessions is valued in academic writing because it acknowledges both complexity and the importance of multiple perspectives. It also acknowledges the fact that information can always be interpreted in different ways.

The Sadkers make a concession when they acknowledge in the last paragraph of the excerpt that "it is difficult to detect sexism unless you know precisely how to observe." And, they explain, "if a lifetime of socialization makes it difficult to spot gender bias even when you're looking for it, how much harder it is to avoid the traps when you are the one doing the teaching."

Notice that these concessions do not weaken their argument. The authors' evidence appears overwhelmingly to support their thesis. The lesson here is that conceding a point in your argument shows that you have acknowledged there are other ways of seeing things, other interpretations. This is an important part of what it means to enter a conversation of ideas.

Often a writer will signal a concession with phrases like the following:

- "It is true that . . ."
- "I agree with X that Y is an important factor to consider."
- "Some studies have convincingly shown that . . ."

Generally, the writer will then go on to address the concession, explaining how it needs to be modified or abandoned in the light of new evidence or the writer's perspective on the issue.

▪ Identify Counterarguments

As the term suggests, a **counterargument** is an argument raised in response to another argument. You want to be aware of and acknowledge what your readers may object to in your argument. Anticipating readers' objections is an important part of developing a conversational argument.

For example, if you were arguing in support of universal health care, you would have to acknowledge that the approach departs dramatically from the traditional role the federal government has played in providing health insurance. That is, most people's access to health insurance has depended on their individual ability to afford and purchase this kind of insurance. You would have to anticipate how readers would respond to your proposal, especially readers who do not feel that the federal government should ever play a role in what has heretofore been an individual responsibility.

Anticipating readers' objections demonstrates that you understand the complexity of the issue and are willing at least to entertain different and conflicting opinions.

In the excerpt from "Hidden Lessons," the Sadkers describe the initial response of *Dateline* staffers to what they observed in the classroom they were videotaping: "This is a fair teacher. . . . [T]here's no gender bias in this teacher's class." Two women whom the Sadkers describe as "intelligent" and "concerned about fair treatment in school" agreed: "We've been playing this over and over. The teacher is terrific. There's no bias in her teaching. Come watch" (para. 9).

Notice the Sadkers' acknowledgment that even intelligent, concerned people may not see the problems that the Sadkers spent more than twenty years studying. In addressing the counterargument—that sexism does not exist—the authors are both empathetic to and respectful of what any reasonable person might or might not see. This is in keeping with what we would call a conversational argument: that writers listen to different points of view, that they respect arguments that diverge from their own, and that they be willing to exchange ideas and revise their own points of view.

In an argument that is more conversational than confrontational, writers establish areas of common ground, both to convey different views that are understood and to acknowledge the conditions under which those different views are valid. Writers do this by making concessions and anticipating and responding to counterarguments.

This conversational approach is what many people call a **Rogerian approach to argument**, based on psychologist Carl Rogers's approach to psychotherapy. The objective of a Rogerian strategy is to reduce listeners' sense of threat so that they are open to alternatives. For academic writers, it involves four steps:

1. Conveying to readers that their different views are understood
2. Acknowledging conditions under which readers' views are valid
3. Helping readers see that the writer shares common ground with them
4. Creating mutually acceptable solutions to agreed-on problems

The structure of an argument, according to the Rogerian approach, grows out of the give-and-take of conversation between two people and the topic under discussion. In a written conversation, the give-and-take of face-to-face conversation takes the form of anticipating readers' counterarguments and uses language that is both empathetic and respectful, to put the readers at ease.

Steps to Analyzing an Argument

1 **Identify the type of claim.** Is it a claim of fact? Value? Policy?

2 **Analyze the reasons used to support the claim.** Are they recent? Relevant? Reliable? Accurate?

3 **Identify concessions.** Is there another argument that even the author acknowledges is legitimate?

4 **Identify counterarguments.** What arguments contradict or challenge the author's position?

AN ANNOTATED STUDENT ARGUMENT

We have annotated the following essay to show the variety of claims the student writer uses, as well as some of the other argumentative moves he performs. The assignment was to write an argument out of personal experience and observation about the cultural impact of a recent innovation. Marques Camp chose to write about the Kindle, an electronic reading device developed by the online retailer Amazon that allows users to download books for a fee. However, the user cannot share the download electronically with other users. Camp touches on a number of issues reflected in his claims.

As you read the essay, imagine how you would respond to his various claims. Which do you agree with, which do you disagree with, and why? What evidence would you present to support or counter his claims? Do you detect a main claim? Do you think his overall essay develops and supports it?

Camp 1

Marques Camp
Professor Fells
English 1020
January 28, 20 —

The End of the World May Be Nigh, and It's the Kindle's Fault

"Libraries will in the end become cities."
— Gottfried Wilhelm Leibniz, German polymath

The future of written human history will come, as they will have us believe, in the form of the Amazon Kindle, all 10.2 ounces of it, all 2 GB and 532 MHz of it, all 240,000+ titles of it, ready to change the way people read, ready to revolutionize the way people see the world.

The student presents a claim of fact that others have made.

The Kindle is a signpost for our times, the final checkpoint in our long and adventurous journey from the world of printed paper to the twenty-first-century world of digitalization. We first saw this paradigm shift with newspapers, where weekly columns were taken over by daily blog posts, where 48-point sans-serif headlines transformed into 12-point Web links. We then moved on into television, where Must-See TV was replaced with On-Demand TV, where consumers no longer sat around in the living room with their families during prime time but rather watched the latest episode of their favorite show commercial-free from the comfortable and convenient confines of their

He lays the basis for a counterargument by questioning whether this is a real threat at all, citing some technological precedents.

1

2

Camp 2

laptop, able to fast-forward, rewind, and pause with a delightful and devilish sense of programming omnipotence. We are now seeing it, slowly but surely, slay the giant that we never thought could be slain: the world of books.

In this paragraph, he makes a claim of fact about unequal access to techno- logical innovation and offers a concession to what many see as the value of the Kindle.

Contrary to popular belief, easier access to a wider quantity of literature is not a universal revolution. The Kindle speaks to the world that measures quantity by the number of cable television channels it has, speed by the connectivity of its wireless networks, and distance by the number of miles a family travels for vacation. Yes, the Kindle is the new paradigm for uni- versal access and literary connectivity. But it is much like a col- lege degree in the sense that it is merely a gateway to a wealth of opportunity. The problem, however, is gaining access to this gateway in the first place.

He supports his claim of fact with evi- dence based on expe- rience: that sharing books provides something technol- ogy cannot offer.

Books often pass from hand to hand, from friend to friend, from generation to generation, many times with the mutual understanding that remuneration is not neces- sary — merely the promise of hope that the new reader is as touched and enlightened by the book as the previous one. This transfer serves more than a utilitarian function; symbolically, it represents the passage of hope, of knowledge, of responsibility.

Evidence from obser- vation: not everyone has access to new technologies, but people will always have access to books.

The book, in many cases, represents the only sort of hope for the poorest among us, the great equalizer in a world full of financial and intellectual capital and highly concentrated access to this capital. The wonderful quality of the book is that its intellectual value is very rarely proportional to its financial value; people often consider their most valuable book to be one they happened to pick up one day for free.

An evaluative claim — that the widening gap between rich and poor is dangerous — adds another layer to the argument.

The proliferation of the Kindle technology, however, will result in a wider disconnect between the elite and the non- elite — as the old saying goes, the rich will get richer and the poor will get poorer. Unfortunately for the poor, this is no finan- cial disconnect — this is a widening of the gap in the world of ideas. And this is, perhaps, the most dangerous gap of all.

A further evaluative claim — that new technological devices offer little hope to "victims" of illit- eracy — is followed by

The Kindle Revolution, ironically, may end up contribut- ing to the very disease that is antithetical to its implied func- tion: illiteracy. Make no mistake, the Kindle was not designed with the poor in mind. For those in most need of the printed

Camp 3

a claim of fact that books inspire people to create change in the world.

word, for those who are the most vulnerable victims of the illiteracy threat, the $359 Kindle offers little in the way of hope.
One book for a poor person is all he or she needs to be inspired
and change the world; with the Kindle, that one book is consoli-
dated and digitized, transformed from a tangible piece of hope
and the future into a mere collection of words in the theoreti-
cally infinite dimension of cyberspace. A "book" on the Kindle is
a book wedged among many other books, separated by nothing
more than title, devoid of essence, devoid of uniqueness, devoid
of personality, devoid of its unique position in space — precisely
what makes a book a "book," as opposed to a mere collection
of words. It is no longer singular, no longer serendipitous, no
longer distinguishable.

The e-book cannot, like a bound book, pass through   *8*
multiple hands and eventually settle itself on the right person,
ready to be unleashed as a tool to change the world. Due to the

An evaluative claim in which the author observes that tech-nology can make reading passive. Then a claim of fact: that the experience of reading can be trans-formative.

restrictions on sharing and reselling e-books with the Kindle,
the very nature of reading books transforms from highly communal to individualistic, from highly active to somewhat passive.
The Kindle will lead to the mystification of books, wherein they
become less unique capsules of thoughts and ideas and experiences and more utility-oriented modes of information-giving.
What many Kindle advocates fail to realize is that oftentimes,
the transformative quality of books resides less in the actual
words comprising the book and more in the actual experience of
reading.

There is also something to be said for the utter cor-   *9*
poreality of books that lies at the heart of Leibniz's metaphor.
Libraries are physical testaments to all that we have learned and
recorded during human history. The sheer size of libraries, the
sheer number of volumes residing in them, tell us, in a spatial
sense, of all the theoretical knowledge we have accumulated in
the course of our existence, and all the power we have to further

The student offers a final evaluative claim, observing that the Kindle threatens to mask the relation-ship between ideas and the world.

shape and define the world we live in. The Kindle and other
digital literary technologies are threatening the very connection
between the world of ideas and the material world, threatening
to take our literal measures of progress and hide them away in

Camp 4

His concluding claim
falls just short
of making a pro-
posal—but he does
suggest that those
in positions of power
must ensure the pro-
liferation of books.

the vast database of words and ideas, available only to those with $359 to spare and a credit card for further purchases.

If libraries will indeed become cities, then we need to carefully begin to lay the foundations, book on top of book on top of book, and we are going to have to ensure that we have enough manpower to do it.

10

ANALYZING AND COMPARING ARGUMENTS

As an academic writer, you will often need to compare disparate claims and evidence from multiple arguments addressing the same topic. Rarely, however, will those arguments be simplistic pro/con pairs meant to represent two opposing sides to an issue. Certainly the news media thrive on such black-and-white conflict, but academic writers seek greater complexity and do not expect to find simple answers. Analyzing and comparing essays on the same topic or issue will often reveal the ways writers work with similar evidence to come up with different, and not necessarily opposed, arguments.

The next two selections are arguments about grade inflation. Both are brief, and we recommend you read through them quickly as a prelude to the activity in analyzing and comparing arguments that follows them. As you read, try to note their claims, the reasons used to support them, concessions, and counterarguments.

STUART ROJSTACZER

Grade Inflation Gone Wild

A former professor of geophysics at Duke University with a PhD in applied earth sciences, Stuart Rojstaczer has written or coauthored many geological studies in his career as a scientist. He has also published a book, *Gone for Good: Tales of University Life After the Golden Age* (1999), and numerous articles on higher education and grading. He is the creator of gradeinflation.com, where he posts a variety of charts and graphs chronicling his data about grade inflation. This op-ed piece appeared in the *Christian Science Monitor* on March 24, 2009.

■ ■ ■

About six years ago, I was sitting in the student union of a small lib-   *1*
eral arts college when I saw a graph on the cover of the student
newspaper that showed the history of grades given at that institution in
the past 30 years.

Grades were up. Way up.   *2*

I'm a scientist by training and I love numbers. So when I looked at that   *3*
graph, I wondered, "How many colleges and universities have data like
this that I can find?" The answer is that a lot of schools have data like this
hidden somewhere. Back then, I found more than 80 colleges and universities with data on grades, mostly by poking around the Web. Then I created a website (gradeinflation.com) so that others could find this data.
I learned that grades started to shoot up nationwide in the 1960s, leveled off in the 1970s, and then started rising again in the 1980s. Private
schools had much higher grades than public schools, but virtually everyone was experiencing grade inflation.

What about today?   *4*

Grades continue to go up regardless of the quality of education. At a   *5*
time when many are raising questions about the quality of US higher education, the average GPA at public schools is 3.0, with many flagship state
schools having average GPAs higher than 3.2. At a private college, the
average is now 3.3. At some schools, it tops 3.5 and even 3.6. "A" is average at those schools! At elite Brown University, two-thirds of all letter
grades given are now A's.

These changes in grading have had a profound influence on college life   *6*
and learning. When students walk into a classroom knowing that they can
go through the motions and get a B+ or better, that's what they tend to do,
give minimal effort. Our college classrooms are filled with students who
do not prepare for class. Many study less than 10 hours a week—that's
less than half the hours they spent studying 40 years ago. Paradoxically,
students are spending more and more money for an education that seems
to deliver less and less content.

With so few hours filled with learning, boredom sets in and students   *7*
have to find something to pass the time. Instead of learning, they drink. A
recent survey of more than 30,000 first-year students across the country
showed that nearly half were spending more hours drinking than they
were studying. If we continue along this path, we'll end up with a generation of poorly educated college graduates who have used their four years
principally to develop an addiction to alcohol.

There are many who say that grade inflation is a complicated issue   *8*
with no easy fix. But there are solutions. At about the same time that I
started to collect data on rising grades, Princeton University began to
actually do something about its grade-inflation problem. Its guidelines
have the effect of now limiting A's on average to 35 percent of students
in a class. Those guidelines have worked. Grades are going back down
at Princeton and academic rigor is making a comeback. A similar suc-

cessful effort has taken place at Wellesley College in Massachusetts. And through a concerted effort on the part of faculty and leadership, grades at Reed College in Oregon have stayed essentially constant for 20 years.

Princeton, Wellesley, and Reed provide evidence that the effort to keep grade inflation in check is not impossible. This effort takes two major steps. First, school officials must admit that there is a problem. Then they must implement policies or guidelines that truly restore excellence.

I asked Dean Nancy Malkiel at Princeton why so few schools seem to be following Princeton's lead. "Because it's hard work," she answered. "Because you have to persuade the faculty that it's important to do the work."

Making a switch will take hard work, but the effort is worthwhile. The alternative is a student body that barely studies and drinks out of boredom. That's not acceptable. Colleges and universities must roll up their sleeves, bring down inflated grades, and encourage real learning. It's not an impossible task. There are successful examples that can be followed. I'm looking forward to the day when we can return to being proud of the education that our nation's colleges and universities provide.

PHIL PRIMACK

Doesn't Anybody Get a C Anymore?

Phil Primack is a journalist, editor, and policy analyst who teaches journalism at Tufts University, where he is a senior fellow at the Jonathan M. Tisch College of Citizenship and Public Service. His articles have appeared in many regional and national publications, including the *New York Times*, the *Boston Globe*, and *Columbia Journalism Review*. The following piece appeared in the *Boston Globe* on October 5, 2008.

■ ■ ■

The student deserved a B-minus. Maybe even a C-plus, I had decided. One paper was especially weak; another was late. But then I began to rationalize. The student had been generally prepared and contributed to class discussion, so I relented and gave what I thought was a very generous B. At least I wouldn't get a complaint about this grade, I figured. Then came the e-mail.

Why such a "low grade," the indignant student wrote.

"Low grade"? Back when I attended Tufts in the late 1960s, a B in certain courses was something I could only dream about. But grade inflation, the steady rise in grade point averages that began in the 1960s, now leaves many students regarding even the once-acceptable B—which has always stood for "good"—as a transcript wrecker, and a C—that is, "average"—as unmitigated disaster. More and more academic leaders may lament grade inflation, but precious few have been willing to act against it, leaving their professors all alone in the minefield between giving marks that reflect true merit and facing the wrath of students for whom entitlement begins with the letter A.

Grade inflation "is a huge problem," says former US senator Hank Brown, who tried to make it a priority issue as president of the University of Colorado in 2006. "Under the current system at a lot of schools, there is no way to recognize the difference between an outstanding job and a good job. Grade inflation hides laziness on the part of the students, and as long as it exists, even faculty who want to do a good job [in grading] don't feel they can."   4

That's because many professors fear that "tough grading" will trigger poor student evaluations or worse, which in turn can jeopardize the academic career track. "In my early years, students would say they liked my class, but the grades were low and the work level high," says retired Duke University professor Stuart Rojstaczer. "I had to get with the program and reduce my own expectations of workload and increase grades in order to have students leave my class with a positive impression to give to other students so they would attend [next year]. I was teaching worse, but the student response was much more positive."   5

Harvard University is the poster campus for academic prestige—and for grade inflation, even though some of its top officials have warned about grade creep. About 15 percent of Harvard students got a B-plus or better in 1950, according to one study. In 2007, more than half of all Harvard grades were in the A range. Harvard declined to release more current data or officially comment for this article. At the University of Massachusetts at Amherst, the average GPA in 2007 was 3.19 (on a four-point scale), up from 3.02 a decade earlier. That "modest increase" simply reflects better students, UMass spokesman Ed Blaguszewski says in an e-mail. "Since our students have been increasingly well-prepared . . . it makes sense that their UMass grades have crept up. Essentially, the profile of the population has changed over time, so we don't consider this to be grade inflation."   6

That's certainly the most common argument to explain away grade inflation—smarter students naturally get higher grades. But is it that simple? Privately, many faculty members and administrators say colleges are unwilling to challenge and possibly offend students and their hovering, tuition-paying parents with some tough grade love. And without institutional backing, individual faculty members simply yield to whining students.   7

But not everywhere. The most cited—and extreme—case of taking on grade inflation is at Princeton University, which in 2004 directed that A's account for less than 35 percent of undergraduate course grades. From 2004 to 2007, A's (A-plus, A, A-minus) accounted for 40.6 percent of   8 undergraduate course grades, down from 47 percent in the period 2001 to 2004.

Closer to home, Wellesley College calls for the average grade in basic undergraduate courses to be no higher than a B-plus (3.33 GPA). "It's not that we're trying to get grades down, but we're trying to get grades to mean something," says associate dean of the college Adele Wolfson, who teaches chemistry. Wellesley's GPA, which stood at 3.47 in 2002 and was 3.4 when the policy was implemented two years later, fell to 3.3 this year, mainly because of more B grades and fewer A's. "The A has really become the mark of excellence," she says, "which is what it should be." *9*

The problem, says Rojstaczer, is that such policies are the exceptions, and that grade inflation will be reduced only through consistent prodding and action by top officials. "In truth, some university leaders are embarrassed that grading is so lax, but they are loath to make any changes," he says in an e-mail. "Grade inflation in academia is like the alcoholic brother you pretend is doing just fine. When someone calls your brother a drunk, you get angry and defend him, although privately you worry. That's where we are with grade inflation: public denial and private concern." *10*

A Practice Sequence: Analyzing and Comparing Arguments

1 To practice these strategies, first break up into small groups to discuss four different concerns surrounding grade inflation:

Group 1: Define what you think grade inflation is.

Group 2: Discuss whether you think grade inflation is a problem at the university or college you attend. What evidence can you provide to suggest that it is or is not a problem?

Group 3: Why should students or faculty be concerned with grade inflation? What's at stake?

Group 4: How would you respond if the administration at your university or college decided to limit the number of A's that faculty could give students?

Reassemble as a class and briefly report on the discussions.

2 Analyze Stuart Rojstaczer's argument in "Grade Inflation Gone Wild," addressing the following questions:

• What evidence does Rojstaczer use to indicate that there is a problem?

• How would you characterize this evidence (for example, scientific, anecdotal), and to what extent are you persuaded by the evidence he provides to suggest that grade inflation has a profound effect on "life and learning"?

- To what extent does he persuade you that a change in policy is necessary or that such a change would make a difference?

3 Now compare Phil Primack's and Stuart Rojstaczer's strategies for developing an argument.

- How does Primack establish that there is a problem? To what extent is his approach as persuasive as Rojstaczer's?

- What strategies would you identify in either argument as strategies that you might employ to develop your own argument?

- To what extent are you persuaded by the counterargument that Primack introduces?

- What do you think Primack wants you to do or think about in his analysis?

- In the end, does Primack add anything to your understanding of the problem of whether your college or university should introduce a policy to limit grade inflation?

From Identifying Issues to Forming Questions

Remember that inquiry is central to the process of composing. As you move from reading texts to writing them, you will discover that writing grows out of answering these questions:

- What are the concerns of the authors I've been reading?
- What situations motivate them to write?
- What frames or contexts do they use to construct their arguments?
- What is my argument in response to their writing?
- What is at stake in my argument?
- Who will be interested in reading what I have to say?
- How can I connect with both sympathetic and antagonistic readers?
- What kinds of evidence will persuade my readers?
- What objections are they likely to raise?

To answer these questions, you must read in the role of writer, with an eye toward

- *identifying an issue* (an idea or a statement that is open to dispute) that compels you to respond in writing
- *understanding the situation* (the factors that give rise to the issue and shape your response)
- *formulating a question* (what you intend to answer in response to the issue)

In Table 4.1, we identify a series of situations and one of the issues and questions that derive from each of them. Notice that the question you

TABLE 4.1   A Series of Situations with Related Issues and Questions

SITUATION	ISSUE	QUESTION
Different state legislatures are passing legislation to prevent Spanish-speaking students from using their own language in schools.	Most research on learning contradicts the idea that students should be prevented from using their own language in the process of learning a new language.	Under what conditions should students be allowed to use their own language while they learn English?
A manufacturing company has plans to move to your city with the promise of creating new jobs in a period of high unemployment.	You feel that this company will compromise the quality of life for the surrounding community because the manufacturing process will pollute the air.	What would persuade the city to prevent this company from moving in, even though the company will provide much-needed jobs?
Your school has made an agreement with a local company to supply vending machines that sell drinks and food. The school plans to use its share of the profit to improve the library and purchase a new scoreboard for the football field.	You see that the school has much to gain from this arrangement, but you also know that obesity is a growing problem at the school.	Is there another way for the school to generate needed revenue without putting students' health at risk?
An increasing number of homeless people are seeking shelter on your college campus.	Campus security has stepped up its efforts to remove the homeless, even though the shelters off campus are overcrowded.	How can you persuade the school to shelter the homeless and to provide funds to support the needs of the homeless in your city?

ask defines the area of inquiry as you read; it also can help you formulate your working thesis, the statement that answers your question. (We say more about developing a thesis in Chapter 5.) In this chapter, in addition to further discussing the importance of situation, we look at how you can identify issues and formulate questions to guide your reading and writing.

IDENTIFYING ISSUES

Below we present several steps to identifying an issue. You don't have to follow them in this particular order, and you may find yourself going back and forth among them as you try to bring an issue into focus.

Keep in mind that issues do not simply exist in the world well formed. Instead, writers construct what they see as issues from the situations they observe. For example, consider legislation to limit downloads from the Internet. If such legislation conflicts with your own practices and sense of freedom, you may have begun to identify an issue: the clash of values over what constitutes fair use and what does not. Be aware that others may not understand your issue and that in your writing you will have to explain carefully what is at stake.

■ Draw on Your Personal Experience

You may have been taught that formal writing is objective, that you must keep a dispassionate distance from your subject, and that you should not use *I* in a college-level paper. The fact is, however, that our personal experiences influence how we read, what we pay attention to, and what inferences we draw. It makes sense, then, to begin with you—where you are and what you think and believe.

We all use personal experience to make arguments in our everyday lives. In an academic context, the challenge is to use personal experience to argue a point, to illustrate something, or to illuminate a connection between theories and the sense we make of our daily experience. You don't want simply to tell your story. You want your story to strengthen your argument.

For example, in *Cultural Literacy*, E. D. Hirsch personalizes his interest in reversing the cycle of illiteracy in America's cities. To establish the nature of the problem in the situation he describes, he cites research showing that student performance on standardized tests in the United States is falling. But he also reflects on his own teaching in the 1970s, when he first perceived "the widening knowledge gap [that] caused me to recognize the connection between specific background knowledge and mature literacy." And he injects anecdotal evidence from conversations with his son, a teacher. Those stories heighten readers' awareness that school-aged children do not know much about literature, history, or government. (For example, his son mentions a student who challenged his claim that Latin is a "dead language" by demanding, "What do they speak in Latin America?")

Hirsch's use of his son's testimony makes him vulnerable to criticism, as readers might question whether Hirsch can legitimately use his son's experience to make generalizations about education. But in fact, Hirsch is using personal testimony—his own and his son's—to augment and put a human face on the research he cites. He presents his issue, that schools must teach cultural literacy, both as something personal and as something with which we should all be concerned. The personal note helps readers see Hirsch as someone who has long been concerned with education and who has even raised a son who is an educator.

■ Identify What Is Open to Dispute

An issue is something that is open to dispute. Sometimes the way to clarify an issue is to think of it as a *fundamental tension* between two or more conflicting points of view. If you can identify conflicting points of view, an issue may become clear.

Consider E. D. Hirsch, who believes that the best approach to educational reform (the subject he writes about) is to change the curriculum in schools. His position: A curriculum based on cultural literacy is the one sure way to reverse the cycle of poverty and illiteracy in urban areas.

What is the issue? Hirsch's issue emerges in the presence of an alternative position. Jonathan Kozol, a social activist who has written extensively about educational reform, believes that policymakers need to address reform by providing the necessary resources that all students need to learn. Kozol points out that students in many inner-city schools are reading outdated textbooks and that the dilapidated conditions in these schools—windows that won't close, for example—make it impossible for students to learn.

In tension are two different views of the reform that can reverse illiteracy: Hirsch's view that educational reform should occur through curricular changes, and Kozol's view that educational reform demands socioeconomic resources.

■ Resist Binary Thinking

As you begin to define what is at issue, try to tease out complexities that may not be immediately apparent. That is, try to resist the either/or mindset that signals binary thinking.

If you considered only what Hirsch and Kozol have to say, it would be easy to characterize the problems facing our schools as either curricular or socioeconomic. But it may be that the real issue combines these arguments with a third or even a fourth, that neither curricular nor socioeconomic changes by themselves can resolve the problems with American schools.

After reading essays by both Hirsch and Kozol, one of our students pointed out that both Hirsch's focus on curriculum and Kozol's socioeconomic focus ignore another concern. She went on to describe her school experience in racial terms. In the excerpt below, notice how this writer uses personal experience (in a new school, she is not treated as she had expected to be treated) to formulate an issue.

> Moving from Colorado Springs to Tallahassee, I was immediately struck by the differences apparent in local home life, school life, and community unity, or lack thereof. Ripped from my sheltered world at a small Catholic school characterized by racial harmony, I was thrown into a large public school where outward prejudice from classmates and teachers and "race wars" were common and tolerated. . . .
>
> In a school where students and teachers had free rein to abuse anyone different from them, I was constantly abused. As the only black student in English honors, I was commonly belittled in front of my "peers" by my teacher. If I developed courage enough to ask a question, I was always answered with the use of improper grammar and such words as "ain't" as my teacher attempted to simplify the mate-

rial to "my level" and to give me what he called "a little learning." After discussing several subjects, he often turned to me, singling me out of a sea of white faces, and asked, "Do *you* understand, Mila?" When asking my opinion of a subject, he frequently questioned, "What do *your* people think about this?" Although he insisted on including such readings as Martin Luther King's "I Have a Dream" speech in the curriculum, the speech's themes of tolerance and equity did not accompany his lesson.

Through her reading, this student discovered that few prominent scholars have confronted the issue of racism in schools directly. Although she grants that curricular reform and increased funding may be necessary to improve education, she argues that scholars also need to address race in their studies of teaching and learning.

Our point is that issues may be more complex than you first think they are. For this student, the issue wasn't one of two positions—reform the curriculum or provide more funding. Instead, it combined a number of different positions, including race ("prejudice" and "race wars") and the relationship between student and teacher ("Do *you* understand, Mila?") in a classroom.

In this passage, the writer uses her experience to challenge binary thinking. Like the student writer, you should examine issues from different perspectives, avoiding either/or propositions that oversimplify the world.

■ Build on and Extend the Ideas of Others

Academic writing builds on and extends the ideas of others. As an academic writer, you will find that by extending other people's ideas, you will extend your own. You may begin in a familiar place, but as you read more and pursue connections to other readings, you may well end up at an unexpected destination.

For example, one of our students was troubled when he read Melissa Stormont-Spurgin's description of homeless children. The student uses details from her work (giving credit, of course) in his own:

The children . . . went to school after less than three hours of sleep. They wore the same wrinkled clothes that they had worn the day before. What will their teachers think when they fall asleep in class? How will they get food for lunch? What will their peers think? What could these homeless children talk about with their peers? They have had to grow up too fast. Their worries are not the same as other children's worries. They are worried about their next meal and where they will seek shelter. Their needs, however, are the same. They need a home and all of the securities that come with it. They also need an education (Stormont-Spurgin 156).

Initially the student was troubled by his own access to quality schools, and the contrast between his life and the lives of the children Stormont-Spurgin describes. Initially, then, his issue was the fundamental tension between his own privileged status, something he had taken for granted, and the struggle that homeless children face every day.

However, as he read further and grew to understand homelessness as a concern in a number of studies, he connected his personal response to a larger conversation about democracy, fairness, and education:

> Melissa Stormont-Spurgin, an author of several articles on educational studies, addresses a very real and important, yet avoided issue in education today. Statistics show that a very high percentage of children who are born into homeless families will remain homeless, or in poverty, for the rest of their lives. How can this be, if everyone actually does have the same educational opportunities? There must be significant educational disadvantages for children without homes. In a democratic society, I feel that we must pay close attention to these disadvantages and do everything in our power to replace them with equality.

Ultimately, the student refined his sense of what was at issue: *Although all people should have access to public education in a democratic society, not everyone has the opportunity to attend quality schools in order to achieve personal success.* In turn, his definition of the issue began to shape his argument:

> Parents, teachers, homeless shelters, and the citizens of the United States who fund [homeless] shelters must address the educational needs of homeless children, while steering them away from any more financial or psychological struggles. Without this emphasis on education, the current trend upward in the number of homeless families will inevitably continue in the future of American society.

The student shifted away from a personal issue—the difference between his status and that of homeless children—to an issue of clashing values: the principle of egalitarian democracy on the one hand and the reality of citizens in a democracy living in abject poverty on the other. When he started to read about homeless children, he could not have made the claim he ends up making, that policymakers must make education a basic human right.

This student offers us an important lesson about the role of inquiry and the value of resisting easy answers. He has built on and extended his own ideas—and the ideas of others—after repeating the process of reading, raising questions, writing, and seeing problems a number of times.

■ Read to Discover a Writer's Frame

A more specialized strategy of building on and extending the ideas of others involves reading to discover a writer's **frame**, the perspective through which a writer presents his or her arguments. Writers want us to see the world a certain way, so they frame their arguments much the same way photographers and artists frame their pictures.

For example, if you were to take a picture of friends in front of the football stadium on campus, you would focus on what you would most like to remember—your friends' faces—blurring the images of the people walking behind your friends. Setting up the picture, or framing it, might require using light and shade to make some details stand out more than others. Writers do the same with language.

E. D. Hirsch uses the concept of *cultural literacy* to frame his argument for curricular reform. For Hirsch, the term is a benchmark, a standard: People who are culturally literate are familiar with the body of information that every educated citizen should know. Hirsch's implication, of course, is that people who are not culturally literate are not well educated. But that is not necessarily true. In fact, a number of educators insist that literacy is simply a means to an end—reading to complete an assignment, for example, or to understand the ramifications of a decision—not an end in itself. By defining and using *cultural literacy* as the goal of education, Hirsch is framing his argument; he is bringing his ideas into focus.

When writers use framing strategies, they also call attention to the specific conversations that set up the situation for their arguments. Framing often entails quoting specific theories and ideas from other authors and then using those quotations as a perspective, or lens, through which to examine other material. In his memoir *Hunger of Memory: The Education of Richard Rodriguez* (1982), Richard Rodriguez uses this method to examine his situation as a nonnative speaker of English desperate to enter the mainstream culture, even if it means sacrificing his identity as the son of Mexican immigrants. Reflecting on his life as a student, Rodriguez comes across Richard Hoggart's book *The Uses of Literacy* (1957). Hoggart's description of "the scholarship boy" presents a lens through which Rodriguez can see his own experience. Hoggart writes:

> With his family, the boy has the intense pleasure of intimacy, the family's consolation in feeling public alienation. Lavish emotions texture home life. *Then*, at school, the instruction bids him to trust lonely reason primarily. Immediate needs set the pace of his parents' lives. From his mother and father the boy learns to trust spontaneity and nonrational ways of knowing. *Then*, at school, there is mental calm. Teachers emphasize the value of a reflectiveness that opens a space between thinking and immediate action.
>
> Years of schooling must pass before the boy will be able to sketch the cultural differences in his day as abstractly as this. But he senses those differences early. Perhaps as early as the night he brings home an assignment from school and finds the house too noisy for study. He has to be more and more alone, if he is going to "get on." He will have, probably unconsciously, to oppose the ethos of the hearth, the intense gregariousness of the working-class family group. . . . The boy has to cut himself off mentally, so as to do his homework, as well as he can.

Here is Rodriguez's response to Hoggart's description of the scholarship boy:

> For weeks I read, speed-read, books by modern educational theorists, only
> to find infrequent and slight mention of students like me. . . . Then one day,
> leafing through Richard Hoggart's *The Uses of Literacy*, I found, in his descrip-
> tion of the scholarship boy, myself. For the first time I realized that there were
> other students like me, and so I was able to frame the meaning of my aca-
> demic success, its consequent price—the loss.

Notice how Rodriguez introduces ideas from Hoggart "to frame" his
own ideas: "I found, in his description of the scholarship boy, myself. For
the first time I realized that there were other students like me, and so I
was able to frame the meaning of my academic success, its consequent
price—the loss." Hoggart's scholarship boy enables Rodriguez to revisit
his own experience with a new perspective. Hoggart's words and idea advance Rodriguez's understanding of the problem he identifies in his life:
his inability to find solace at home and within his working-class roots.
Hoggart's description of the scholarship boy's moving between cultural
extremes—spontaneity at home and reflection at school—helps Rodriguez bring his own youthful discontent into focus.

Rodriguez's response to Hoggart's text shows how another writer's lens
can help frame an issue. If you were using Hoggart's term *scholarship boy*
as a lens through which to clarify an issue in education, you might ask how
the term illuminates new aspects of another writer's examples or your own.
And then you might ask, "To what extent does Hirsch's cultural literacy
throw a more positive light on what Rodriguez and Hoggart describe?" or
"How do my experiences challenge, extend, or complicate the scholarship-
boy concept?"

■ Consider the Constraints of the Situation

In identifying an issue, you have to understand the situation that gives
rise to the issue, including the contexts in which it is raised and debated.
One of the contexts is the *audience*. In thinking about your issue, you must
consider the extent to which your potential readers are involved in the dialogue you want to enter, and what they know and need to know. In a sense,
audience functions as both context and **constraint**, a factor that narrows
the choices you can make in responding to an issue. An understanding of
your potential readers will help you choose the depth of your discussion; it
will also determine the kind of evidence you can present and the language
you can use.

Another constraint on your response to an issue is the form that response takes. For example, if you decide to make an issue of government-
imposed limits on what you can download from the Internet, your response
in writing might take the form of an editorial or a letter to a legislator. In
this situation, length is an obvious constraint: Newspapers limit the word
count of editorials, and the best letters to legislators tend to be brief and
very selective about the evidence they cite. A few personal examples and a
few statistics may be all you can include to support your claim about the

issue. By contrast, if you were making your case in an academic journal, a very different set of constraints would apply. You would have more space for illustrations and support, for example.

Finally, the situation itself can function as a major constraint. For instance, suppose your topic is the decline of educational standards. It's difficult to imagine any writer making the case for accelerating that decline, or any audience being receptive to the idea that a decline in standards is a good thing.

Steps to Identifying Issues

1 Draw on your personal experience. Start with your own sense of what's important, what puzzles you, or what you are curious about. (Then build your argument by moving on to other sources to support your point of view.)

2 Identify what is open to dispute. Identify a phenomenon or some idea in a written argument that challenges what you think or believe.

3 Resist binary thinking. Think about the issue from multiple perspectives.

4 Build on and extend the ideas of others. As you read, be open to new ways of looking at the issue. The issue you finally write about may be very different from what you set out to write about.

5 Read to discover a writer's frame. What theories or ideas shape the writer's focus? How can these theories or ideas help you frame your argument?

6 Consider the constraints of the situation. Craft your argument to meet the needs of and constraints imposed by your audience and form.

■ Identify Issues in an Essay

In the following editorial, published in 2002 in *Newsweek*, writer Anna Quindlen addresses her concern that middle-class parents overschedule their children's lives. She calls attention to the ways leisure time helped her develop as a writer and urges parents to consider the extent to which children's creativity depends on having some downtime. They don't always have to have their time scheduled. As you read Quindlen's "Doing Nothing Is Something," note what words and phrases Quindlen uses to identify the situation and to indicate who her audience is. Identify her main claim as one of fact, value, or policy. Finally, answer the questions that follow the selection to see if you can discern how she locates, defines, and advances her issue.

ANNA QUINDLEN

Doing Nothing Is Something

Anna Quindlen is a best-selling author of novels and children's books, but she is perhaps most widely known for her nonfiction and commentary on current events and contemporary life. She won a Pulitzer Prize in 1992 for her "Public and Private" column in the *New York Times*, and for ten years wrote a biweekly column for *Newsweek*. Some of her novels are *Object Lessons* (1991), *Blessings* (2002), and *Every Last One* (2010). Her nonfiction works and collections include *Living Out Loud* (1988), *Thinking Out Loud* (1994), *Loud and Clear* (2004), and *Good Dog. Stay.* (2007).

Summer is coming soon. I can feel it in the softening of the air, but I can see it, too, in the textbooks on my children's desks. The number of uncut pages at the back grows smaller and smaller. The loose-leaf is ragged at the edges, the binder plastic ripped at the corners. An old remembered glee rises inside me. Summer is coming. Uniform skirts in mothballs. Pencils with their points left broken. Open windows. Day trips to the beach. Pickup games. Hanging out.   1

How boring it was.   2

Of course, it was the making of me, as a human being and a writer. Downtime is where we become ourselves, looking into the middle distance, kicking at the curb, lying on the grass, or sitting on the stoop and staring at the tedious blue of the summer sky. I don't believe you can write poetry, or compose music, or become an actor without downtime, and plenty of it, a hiatus that passes for boredom but is really the quiet moving of the wheels inside that fuel creativity.   3

And that, to me, is one of the saddest things about the lives of American children today. Soccer leagues, acting classes, tutors—the calendar of the average middle-class kid is so over the top that soon Palm handhelds will be sold in Toys "R" Us. Our children are as overscheduled as we are, and that is saying something.   4

This has become so bad that parents have arranged to schedule times for unscheduled time. Earlier this year the privileged suburb of Ridgewood, New Jersey, announced a Family Night, when there would be no homework, no athletic practices, and no after-school events. This was terribly exciting until I realized that this was not one night a week, but one single night. There is even a free-time movement, and Web site: familylife1st.org. Among the frequently asked questions provided online: "What would families do with family time if they took it back?"   5

Let me make a suggestion for the kids involved: How about nothing? It is not simply that it is pathetic to consider the lives of children who don't have a moment between piano and dance and homework to talk about their day or just search for split ends, an enormously satisfying leisure-   6 time activity of my youth. There is also ample psychological research suggesting that what we might call "doing nothing" is when human beings actually do their best thinking, and when creativity comes to call. Perhaps we are creating an entire generation of people whose ability to think outside the box, as the current parlance of business has it, is being systematically stunted by scheduling.

A study by the University of Michigan quantified the downtime deficit; in the last 20 years American kids have lost about four unstructured hours a week. There has even arisen a global Right to Play movement: in the Third World it is often about child labor, but in the United States it is about the sheer labor of being a perpetually busy child. In Omaha, Nebraska, a group of parents recently lobbied for additional recess. Hooray, and yikes. 7

How did this happen? Adults did it. There is a culture of adult distrust that suggests that a kid who is not playing softball or attending science-enrichment programs—or both—is huffing or boosting cars: if kids are left alone, they will not stare into the middle distance and consider the meaning of life and how come your nose in pictures never looks the way you think it should, but instead will get into trouble. There is also the culture of cutthroat and unquestioning competition that leads even the parents of preschoolers to gab about prestigious colleges without a trace of irony: this suggests that any class in which you do not enroll your first grader will put him at a disadvantage in, say, law school. 8

Finally, there is a culture of workplace presence (as opposed to productivity). Try as we might to suggest that all these enrichment activities are for the good of the kid, there is ample evidence that they are really for the convenience of parents with way too little leisure time of their own. Stories about the resignation of presidential aide Karen Hughes unfailingly reported her dedication to family time by noting that she arranged to get home at 5:30 one night a week to have dinner with her son. If one weekday dinner out of five is considered laudable, what does that say about what's become commonplace? 9

Summer is coming. It used to be a time apart for kids, a respite from the clock and the copybook, the organized day. Every once in a while, either guilty or overwhelmed or tired of listening to me keen about my monumental boredom, my mother would send me to some rinky-dink park program that consisted almost entirely of three-legged races and making things out of Popsicle sticks. Now, instead, there are music camps, sports camps, fat camps, probably thin camps. I mourn hanging out in the backyard. I mourn playing Wiffle ball in the street without a sponsor and matching shirts. I mourn drawing in the dirt with a stick. 10

Maybe that kind of summer is gone for good. Maybe this is the leading edge of a new way of living that not only has no room for contemplation but is contemptuous of it. But if downtime cannot be squeezed during the school year into the life of frantic and often joyless activity with 11 which our children are saddled while their parents pursue frantic and often joyless activity of their own, what about summer? Do most adults really want to stand in line for Space Mountain or sit in traffic to get to a shore house that doesn't have enough saucepans? Might it be even more enriching for their children to stay at home and do nothing? For those who say they will only watch TV or play on the computer, a piece of technical advice: the cable box can be unhooked, the modem removed. Perhaps it is not too late for American kids to be given the gift of enforced boredom for at least a week or two, staring into space, bored out of their gourds, exploring the inside of their own heads. "To contemplate is to toil, to think is to do," said Victor Hugo. "Go outside and play," said Prudence Quindlen. Both of them were right.

Reading as a Writer

1. What evidence of Quindlen's personal responses and experiences can you identify?
2. What phenomenon has prompted her to reflect on what she thinks and believes? How has she made it into an issue?
3. Where does she indicate that she has considered the issue from multiple perspectives and is placing her ideas in conversation with those of others?
4. What sort of lens does she seem to be using to frame her argument?
5. What constraints (such as the format of an editorial) seem to be in play in the essay?

A Practice Sequence: Identifying Issues

This sequence of activities will give you practice in identifying and clarifying issues based on your own choice of reading and collaboration with your classmates.

1   Draw on your personal experience. Reflect on your own responses to what you have been reading in this class or in other classes, or issues that writers have posed in the media. What concerns you most? Choose a story that supports or challenges the claims people are making in what you have read or listened to. What questions do you have? Make some notes in response to these questions, explaining your personal stake in the issues and questions you formulate.

2   Identify what is open to dispute. Take what you have written and formulate your ideas as an issue, using the structure we used in our example of Hirsch's and Kozol's competing arguments:

- Part 1: Your view of a given topic
- Part 2: At least one view that is in tension with your own

If you need to, read further to understand what others have to say about this issue.

3 Resist binary thinking. Share your statement of the issue with one or more peers and ask them if they see other ways to formulate the issue that you may not have thought about. What objections, if any, do they make to your statement in part 1? Write these objections down in part 2 so that you begin to look at the issue from multiple perspectives.

4 Build on and extend the ideas of others. Now that you have formulated an issue from different perspectives, explaining your personal stake in the issue, connect what you think to a broader conversation in what you are reading. Then try making a claim using this structure: "Although some people would argue _____, I think that _____."

5 Read to discover a writer's frame. As an experiment in trying out multiple perspectives, revise the claim you make in exercise 4 by introducing the frame, or lens, through which you want readers to understand your argument. You can employ the same sentence structure. For example, here is a claim framed in terms of race: "Although people should have access to public education, recent policies have worsened racial inequalities in public schools." In contrast, here is a claim that focuses on economics: "Although people should have access to public education, the unequal distribution of tax money has created what some would call an 'economy of education.'" The lens may come from reading you have done in other courses or from conversations with your classmates, and you may want to attribute the lens to a particular author or classmate: "Although some people would argue_____, I use E. D. Hirsch's notion of cultural literacy to show_____."

6 Consider the constraints of the situation. Building on these exercises, develop an argument in the form of an editorial for your local newspaper. This means that you will need to limit your argument to about 250 words. You also will need to consider the extent to which your potential readers are involved in the conversation. What do they know? What do they need to know? What kind of evidence do you need to use to persuade readers?

FORMULATING ISSUE-BASED QUESTIONS

As we have said, when you identify an issue, you need to understand it in the context of its situation. Ideally, the situation and the issue will be both relevant and recent, making the task of connecting to your audience that much easier when you write about the issue. For example, the student writer who was concerned about long-standing issues of homelessness and lack of educational opportunity connected to his readers by citing recent statistics and giving the problem of homelessness a face: "The children . . . went to school after less than three hours of sleep. They wore the same wrinkled clothes that they had worn the day before." If your issue does not immediately fulfill the criteria of relevance and timeliness, you need to take that into consideration as you continue your reading and research on the issue. Ask yourself, "What is on people's minds these days?" "What do they need to know about?" Think about why the issue matters to you, and imagine why it might matter to others. By the time you write, you should be prepared to make the issue relevant for your readers.

In addition to understanding the situation and defining the issue that you feel is most relevant and timely, you can formulate an issue-based question that can help you think through what you might be interested in writing about. This question should be specific enough to guide inquiry into what others have written. An issue-based question can also help you accomplish the following:

- Clarify what you know about the issue and what you still need to know
- Guide your inquiry with a clear focus
- Organize your inquiry around a specific issue
- Develop an argument, rather than simply collecting information by asking "how," "why," "should," or "the extent to which something is or is not true"
- Consider who your audience is
- Determine what resources you have, so that you can ask a question that you will be able to answer with the resources available to you

A good question develops out of an issue, some fundamental tension that you identify within a conversation. In "Doing Nothing Is Something," Anna Quindlen identifies a problem that middle-class parents need to know about: that overscheduling their children's lives may limit their children's potential for developing their creativity. As she explores the reasons why children do not have sufficient downtime, she raises a question that encourages parents to consider what would happen if they gave their children time to do nothing: "Might it be even more enriching for their children to stay at home and do nothing?" (para. 11). Through identifying what is at issue, you should begin to understand for whom it is an issue— for whom you are answering the question. In turn, the answer to your question will help you craft your thesis.

In the following paragraphs, we trace the steps one of our students took to formulate an issue-based question on the broad topic of language diversity. Although we present the steps in sequence, be aware that they are guidelines only: The steps often overlap, and there is a good deal of room for rethinking and refining along the way.

■ Refine Your Topic

Generally speaking, a **topic** is the subject you want to write about. For example, homelessness, tests, and violence are all topics. So are urban homelessness, standardized tests, and video game violence. And so are homelessness in New York City, aptitude tests versus achievement tests, and mayhem in the video game Grand Theft Auto. As our list suggests, even a specific topic needs refining into an issue before it can be explored effectively in writing.

The topic our student wanted to focus on was language diversity, a subject her linguistics class had been discussing. She was fascinated by the extraordinary range of languages spoken in the United States, not just by immigrant groups but by native speakers whose dialects and varieties of English are considered nonstandard. She herself had relatives for whom English was not a first language. She began refining her topic by putting her thoughts into words:

> I want to describe the experience of being raised in a home where non–Standard English is spoken.
>
> I'd like to know the benefits and liabilities of growing up bilingual.
>
> I am curious to know what it's like to live in a community of nonnative speakers of English while trying to make a living in a country where the dominant language is English.

Although she had yet to identify an issue, her attempts to articulate what interested her about the topic were moving her toward the situation of people in the United States who don't speak Standard English or don't have English as their first language.

■ Explain Your Interest in the Topic

At this point, the student encountered E. D. Hirsch's *Cultural Literacy* in her reading, which had both a provocative and a clarifying effect on her thinking. She began to build on and extend Hirsch's ideas. Reacting to Hirsch's assumption that students should acquire the same base of knowledge and write in Standard Written English, her first, somewhat mischievous thought was, "I wonder what Hirsch would think about cultural literacy being taught in a bilingual classroom?" But then her thinking took another turn, and she began to contemplate the effect of Hirsch's cultural-literacy agenda on speakers whose English is not standard or for whom English is not a first language. She used a demographic fact that she had learned in her linguistics class in her explanation of her interest in the topic: "I'm curious about the consequences of limiting language diversity when the presence of ethnic minorities in our educational system is growing."

■ Identify an Issue

The more she thought about Hirsch's ideas, and the more she read about language diversity, the more concerned our student grew. It seemed to her that Hirsch's interest in producing students who all share the same base of knowledge and all write in Standard Written English was in tension with her sense that this kind of approach places a burden on people whose first language is not English. That tension clarified the issue for her. In identifying the issue, she wrote:

> Hirsch's book actually sets some priorities, most notably through his list of words and phrases that form the foundations of what it means to be "American." However, this list certainly overlooks several crucial influences in American culture. Most oversights generally come at the expense of the minority populations.

These two concerns—with inclusion and with exclusion—helped focus the student's inquiry.

■ Formulate Your Topic as a Question

To further define her inquiry, the student formulated her topic as a question that pointed toward an argument: "To what extent can E. D. Hirsch's notion of 'cultural literacy' coexist with our country's principles of democracy and inclusion?" Notice that her choice of the phrase *To what extent* implies that both goals do not go hand in hand. If she had asked, "Can common culture coexist with pluralism?" her phrasing would imply that a yes or no answer would suffice, possibly foreclosing avenues of inquiry and certainly ignoring the complexity of the issue.

Instead, despite her misgivings about the implications of Hirsch's agenda, the student suspended judgment, opening the way to genuine inquiry. She acknowledged the usefulness and value of sharing a common language and conceded that Hirsch's points were well taken. She wrote:

> Some sort of unification is necessary. Language, . . . on the most fundamental level of human interaction, demands some compromise and chosen guidelines. . . . How can we learn from one another if we cannot even say hello to each other?

Suspending judgment led her to recognize the complexity of the issue, and her willingness to examine the issue from different perspectives indicated the empathy that is a central component of developing a conversational argument.

■ Acknowledge Your Audience

This student's question ("To what extent can E. D. Hirsch's notion of 'cultural literacy' coexist with our country's principles of democracy and inclusion?") also acknowledged an audience. By invoking cultural literacy, she assumed an audience of readers who are familiar with Hirsch's ideas, probably including policymakers and educational administrators. In gesturing toward democracy, she cast her net very wide: Most Americans probably admire the "principles of democracy." But in specifying inclusion as a democratic principle, she wisely linked all Americans who believe in democratic principles, including the parents of schoolchildren, with all people who have reason to feel excluded by Hirsch's ideas, especially nonnative speakers of English, among them immigrants from Mexico and speakers of African American Vernacular English. Thus, this student was acknowledging an audience of policymakers, administrators, parents (both mainstream and marginalized), and those who knew about and perhaps supported cultural literacy.

Steps to Formulating an Issue-Based Question

1 **Refine your topic.** Examine your topic from different perspectives. For example, what are the causes of homelessness? What are its consequences?

2 **Explain your interest in the topic.** Explore the source of your interest in this topic and what you want to learn.

3 **Identify an issue.** Determine what is open to dispute.

4 **Formulate your topic as a question.** Use your question to focus your inquiry.

5 **Acknowledge your audience.** Reflect on what readers may know about the issue, why they may be interested, and what you would like to teach them.

A Practice Sequence: Formulating an Issue-Based Question

As you start developing your own issue-based question, it might be useful to practice a five-step process that begins with a topic, a word or phrase that describes the focus of your interests. Here, apply the process to the one-word topic homelessness.

1 Expand your topic into a phrase. "I am interested in the *consequences* of homelessness," "I want to *describe* what it means to be homeless," or "I am interested in discussing the *cause* of homelessness."

2 Explain your interest in this topic. "I am interested in the consequences of homelessness because it challenges democratic principles of fairness."

3 Identify an issue. "The persistence of homelessness contradicts my belief in social justice."

4 Formulate your topic as a question. "To what extent can we allow homelessness to persist in a democratic nation that prides itself on providing equal opportunity to all?"

5 Acknowledge your audience. "I am interested in the consequences of homelessness because I want people who believe in democracy to understand that we need to work harder to make sure that everyone has access to food, shelter, and employment."

The answer to the question you formulate in step 4 should lead to an assertion, your main claim, or *thesis*. For example, you could state your main claim this way: "Although homelessness persists as a widespread problem in our nation, we must develop policies that eliminate homelessness, ensuring that everyone has access to food, shelter, and employment. This is especially important in a democracy that embraces social justice and equality."

The thesis introduces a problem and makes an assertion that you will need to support: "We must develop policies that eliminate homelessness, ensuring that everyone has access to food, shelter, and employment." What is at issue? Not everyone would agree that policies must be implemented to solve the problem. In fact, many would argue that homelessness is an individual problem, that individuals must take responsibility for lifting themselves out of poverty, homelessness, and unemployment. Of course, you would need to read quite a bit to reach this final stage of formulating your thesis.

Try using the five-step process we describe above to formulate your own topic as a question, or try formulating the following topics as questions:

- Violence in video games
- Recycling
- The popularity of a cultural phenomenon (a book, a film, a performer, an icon)
- Standardized tests
- Professional sports injuries
- Town-gown relationships
- Media and representation
- Government and religion
- Vegetarianism

AN ACADEMIC ESSAY FOR ANALYSIS

The following essay by William Deresiewicz provides an intriguing academic extension of the homely topic that Anna Quindlen writes about (p. 82): the need for the young to have solitary, unscheduled time. His essay illustrates many of the strategies we have discussed thus far: raising questions, stating a thesis by placing an argument in the stream of a broader conversation, using evidence to support his claims. As you read Deresiewicz's essay, you might use the following questions as a guide:

- What is Deresiewicz's thesis? Would you characterize his claim as one of fact? Value?
- What types of evidence does he use to support his claim?
- What do Deresiewicz's vocabulary and citations indicate about his target audience?
- What does Deresiewicz want his readers to do or think about?

WILLIAM DERESIEWICZ

The End of Solitude

William Deresiewicz taught English at Yale University from 1998 to 2008. He is now a contributing writer at *The Nation* and was nominated for a 2009 National Magazine Award for his reviews and criticism. His essay "The End of Solitude" appeared in *The Chronicle of Higher Education* in January 2009 and represents one of many debates about literacy that scholars have waged concerning the benefits and limits of new technologies. Deresiewicz observes that technology fulfills a human impulse to be known, to be connected with others. Posting on MySpace, Twitter, and Facebook enables us to be visible and helps validate who we are as individuals. However, he worries that this instinct to be connected also has an adverse effect: We lose a sense of solitude and the space he believes we all need to have in order to understand who we are, what we believe, and what we value. He worries, too, that a new generation does not see the point of solitude because so many young people equate solitude with loneliness.

■ ■ ■

What does the contemporary self want? The camera has created a culture of celebrity; the computer is creating a culture of connectivity. As the two technologies converge—broadband tipping the Web from text to image, social-networking sites spreading the mesh of interconnection ever wider—the two cultures betray a common impulse. Celebrity and connectivity are both ways of becoming known. This is what the contemporary self wants. It wants to be recognized, wants to be connected: It wants to be visible. If not to the millions, on *Survivor* or

Oprah, then to the hundreds, on Twitter or Facebook. This is the quality that validates us, this is how we become real to ourselves—by being seen by others. The great contemporary terror is anonymity. If Lionel Trilling was right, if the property that grounded the self, in Romanticism, was sincerity, and in modernism it was authenticity, then in postmodernism it is visibility.

So we live exclusively in relation to others, and what disappears from   2
our lives is solitude. Technology is taking away our privacy and our concentration, but it is also taking away our ability to be alone. Though I shouldn't say taking away. We are doing this to ourselves; we are discarding these riches as fast as we can. I was told by one of her older relatives that a teenager I know had sent 3,000 text messages one recent month. That's 100 a day, or about one every 10 waking minutes, morning, noon, and night, weekdays and weekends, class time, lunch time, homework time, and toothbrushing time. So on average, she's never alone for more than 10 minutes at once. Which means, she's never alone.

I once asked my students about the place that solitude has in their   3
lives. One of them admitted that she finds the prospect of being alone so unsettling that she'll sit with a friend even when she has a paper to write. Another said, why would anyone want to be alone?

To that remarkable question, history offers a number of answers. Man   4
may be a social animal, but solitude has traditionally been a societal value. In particular, the act of being alone has been understood as an essential dimension of religious experience, albeit one restricted to a self-selected few. Through the solitude of rare spirits, the collective renews its relationship with divinity. The prophet and the hermit, the sadhu and the yogi, pursue their vision quests, invite their trances, in desert or forest or cave. For the still, small voice speaks only in silence. Social life is a bustle of petty concerns, a jostle of quotidian interests, and religious institutions are no exception. You cannot hear God when people are chattering at you, and the divine word, their pretensions notwithstanding, demurs at descending on the monarch and the priest. Communal experience is the human norm, but the solitary encounter with God is the egregious act that refreshes that norm. (Egregious, for no man is a prophet in his own land. Tiresias was reviled before he was vindicated, Teresa interrogated before she was canonized.) Religious solitude is a kind of self-correcting social mechanism, a way of burning out the underbrush of moral habit and spiritual custom. The seer returns with new tablets or new dances, his face bright with the old truth.

Like other religious values, solitude was democratized by the Refor-   5
mation and secularized by Romanticism. In Marilynne Robinson's interpretation, Calvinism created the modern self by focusing the soul inward, leaving it to encounter God, like a prophet of old, in "profound isolation." To her enumeration of Calvin, Marguerite de Navarre, and Milton as pioneering early-modern selves we can add Montaigne, Hamlet, and even

Don Quixote. The last figure alerts us to reading's essential role in this transformation, the printing press serving an analogous function in the sixteenth and subsequent centuries to that of television and the Internet in our own. Reading, as Robinson puts it, "is an act of great inwardness and subjectivity." "The soul encountered itself in response to a text, first Genesis or Matthew and then *Paradise Lost* or *Leaves of Grass*." With Protestantism and printing, the quest for the divine voice became available to, even incumbent upon, everyone.

But it is with Romanticism that solitude achieved its greatest cultural salience, becoming both literal and literary. Protestant solitude is still only figurative. Rousseau and Wordsworth made it physical. The self was now encountered not in God but in Nature, and to encounter Nature one had to go to it. And go to it with a special sensibility: The poet displaced the saint as social seer and cultural model. But because Romanticism also inherited the eighteenth-century idea of social sympathy, Romantic solitude existed in a dialectical relationship with sociability—if less for Rousseau and still less for Thoreau, the most famous solitary of all, then certainly for Wordsworth, Melville, Whitman, and many others. For Emerson, "the soul environs itself with friends, that it may enter into a grander self-acquaintance or solitude; and it goes alone, for a season, that it may exalt its conversation or society." The Romantic practice of solitude is neatly captured by Trilling's "sincerity": the belief that the self is validated by a congruity of public appearance and private essence, one that stabilizes its relationship with both itself and others. Especially, as Emerson suggests, one beloved other. Hence the famous Romantic friendship pairs: Goethe and Schiller, Wordsworth and Coleridge, Hawthorne and Melville.

Modernism decoupled this dialectic. Its notion of solitude was harsher, more adversarial, more isolating. As a model of the self and its interactions, Hume's social sympathy gave way to Pater's thick wall of personality and Freud's narcissism—the sense that the soul, self-enclosed and inaccessible to others, can't choose but be alone. With exceptions, like Woolf, the modernists fought shy of friendship. Joyce and Proust disparaged it; D. H. Lawrence was wary of it; the modernist friendship pairs—Conrad and Ford, Eliot and Pound, Hemingway and Fitzgerald—were altogether cooler than their Romantic counterparts. The world was now understood as an assault on the self, and with good reason.

The Romantic ideal of solitude developed in part as a reaction to the emergence of the modern city. In modernism, the city is not only more menacing than ever, it has become inescapable, a labyrinth: Eliot's London, Joyce's Dublin. The mob, the human mass, presses in. Hell is other people. The soul is forced back into itself—hence the development of a more austere, more embattled form of self-validation, Trilling's "authenticity," where the essential relationship is only with oneself. (Just as there are few good friendships in modernism, so are there few good marriages.)

Solitude becomes, more than ever, the arena of heroic self-discovery, a voyage through interior realms made vast and terrifying by Nietzschean and Freudian insights. To achieve authenticity is to look upon these visions without flinching; Trilling's exemplar here is Kurtz. Protestant self-examination becomes Freudian analysis, and the culture hero, once a prophet of God and then a poet of Nature, is now a novelist of self—a Dostoyevsky, a Joyce, a Proust.

But we no longer live in the modernist city, and our great fear is not   9
submersion by the mass but isolation from the herd. Urbanization gave way to suburbanization, and with it the universal threat of loneliness. What technologies of transportation exacerbated—we could live farther and farther apart—technologies of communication redressed—we could bring ourselves closer and closer together. Or at least, so we have imagined. The first of these technologies, the first simulacrum of proximity, was the telephone. "Reach out and touch someone." But through the 1970s and 1980s, our isolation grew. Suburbs, sprawling ever farther, became exurbs. Families grew smaller or splintered apart, mothers left the home to work. The electronic hearth became the television in every room. Even in childhood, certainly in adolescence, we were each trapped inside our own cocoon. Soaring crime rates, and even more sharply escalating rates of moral panic, pulled children off the streets. The idea that you could go outside and run around the neighborhood with your friends, once unquestionable, has now become unthinkable. The child who grew up between the world wars as part of an extended family within a tight-knit urban community became the grandparent of a kid who sat alone in front of a big television, in a big house, on a big lot. We were lost in space.

Under those circumstances, the Internet arrived as an incalculable   10
blessing. We should never forget that. It has allowed isolated people to communicate with one another and marginalized people to find one another. The busy parent can stay in touch with far-flung friends. The gay teenager no longer has to feel like a freak. But as the Internet's dimensionality has grown, it has quickly become too much of a good thing. Ten years ago we were writing e-mail messages on desktop computers and transmitting them over dial-up connections. Now we are sending text messages on our cellphones, posting pictures on our Facebook pages, and following complete strangers on Twitter. A constant stream of mediated contact, virtual, notional, or simulated, keeps us wired in to the electronic hive—though contact, or at least two-way contact, seems increasingly beside the point. The goal now, it seems, is simply to become known, to turn oneself into a sort of miniature celebrity. How many friends do I have on Facebook? How many people are reading my blog? How many Google hits does my name generate? Visibility secures our self-esteem, becoming a substitute, twice removed, for genuine connection. Not long ago, it was easy to feel lonely. Now, it is impossible to be alone.

As a result, we are losing both sides of the Romantic dialectic. What *11* does friendship mean when you have 532 "friends"? How does it enhance my sense of closeness when my Facebook News Feed tells me that Sally Smith (whom I haven't seen since high school, and wasn't all that friendly with even then) "is making coffee and staring off into space"? My students told me they have little time for intimacy. And of course, they have no time at all for solitude.

But at least friendship, if not intimacy, is still something they want. As *12* jarring as the new dispensation may be for people in their 30s and 40s, the real problem is that it has become completely natural for people in their teens and 20s. Young people today seem to have no desire for solitude, have never heard of it, can't imagine why it would be worth having. In fact, their use of technology—or to be fair, our use of technology—seems to involve a constant effort to stave off the possibility of solitude, a continuous attempt, as we sit alone at our computers, to maintain the imaginative presence of others. As long ago as 1952, Trilling wrote about "the modern fear of being cut off from the social group even for a moment." Now we have equipped ourselves with the means to prevent that fear from ever being realized. Which does not mean that we have put it to rest. Quite the contrary. Remember my student, who couldn't even write a paper by herself. The more we keep aloneness at bay, the less are we able to deal with it and the more terrifying it gets.

There is an analogy, it seems to me, with the previous generation's *13* experience of boredom. The two emotions, loneliness and boredom, are closely allied. They are also both characteristically modern. The *Oxford English Dictionary*'s earliest citations of either word, at least in the contemporary sense, date from the nineteenth century. Suburbanization, by eliminating the stimulation as well as the sociability of urban or traditional village life, exacerbated the tendency to both. But the great age of boredom, I believe, came in with television, precisely because television was designed to palliate that feeling. Boredom is not a necessary consequence of having nothing to do, it is only the negative experience of that state. Television, by obviating the need to learn how to make use of one's lack of occupation, precludes one from ever discovering how to enjoy it. In fact, it renders that condition fearsome, its prospect intolerable. You are terrified of being bored—so you turn on the television.

I speak from experience. I grew up in the 1960s and 1970s, the age of *14* television. I was trained to be bored; boredom was cultivated within me like a precious crop. (It has been said that consumer society wants to condition us to feel bored, since boredom creates a market for stimulation.) It took me years to discover—and my nervous system will never fully adjust to this idea; I still have to fight against boredom, am permanently damaged in this respect—that having nothing to do doesn't have to be a bad thing. The alternative to boredom is what Whitman called idleness: a passive receptivity to the world.

So it is with the current generation's experience of being alone. That is   *15*
precisely the recognition implicit in the idea of solitude, which is to loneliness what idleness is to boredom. Loneliness is not the absence of company, it is grief over that absence. The lost sheep is lonely; the shepherd
is not lonely. But the Internet is as powerful a machine for the production of loneliness as television is for the manufacture of boredom. If six
hours of television a day creates the aptitude for boredom, the inability
to sit still, a hundred text messages a day creates the aptitude for loneliness, the inability to be by yourself. Some degree of boredom and loneliness is to be expected, especially among young people, given the way our
human environment has been attenuated. But technology amplifies those
tendencies. You could call your schoolmates when I was a teenager, but
you couldn't call them 100 times a day. You could get together with your
friends when I was in college, but you couldn't always get together with
them when you wanted to, for the simple reason that you couldn't always
find them. If boredom is the great emotion of the TV generation, loneliness is the great emotion of the Web generation. We lost the ability to be
still, our capacity for idleness. They have lost the ability to be alone, their
capacity for solitude.

And losing solitude, what have they lost? First, the propensity for in-   *16*
trospection, that examination of the self that the Puritans, and the
Romantics, and the modernists (and Socrates, for that matter) placed at
the center of spiritual life—of wisdom, of conduct. Thoreau called it fish-
ing "in the Walden Pond of [our] own natures," "bait[ing our] hooks with
darkness." Lost, too, is the related propensity for sustained reading. The
Internet brought text back into a televisual world, but it brought it back
on terms dictated by that world—that is, by its remapping of our attention spans. Reading now means skipping and skimming; five minutes on
the same Web page is considered an eternity. This is not reading as
Marilynne Robinson described it: the encounter with a second self in the
silence of mental solitude.

But we no longer believe in the solitary mind. If the Romantics had   *17*
Hume and the modernists had Freud, the current psychological model—
and this should come as no surprise—is that of the networked or social
mind. Evolutionary psychology tells us that our brains developed to
interpret complex social signals. According to David Brooks, that reliable
index of the social-scientific zeitgeist, cognitive scientists tell us that "our
decision-making is powerfully influenced by social context"; neurosci-
entists, that we have "permeable minds" that function in part through a
process of "deep imitation"; psychologists, that "we are organized by our
attachments"; sociologists, that our behavior is affected by "the power
of social networks." The ultimate implication is that there is no mental
space that is not social (contemporary social science dovetailing here
with postmodern critical theory). One of the most striking things about
the way young people relate to one another today is that they no longer
seem to believe in the existence of Thoreau's "darkness."

The MySpace page, with its shrieking typography and clamorous im-   18
agery, has replaced the journal and the letter as a way of creating and
communicating one's sense of self. The suggestion is not only that such
communication is to be made to the world at large rather than to oneself or one's intimates, or graphically rather than verbally, or performa-
tively rather than narratively or analytically, but also that it can be made
completely. Today's young people seem to feel that they can make themselves fully known to one another. They seem to lack a sense of their own
depths, and of the value of keeping them hidden.

If they didn't, they would understand that solitude enables us to secure   19
the integrity of the self as well as to explore it. Few have shown this more
beautifully than Woolf. In the middle of *Mrs. Dalloway*, between her navigation of the streets and her orchestration of the party, between the urban
jostle and the social bustle, Clarissa goes up, "like a nun withdrawing," to
her attic room. Like a nun: She returns to a state that she herself thinks of
as a kind of virginity. This does not mean she's a prude. Virginity is classi-
cally the outward sign of spiritual inviolability, of a self untouched by the
world, a soul that has preserved its integrity by refusing to descend into
the chaos and self-division of sexual and social relations. It is the mark
of the saint and the monk, of Hippolytus and Antigone and Joan of Arc.
Solitude is both the social image of that state and the means by which
we can approximate it. And the supreme image in *Mrs. Dalloway* of the
dignity of solitude itself is the old woman whom Clarissa catches sight of
through her window. "Here was one room," she thinks, "there another."
We are not merely social beings. We are each also separate, each solitary,
each alone in our own room, each miraculously our unique selves and
mysteriously enclosed in that selfhood.

To remember this, to hold oneself apart from society, is to begin to   20
think one's way beyond it. Solitude, Emerson said, "is to genius the stern
friend." "He who should inspire and lead his race must be defended from
traveling with the souls of other men, from living, breathing, reading, and
writing in the daily, time-worn yoke of their opinions." One must protect
oneself from the momentum of intellectual and moral consensus—especially, Emerson added, during youth. "God is alone," Thoreau said, "but
the Devil, he is far from being alone; he sees a great deal of company; he
is legion." The university was to be praised, Emerson believed, if only
because it provided its charges with "a separate chamber and fire"—the
physical space of solitude. Today, of course, universities do everything
they can to keep their students from being alone, lest they perpetrate self-
destructive acts, and also, perhaps, unfashionable thoughts. But no real
excellence, personal or social, artistic, philosophical, scientific, or moral,
can arise without solitude. "The saint and poet seek privacy," Emerson
said, "to ends the most public and universal." We are back to the seer,
seeking signposts for the future in splendid isolation.

Solitude isn't easy, and isn't for everyone. It has undoubtedly never   21
been the province of more than a few. "I believe," Thoreau said, "that

men are generally still a little afraid of the dark." Teresa and Tiresias will always be the exceptions, or to speak in more relevant terms, the young people—and they still exist—who prefer to loaf and invite their soul, who step to the beat of a different drummer. But if solitude disappears as a social value and social idea, will even the exceptions remain possible? Still, one is powerless to reverse the drift of the culture. One can only save oneself—and whatever else happens, one can still always do that. But it takes a willingness to be unpopular.

The last thing to say about solitude is that it isn't very polite. Thoreau   22
knew that the "doubleness" that solitude cultivates, the ability to stand back and observe life dispassionately, is apt to make us a little unpleasant to our fellows, to say nothing of the offense implicit in avoiding their company. But then, he didn't worry overmuch about being genial. He didn't even like having to talk to people three times a day, at meals; one can only imagine what he would have made of text-messaging. We, however, have made of geniality—the weak smile, the polite interest, the fake invitation—a cardinal virtue. Friendship may be slipping from our grasp, but our friendliness is universal. Not for nothing does "gregarious" mean "part of the herd." But Thoreau understood that securing one's self-possession was worth a few wounded feelings. He may have put his neighbors off, but at least he was sure of himself. Those who would find solitude must not be afraid to stand alone.

Writing as a Reader

1. Recast Deresiewicz's essay as Anna Quindlen might in her *Newsweek* column. Obviously, her *Newsweek* column is much shorter (an important constraint). She also writes for a more general audience than Deresiewicz, and her tone is quite different. To strengthen your sense of her approach, you may want to browse some of Quindlen's other essays in editions of *Newsweek* or in some of her essay collections listed in the headnote on page 82.

2. Recast Deresiewicz's essay in terms of a writer you read regularly—for example, a columnist in your local newspaper or a blogger in some online venue. Use your imagination. What is the audience, and how will you have to present the issue to engage and persuade them?

From Formulating to Developing a Thesis

Academic writing explores complex issues that grow out of relevant, timely conversations in which something is at stake. An academic writer reads as a writer to understand the issues, situations, and questions that lead other writers to make claims. Readers expect academic writers to take a clear, specific, logical stand on an issue, and they evaluate how writers support their claims and anticipate counterarguments. The logical stand is the **thesis**, an assertion that academic writers make at the beginning of what they write and then support with evidence throughout their essay. The illustrations and examples that a writer includes must relate to and support the thesis. Thus, a thesis encompasses all of the information writers use to further their arguments; it is not simply a single assertion at the beginning of an essay.

One of our students aptly described the thesis using the metaphor of a shish kebab: The thesis penetrates every paragraph, holding the paragraphs together, just as a skewer penetrates and holds the ingredients of a shish kebab together. Moreover, the thesis serves as a signpost throughout an essay, reminding readers what the argument is and why the writer has included evidence—examples, illustrations, quotations—relevant to that argument.

An academic thesis

- makes an assertion that is clearly defined, focused, and supported.
- reflects an awareness of the conversation from which the writer has taken up the issue.
- is placed at the beginning of the essay.

- penetrates every paragraph like the skewer in a shish kebab.
- acknowledges points of view that differ from the writer's own, reflecting the complexity of the issue.
- demonstrates an awareness of the readers' assumptions and anticipates possible counterarguments.
- conveys a significant fresh perspective.

It is a myth that writers first come up with a thesis and then write their essays. The reality is that writers use issue-based questions to read, learn, and develop a thesis throughout the process of writing. Through revising and discussing their ideas, writers hone their thesis, making sure that it threads through every paragraph of the final draft. The position writers ultimately take in writing—their thesis—comes at the end of the writing process, after not one draft but many.

WORKING VERSUS DEFINITIVE THESES

Writers are continually challenged by the need to establish their purpose and to make a clear and specific assertion of it. To reach that assertion, you must first engage in a prolonged process of inquiry, aided by a well-formulated question. The question serves as a tool for inquiry that will help you formulate your **working thesis**, your first attempt at an assertion of your position. A working thesis is valuable in the early stages of writing because it helps you read selectively, in the same way that your issue-based question guides your inquiry. Reading raises questions, helping you see what you know and need to know, and challenging you to read on.

Never accept your working thesis as your final position. Instead, continue testing your assertion as you read and write, and modify your working thesis as necessary. A more definitive thesis will come once you are satisfied that you have examined the issue from multiple perspectives.

For example, one of our students wanted to study representations of femininity in the media. In particular, she focused on why the Barbie doll has become an icon of femininity despite what many cultural critics consider Barbie's "outrageous and ultimately unattainable physical characteristics." Our student's working thesis suggested she would develop an argument about the need for change:

> The harmful implications of ongoing exposure to these unattainable ideals, such as low self-esteem, eating disorders, unhealthy body image, and acceptance of violence, make urgent the need for change.

The student assumed that her research would lead her to argue that Barbie's unattainable proportions have a damaging effect on women's self-image and that something needs to be done about it. However, as she read scholarly research to support her tentative thesis, she realized that a more compelling project would be less Barbie-centric. Instead, she chose to examine the broader phenomenon of how the idea of femininity is created and reinforced by society. That is, her personal interest in Barbie was supplanted by her discoveries about cultural norms of beauty and the power they have to influence self-perception and behavior. In her final draft, this was her definitive thesis:

> Although evidence may be provided to argue that gender is an innate characteristic, I will show that it is actually the result of one's actions, which are then labeled *masculine* or *feminine* according to society's definitions of ideal gender. Furthermore, I will discuss the communication of such definitions through the media, specifically in music videos, on TV, and in magazines, and the harmful implications of being exposed to these ideals.

Instead of arguing for change, the student chose to show her readers how they were being manipulated, leaving it to them to decide what actions they might want to take.

DEVELOPING A WORKING THESIS: THREE MODELS

What are some ways to develop a working thesis? We suggest three models that may help you organize the information you gather in response to the question guiding your inquiry.

■ The Correcting-Misinterpretations Model

This model is used to correct writers whose arguments you believe have misconstrued one or more important aspects of an issue. The thesis typically takes the form of a factual claim. Consider this example and the words we have underlined:

> <u>Although scholars have addressed curriculum</u> to explain low achievement in schools, <u>they have failed to fully appreciate the impact of limited resources</u> to fund up-to-date textbooks, quality teachers, and computers. Therefore, reform in schools must focus on economic need as well as curriculum.

The clause beginning with "Although" lays out the assumption that many scholars make, that curriculum explains low educational achievement; the clause beginning with "they have failed" identifies the error those scholars have made by ignoring the economic reasons for low achievement in schools. Notice that the structure of the sentence reinforces the author's position. He offers the faulty assumption in a subordinate clause, reserving the main clause for his own position. The two clauses also reinforce that there are conflicting opinions here. One more thing: Although it is a common myth that a thesis must be phrased in a single sentence, this example shows that a thesis can be written in two (or more) sentences.

■ The Filling-the-Gap Model

The gap model points to what other writers may have overlooked or ignored in discussing a given issue. The gap model typically makes a claim of value. Consider this student's argument that discussions of cultural diversity in the United States are often framed in terms of black and white. Our underlining indicates the gap the writer has identified:

> If America is truly a "melting pot" of cultures, as it is often called, then <u>why is it that stories and events seem only to be in black and white? Why is it that when history courses are taught about the period of the civil rights movement, only the memoirs of African Americans are read</u>, like those of Melba Pattillo Beals and Ida Mae Holland? Where are <u>the works of Maxine Hong Kingston</u>, who tells the story of alienation and segregation in schools through the eyes of a Chinese child? African Americans were denied the right to vote, and many other citizenship rights; but Chinese Americans were denied even the opportunity to become citizens. I am not diminishing the issue of discrimination against African Americans, or belittling the struggles they went through. <u>I simply want to call attention to discrimination against other minority groups and their often-overlooked struggles to achieve equality.</u>

In the student's thesis, the gap in people's knowledge stems from their limited understanding of history. They need to understand that many minority groups were denied their rights.

A variation on the gap model also occurs when a writer suggests that although something might appear to be the case, a closer look reveals something different. For example: "Although it would *appear* that women have achieved equality in the workplace, their paychecks suggest that this is not true."

One of our students examined two poems by the same author that appeared to contradict each other. She noticed a gap others had not seen:

> In both "The Albatross" and "Beauty," Charles Baudelaire chooses to explore the plight of the poet. Interestingly, despite their common author, the two poems' portrayals of the poet's struggles appear contradictory. "The Albatross" seems to give a somewhat sympathetic glimpse into the exile of the poet — the "winged voyager" so awkward in the ordinary world. "Beauty" takes what appears to be a less forgiving stance: The poet here is docile, simply a mirror. Although both pieces depict the poet's struggles, a closer examination demonstrates how the portrayals differ.

In stating her thesis, the student indicates that although readers might expect Baudelaire's images of poets to be similar, a closer examination of his words would prove them wrong.

■ The Modifying-What-Others-Have-Said Model

The modification model of thesis writing assumes that mutual understanding is possible. For example, in proposing a change in policy, one student asserts:

> Although scholars have claimed that the only sure way to reverse the cycle of homelessness in America is to provide an adequate education, we need to build on this work, providing school-to-work programs that ensure graduates have access to employment.

Here the writer seeks to modify other writers' claims, suggesting that education alone does not solve the problem of homelessness. The challenge he sets for himself is to understand the complexity of the problem by building on and extending the ideas of others. In effect, he is in a constructive conversation with those whose work he wants to build on, helping readers see that he shares common ground with the other writers and that he hopes to find a mutually acceptable solution to the agreed-on problem.

Steps to Formulating a Working Thesis: Three Models

1 **Misinterpretations model:** "Although many scholars have argued about X and Y, a careful examination suggests Z."

2 **Gap model:** "Although scholars have noted X and Y, they have missed the importance of Z."

3 **Modification model:** "Although I agree with the X and Y ideas of other writers, it is important to extend/refine/limit their ideas with Z."

A Practice Sequence: Identifying Types of Theses

Below is a series of working theses. Read each one and then identify the model—misinterpretations, gap, or modification—that it represents.

1 A number of studies indicate that violence on television has a detrimental effect on adolescent behavior. However, few researchers have examined key environmental factors like peer pressure, music, and home life. In fact, I would argue that many researchers have oversimplified the problem.

2 Although research indicates that an increasing number of African American and Hispanic students are dropping out of high school, researchers have failed to fully grasp the reasons why this has occurred.

3   I want to argue that studies supporting single-sex education are relatively sound. However, we don't really know the long-term effects of single-sex education, particularly on young women's career paths.

4   Although recent studies of voting patterns in the United States indicate that young people between the ages of 18 and 24 are apathetic, I want to suggest that not all of the reasons these studies provide are valid.

5   Indeed, it's not surprising that students are majoring in fields that will enable them to get a job after graduation. But students may not be as pragmatic as we think. Many students choose majors because they feel that learning is an important end in itself.

6   Although good teachers are essential to learning, we cannot ignore the roles that race and class play in students' access to a quality education.

7   It is clear that cities need to clean up the dilapidated housing projects that were built over half a century ago; but few, if any, studies have examined the effects of doing so on the life chances of those people who are being displaced.

8   In addition to its efforts to advance the cause of social justice in the new global economy, the university must make a commitment to ending poverty on the edge of campus.

9   Although the writer offers evidence to explain the sources of illiteracy in America, he overstates his case when he ignores other factors, among them history, culture, and economic well-being. Therefore, I will argue that we place the discussion in a broader context.

10   More and more policymakers argue that English should be the national language in the United States. Although I agree that English is important, we should not limit people's right to maintain their own linguistic and cultural identity.

ESTABLISHING A CONTEXT FOR A THESIS

In addition to defining the purpose and focus of an essay, a thesis must set up a **context** for the writer's claim. The process of establishing a background for understanding an issue typically involves four steps:

1. Establish that the topic of conversation, the issue, is current and relevant—that it is on people's minds or should be.

2. Briefly summarize what others have said to show that you are familiar with the topic or issue.

3. Explain what you see as the problem—a misinterpretation, a gap, or a modification that needs to be made in how others have addressed the topic or issue—perhaps by raising the questions you believe need to be answered.

4. State your thesis, suggesting that your view on the issue may present readers with something new to think about as it builds on and extends what others have argued.

You need not follow these steps in this order as long as your readers come away from the first part of your essay knowing why you are discussing a given issue and what your argument is.

AN ANNOTATED STUDENT INTRODUCTION: PROVIDING A CONTEXT FOR A THESIS

We trace these four steps below in our analysis of the opening paragraphs of a student's essay. She wrote in response to what many call the English-only movement. Specifically, she responds to the effects of Proposition 227 in California, a piece of legislation that prevents non-English-speaking students from using their first language in school. Our discussion of how she provides a context for her thesis follows the excerpt.[1]

NUESTRA CLASE   1

Jenny Eck
English 200
Professor Walters
March 18, 20 —

Nuestra Clase: Making the Classroom a Welcoming Place
for English Language Learners

Notes the impor-tance of the issue.   With the Latino population growing exponentially and Spanish quickly becoming one of the most widely spoken languages in the United States, the question arises of how the American educational system is meeting the needs of a growing

---

[1] This excerpt follows APA citation style (see Appendix). For brevity, we have omitted the references page at the end of the excerpt.

NUESTRA CLASE   2

Hispanic population. What does our educational system do to address the needs of students whose primary language is not English?

Sets the stage with background on Proposition 227.

In 1998, the state of California passed Proposition 227, which prohibited bilingual instruction in public schools. Ron Unz, a former Republican gubernatorial candidate and software developer, launched the initiative under the name "English for the Children." Unz argued that the initiative would help Latinos and other recent immigrants free themselves from bilingual education, which he avowed would hinder the ability of immigrants to assimilate into American culture (Stritikus, 2002). Supporters of Proposition 227 assert that bilingual education has failed English language learners (ELLs) because it does not adequately equip them with the English language skills essential to success in school. Eradicating bilingual education, they believe, will help students learn English more effectively and consequently achieve more in their educational careers.

The issue remains relevant.

Since its passage, Proposition 227 has been hotly debated. Many researchers claim that its strictures have stunted the education of Spanish-speaking students (Halcón, 2001; Stritikus, 2002). Many studies have indicated the harmful effects of what Gutiérrez and her colleagues describe as "backlash pedagogy" (Gutiérrez, Asato, Santos, & Gotanda, 2002),

Represents what others have said in the conversation.

which prohibits the use of students' complete linguistic, sociocultural, and academic repertoire. In essence, they claim that Proposition 227's backlash pedagogy, in attempting to emphasize "colorblindness" in education, has instead eradicated differences that are crucial to students' efforts to become educated. They argue that by devaluing these differences, the educational system devalues the very students it is attempting to help.

Introduces a frame or lens for thinking about the issue.

A sociocultural theory of learning, with its emphasis on the significant impact that factors such as language, culture, family, and community have on a student's potential for educational success (Halcón, 2001), calls attention to growing concerns that schools may not be meeting the needs of ELLs. Russian psychologist Lev Vygotsky (1978) introduced this viewpoint to educators when he proposed that development and learning are firmly embedded in and influenced by society and culture. With Vygotsky's theory in mind, other researchers have embraced the idea that the failure of minority students is more often than not a systematic failure, rather than an individual failure (Trueba, 1989). Sociocultural theory posits that learning needs to be understood not only in the broader context of the sociocultural lives of students, teachers, and schools, but also in their sociopolitical lives. A sociocultural context takes a student's culture, race, religion, language, family, community, and other similar factors into consideration, while a sociopolitical context takes into account the inherent ideologies and prejudices that exist in society today. In order for teaching to be effective, both sociocultural and sociopolitical factors must be identified and addressed.

Explains what she sees as the problem.

Many educators seem to dismiss sociocultural and sociopolitical factors, perhaps not realizing that by ignoring these factors, they are inadvertently privileging the students in their classrooms for whom English is a first language (Larson, 2003). Such a dismissive attitude does not reckon with other studies that have shown how important it is for English language learners to explore and express their bilingual/bicultural identities (McCarthey, García, López-Velásquez, Lin, & Guo, 2004). Some of these other studies have even proposed that schooling acts as a "subtractive process" for minority students, not only denying them opportunities to express their identities, but also divesting them of important social and cultural resources, which ultimately leaves them vulnerable to academic failure (Valenzuela, 1999). These other studies convincingly show that sociocultural factors are essential to the educational success of

States her thesis.

English language learners. Therefore, although many educators believe they know the best way to teach these students, I will argue that the educational system, by not taking into account factors that sociocultural theory emphasizes, has mostly failed to create classrooms that embrace cultural differences, and by so doing has failed to create optimal conditions for teaching and learning.

5

■ Establish That the Issue Is Current and Relevant

Ideally, you should convey to readers that the issue you are discussing is both current (what's on people's minds) and relevant (of sufficient importance to have generated some discussion and written conversation). In the first sentence, Eck tells readers of a trend she feels they need to be aware of, the dramatic growth of the Hispanic population in the United States. Her issue is what the schools are doing to meet the needs of a growing population of students "whose primary language is not English." At the beginning of the third paragraph, she signals the relevance of the issue when she observes that the passage of Proposition 227 has been "hotly debated."

■ Briefly Present What Others Have Said

It is important to introduce who has said what in the conversation you are entering. After all, you are interrupting that conversation to make your contribution, and those who are already in that conversation expect you to have done your homework and acknowledge those who have already made important contributions.

In the second paragraph, Eck sets the stage for her review with a brief history of Proposition 227. Here she describes what was at issue for supporters of the law and what they hoped the law would accomplish. Starting with paragraph 3, Eck acknowledges the researchers who have participated in the debate surrounding Proposition 227 and reviews a number of studies that challenge the premises on which Proposition 227 rested.

In paragraph 4, notice that Eck introduces the frame of sociocultural theory to help her readers see that denying students the use of their native language in the classroom is a problem.

By pointing out the ways that researchers on language learning challenge the assumptions underlying the English-only movement, Eck is doing more than listing sources. She is establishing that a problem, or issue, exists. Moreover, her review gives readers intellectual touchstones, the scholars who need to be cited in any academic conversation about bilingual education. A review is not a catchall for anyone writing on a topic; instead, it should reflect a writer's selection of the most relevant participants in the conversation. Eck's choice of sources, and how she presents them, conveys that she is knowledgeable about her subject. (Of course, it is her readers' responsibility to read further to determine whether she has reviewed the most relevant work and has presented the ideas of others accurately. If she has, readers will trust her, whether or not they end up agreeing with her on the issue.)

■ Explain What You See as the Problem

If a review indicates a problem, as Eck's review does, the problem can often be couched in terms of the models we discussed earlier: misinterpretations, gap, or modification. In paragraph 5, Eck identifies what she concludes is a misunderstanding of how students learn a new language. She suggests that the misunderstanding stems from a gap in knowledge (notice our underlining):

> <u>Many educators seem to dismiss sociocultural and sociopolitical factors, perhaps not realizing that by ignoring these factors, they are inadvertently privileging the students in their classrooms for whom English is a first language</u> (Larson, 2003). Such a dismissive attitude does not reckon with other studies that have shown how important it is for English language learners to explore and express their bilingual/bicultural identities (McCarthey, García, López-Velásquez, Lin, & Guo, 2004). Some of these other studies have even proposed that schooling acts as a "subtractive process" for minority students, not only denying them opportunities to express their identities, but also divesting them of important social and cultural resources, which ultimately leaves them vulnerable to academic failure (Valenzuela, 1999).

While Eck concedes that efforts to understand the problems of language learning have been extensive and multifaceted, her review of the research culminates with her assertion that ignoring students' language practices could have devastating results—that educators, by denying students "important social and cultural resources," may be leaving those students "vulnerable to academic failure."

■ State Your Thesis

An effective thesis statement helps readers see the reasoning behind the author's claim; it also signals what readers should look for in the remainder of the essay. Eck closes paragraph 5 with a statement that speaks to both the purpose and the substance of her writing:

> Therefore, although many educators believe they know the best way to teach ELL students, I will argue that the educational system, by not taking into account factors that sociocultural theory emphasizes, has mostly failed to create classrooms that embrace cultural differences, and by so doing has failed to create optimal conditions for teaching and learning.

In your own writing, you can make use of the strategies that Eck uses in her essay. Words like *although* and *though* can set up problem statements: "Although [Though] some people think that nonnative speakers of English can best learn English by not using their first language, the issue is more complex than most people realize." Words like *but*, *however*, and *yet* can serve the same purpose: "One might argue that nonnative speakers of English can best learn English by not using their first language; but [however, yet] the issue is more complex than most people realize."

Steps to Establishing a Context for a Thesis

1 Establish that the issue is current and relevant. Point out the extent to which others have recognized the problem, issue, or question that you are writing about.

2 Briefly present what others have said. Explain how others have addressed the problem, issue, or question you are focusing on.

3 Explain what you see as the problem. Identify what is open to dispute.

4 State your thesis. Help readers see your purpose and how you intend to achieve it—by correcting a misconception, filling a gap, or modifying a claim others have accepted.

■ Analyze the Context of a Thesis

In "Protean Shapes in Literacy Events," cultural anthropologist and linguist Shirley Brice Heath argues that communities of practice shape the ways in which people use reading and writing. Heath points out the problem of holding up a standard of literacy from one community to measure the extent to which another community is or is not literate. Her essay, originally published in 1982, is addressed to a community of scholars who study literacy. As you read the excerpt that follows, you will likely find yourself puzzled by Heath's vocabulary and possibly even excluded from the conversation at times. Our point in reprinting this excerpt is not to initiate you into Heath's academic community but to show, through our annotations, how Heath has applied the strategies we have been discussing in this chapter. As you read, feel free to make your own annotations, and then try to answer the questions—which may involve some careful rereading—that we pose after the excerpt. In particular, watch for signpost words (*but*, *few*, *little*, *however*) that signal the ideas the writer is challenging.

SHIRLEY BRICE HEATH

From Protean Shapes in Literacy Events: Ever-Shifting Oral and Literate Traditions

The first sentence establishes that the issue that interests Heath has been discussed for more than a few years, helping us see the continuing relevance of the area of study.

Since the mid-1970s, anthropologists, linguists, historians, and psychologists have turned with new tools of analysis to the study of oral and literate societies. They have used discourse analysis, econometrics, theories of schemata and frames, and proposals of developmental performance to consider the possible links between oral and written language, and between

1

literacy and its individual and societal consequences. Much of this research is predicated on a dichotomous view of oral and literate traditions, usually attributed to researchers active in the 1960s. Repeatedly, Goody and Watt (1963), Ong (1967), Goody (1968), and Havelock (1963) are cited as having suggested a dichotomous view of oral and literate societies and as having asserted certain cognitive, social, and linguistic effects of literacy on both the society and the individual. Survey research tracing the invention and diffusion of writing systems across numerous societies (Kroeber, 1948) and positing the effects of the spread of literacy on social and individual memory (Goody and Watt, 1963; Havelock, 1963, 1976) is cited as supporting a contrastive view of oral and literate social groups. Research which examined oral performance in particular groups is said to support the notion that as members of a society increasingly participate in literacy, they lose habits associated with the oral tradition (Lord, 1965).

In short, existing scholarship makes it easy to interpret a picture which depicts societies existing along a continuum of development from an oral tradition to a literate one, with some societies having a restricted literacy, and others having reached a full development of literacy (Goody, 1968:11). One also finds in this research specific characterizations of oral and written language associated with these traditions.

But a close reading of these scholars, especially Goody (1968) and Goody and Watt (1963), leaves some room for questioning such a picture of consistent and universal processes or products—individual or societal—of literacy. Goody pointed out that in any traditional society, factors such as secrecy, religious ideology, limited social mobility, lack of access to writing materials and alphabetic scripts could lead to restricted literacy. Furthermore, Goody warned that the advent of a writing system did not amount to technological determinism or to sufficient cause of certain changes in either the individual or the society. Goody went on to propose exploring the concrete context of written communication (1968:4) to determine how the

From the sentence that begins "Much of this research" to the end of the paragraph, Heath reviews some of the relevant literature and points to a problem: that previous work has seen literate and oral cultures as somehow opposed to one another. The author gives us more than a list of sources.

In the first sentence in this paragraph, Heath suggests that a close reading would raise some important unanswered questions about the relationship between orality and literacy.

2

3

potentialities of literacy developed in traditional societies. He brought together a collection of essays based on the ethnography of literacy in traditional societies to illustrate the wide variety of ways in which *traditional*, i.e., pre-industrial but not necessarily preliterate, societies played out their uses of oral and literate traditions.

The previous paragraph sets up the problem and the gap that Heath believes her research — indicated in the first two sentences of this paragraph — should address.

Few researchers in the 1970s have, however, heeded Goody's warning about the possible wide-ranging effects of societal and cultural factors on literacy and its uses. In particular, little attention has been given in *modern* complex industrial societies to the social and cultural correlates of literacy or to the work experiences adults have which may affect the maintenance and retention of literacy skills acquired in formal schooling. The public media today give much attention to the decline of literacy skills as measured in school settings and the failure of students to acquire certain

This sentence indicates the gap: The media focus on one set of concerns when they should be attending to a very different set of issues.

levels of literacy. However, the media pay little attention to occasions for literacy retention — to the actual uses of literacy in work settings, daily interactions in religious, economic, and legal institutions, and family habits of socializing the young into uses of literacy. In the clamor over the need to increase the teaching of basic skills, there is much emphasis on the positive effects extensive and critical reading can have on im-

Heath elaborates on what she sees as a troubling gap between what educators know and what they need to know.

proving oral language. Yet there are scarcely any data comparing the forms and functions of oral language with those of written language produced and used by members of social groups within a complex society. One of the most appropriate sources of data for informing discussions of these issues is that which Goody proposed for traditional societies: the concrete context of written communication. Where, when, how, for whom, and with what results are individuals in different social groups of today's highly industrialized

In the last four sentences of the excerpt, Heath raises the questions that she wants readers to consider and that guide her own research.

society using reading and writing skills? How have the potentialities of the literacy skills learned in school developed in the lives of today's adults? Does modern society contain certain conditions which restrict literacy just as some traditional societies do? If so, what are these factors, and are groups with restricted literacy

> denied benefits widely attributed to full literacy, such as upward socioeconomic mobility, the development of logical reasoning, and access to the information necessary to make well-informed political judgments?

Reading as a Writer

1. What specific places can you point to in the selection that illustrate what is at issue for Heath?

2. How does Heath use her review to set up her argument?

3. What specific words and phrases does Heath use to establish what she sees as the problem? Is she correcting misinterpretations, filling a gap, or modifying what others have said?

4. What would you say is Heath's thesis? What specifics can you point to in the text to support your answer?

5. What would you say are the arguments Heath wants you to avoid? Again, what specific details can you point to in the text to support your answer?

A Practice Sequence: Building a Thesis

We would like you to practice some of the strategies we have covered in this chapter. If you have already started working on an essay, exercises 1 through 4 present an opportunity to take stock of your progress, a chance to sort through what you've discovered, identify what you still need to discover, and move toward refining your thesis. Jot down your answer to each of the questions below and make lists of what you know and what you need to learn.

1 Have you established that your issue is current and relevant, that it is or should be on people's minds? What information would you need to do so?

2 Can you summarize briefly what others have said in the past to show that you are familiar with how others have addressed the issue? List some of the key texts you have read and the key points they make.

3 Have you identified any misunderstandings or gaps in how others have addressed the issue? Describe them. Do you have any ideas or information that would address these misunderstandings or help fill these gaps? Where might you find the information you need? Can you think of any sources you should reread to learn more? (For example, have you looked at the works cited or bibliographies in the texts you've already read?)

4   At this point, what is your take on the issue? Try drafting a work-
    ing thesis statement that will present readers with something
    new to think about, building on and extending what others have
    argued. In drafting your thesis statement, try out the three models
    discussed in this chapter and see if one is an especially good fit:

  - *Misinterpretations model*: "Although many scholars have
    argued about X and Y, a careful examination suggests Z."

  - *Gap model*: "Although scholars have noted X and Y, they have
    missed the importance of Z."

  - *Modification model*: "Although I agree with X and Y ideas of
    other writers, it is important to extend/refine/limit their ideas
    with Z."

5   If you haven't chosen a topic yet, try a group exercise. Sit down
    with a few of your classmates and choose one of the following top-
    ics to brainstorm about as a group. Choose a topic that everyone in
    the group finds interesting, and work through exercises 1 through
    4 in this practice sequence. Here are some suggestions:

  - The moral obligation to vote

  - The causes or consequences of poverty

  - The limits of academic freedom

  - Equity in education

  - The popularity of _____

  - The causes or consequences of teen violence

  - Gender stereotypes in the media

  - Linguistic diversity

  - The uses of a liberal education

  - Journalism and truth

AN ANNOTATED STUDENT ESSAY: STATING AND SUPPORTING A THESIS

We have annotated the following student essay to illustrate the strategies
we have discussed in this chapter for stating a thesis that responds to a relevant, timely problem in a given context. The assignment was to write an
argument focusing on literacy based on research. Veronica Stafford chose
to write about her peers' habit of texting and the ways in which this type of
social interaction affects their intellectual development. Stafford develops
a thesis that provides a corrective to a misconception that she sees in the

ongoing conversations about texting. Her approach is a variation on the strategy in which writers correct a misinterpretation. In turn, you will see that she makes claims of fact and evaluation in making an argument for changing her peers' penchant for texting.

As you read the essay, reflect on your own experiences: Do you think the issue she raises is both timely and relevant? How well do you think she places her ideas in conversation with others? How would you respond to her various claims? Which do you agree with and disagree with, and why? What evidence would you present to support or counter her claims? Do you think she offers a reasonable corrective to what she believes is a misconception about texting?

Stafford 1

Veronica Stafford
Professor Wilson
English 1102
April 20 —

Texting and Literacy

As students walk to class each day, most do not notice the other people around them. Rather than talking with others, they are texting their friends in the next building, in their dorm, or back home. Although social networking is the most common use for text messages, they are not used solely for socializing. While texting is a quick and easy way to keep up with friends, it threatens other aspects of our lives. When students spend time texting rather than focusing on those other important aspects, texting becomes detrimental. Students' enjoyment of reading, their schoolwork, and their relationships with others are all negatively affected by text messaging.

The student identifies an issue, or problem, and states her thesis as an evaluative claim that attempts to correct a misconception.

Due to the mass appeal of text messaging, students pass their free time chatting through their cell phones rather than enjoying a great book. Texting is so widespread because 25% of students under age eight, 89% of students ages eleven to thirteen, and over 95% of students over age fifteen have a cell phone ("Mobile Phones"). On average, 75.6 million text messages are sent in a day, with 54% of the population texting more than five times per day ("Mobile Phones"). In contrast to

She summarizes research, placing the conversation in a larger context. Her citations also indicate that the problem she identifies is relevant and timely.

1

2

Stafford 2

the time they spend texting, fifteen- to twenty-four-year-olds read a mere seven minutes per day for fun and only 1.25 hours a week ("To Read" 10), which is less than half the time that seventh-grade students spend texting: 2.82 hours a week (Bryant, Sanders-Jackson and Smallwood). While more than half of the population texts every day, almost as many (43%) have not read a single book in the past year ("To Read" 7). It seems there is a direct correlation between reading and texting because, as text messaging increases in popularity, reading decreases. The National Endowment for the Arts surveyed eighteen- to twenty-four-year-olds and discovered that the enjoyment of reading in this age group is declining the fastest. Inversely, it is the group that sends the most text messages: 142 billion a year ("To Read" 10). From 1992 to 2002, 2.1 million potential readers, aged eighteen to twenty-four years old, were lost ("To Read" 27). As proved by the direct correlation, reading does not have the same appeal because of texting. Students prefer to spend time in the technological world rather than sitting with a book.

However, reading well is essential to being successful academically. Although some argue that text messages force students to think quickly and allow them to formulate brief responses to questions, their habit is actually stifling creativity. When a group of twenty students was given a chance to write responses to open-ended questions, the students who owned cell phones with text messaging wrote much less. They also had more grammatical errors, such as leaving apostrophes out of contractions and substituting the letter "r" for the word "are" (Ward). Because of text messages, students perceive writing as a fun way to communicate with friends and not as a way to strongly voice an opinion. Students no longer think of writing as academic, but rather they consider it social. For instance, in Scotland, a thirteen-year-old student wrote this in a school essay about her summer vacation: "My smmr hols wr CWOT. B4 we used 2 go to NY 2C my bro, & 3 kids FTF ILNY, its gr8 . . ." (Ward). She used writing that would appear in a text message for a friend rather than in a report for school. Furthermore,

She uses evidence to support her thesis—that we take for granted a mode of communication that actually threatens the development of literacy.

She refines her thesis, first stating what people assume is true and then offering a corrective in the second part of her thesis.

She also makes a secondary claim related to her thesis.

3

Stafford 3

And she elaborates on this claim to point out one of the detrimental effects of texting.

students who text become so accustomed to reading this type of shorthand lingo that they often overlook it in their own writing (O'Connor). This means that teachers have to spend even longer correcting these bad habits. Regardless, Lily Huang, a writer for *Newsweek*, believes that text messages increase literacy because a student must first know how to spell a word to abbreviate it in texting.

The student presents a possible counterargument from a published writer and then restates her thesis in an effort to correct a misconception.

However, texting affects not only the way that students write, but also the way in which they think about language. As a critic of Huang's article writes, "Habitual use of shorthand isn't just about choppy English, but choppy thinking" (Muffie). Writers who text will have trouble thinking creatively, and will especially have trouble composing intricate works like poetry because of the abridged way of thinking to which they are accustomed.

Outside of school, students' interactions with one another are similarly altered. Three in five teens would argue with a friend and one in three would break up with someone through a text message ("Technology Has Tremendous Impact"). Text messaging is now the most popular way for students to arrange to meet with friends, have a quick conversation, contact a friend when bored, or invite friends to a party ("Technology Has Tremendous Impact"). Eight out of ten teens would rather

She restates an evaluative claim that runs through the essay like the skewer we discussed earlier.

text than call ("Mobile Phones"). Although it is true that text messaging has made conversations much simpler and faster, it has not improved communication. Texting may make it more convenient to stay in contact with friends, but it does not ensure that the contact is as beneficial as talking in person. Text messages do not incorporate all of the body language and vocal inflections that a face-to-face conversation does. These nonverbal cues are essential to fully comprehending what is

She provides current research to support her thesis.

being communicated. Only 7% of a message is verbal. When the message is not communicated face-to-face, 93% of that message is lost ("Importance of Nonverbal"), and this nonverbal message is crucial to maintaining close relationships. According to Don McKay, a contributor to healthinfosource.com, the most important aspect of lasting friendships is effective

4

Stafford 4

communication. Friends must be able to convey emotions and empathize with others (McKay). However, friends who communicate solely through text messages will miss out on any truly personal interaction because they can never see the other person's posture, body language, or gestures.

She concludes by restating her premise about the value of reading and her evaluation of texting as a form of communication that erodes what she considers the very definition of literacy.

All of the negative effects of text messaging additionally deteriorate literacy. The enjoyment of reading leads to avid readers who eagerly absorb written words. A devotion to schoolwork encourages students to read so that they may be informed about important topics. Through book clubs and conversations about great literature, even relationships can foster a love for reading. However, text messaging is detracting from all three. In today's society, literacy is important. Schools focus on teaching English at an early age because of the active role that it forces students to take (Le Guin). While students can passively text message their friends, they need to focus on reading to enjoy it. In order to really immerse themselves in the story, they need to use a higher level of thinking than that of texting. This learning is what causes avid readers to become so successful. Those who read for fun when they are young score better on standardized tests, are admitted to more selective universities, and are able to secure the most competitive jobs ("To Read" 69). The decline in literacy caused by text messaging could inevitably cost a student a selective job. If students spent less time texting and more time reading, it could give them an advantage over their peers. Imagine a scenario between classes without any students' eyes to the ground. Imagine that Notre Dame students are not texting acquaintances hours away. Perhaps instead they are all carrying a pen and notebook and writing a letter to their friends. Maybe they are conversing with those around them. Instead of spending time every week text messaging, they are reading. When those other students text "lol," it no longer is an abbreviation for "laugh out loud," but for "loss of literacy."

She also concludes with a claim in which she proposes that students need to elevate the way they read and write.

5

Stafford 5

Works Cited

Bryant, J. Alison, Ashley Sanders-Jackson, and Amber M. K. Smallwood. "IMing, Text Messaging, and Adolescent Social Networks." *Journal of Computer-Mediated Communication* 11.2 (2006): n. pag Web. 28 Mar. 20--.

Huang, Lily. "The Death of English (LOL)." *Newsweek*. Newsweek, 2 Aug. 2008. Web. 28 Mar. 20--.

"The Importance of Nonverbal Communication." *EruptingMind Self Improvement Tips*. N.p., 2008. Web. 1 Apr. 20--.

Le Guin, Ursula K. "Staying Awake: Notes on the Alleged Decline of Reading." *Harper's Magazine*. The Harper's Magazine Foundation, Feb. 2008. Web. 30 Mar. 20--.

McKay, Don. "Communication and Friendship." *EzineArticles*. EzineArticles.com, 22 Feb. 2006. Web. 27 Mar. 20--.

"Mobile Phones, Texting, and Literacy." *National Literacy Trust*. NLT, 2008. Web. 1 Apr. 20--.

Muffie. Member comment. "The Death of English (LOL)." *Newsweek*. Newsweek, 18 Aug. 2008. Web. 28 Mar. 20--.

National Endowment for the Arts. *To Read or Not To Read: A Question of National Consequence*. Washington, NEA, Nov. 2007. PDF file.

O'Connor, Amanda. "Instant Messaging: Friend or Foe of Student Writing." *New Horizons for Learning*. New Horizons for Learning, Mar. 2005. Web. 27 Mar. 20--.

"Technology Has Tremendous Impact on How Teens Communicate." *Cellular-news*. Cellular-news, 20 Feb. 2007. Web. 27 Mar. 20--.

Ward, Lucy. "Texting 'Is No Bar to Literacy.'" *Guardian.co.uk*. Guardian News and Media Limited, 23 Dec. 2004. Web. 2 Apr. 20--.

6

From Finding to Evaluating Sources

In this chapter, we look at strategies for expanding the base of sources you work with to support your argument. The habits and skills of close reading and analysis that we have discussed and that you have practiced are essential for evaluating the sources you find. Once you find sources, you will need to assess the claims the writers make, the extent to which they provide evidence in support of those claims, and the recency, relevance, accuracy, and reliability of the evidence. The specific strategies we discuss here are those you will use to find and evaluate the sources you find in your library's electronic catalog or on the Internet. These strategies are core skills for developing a researched academic argument. They are also essential to avoid being overwhelmed by the torrent of information unleashed at the click of a computer mouse.

Finding sources is not difficult; finding and identifying good sources is challenging. You know how simple it is to look up a subject in an encyclopedia or to use a search engine like Google or Yahoo! to discover basic information on a subject or topic. Unfortunately, this kind of research will only take you so far. What if the information you find doesn't really address your question? True, we have emphasized the importance of thinking about an issue from multiple perspectives—and finding multiple perspectives is easy when you search the Internet. But how do you know whether a perspective is authoritative or trustworthy or even legitimate? Without knowing how to find and identify good sources, you can waste a lot of time reading material that will not contribute to your essay. Our goal is to help you use your time wisely to collect the sources you need to support your argument.

IDENTIFYING SOURCES

We assume that by the time you visit the library or log on to the Internet to find sources, you are not flying blind. At the very least, you will have chosen a topic to explore (something in general you want to write about), possibly will have identified an issue (a question or problem about the topic that is arguable), and perhaps will even have a working thesis (a main claim that you want to test against other sources) in mind. Let's say you are already interested in the topic of mad cow disease. Perhaps you have identified an issue: Is mad cow disease a significant threat in the United States given the massive scale of factory farming? And maybe you have drafted a working thesis: "Although factory farming is rightly criticized for its often unsanitary practices and lapses in quality control, the danger of an epidemic of mad cow disease in the United States is minimal." The closer you are to having a working thesis, the more purposeful your research will be. With the working thesis above, instead of trying to sift through hundreds of articles about mad cow disease, you can probably home in on materials that examine mad cow disease in relation to epidemiology and agribusiness.

Once you start expanding your research, however, even a working thesis is just a place to begin. As you digest all the perspectives your research yields, you may discover that your thesis, issue, and perhaps even interest in the topic will shift significantly. Maybe you'll end up writing about factory farming rather than mad cow disease. This kind of shift happens more often than you may think. What is important is to follow what interests you and to keep in mind what is going to matter to your readers.

■ Consult Experts Who Can Guide Your Research

Before you embark on a systematic hunt for sources, you may want to consult with experts who can help guide your research. The following experts are nearer to hand and more approachable than you may think.

Your Writing Instructor.   Your first and best expert is likely to be your writing instructor, who can help you define the limits of your research and the kinds of sources that would prove most helpful. Your writing instructor can probably advise you on whether your topic is too broad or too narrow, help you identify your issue, and perhaps even point you to specific reference works or readings you should consult. He or she can also help you figure out whether you should concentrate mainly on popular or scholarly sources (for more about popular and scholarly sources, see pages 125–26).

Librarians at Your Campus or Local Library.   In all likelihood, there is no better repository of research material than your campus or local library, and no better guide to those resources than the librarians who work there. Their job is to help you find what you need (although it's up to you to make the most of what you find). Librarians can give you a map or tour of the library and provide you with booklets or other handouts that instruct you in the specific resources available and their uses. They can explain the catalog system and reference system. And, time allowing, most librarians are willing to give you personal help in finding and using specific sources, from books and journals to indexes and databases.

Experts in Other Fields.   Perhaps the idea for your paper originated outside your writing course, in response to a reading assigned in, say, your psychology or economics course. If so, you may want to discuss your topic or issue with the instructor in that course, who can probably point you to other readings or journals you should consult. If your topic originated outside the classroom, you can still seek out an expert in the appropriate field. If so, you may want to read the advice on interviewing we present in Chapter 11.

Manuals, Handbooks, and Dedicated Web Sites.   These exist in abundance, for general research as well as for discipline-specific research. They are especially helpful in identifying a wide range of authoritative search tools and resources, although they also offer practical advice on how to use and cite them. Indeed, your writing instructor may assign one of these manuals or handbooks, or recommend a Web site, at the beginning of the course. If not, he or she can probably point you to the one that is best suited to your research.

■ Develop a Working Knowledge of Standard Sources

As you start your hunt for sources, it helps to know broadly what kinds of sources are available and what they can help you accomplish. Table 6.1 lists a number of the resources you are likely to rely on when you are looking for material, the purpose and limitations of each type of resource, and some well-known examples. Although it may not help you pinpoint specific resources that are most appropriate for your research, the table does provide a basis for finding sources in any discipline. And familiarizing yourself with the types of resources here should make your conversations with the experts more productive.

■ Distinguish Between Primary and Secondary Sources

As you define the research task before you, you will need to understand the difference between primary and secondary sources and figure out which you will need to answer your question. Your instructor may specify which he or she prefers, but chances are you will have to make the decision yourself. A **primary source** is a firsthand, or eyewitness, account, the kind

TABLE 6.1   Standard Types of Sources for Doing Research

SOURCE	TYPE OF INFORMATION	PURPOSE	LIMITATIONS	EXAMPLES
Abstract	Brief summary of a text and the bibliographic information needed to locate the complete text	To help researchers decide whether they want to read the entire source		*Biological Abstracts* *Historical Abstracts* *New Testament Abstracts* *Reference Sources in History: An Introductory Guide*
Bibliography	List of works, usually by subject and author, with full publication information	For an overview of what has been published in a field and who the principal researchers in the field are	Difficult to distinguish the best sources and the most prominent researchers	Bibliography of the History of Art *MLA International Bibliography*
Biography	Story of an individual's life and the historical, cultural, or social context in which he or she lived	For background on a person of importance	Lengthy and reflects the author's bias	Biography and Genealogy Master Index Biography Resource Center Biography.com Literature Resource Center *Oxford Dictionary of National Biography*
Book review	Description and usually an evaluation of a recently published book	To help readers stay current with research and thought in their field and to evaluate scholarship	Reflects the reviewer's bias	ALA *Booklist* *Book Review Digest* Book Review Index *Books in Print* with Book Reviews on Disc
Database, index	Large collection of citations and abstracts from books, journals, and digests, often updated daily	To give researchers access to a wide range of current sources	Lacks evaluative information	Education Resources Information Center (ERIC) Humanities International Index Index to Scientific & Technical Proceedings

(continued on next page)

TABLE 6.1   (*continued*)

Source	Type of Information	Purpose	Limitations	Examples
				United Nations Bibliographic Information System
Data, statistics	Measurements derived from studies or surveys	To help researchers identify important trends (e.g., in voting, housing, residential segregation)	Requires a great deal of scrutiny and interpretation	American Fact-Finder American National Election Studies Current Index to Statistics Current Population Survey *Statistical Abstract of the United States*
Dictionary	Alphabetical list of words and their definitions	To explain key terms and how they are used		*Merriam-Webster's Collegiate Dictionary* *Oxford English Dictionary*
Encyclopedia	Concise articles about people, places, concepts, and things	A starting point for very basic information	Lack of in-depth information	*The CQ Researcher* Encyclopedia Brittanica Online *Information Please Almanac* *McGraw-Hill Encyclopedia of Science & Technology*
Internet search engine	Web site that locates online information by keyword or search term	For quickly locating a broad array of current resources	Reliability of information open to question	Google Yahoo!
Newspaper, other news sources	Up-to-date information	To locate timely information	May reflect reporter's or medium's bias	America's Historical Newspapers LexisNexis Academic Newspaper Source ProQuest Historical Newspapers World News Connection
Thesaurus	Alphabetical list of words and their synonyms	For alternative search terms		*Roget's II: The New Thesaurus*

of account you find in letters or newspapers or research reports in which the researcher explains his or her impressions of a particular phenomenon. For example, "Hidden Lessons," the Sadkers' study of gender bias in schools, is a primary source. The authors report their own experiences of the phenomenon in the classroom. A **secondary source** is an analysis of information reported in a primary source. For example, even though it may cite the Sadkers' primary research, an essay that analyzes the Sadkers' findings along with other studies of gender dynamics in the classroom would be considered a secondary source.

If you were exploring issues of language diversity and the English-only movement, you would draw on both primary and secondary sources. You would be interested in researchers' firsthand (primary) accounts of language learning and use by diverse learners for examples of the challenges nonnative speakers face in learning a standard language. And you would also want to know from secondary sources what others think about whether national unity and individuality can and should coexist in communities and homes as well as in schools. You will find that you are often expected to use both primary and secondary sources in your research.

■ Distinguish Between Popular and Scholarly Sources

To determine the type of information to use, you also need to decide whether you should look for popular or scholarly books and articles. **Popular sources** of information—newspapers like *USA Today* and *The Chronicle of Higher Education*, and large-circulation magazines like *Newsweek* and *Field & Stream*—are written for a general audience. This is not to say that popular sources cannot be specialized: *The Chronicle of Higher Education* is read mostly by academics; *Field & Stream*, by people who love the outdoors. But they are written so that any educated reader can understand them. **Scholarly sources**, by contrast, are written for experts in a particular field. *The New England Journal of Medicine* may be read by people who are not physicians, but they are not the journal's primary audience. In a manner of speaking, these readers are eavesdropping on the journal's conversation of ideas; they are not expected to contribute to it (and in fact would be hard pressed to do so). The articles in scholarly journals undergo **peer review**. That is, they do not get published until they have been carefully evaluated by the author's peers, other experts in the academic conversation being conducted in the journal. Reviewers may comment at length about an article's level of research and writing, and an author may have to revise an article several times before it sees print. And if the reviewers cannot reach a consensus that the research makes an important contribution to the academic conversation, the article will not be published.

When you begin your research, you may find that popular sources provide helpful information about a topic or an issue—the results of a national poll, for example. Later, however, you will want to use scholarly sources to advance your argument. You can see from Table 6.2 that popular

TABLE 6.2   Popular Magazines Versus Scholarly Journals

CRITERIA	POPULAR MAGAZINES	SCHOLARLY JOURNALS
Advertisements	Numerous full-page color ads	Few if any ads
Appearance	Eye-catching; glossy; pictures and illustrations	Plain; black-and-white graphics, tables, charts, and diagrams
Audience	General	Professors, researchers, and college students
Author	Journalists	Professionals in an academic field or discipline
Bibliography	Occasional and brief	Extensive bibliography at the end of each article; footnotes and other documentation
Content	General articles to inform, update, or introduce a contemporary issue	Research projects, methodology, and theory
Examples	*Newsweek, National Review, PC World, Psychology Today*	*International Journal of Applied Engineering Research, New England Journal of Medicine*
Language	Nontechnical, simple vocabulary	Specialized vocabulary
Publisher	Commercial publisher	Professional organization, university, research institute, or scholarly press

SOURCE: Adapted from materials at the Hesburgh Library, University of Notre Dame.

magazines and scholarly journals can be distinguished by a number of characteristics. Does the source contain advertisements? If so, what kinds of advertisements? For commercial products? Or for academic events and resources? How do the advertisements appear? If you find ads and glossy pictures and illustrations, you are probably looking at a popular magazine. This is in contrast to the tables, charts, and diagrams you are likely to find in an education, psychology, or microbiology journal. Given your experience with rhetorical analyses, you should also be able to determine the makeup of your audience—specialists or nonspecialists—and the level of language you need to use in your writing.

Again, as you define your task for yourself, it is important to consider why you would use one source or another. Do you want facts? Opinions? News reports? Research studies? Analyses? Personal reflections? The extent to which the information can help you make your argument will serve as your basis for determining whether a source of information is of value.

Steps to Identifying Sources

1 **Consult experts who can guide your research.** Talk to people who can help you formulate issues and questions.

2 **Develop a working knowledge of standard sources.** Identify the different kinds of information that different types of sources provide.

3 **Distinguish between primary and secondary sources.** Decide what type of information can best help you answer your research question.

4 **Distinguish between popular and scholarly sources.** Determine what kind of information will persuade your readers.

A Practice Sequence: Identifying Sources

We would now like you to practice using some of the strategies we have discussed so far: talking with experts, deciding what sources of information you should use, and determining what types of information can best help you develop your paper and persuade your readers. We assume you have chosen a topic for your paper, identified an issue, and perhaps formulated a working thesis. If not, think back to some of the topics mentioned in earlier chapters. Have any of them piqued your interest? If not, here are five very broad topics you might work with:

- The civil rights movement
- The media and gender
- Global health
- Science and religion
- Immigration

Once you've decided on a topic, talk to experts and decide which types of sources you should use: primary or secondary, popular or scholarly. Consult with your classmates to evaluate the strengths and weaknesses of different sources of information and the appropriateness of using different types of information. Here are the steps to follow:

1 Talk to a librarian about the sources you might use to get information about your topic (for example, databases, abstracts, or bibliographies). Be sure to take notes.

2 Talk to an expert who can provide you with some ideas about current issues in the field of interest. Be sure to take detailed notes.

3 Decide whether you should use primary or secondary sources. What type of information would help you develop your argument?

4 Decide whether you should use popular or scholarly sources. What type of information would your readers find compelling?

SEARCHING FOR SOURCES

Once you've decided on the types of sources you want to use—primary or secondary, popular or scholarly—you can take steps to locate the information you need. You might begin with a tour of your university or local library, so that you know where the library keeps newspapers, government documents, books, journals, and other sources of information. Notice where the reference desk is: This is where you should head to ask a librarian for help if you get stuck. You also want to find a computer where you can log on to your library's catalog to start your search. Once you have located your sources in the library, you can begin to look through them for the information you need.

You may be tempted to rely on the Internet and a search engine like Google or Yahoo! But keep in mind that the information you retrieve from the Internet may not be trustworthy: Anyone can post his or her thoughts on a Web site. Of course, you can also find excellent scholarly sources on the Internet. (For example, Johns Hopkins University Press manages Project MUSE, a collection of 300-plus academic journals that can be accessed online through institutional subscription.) School libraries also offer efficient access to government records and other sources essential to scholarly writing.

Let's say you are about to start researching a paper on language diversity and the English-only movement. When you log on to the library's site, you find a menu of choices: Catalog, Electronic Resources, Virtual Reference Desk, and Services & Collections. (The wording may vary slightly from library to library, but the means of locating information will be the same.) When you click on Catalog, another menu of search choices appears: Keyword, Title, Author, and Subject (Figure 6.1). The hunt is on.

Search type:

Keyword Anywhere
Title begins with...
Title Keyword
Author (last name first)
Author Keyword
Subject begins with...
Subject Keyword
Call Number begins with...

More Search Options

FIGURE 6.1   Menu of Basic Search Strategies

▪ Perform a Keyword Search

A **keyword** is essentially your topic: It defines the topic of your search. To run a keyword search, you can look up information by author, title, or subject. You would search by author to locate all the works a particular author has written on a subject. So, for example, if you know that Paul Lang is an expert on the consequences of the English-only movement, you might begin with an author search. You can use the title search to locate all works with a key word or phrase in the title. The search results are likely to include a number of irrelevant titles, but you should end up with a list of authors, titles, and subject headings to guide another search.

A search by subject is particularly helpful as you begin your research, while you are still formulating your thesis. You want to start by thinking of as many words as possible that relate to your topic. (A thesaurus can help you come up with different words you can use in a keyword search.) Suppose you type in the phrase "English only." A number of different sources appear on the screen, but the most promising is Paul Lang's book *The English Language Debate: One Nation, One Language?* You click on this record, and another screen appears with some valuable pieces of information, including the call number (which tells you where in the library you can find the book) and an indication that the book has a bibliography, something you can make use of once you find the book (Figure 6.2). Notice that the subject listings—*Language policy, English language–Political aspects, English-only movement, Bilingual education*—also give you additional keywords to use in finding relevant information. The lesson here is that it is important to generate keywords to get initial information and then to look

Full View of Record

Record 12 out of 18

	Author :	Lang, Paul (Paul C.)
Source	**Title :**	The English language debate : one nation, one language? / Paul Lang.
	Published :	Springfield, N.J. : Enslow Publishers, c1995.
		112 p. : ill. ; 24 cm.

ND Has : All items

Hesburgh Library General Collection
P 119.32 .U6 E55 1995   [Call number

Notes : Includes bibliographical references (p. 107-109) and index.   ] Indicates book has a bibliography

Series : Multicultural issues

Subjects : Language policy – United States – Juvenile literature.
English language – Political aspects – United States – Juvenile literature.
Additional list of related subjects **English-only** movement – United States – Juvenile literature.
Education, Bilingual – United States – Juvenile literature.
English-only movement.
English language – Political aspects.
Education, Bilingual.

Done

FIGURE 6.2   Full-View Bibliographic Entry

at that information carefully for more keywords and to determine if the source has a bibliography. Even if this particular source isn't relevant, it may lead you to other sources that are.

■ Try Browsing

Browse is a headings search; it appears in the menu of choices in Figure 6.1 as "Subject begins with . . ." This type of search allows you to scroll through an alphabetical index. Some of the indexes available are the Author Index, the Title Index, and the Library of Congress Subject Headings, a subject index. Browse

- displays an alphabetical list of entries;
- shows the number of records for each entry;
- indicates whether there are cross-references for each entry.

What appears in the window is "Browse List: Choose a field, enter a phrase and click the 'go' button." Figure 6.3 shows the results of a preliminary browse when the words "English-only" are entered. Notice that a list of headings or titles appears on the screen. This is not a list of books, and not all of the entries are relevant. But you can use the list to determine which headings are relevant to your topic, issue, or question.

For your paper on the English-only movement, the first two headings seem relevant: *English-only debate* and *English-only movement*. A further click would reveal the title of a relevant book and a new list of subject headings (Figure 6.4) that differs from those of your initial search. This list gives you a new bibliography from which you can gather new leads and a list of subject headings to investigate.

Browse List: Subjects

No. of Recs	Entry
	English one-act plays - [LC Authority Record] See: One-act plays, English
	English-only debate - [LC Authority Record] See: English-only movement
4	English-only movement - [LC Authority Record]
1	English-only movement — California — Case studies
1	English-only movement — Colorado
4	English-only movement — United States
1	English-only movement — United States — Juvenile literature
	English-only question - [LC Authority Record] See: English-only movement
1	English — Ontario — Correspondence
1	English oration

FIGURE 6.3   Preliminary Browse of "English-only" Subject Heading

We suggest that you do a keyword search first and then a browse search to home in on a subject. Especially when you don't know the exact subject, you can do a quick keyword search, retrieve many sets of results, and then begin looking at the subjects that correspond to each title. Once you find a subject that fits your needs, you can click on the direct subject (found in each bibliographic record) and execute a new search that will yield more-relevant results.

■ Perform a Journal or Newspaper Title Search

Finally, you can search by journal or newspaper title. For this kind of search, you will need exact information. You can take the name of a journal, magazine, or newspaper cited in your keyword or browse search. The journal or newspaper title search will tell you if your library subscribes to the publication and in what format—print, microform or microfilm, or electronic.

Suppose you want to continue your search in the *New York Times* for information on the English-only movement by searching for articles in the *New York Times*. You would run a basic search under the category "Periodicals": "Periodical Title begins with . . ." That would give you access to a limited number of articles that focused on the debate surrounding the English-only movement. To find more recent articles, you could go to the *New York Times* Web site (nytimes.com), where you could find many potentially useful listings. Recent newspaper articles will lack the depth and complexity of more scholarly studies, but they are undeniably useful in helping you establish the timeliness and relevance of your research. To see the full text of the articles, you must subscribe or pay a nominal fee, although you can usually preview the articles because the Web site will include a few sentences describing the content of each article.

#	Year	Author	Title
1 ☐	2006	United States.	English as the official language : hearing before the Subcommittee on Education Reform of the Co <Book> Click for ONLINE ACCESS { Text version: } Documents Center Owned: 1 Checked Out: 0 Display full record
2 ☐	1996	United States.	S. 356—Language of Government Act of 1995 : hearings before the Committee on Governmental Affai <Book> Documents Center Display full record
3 ☐	1996	United States.	Hearing on English as the common language : hearing before the Subcommittee on Early Childhood, <Book> Documents Center Display full record
4 ☐	1995	United States.	Hearing on English as a common language : hearing before the Subcommittee on Early Childhood, Yo <Book> Documents Center Display full record

Done

FIGURE 6.4   Results of Browsing Deeper: A New List of Sources

---

Steps to Searching for Sources

1 **Perform a keyword search.** Choose a word or phrase that best describes your topic.

2 **Try browsing.** Search an alphabetical list by subject.

3 **Perform a journal or newspaper title search.** Find relevant citations by identifying the exact title of a journal or newspaper, or by subject.

A Practice Sequence: Searching for Sources

If you tried the practice sequence on identifying sources (p. 127), explore your topic further by practicing the types of searches discussed in this section: a keyword search; a browse; and a journal or newspaper title search (or a subject search).

EVALUATING LIBRARY SOURCES

The information you collect can and will vary in terms of its relevance and overall quality. You will want to evaluate this information as systematically as possible to be sure that you are using the most appropriate sources to develop your argument. Once you have obtained at least some of the sources you located by searching your library's catalog, you should evaluate the material as you read it. In particular, you want to evaluate the following information for each article or book:

- the author's background and credentials (What is the author's educational background? What has he or she written about in the past? Is this person an expert in the field?)
- the writer's purpose
- the topic of discussion
- the audience the writer invokes and whether you are a member of that audience
- the nature of the conversation (How have others addressed the problem?)
- what the author identifies as a misinterpretation or a gap in knowledge, or an argument that needs modifying
- what the author's own view is
- how the author supports his or her argument (that is, with primary or secondary sources, with facts or opinions)
- the accuracy of the author's evidence (Can you find similar information elsewhere?)

If your topic is current and relevant, chances are your searches are going to turn up a large number of possible sources. How do you go about choosing which sources to rely on in your writing? Of course, if time were not an issue, you would read them all from start to finish. But in the real world, assignments come with due dates. To decide whether a library source merits a close reading and evaluation, begin by skimming each book or article. **Skimming**—briefly examining the material to get a sense of the information it offers—involves four steps:

1. Read the introductory sections.
2. Examine the table of contents and index.
3. Check the notes and bibliographic references.
4. Skim deeper.

■ Read the Introductory Sections

Turn to the introductory sections of the text first. Many authors use a preface or an introduction to explain the themes they focus on in a book. An **abstract** serves a similar purpose, but article abstracts are usually only 250 words long. In the introductory sections, writers typically describe the issue that motivated them to write and indicate whether they believe the work corrects a misconception, fills a gap, or builds on and extends the research of others. For example, in the preface to her book *Learning and Not Learning English: Latino Students in American Schools* (2001), Guadalupe Valdés explains that even after two years of language instruction, many students remain at a low level of language competence. In this passage, Valdés makes clear the purpose of her work:

> This book examines the learning of English in American schools by immigrant children. It focuses on the realities that such youngsters face in trying to acquire English in settings in which they interact exclusively with other non-English-speaking youngsters the entire school day. It is designed to fill a gap in the existing literature on non-English-background youngsters by offering a glimpse of the challenges and difficulties faced by four middle-school students enrolled in the United States for the first time when they were 12 or 13 years old. It is my purpose here to use these youngsters' lives and experiences as a lens through which to examine the policy and instructional dilemmas that now surround the education of immigrant children in this country. (p. 2)

If you were looking for sources for a paper on the English-only movement, in particular the consequences of that movement for young students, you might very well find Valdés's words compelling and decide the book is worth a closer reading.

■ Examine the Table of Contents and Index

After reading the introductory sections, you will find it useful to analyze the table of contents to see how much emphasis the writer gives to topics that are relevant to your own research. For example, the table of contents to *Learning and Not Learning English* includes several headings that may relate to your interest: "Educating English-Language Learners," "Challenges and Realities," "Implications for Policy and Practice," and the "Politics of Teaching English." You also should turn to the back of the book to examine the **index**, an alphabetical list of the important and recurring concepts in a book, and the page numbers on which they appear. An index also would include the names of authors cited in the book. In the index to Valdés's book, you would find references to "English-language abilities and instruction" with specific page numbers where you can read what the author has to say on this subject. You would also find references to "English-only instruction," "equal educational opportunities," and "sheltered instruction."

■ Check the Notes and Bibliographic References

Especially in the initial stages of writing, you should look closely at writers' notes and bibliographies to discern who they feel are the important voices in the field. Frequent citation of a particular researcher's work may indicate that the individual is considered to be an expert in the field you are studying. Notes usually provide brief references to people, concepts, or context; the bibliography includes a long list of related works. Mining Valdés's bibliography, you would find such titles as "Perspectives on Official English," "Language Policy in Schools," "Not Only English," "Language and Power," and "The Cultural Politics of English."

■ Skim Deeper

Skimming a book or an article entails briefly looking over the elements we have discussed so far: the preface or abstract, the table of contents and the index, and the notes and bibliography. Skimming also can mean reading chapter titles, headings, and the first sentence of each paragraph to determine the relevance of a book or an article.

Skimming the first chapter of *Learning and Not Learning English*, you would find several topic sentences that reveal the writer's purpose:

> "In this book, then, I examine and describe different expressions that both learning and not-learning English took among four youngsters."

> "In the chapters that follow . . ."

> "What I hope to suggest . . ."

These are the types of phrases you should look for to get a sense of what the writer is trying to accomplish and whether the writer's work will be of use to you.

If, after you've taken these steps, a source still seems promising, you should read it closely, from start to finish, to determine how effectively it can help you answer your research question. Keep in mind all you've learned about critical reading. Those skills are what you'll rely on most as you work through the texts and choose the ones you should use in your paper. Remember the steps of rhetorical analysis: identifying the writer's situation, purpose, claims, and audience. And remember how to identify claims and evaluate the reasons used to support the claims: Is the evidence recent, relevant, accurate, and reliable?

Steps to Evaluating Library Sources

1 **Read the introductory sections.** Get an overview of the researcher's argument.

2 **Examine the table of contents and index.** Consider the most relevant chapters to your topic and the list of relevant subjects.

3 **Check the notes and bibliographic references.** Identify the authors a researcher refers to (do the names come up in many different books?) and the titles of both books and articles.

4 **Skim deeper.** Read chapter titles and headings and topic sentences to determine the relevance of what you are reading for your own research.

A Practice Sequence: Evaluating Library Sources

For this exercise, we would like you to choose a specific book or article to examine in order to practice these strategies. If you are far along on your own research, use a book or an article you have identified as potentially useful.

1 Read the introductory sections. What issue is the author responding to? What is the writer's purpose? To correct a misconception? To fill a gap? To build on or extend the work of others?

2 Examine the table of contents and index. What key words or phrases are related to your own research? Which topics does the author focus on? Are you intending to give these topics similar emphasis? (Will you give more or less emphasis?)

3 Check the notes and bibliographic references. Make a list of the sources you think you want to look up for your own research. Do certain sources seem more important than others?

4 Skim deeper. What is the writer's focus? Is that focus relevant to your own topic, issue, question, or working thesis?

EVALUATING INTERNET SOURCES

Without question, the World Wide Web has revolutionized how research is conducted. It has been a particular boon to experienced researchers who have a clear sense of what they are looking for, giving them access to more information more quickly than ever before. But the Internet is rife with pitfalls for inexperienced researchers. That is, sites that appear accurate and reliable may prove not to be. The sources you find on the Internet outside your school library's catalog pose problems because anyone can post anything he or she wants. Unfortunately, there is no way to monitor the accuracy of what is published on the Internet. Although Internet sources can be useful, particularly because they are current, you must take steps to evaluate them before using information from them.

■ Evaluate the Author of the Site

If an author's name appears on a Web site, ask: Who is this person? What is this person's background? Can I contact this person?

One of our students googled "English only" and clicked on the first result, "Language Policy—English Only Movement," which eventually led her to James Crawford's Language Policy Web Site & Emporium. On the site, Crawford explains that he is "a writer and lecturer—formerly the Washington editor of *Education Week*—who specializes in the politics of language."* He notes that "since 1985, I have been reporting on the English Only movement, English Plus, bilingual education, Native American language revitalization, and language rights in the U.S.A." Between 2004 and 2006, he served as executive director of the National Association for Bilingual Education. Perhaps most important, Crawford has authored four books and a number of articles and has testified before Congress on "Official English Legislation." From this biographical sketch, the student inferred that Crawford is credentialed to write about the English-only movement.

Less certain, however, are the credentials of the writer who penned an article titled "Should the National Anthem Be Sung in English Only?" which appeared on another Web site our student visited. Why? Because the writer's name never appears on the site. An anonymous posting is the first clue that you want to move on to a more legitimate source of information.

■ Evaluate the Organization That Supports the Site

You have probably noticed that Internet addresses usually end with a suffix: .edu, .gov, .org, or .com. The .edu suffix means the site is associated

---

Education Week has been published since 1981 by Editorial Projects in Education, a nonprofit organization that was founded with the help of a Carnegie grant. The publication covers issues related to primary and secondary education. If you are not familiar with a publication and are uncertain about its legitimacy, you can always ask your instructor, a librarian, or another expert to vouch for its reliability.

with a university or college, which gives it credibility. The same holds true for .gov, which indicates a government agency. Both types of sites have a regulatory body that oversees their content. The suffix .org indicates a nonprofit organization; .com, a commercial organization. You will need to approach these Web sites with a degree of skepticism because you cannot be sure that they are as carefully monitored by a credentialed regulatory body. (In fact, even .edu sites may turn out to be postings by a student at a college or university.)

Our student was intrigued by James Crawford's site because he appears to be a credible source on the English-only movement. She was less sure about the reference to the Institute for Language and Education Policy. Is the institute a regulatory body that oversees what appears on the site? How long has the institute existed? Who belongs to the institute? Who sits on its board of directors? As a critical thinker, the student had to ask these questions.

■ Evaluate the Purpose of the Site

Information is never objective, so whenever you evaluate a book, an article, or a Web site, you should consider the point of view the writer or sponsor is taking. It's especially important to ask if there is a particular bias among members of the group that sponsors the site. Can you tell what the sponsors of the site advocate? Are they hoping to sell or promote a product, or to influence opinion?

Not all Web sites provide easy answers to these questions. However, James Crawford's Language Policy Web Site & Emporium is quite explicit. In fact, Crawford writes that "the site is designed to encourage discussion of language policy issues, expose misguided school 'reforms,'" and, among other goals, "promote [his] own publications." (Notice "Emporium" in the name of the site.) He is candid about his self-interest, which does raise a question about his degree of objectivity.

What about a site like Wikipedia ("The Free Encyclopedia")? The site appears to exist to convey basic information. Although the popularity of Wikipedia recommends it as a basic resource, you should approach the site with caution because it is not clear whether and how the information posted on the site is regulated. It is prudent to confirm information from Wikipedia by checking on sites that are regulated more transparently rather than take Wikipedia as an authoritative source.

■ Evaluate the Information on the Site

In addition to assessing the purpose of a Web site like Wikipedia, you need to evaluate the extent to which the information is recent, accurate, and consistent with information you find in print sources and clearly regulated sites. For example, clicking on "The modern English-only movement" on Wikipedia takes you to a timeline of sorts with a number of links to other sites. But again, what is the source of this information? What is included?

What is left out? You should check further into some of these links, read-ing the sources cited and keeping in mind the four criteria for evaluating a claim—recency, relevance, accuracy, and reliability. Because you cannot be certain that Internet sources are reviewed or monitored, you need to be scrupulous about examining the claims they make: How much and what kind of evidence supports the writer's (or site's) argument? Can you offer counterarguments?

In the last analysis, it comes down to whether the information you find stands up to the criteria you've learned to apply as a critical reader and writer. If not, move on to other sources. In a Web-based world of informa-tion, there is no shortage of material, but you have to train yourself not to settle for the information that is most readily available if it is clearly not credible.

Steps to Evaluating Internet Sources

1 **Evaluate the author of the site.** Determine whether the author is an expert.

2 **Evaluate the organization that supports the site.** Find out what the organization stands for and the extent of its credibility.

3 **Evaluate the purpose of the site.** What interests are represented on the site? What is the site trying to do? Provide access to legiti-mate statistics and information? Advance an argument? Spread propaganda?

4 **Evaluate the information on the site.** Identify the type of infor-mation on the site and the extent to which the information is recent, relevant, accurate, and reliable.

A Practice Sequence: Evaluating Internet Sources

For this exercise, we would like you to work in groups on a common topic. The class can choose its own topic or use one of the topics we suggest on page 127. Then google the topic and agree on a Web site to analyze:

Group 1: Evaluate the author of the site.

Group 2: Evaluate the organization that supports the site.

Group 3: Evaluate the purpose of the site.

Group 4: Evaluate the information on the site.

Next, each group should share its evaluation. The goal is to determine the extent to which you believe you could use the information on this site in writing an academic essay.

7

From Summary to Synthesis
Using Sources to Build an Argument

When you start to use sources to build your argument, there are certain strategies for working with the words and ideas of others that you will need to learn. Often you can quote the words of an author directly; but just as often you will restate and condense the arguments of others (paraphrasing and summarizing) or make comparisons to the ideas of others in the process of developing your own argument (synthesizing). We walk you through these more challenging strategies in this chapter. We also briefly discuss plagiarism and ways to avoid it and how to integrate quotations into your writing.

SUMMARIES, PARAPHRASES, AND QUOTATIONS

In contrast to quotations, which involve using another writer's exact words, paraphrases and summaries are both restatements of another writer's ideas in your own words, but they differ in length:

- A paraphrase is usually about the same length as the original passage.
- A summary generally condenses a significantly longer text, conveying the argument not only of a few sentences but also of entire paragraphs, essays, or books.

In your own writing, you might paraphrase a few sentences or even a few paragraphs, but you certainly would not paraphrase a whole essay (much less a whole book). In constructing your arguments, however, you will often have to summarize the main points of the lengthy texts with which you are in conversation.

Both paraphrasing and summarizing are means to inquiry. That is, the act of recasting someone else's words or ideas into your own language, to suit your argument and reach your readers, forces you to think critically: What does this passage really mean? What is most important about it for my argument? How can I best present it to my readers? It requires making choices, not least of which is the best way to present the information—through paraphrase, summary, or direct quotation. In general, the following rules apply:

- *Paraphrase* when all the information in the passage is important, but the language may be difficult for your readers to understand.
- *Summarize* when you need to present only the key ideas of a passage (or an essay or a book) to advance your argument.
- *Quote* when the passage is so effective—so clear, so concise, so authoritative, so memorable—that you would be hard-pressed to improve on it.

WRITING A PARAPHRASE

A **paraphrase** is a restatement of all the information in a passage in your own words, using your own sentence structure and composed with your own audience in mind to advance your argument.

- When you paraphrase a passage, start by identifying key words and phrases and substituting synonyms for them. A dictionary or thesaurus can help, but you may also have to reread what led up to the passage to remind yourself of the context. For example, did the writer define terms earlier that he or she uses in the passage and now expects you to know?
- Continue by experimenting with word order and sentence structure, combining and recombining phrases to convey what the writer says without replicating his or her style, in the best sequence for your readers. As you shuffle words and phrases, you should begin arriving at a much better understanding of what the writer is saying. By thinking critically, then, you are clarifying the passage for yourself as much as for your readers.

Let's look at a paraphrase of a passage from science fiction writer and scholar James Gunn's essay "Harry Potter as Schooldays Novel"*:

ORIGINAL PASSAGE

The situation and portrayal of Harry as an ordinary child with an extraordinary talent make him interesting. He elicits our sympathy at every turn. He plays a Cinderella-like role as the abused child of mean-spirited foster parents

*Gunn's essay appears in *Mapping the World of Harry Potter: An Unauthorized Exploration of the Bestselling Fantasy Series of All Time*, edited by Mercedes Lackey (Dallas: BenBella, 2006).

who favor other, less-worthy children, and also fits another fantasy role, that of changeling. Millions of children have nursed the notion that they cannot be the offspring of such unremarkable parents; in the Harry Potter books, the metaphor is often literal truth.

PARAPHRASE

According to James Gunn, the circumstances and depiction of Harry Potter as a normal boy with special abilities captivate us by playing on our empathy. Gunn observes that, like Cinderella, Harry is scorned by his guardians, who treat him far worse than they treat his less-admirable peers. And like another fairy-tale figure, the changeling, Harry embodies the fantasies of children who refuse to believe that they were born of their undistinguished parents (146).

In this paraphrase, synonyms have replaced main words (*circumstances and depiction* for "situation and portrayal," *guardians* for "foster parents"), and the structure of the original sentences has been rearranged. But the paraphrase is about the same length as the original and says essentially the same things as Gunn's original.

Now, compare the paraphrase with this summary:

SUMMARY

James Gunn observes that Harry Potter's character is compelling because readers empathize with Harry's fairy tale–like plight as an orphan whose gifts are ignored by his foster parents (144–45).

The summary condenses the passage, conveying Gunn's main point without restating the details. Notice how both the paraphrase and the summary indicate that the ideas are James Gunn's, not the writer's—"According to James Gunn," "James Gunn observes"—and signal, with page references, where Gunn's ideas end. *It is essential that you acknowledge your sources*, a subject we come back to in our discussion of plagiarism on page 180. The point we want to make here is that borrowing from the work of others is not always intentional. Many students stumble into plagiarism, especially when they are attempting to paraphrase. Remember that it's not enough to change the words in a paraphrase; you must also change the structure of the sentences. The only sure way to protect yourself is to cite your source.

You may be wondering: "If paraphrasing is so tricky, why bother? What does it add? I can see how the summary of Gunn's paragraph presents information more concisely and efficiently than the original, but the paraphrase doesn't seem to be all that different from the source and doesn't seem to add anything to it. Why not simply quote the original or summarize it?"

Good questions. The answer is that you paraphrase when the ideas in a passage are important but are conveyed in language your readers may have difficulty understanding. When academics write for their peers, they draw on the specialized vocabulary of their disciplines to make their arguments. By paraphrasing, you may be helping your readers, providing a translation of sorts for those who do not speak the language.

Consider this paragraph by George Lipsitz from his academic book *Time Passages: Collective Memory and American Popular Culture*, 1990), and compare the paraphrase that follows it:

ORIGINAL PASSAGE

The transformations in behavior and collective memory fueled by the contradictions of the nineteenth century have passed through three major stages in the United States. The first involved the establishment and codification of commercialized leisure from the invention of the tele-graph to the 1890s. The second involved the transition from Victorian to consumer-hedonist values between 1890 and 1945. The third and most impor-tant stage, from World War II to the present, involved extraordinary expan-sion in both the distribution of consumer purchasing power and in both the reach and scope of electronic mass media. The dislocations of urban renewal, suburbanization, and deindustrialization accelerated the demise of tradi-tion in America, while the worldwide pace of change undermined stability elsewhere. The period from World War II to the present marks the final triumph of commercialized leisure, and with it an augmented crisis over the loss of connection to the past.

PARAPHRASE

Historian George Lipsitz argues that Americans' sense of the past is rooted in cultural changes dating from the 1800s and has evolved through three stages. In the first stage, technological innovations of the nineteenth century gave rise to widespread commercial entertainment. In the second stage, dating from the 1890s to about 1945, attitudes toward the consumption of goods and ser-vices changed. Since 1945, in the third stage, increased consumer spending and the growth of the mass media have led to a crisis in which Americans find themselves cut off from their traditions and the memories that give meaning to them (12).

Notice that the paraphrase is not a word-for-word translation of the origi-nal. Instead, the writer has made choices that resulted in a slightly briefer and more accessible restatement of Lipsitz's thinking. (Although this para-phrase is shorter than the original passage, a paraphrase can also be a little longer than the original if extra words are needed to help readers understand the original.)

Notice too that several specialized terms and phrases from the origi-nal passage—the "codification of commercialized leisure," "the transition from Victorian to consumer-hedonist values," "the dislocations of urban renewal, suburbanization, and deindustrialization"—have disappeared. The writer not only looked up these terms and phrases in the dictionary but also reread the several pages that preceded the original passage to understand what Lipsitz meant by them.

The paraphrase is not an improvement on the original passage—in fact, historians would probably prefer what Lipsitz wrote—but it may help readers who do not share Lipsitz's expertise understand his point without distorting his argument.

Now compare this summary to the paraphrase:

SUMMARY

Historian George Lipsitz argues that technological, social, and economic changes dating from the nineteenth century have culminated in what he calls a "crisis over the loss of connection to the past," in which Americans find themselves cut off from the memories of their traditions (12).

Which is better, the paraphrase or the summary? Neither is better or worse in and of itself. Their correctness and appropriateness depend on how the restatements are used in a given argument. That is, the decision to paraphrase or summarize depends entirely on the information you need to convey. Would the details in the paraphrase strengthen your argument? Or is a summary sufficient? In this case, if you plan to focus your argument on the causes of America's loss of cultural memory (the rise of commercial entertainment, changes in spending habits, globalization), then a paraphrase might be more helpful. But if you plan to define *loss of cultural memory*, then a summary may provide enough context for the next stage of your argument.

Steps to Writing a Paraphrase

1 **Decide whether to paraphrase.** If your readers don't need all the information in the passage, consider summarizing it or presenting the key points as part of a summary of a longer passage. If a passage is clear, concise, and memorable as originally written, consider quoting instead of paraphrasing. Otherwise, and especially if the original was written for an academic audience, you may want to paraphrase the original to make its substance more accessible to your readers.

2 **Understand the passage.** Start by identifying key words, phrases, and ideas. If necessary, reread the pages leading up to the passage, to place it in context.

3 **Draft your paraphrase.** Replace key words and phrases with synonyms and alternative phrases (possibly gleaned from the context provided by the surrounding text). Experiment with word order and sentence structure until the paraphrase captures your understanding of the passage, in your own language, for your readers.

4 **Acknowledge your source.** That's the only sure way to protect yourself from a charge of plagiarism.

A Practice Sequence: Paraphrasing

1 In one of the sources you've located in your research, find a sentence of some length and complexity, and paraphrase it. Share the original and your paraphrase of it with a classmate, and discuss the effectiveness of your restatement. Is the meaning clear to your reader? Is the paraphrase written in your own language, using your own sentence structure?

2 Repeat the activity using a short paragraph from the same source. You and your classmate may want to attempt to paraphrase the same paragraph and then compare results. What differences do you detect?

WRITING A SUMMARY

As you have seen, a **summary** condenses a body of information, presenting the key ideas and acknowledging their source. Summarizing is not an active way to make an argument, but summaries do provide a common ground of information for readers so that you can make your argument more effectively. You can summarize a paragraph, several paragraphs, an essay, a chapter in a book, or even an entire book, depending on the use you plan to make of the information in your argument.

We suggest a method of summarizing that involves

1. describing the author's key claims,
2. selecting examples to illustrate the author's argument,
3. presenting the gist of the author's argument, and
4. contextualizing what you summarize.

We demonstrate these steps for writing a summary following Clive Thompson's article "On the New Literacy."

CLIVE THOMPSON

On the New Literacy

A print journalist at *New York Magazine*, Clive Thompson started his blog, Collision Detection, in September 2002, when he was beginning his year as a Knight Fellow in Science Journalism at MIT. Collision Detection has become one of the most well-regarded blogs on technology and culture. The blog receives approximately 3,000 to 4,000 hits a day. His piece on literacy appeared in *Wired* magazine in 2009.

■ ▓ ▒

As the school year begins, be ready to hear pundits fretting once again about how kids today can't write—and technology is to blame. Facebook encourages narcissistic blabbering, video and Power-Point have replaced carefully crafted essays, and texting has dehydrated language into "bleak, bald, sad shorthand" (as University College of London English professor John Sutherland has moaned). An age of illiteracy is at hand, right? *1*

Andrea Lunsford isn't so sure. Lunsford is a professor of writing and rhetoric at Stanford University, where she has organized a mammoth project called the Stanford Study of Writing to scrutinize college students' prose. From 2001 to 2006, she collected 14,672 student writing samples—everything from in-class assignments, formal essays, and journal entries to emails, blog posts, and chat sessions. Her conclusions are stirring. *2*

"I think we're in the midst of a literacy revolution the likes of which we haven't seen since Greek civilization," she says. For Lunsford, technology isn't killing our ability to write. It's reviving it—and pushing our literacy in bold new directions. *3*

The first thing she found is that young people today write far more than any generation before them. That's because so much socializing takes place online, and it almost always involves text. Of all the writing that the Stanford students did, a stunning 38 percent of it took place out of the classroom—life writing, as Lunsford calls it. Those Twitter updates and lists of 25 things about yourself add up. *4*

It's almost hard to remember how big a paradigm shift this is. Before the Internet came along, most Americans never wrote anything, ever, that wasn't a school assignment. Unless they got a job that required producing text (like in law, advertising, or media), they'd leave school and virtually never construct a paragraph again. *5*

But is this explosion of prose good, on a technical level? Yes. Lunsford's team found that the students were remarkably adept at what rhetoricians call *kairos*—assessing their audience and adapting their tone and technique to best get their point across. The modern world of online writing, particularly in chat and on discussion threads, is conversational and public, which makes it closer to the Greek tradition of argument than the asynchronous letter and essay writing of 50 years ago. *6*

The fact that students today almost always write for an audience (something virtually no one in my generation did) gives them a different sense of what constitutes good writing. In interviews, they defined good *7* prose as something that had an effect on the world. For them, writing is about persuading and organizing and debating, even if it's over something as quotidian as what movie to go see. The Stanford students were almost always less enthusiastic about their in-class writing because it had no audience but the professor: It didn't serve any purpose other than to get them a grade. As for those texting short-forms and smileys defiling *serious* academic writing? Another myth. When Lunsford examined the work of first-year students, she didn't find a single example of texting speak in an academic paper.

Of course, good teaching is always going to be crucial, as is the mastering of formal academic prose. But it's also becoming clear that online media are pushing literacy into cool directions. The brevity of texting and status updating teaches young people to deploy haiku-like concision. At the same time, the proliferation of new forms of online pop-cultural exegesis—from sprawling TV-show recaps to 15,000-word videogame walkthroughs—has given them a chance to write enormously long and complex pieces of prose, often while working collaboratively with others.   8

We think of writing as either good or bad. What today's young people know is that knowing who you're writing for and why you're writing might be the most crucial factor of all.   9

■ Describe the Key Claims of the Text

As you read through a text with the purpose of summarizing it, you want to identify how the writer develops his or her argument. You can do this by what we call "chunking," grouping related material together into the argument's key claims. Here are two strategies to try.

Notice how paragraphs begin and end.   Often, focusing on the first and last sentences of paragraphs will alert you to the shape and direction of an author's argument. It is especially helpful if the paragraphs are lengthy and full of supporting information, as much academic writing is.

Because of his particular journalistic forum, *Wired* magazine, Thompson's paragraphs are generally rather short, but it's still worth taking a closer look at the first and last sentences of his opening paragraphs:

> *Paragraph 1:* As the school year begins, be ready to hear pundits fretting once again about how kids today can't write—and technology is to blame. Facebook encourages narcissistic blabbering, video and PowerPoint have replaced carefully crafted essays, and texting has dehydrated language into "bleak, bald, sad shorthand" (as University College of London English professor John Sutherland has moaned). An age of illiteracy is at hand, right?

> *Paragraph 2:* Andrea Lunsford isn't so sure. Lunsford is a professor of writing and rhetoric at Stanford University, where she has organized a mam-

moth project called the Stanford Study of Writing to scrutinize college students' prose. From 2001 to 2006, she collected 14,672 student writing samples—everything from in-class assignments, formal essays, and journal entries to emails, blog posts, and chat sessions. Her conclusions are stirring.

Right away you can see that Thompson has introduced a topic in each paragraph—pundits' criticism of students' use of electronic media in the first, and a national study designed to examine students' literacy in the second—and has indicated a connection between them. In fact, Thompson is explicit in doing so. He asks a question at the end of the first paragraph and then raises doubts as to the legitimacy of critics' denunciation of young people's reliance on blogs and posts to communicate. How will Thompson elaborate on this connection? What major points does he develop?

Notice the author's point of view and use of transitions.   Another strategy for identifying major points is to pay attention to descriptive words and transitions. For example, Thompson uses a rhetorical question ("An age of illiteracy is at hand, right?") and then offers a tentative answer ("Andrea Lunsford isn't so sure") that places some doubt in readers' minds.

Notice, too, the words that Thompson uses to characterize the argument in the first paragraph, which he appears to challenge in the second paragraph. Specifically, he describes these critics as "pundits," a word that traditionally refers to an expert or knowledgeable individual. However, the notion of a pundit, someone who often appears on popular talk shows, has also been used negatively. Thompson's description of pundits "fretting," wringing their hands in worry that literacy levels are declining, underscores this negative association of what it means to be a pundit. Finally, Thompson indicates that he does not identify with those who describe students as engaging in "narcissistic blabbering." This is clear when he characterizes the professor as having "moaned."

Once you identify an author's point of view, you will start noticing contrasts and oppositions in the argument—instances where the words are less positive, or neutral, or even negative—which are often signaled by how the writer uses transitions.

For example, Thompson begins with his own concession to critics' arguments when he acknowledges in paragraph 8 that educators should expect students to "[master] formal academic prose." However, he follows this concession with the transition word "but" to signal his own stance in the debate he frames in the first two paragraphs: "online media are pushing literacy into cool directions." Thompson also recognizes that students who write on blogs tend to write short, abbreviated texts. Still, he qualifies his concern with another transition, "at the same time." This transition serves to introduce Thompson's strongest claim: New media have given students "a chance to write enormously long and complex pieces of prose, often while working collaboratively with others."

These strategies can help you recognize the main points of an essay and explain them in a few sentences. For example, you could describe Thompson's key claims in this way:

1. Electronic media give students opportunities to write more than in previous generations, and students have learned to adapt what they are writing in order to have some tangible effect on what people think and how they act.

2. Arguably, reliance on blogging and posting on Twitter and Facebook can foster some bad habits in writing.

3. But at least one major study demonstrates that the benefits of using the new media outweigh the disadvantages. This study indicates that students write lengthy, complex pieces that contribute to creating significant social networks and collaborations.

■ Select Examples to Illustrate the Author's Argument

A summary should be succinct, which means you should limit the number of examples or illustrations you use. As you distill the major points of the argument, try to choose one or two examples to illustrate each major point. Here are the examples (in italics) you might use to support Thompson's main points:

1. Electronic media give students opportunities to write more than in previous generations, and students have learned to adapt what they are writing in order to have some tangible effect on what people think and how they act. *Examples from the Stanford study: Students "defined good prose as something that had an effect on the world. For them, writing is about persuading and organizing and debating"* (para. 7).

2. Arguably, reliance on blogging and posting on Twitter and Facebook can foster some bad habits in writing. *Examples of these bad habits include critics' charges of "narcissistic blabbering," "bleak, bald, sad shorthand," and "dehydrated language"* (para. 1). *Thompson's description of texting's "haiku-like concision"* (para. 8) *seems to combine praise (haiku can be wonderful poetry) with criticism (it can be obscure and unintelligible).*

3. But at least one major study demonstrates that the benefits of using the new media outweigh the disadvantages. *Examples include Thompson's point that the writing in the new media constitutes a "paradigm shift"* (para. 5). *Andrea Lunsford observes that students are "remarkably adept at what rhetoricians call* kairos—*assessing their audience and adapting their tone and technique to best get their point across"* (para. 6).

A single concrete example may be sufficient to clarify the point you want to make about an author's argument. Throughout the essay, Thompson derives examples from the Stanford study to support his argument in the

WRITING A SUMMARY   **149**

final two paragraphs. The most concrete, specific example of how the new media benefit students as writers appears in paragraph 6, where the primary research of the Stanford study describes students' acquisition of important rhetorical skills of developing writing that is opportune (*kairos*) and purposeful. This one example may be sufficient for the purposes of summarizing Thompson's essay.

■ Present the Gist of the Author's Argument

When you present the **gist** of an argument, you are expressing the author's central idea in a sentence or two. The gist is not quite the same thing as the author's thesis statement. Instead, it is your formulation of the author's main idea, composed for the needs of your own argument.

Thompson's observations in paragraph 8 represent his thesis: "But it's also becoming clear that online media are pushing literacy into cool directions. . . . [T]he proliferation of new forms of online pop-cultural exegesis—from sprawling TV-show recaps to 15,000-word videogame walkthroughs—has given [students] a chance to write enormously long and complex pieces of prose, often while working collaboratively with others." In this paragraph, Thompson clearly expresses his central ideas in two sentences, while also conceding some of the critics' concerns. However, in formulating the gist of his argument, you want to do more than paraphrase Thompson. You want to use his position to support your own. For example, suppose you want to qualify the disapproval that some educators have expressed in drawing their conclusions about the new media. You would want to mention Thompson's own concessions when you describe the gist of his argument:

GIST

In his essay "On the New Literacy," Clive Thompson, while acknowledging some academic criticism of new media, argues that these media give students opportunities to write more than in previous generations and that students have learned to adapt what they are writing in order to have some tangible effect on what people think and how they act.

Notice that this gist could not have been written based only on Thompson's thesis statement. It reflects knowledge of Thompson's major points, his examples, and his concessions.

■ Contextualize What You Summarize

Your summary should help readers understand the context of the conversation:

• Who is the author?
• What is the author's expertise?

- What is the title of the work?
- Where did the work appear?
- What was the occasion of the work's publication? What prompted the author to write the work?
- What are the issues?
- Who else is taking part in the conversation, and what are their perspectives on the issues?

Again, because a summary must be concise, you must make decisions about how much of the conversation your readers need to know. If your assignment is to practice summarizing, it may be sufficient to include only information about the author and the source. However, if you are using the summary to build your own argument, you may need to provide more context. Your practice summary of Thompson's essay should mention that he is a journalist and should cite the title of and page references to his essay. You also may want to include information about Thompson's audience, publication information, and what led to the work's publication. Was it published in response to another essay or book, or to commemorate an important event?

We compiled our notes on Thompson's essay (key claims, examples, gist, context) in a worksheet (Figure 7.1). All of our notes in the worksheet constitute a type of prewriting, our preparation for writing the summary. Creating a worksheet like this can help you track your thoughts as you plan to write a summary. (You can download a template of this worksheet at bedfordstmartins.com/frominquiry.)

KEY CLAIM(S)	EXAMPLES	GIST	CONTEXT
1. Electronic media prompt more student writing than ever before, and students use their writing to make a difference.	The Stanford study: Students "defined good prose as something that had an effect on the world" (para. 7).	In his essay "On the New Literacy," Clive Thompson, while acknowledging some academic criticism of new media, argues that these media give students opportunities to write more than in previous generations and that students have learned to adapt what they are writing in order to have some tangible effect on what people think and how they act.	Thompson is a journalist who has written widely on issues in higher education. His essay "On the New Literacy" appeared in *Wired* in August 2009 (http://www.wired .com/techbiz/people/ magazine/17-09/ st_thompson). Under consideration is the debate that he frames in his opening paragraphs.
2. Arguably, reliance on blogging and posting can foster some bad writing habits.	Complaints of "bleak, bald, sad shorthand" and "narcissistic blabbering" (para. 1); texting can be obscure.		
3. But one major study shows the benefits of new media on student writing.	A "paradigm shift" (para. 5) to fluency in multiple formats and skill in assessing and persuading audiences.		

FIGURE 7.1   Worksheet for Writing a Summary

Here is our summary of Thompson's essay:

The gist of Thompson's argument.

In his essay "On the New Literacy," Clive Thompson, while acknowledging some academic criticism of new media, argues that these media give students opportunities to write more than in previous generations and that students have learned to adapt what they are writing in order to have some tangible effect on what people think and how they act. Arguably, reliance on blogging and posting on Twitter and Facebook can foster some bad habits in writing. But at least one major study demonstrates that the benefits of using the new media outweigh the disadvantages. Students write lengthy, complex pieces that contribute to creating significant social networks and collaborations.

This concession helps to balance enthusiasm based on a single study.

Thompson's main point with example.

Steps to Writing a Summary

1 **Describe the key claims of the text.** To understand the shape and direction of the argument, study how paragraphs begin and end, and pay attention to the author's point of view and use of transitions. Then combine what you have learned into a few sentences describing the key claims.

2 **Select examples to illustrate the author's argument.** Find one or two examples to support each key claim. You may need only one example when you write your summary.

3 **Present the gist of the author's argument.** Describe the author's central idea in your own language with an eye to where you expect your argument to go.

4 **Contextualize what you summarize.** Cue your readers into the conversation. Who is the author? Where and when did the text appear? Why did the author write? Who else is in the conversation?

A Practice Sequence: Summarizing

1 Summarize a text that you have been studying for research or for one of your other classes. You may want to limit yourself to an excerpt of just a few paragraphs or a few pages. Follow the four steps we've described, using a summary worksheet for notes, and write a summary of the text. Then share the excerpt and your summary of it with two of your peers. Be prepared to justify your

choices in composing the summary. Do your peers agree that your summary captures what is important in the original?

2 With a classmate, choose a brief text of about three pages. Each of you should use the method we describe above to write a summary of the text. Exchange your summaries and worksheets, and discuss the effectiveness of your summaries. Each of you should be prepared to discuss your choice of key claims and examples and your wording of the gist. Did you set forth the context effectively?

SYNTHESIS VERSUS SUMMARY

A **synthesis** is a discussion that forges connections between the arguments of two or more authors. Like a summary, a synthesis requires you to understand the key claims of each author's argument, including his or her use of supporting examples and evidence. Also like a summary, a synthesis requires you to present a central idea, a *gist*, to your readers. But in contrast to a summary, which explains the context of a source, a synthesis creates a context for your own argument. That is, when you write a synthesis comparing two or more sources, you demonstrate that you are aware of the larger conversation about the issue and begin to claim your own place in that conversation.

Most academic arguments begin with a synthesis that sets the stage for the argument that follows. By comparing what others have written on a given issue, writers position themselves in relation to what has come before them, acknowledging the contributions of their predecessors as they advance their own points of view.

Like a summary, a synthesis requires analysis: You have to break down arguments and categorize their parts to see how they work together. In our summary of Thompson's essay (p. 151), the parts we looked at were the key claims, the examples and evidence that supported them, the central idea (conveyed in the gist), and the context. But in a synthesis, your main purpose is not simply to report what another author has said. Rather, you must think critically about how multiple points of view intersect on your issue, and decide what those intersections mean.

Comparing different points of view prompts you to ask why they differ. It also makes you more aware of *counterarguments*—passages where claims conflict ("writer X says this, but writer Y asserts just the opposite") or at least differ ("writer X interprets this information this way, while writer Y sees it differently"). And it starts you formulating your own counterarguments: "Neither X nor Y has taken this into account. What if they had?"

Keep in mind that the purpose of a synthesis is not merely to list the similarities and differences you find in different sources or to assert your agreement with one source as opposed to others. Instead, it sets up your argument. Once you discover connections among texts, you have to decide what those connections mean to you and your readers. What bearing do they have on your own thinking? How can you make use of them in your argument?

WRITING A SYNTHESIS

To compose an effective synthesis, you must (1) make connections among ideas in different texts, (2) decide what those connections mean, and (3) formulate the gist of what you've read, much like you did when you wrote a summary. The difference is that in a synthesis, your gist should be a succinct statement that brings into focus not the central idea of one text but the relationship among different ideas in multiple texts.

To help you grasp strategies of writing a synthesis, read the following essays by journalists Cynthia Haven and Josh Keller, which, like Clive Thompson's essay, deal with the effects of new media on the quality of students' writing. We have annotated the Haven and Keller readings not only to comment on their ideas but also to connect their ideas with those of Thompson. Annotating your texts in this manner is a useful first step in writing a synthesis.

Following the Haven and Keller selections, we explain how annotating contributes to writing a synthesis. Then we show how you can use a worksheet to organize your thinking when you are formulating a gist of your synthesis. Finally, we present our own synthesis based on the texts of Thompson, Haven, and Keller.

CYNTHIA HAVEN

The New Literacy: Stanford Study Finds Richness and Complexity in Students' Writing

Cynthia Haven was born in Detroit and educated at the University of Michigan. A writer who has received more than a dozen literary and journalism awards, Haven is currently a literary critic at the *San Francisco Chronicle*. She has long been affiliated with Stanford University and is a regular contributor to its magazine, *Stanford Report*, where this article appeared in 2009.

■ ■ ■

Begins with claims in the first two paragraphs for our consideration.

Today's kids don't just write for grades anymore *1* They write to shake the world.

Moreover, they are writing more than any previous *2* generation, ever, in history. They navigate in a bewildering new arena where writers and their audiences have merged.

Cites a study that supports these claims and sets up the terms of a debate: that new media may not be eroding literacy as "conventional wisdom" might suggest.

These are among the startling findings in the Stanford Study of Writing, spearheaded by Professor Andrea Lunsford, director of Stanford's Program in Writing and Rhetoric. The study refutes conventional wisdom and provides a wholly new context for those who wonder "whether Google is making us stupid and whether Facebook is frying our brains," said Lunsford. 3

The five-year study investigated the writing of Stanford students during their undergraduate careers and their first year afterward, whether at a job or in graduate school. 4

Observing the way the study employed a random sample helps give legitimacy to the study and support for the study's claims.

The study began in September 2001, when Lunsford invited a random sample of the freshman class to participate in the study. Of the 243 invited, 189 accepted the invitation—about 12 percent of that year's class. 5

Students agreed to submit the writing they did for all their classes, including multimedia presentations, problem sets, lab reports, and honors theses. They also submitted as much as they wanted of what Lunsford calls "life writing," that is, the writing they did for themselves, their families, their friends, and the world at large. 6

The volume and range of writing reinforces the initial claim: Today's students are writing more than previous generations.

Lunsford was unprepared for the avalanche of material that ensued: about 15,000 pieces of writing, including emails in 11 languages, blog postings, private journal entries and poetry. The last, in particular, surprised her: "If there's any closeted group at Stanford, it's poets." 7

Only 62 percent of the writing was for their classwork. 8

While data analysis is ongoing, Lunsford said the study's first goal was "to paint a picture of the writing that these young writers do" and to portray "its richness and complexity." 9

Her conclusion: Although today's kids are "writing more than ever before in history," it may not look like the writing of yesterday. The focus of today's writing is "more about instantaneous communication." It's also about audience. 10

Writing as Vehicle of Change

Implied comparison between the current generation, which communicates to create change, and previous generations, who wrote to fulfill classroom assignments.

For these students, "Good writing changes something. It doesn't just sit on the page. It gets up, walks off the page, and changes something," whether it's a website or a poster for a walkathon. *11*

More than earlier generations, said Lunsford, "Young people today are aware of the precarious nature of our lives. They understand the dangers that await us." Hence, "Writing is a way to get a sense of power." *12*

Haven provides a representative case example from the study to illustrate one of the conclusions drawn from the research: that students are writing more outside of class to "get something done."

Twenty-six-year-old Mark Otuteye, one of 36 students in the study group who agreed to be interviewed once a year, is in many ways representative. While at Stanford, he started a performance poetry group in response to 2003 student protests against growing involvement in Iraq. *13*

"Academic writing seemed to be divorced from a public audience. I was used to communicating not only privately, with emails, but publicly, with websites, blogs, and social networks," said Otuteye, CEO of AES Connect, a social media design company (he's also worked at Google). *14*

"I was used to writing transactionally—not just for private reflection, but writing to actually get something done in the world." For Otuteye, a half-Ghanaian student in the Program in African and African American Studies who went on to get a Stanford master's degree in modern thought and literature (2005) and, with a Marshall Scholarship, a master's degree from the University of Sussex in artificial intelligence (2008), academic writing was often "less important" than his writing for the "real world"—for example, the fliers he put up all over Stanford to promote his poetry group. *15*

Lunsford cautioned that "audiences are very slippery," and that, in the Internet age, "in a way the whole world can be your audience. It's inspirational, really, but it's hard to know who they are or what they'll do." *16*

Anyone anywhere can be an overnight pundit with an audience of millions—or can ramble on in *17*

*Haven raises a
question that many
critics have about
students being
trapped in a limited
view of the world.*

an unregarded cyberspace tirade. A lively blog "conversation" may consist largely of one writer assuming
different masks. Does much of this writing, moreover, trap them in a world of other 19-year-olds, their
peers?

Audiences Change over Time

Otuteye noted that the students in the study were   18
already writing for professors, friends, and parents.
Moreover, as they transition into the work world after
graduation, they begin to see "those audiences begin
to mix and overlap. All the communication that they
do online, with the exception of email, can become
public."

*The case example
helps support
the claim that
new media enable
students to learn
to value rhetorical
skills.*

"The skill of being able to manage multiple, over-   19
lapping audiences is a principle of rhetoric, a skill I
was able to hone and perfect not only in academic
writing, but in the performance writing I did and all
the rhetorical activity I was engaged in at Stanford."

He said that even the computer code he writes now   20
follows "the same principles of rhetoric, specifically
around audience, that is used in poetry and academic
writing." A line of code, he said, could have four or more
audiences, including other engineers and computers.

*Is it higher edu-
cation—not
students—that
needs to change to
meet the demands
of new media?*

Lunsford underscored the need for higher educa-   21
tion to adapt; for example, students could post their
essays online, accommodating their preference for an
audience and online discussion. But Lunsford said
adaptation must go even further: What does an English professor say when a student approaches her and
says, "I know you'd like me to write an essay, but I'd
like to make a documentary"?

*This is Haven's
own stand. It's
clear that these
prognosticators
were wrong, and
they may be wrong
again.*

In light of this brave new world, it can be hard to   22
remember that only a few decades ago doomsday
prophets were predicting the death of the written
word, as telephones and television increased their
domination over a culture, and business CEOs dictated their letters into Dictaphones.

In those days, graduation from college largely meant   23
goodbye to writing. An office memo, letters, or "annotated cookbooks" were about the only written expres-

sions of the adult world, said Lunsford, unless they were headed for jobs in the media or in academia. Writing was "instrumental"—designed for a purpose, such as a purchasing agreement, or advertising to sell a product.

Redefining "Writing"

Today's landscape alters fundamental notions of what writing is. According to Lunsford, "The everyday understanding of writing is usually operational as opposed to epistemic."

Defines a specialized term, "epistemic."

Epistemic writing creates knowledge. (Think of all those times when you don't know what to think till you begin writing.) Such epistemic writing is an exploration, rather than declaration. It's the writing that dominates journals, letters, and many blogs. Clearly, the students' sense of agency extends to self-knowledge as well as changing the world.

But is the writing "three times" as effective? Is it good writing?

Comparing the Stanford students' writing with their peers from the mid-1980s, Lunsford found that the writing of today's students is about three times as long—they have "the ability to generate more prose."

They are also likely to make different kinds of errors. The number one error 20 years ago was spelling—a problem easily circumvented today by a spell-checker. Today's number one error is using the wrong word—"constraint" instead of "constrained," for example, or using the wrong preposition.

Lunsford recalls one student writing "I feel necrotic" rather than "neurotic."

Counterargument to Lunsford's position: Students have not mastered the technical aspects of writing. However, the quotation does not really answer the question.

Some nevertheless insist that writing today is substandard, littered with too many LOLs and OMGs. However, Lunsford noted that Stanford students were adept at different writing for different audiences. Moreover, they are changing the game: For a graphic novel such as Chris Ware's *Jimmy Corrigan: The Smartest Kid on Earth*, "traditional reading strategies do not work. Every single word is important." And websites, though they can be skimmed with a click, can be very labor- and thought-intensive.

24

25

26

27

28

29

"College writers need to be able to retain the best   *30*
of print literacy, and know how to deploy it for their
own purposes," said Lunsford. "They also need and
deserve to be exposed to new forms of expression."

With the more playful, inventive and spontaneous   *31*
forms of writing available to them, are today's students losing the taste for more complex English?

Concludes with a
quotation about
how the use of new
media does not
devalue traditional
conceptions of lit-
eracy, writing, and
classic literature.

"Every time I pick up Henry James, I have to   *32*
relearn how to read Henry James. We don't want to
lose the ability to do that kind of reading and writing," said Lunsford.

"Thinking about hard things requires hard prose.   *33*
We can boil things down, prepare for a different audiences, but when it comes to hard things, I don't think
it can be worked out in 140 characters."

JOSH KELLER

Studies Explore Whether the Internet Makes Students Better Writers

Josh Keller is a reporter for *The Chronicle of Higher Education* in Washington, D.C. The weekly publication focuses on issues in higher education
and on news and serves as a job-information source for college and university faculty members, administrators, and students. His piece appeared in
2009.

■ ■ ■

As a student at Stanford University, Mark Otuteye   *1*
wrote in any medium he could find. He wrote
blog posts, slam poetry, to-do lists, teaching guides,
e-mail and Facebook messages, diary entries, short
stories. He wrote a poem in computer code, and he
wrote a computer program that helped him catalog
all the things he had written.

Keller uses the
same student
example as Haven
to make the same
point about college
writing assign-
ments.

But Mr. Otuteye hated writing academic papers.   *2*
Although he had vague dreams of becoming an English professor, he saw academic writing as a "soul-
less exercise" that felt like "jumping through hoops."
When given a writing assignment in class, he says, he

would usually adopt a personal tone and more or less ignore the prompt. "I got away with it," says Mr. Otuteye, who graduated from Stanford in 2006. "Most of the time."

The rise of online media has helped raise a new 3 generation of college students who write far more, and in more-diverse forms, than their predecessors did. But the implications of the shift are hotly debated, both for the future of students' writing and for the college curriculum.

Some scholars say that this new writing is more 4 engaged and more connected to an audience, and that colleges should encourage students to bring lessons from that writing into the classroom. Others argue that tweets and blog posts enforce bad writing habits and have little relevance to the kind of sustained, focused argument that academic work demands.

A new generation of longitudinal studies, which 5 track large numbers of students over several years, is attempting to settle this argument. The "Stanford Study of Writing," a five-year study of the writing lives of Stanford students—including Mr. Otuteye—is probably the most extensive to date.

In a shorter project, undergraduates in a first-year 6 writing class at Michigan State University were asked to keep a diary of the writing they did in any environment, whether blogging, text messaging, or gaming. For each act of writing over a two-week period, they recorded the time, genre, audience, location, and purpose of their writing.

"What was interesting to us was how small a percentage of the total writing the school writing was," 7 says Jeffrey T. Grabill, the study's lead author, who is director of the Writing in Digital Environments Research Center at Michigan State. In the diaries and in follow-up interviews, he says, students often described their social, out-of-class writing as more persistent and meaningful to them than their in-class work was.

"Digital technologies, computer networks, the 8 Web—all of those things have led to an explosion in

Sums up two opposed points of view on the debate.

Goes beyond Haven to cite an additional study at Michigan State that reached similar conclusions as the Stanford study.

Additional evidence that supports the Stanford study.

writing," Mr. Grabill says. "People write more now than ever. In order to interact on the Web, you have to write."

Keller adds the voices of scholars of writing to comment on the value of new media.

Kathleen Blake Yancey, a professor of English at Florida State University and a former president of the National Council of Teachers of English, calls the current period "the age of composition" because, she says, new technologies are driving a greater number of people to compose with words and other media than ever before.   9

"This is a new kind of composing because it's so variegated and because it's so intentionally social," Ms. Yancey says. Although universities may not consider social communication as proper writing, it still has a strong influence on how students learn to write, she says. "We ignore it at our own peril."   10

Unlike Thompson and Haven, Keller provides the counterarguments of scholars who dispute the findings of the Stanford study.

But some scholars argue that students should adapt their writing habits to their college course work, not the other way around. Mark Bauerlein, a professor of English at Emory University, cites the reading and writing scores in the National Assessment of Educational Progress, which have remained fairly flat for decades. It is a paradox, he says: "Why is it that with young people reading and writing more words than ever before in human history, we find no gains in reading and writing scores?"   11

The Right Writing

Underscores the difficulty of drawing conclusions either way.

Determining how students develop as writers, and why they improve or not, is difficult. Analyzing a large enough sample of students to reach general conclusions about how the spread of new technologies affects the writing process, scholars say, is a monumental challenge.   12

The sheer amount of information that is relevant to a student's writing development is daunting and difficult to collect: formal and informal writing, scraps of notes and diagrams, personal histories, and fleeting conversations and thoughts that never make it onto the printed page.   13

This summary of the Stanford study suggests that researchers there have responded to the complexity of measuring outcomes of writing in any medium.

The Stanford study is trying to collect as much of that material as possible. Starting in 2001, researchers at the university began collecting extensive writing samples from 189 students, roughly 12 percent of the freshman class. Students were given access to a database where they could upload copies of their work, and some were interviewed annually about their writing experiences. By 2006 researchers had amassed nearly 14,000 pieces of writing.

Students in the study "almost always" had more enthusiasm for the writing they were doing outside of class than for their academic work, says Andrea A. Lunsford, the study's director. Mr. Otuteye submitted about 700 pieces of writing and became the study's most prolific contributor.

The report's authors say they included nonacademic work to better investigate the links between academic and nonacademic writing in students' writing development. One of the largest existing longitudinal studies of student writing, which started at Harvard University in the late 1990s, limited its sample to academic writing, which prevented researchers from drawing direct conclusions about that done outside of class.

In looking at students' out-of-class writing, the Stanford researchers say they found several traits that were distinct from in-class work. Not surprisingly, the writing was self-directed; it was often used to connect with peers, as in social networks; and it usually had a broader audience.

Cites the study at George Mason. Writing on blogs is more engaging than writing in school, and it represents the ways students sustain social networks (paras. 17–20).

The writing was also often associated with accomplishing an immediate, concrete goal, such as organizing a group of people or accomplishing a political end, says Paul M. Rogers, one of the study's authors. The immediacy might help explain why students stayed so engaged, he says. "When you talked to them about their out-of-class writing, they would talk about writing to coordinate out-of-class activity," says Mr. Rogers, an assistant professor of English at George Mason University. "A lot of them were a lot more

14

15

16

17

18

conscious of the effect their writing was having on other people."

Mr. Rogers believes from interviews with students that the data in the study will help show that students routinely learn the basics of writing concepts wherever they write the most. For instance, he says, students who compose messages for an audience of their peers on a social-networking Web site were forced to be acutely aware of issues like audience, tone, and voice. *19*

"The out-of-class writing actually made them more conscious of the things writing teachers want them to think about," the professor says. *20*

Mr. Otuteye, who recently started a company that develops Web applications, says he paid close attention to the writing skills of his peers at Stanford as the co-founder of a poetry slam. It was the students who took their out-of-class writing seriously who made the most progress, he says. "Everybody was writing in class, but the people who were writing out of and inside of class, that was sort of critical to accelerating their growth as writers." *21*

Although analysis of the Stanford study is still at an early stage, other scholars say they would like to start similar studies. At the University of California, several writing researchers say they are trying to get financial support for a longitudinal study of 300 students on the campuses in Irvine, Santa Barbara, and Davis. *22*

Curricular Implications

The implications of the change in students' writing habits for writing and literature curricula are up for debate. Much of the argument turns on whether online writing should be seen as a welcome new direction or a harmful distraction. *23*

Why does it have to be "either/or"? Isn't it possible that there's a middle ground?

Mr. Grabill, from Michigan State, says college writing instruction should have two goals: to help students become better academic writers, and to help them become better writers in the outside world. The second, broader goal is often lost, he says, either *24*

Grabill criticizes the critics, pointing out that they have lost sight of an important goal: Students should be able to write to a general, public audience, not just academic readers (paras. 24–30).

because it is seen as not the college's responsibility, or because it seems unnecessary.

"The unstated assumption there is that if you can write a good essay for your literature professor, you can write anything," Mr. Grabill says. "That's utter nonsense." 25

The writing done outside of class is, in some ways, the opposite of a traditional academic paper, he says. Much out-of-class writing, he says, is for a broad audience instead of a single professor, tries to solve real-world problems rather than accomplish academic goals, and resembles a conversation more than an argument. 26

Rather than being seen as an impoverished, secondary form, online writing should be seen as "the new normal," he says, and treated in the curriculum as such: "The writing that students do in their lives is a tremendous resource." 27

This seems rather anecdotal.

Ms. Yancey, at Florida State, says out-of-class writing can be used in a classroom setting to help students draw connections among disparate types of writing. In one exercise she uses, students are asked to trace the spread of a claim from an academic journal to less prestigious forms of media, like magazines and newspapers, in order to see how arguments are diluted. In another, students are asked to pursue the answer to a research question using only blogs, and to create a map showing how they know if certain information is trustworthy or not. 28

But does this occur—avoiding a "fire wall"?

The idea, she says, is to avoid creating a "fire wall" between in-class and out-of-class writing. 29

"If we don't invite students to figure out the lessons they've learned from that writing outside of school and bring those inside of school, what will happen is only the very bright students" will do it themselves, Ms. Yancey says. "It's the rest of the population that we're worried about." 30

One critic concedes that writing in electronic media can help struggling writers, but he also

Writing in electronic media probably does benefit struggling students in a rudimentary way, says Emory's Mr. Bauerlein, because they are at least forced to string sentences together: "For those kids who 31 *warns that educators should temper their enthusiasm for blogging and other online writing (paras. 32–35).*

wouldn't be writing any words anyway, that's going to improve their very low-level skills."

But he spends more of his time correcting, not integrating, the writing habits that students pick up outside of class. The students in his English courses often turn in papers that are "stylistically impoverished," and the Internet is partly to blame, he says. Writing for one's peers online, he says, encourages the kind of quick, unfocused thought that results in a scarcity of coherent sentences and a limited vocabulary.   32

Has he studied this?

"When you are writing so much to your peers, you're writing to other 17-year-olds, so your vocabulary is going to be the conventional vocabulary of the 17-year-old idiom," Mr. Bauerlein says.   33

Students must be taught to home in on the words they write and to resist the tendency to move quickly from sentence to sentence, he says. Writing scholars, too, should temper their enthusiasm for new technologies before they have fully understood the implications, he says. Claims that new forms of writing should take a greater prominence in the curriculum, he says, are premature.   34

"The sweeping nature of their pronouncements to me is either grandiose or flatulent, or you could say that this is a little irresponsible to be pushing for practices so hard that are so new," Mr. Bauerlein says. "We don't know what the implications of these things will be. Slow down!?"   35

Another scholar reaffirms a finding in the Stanford study: that electronic media represent a cultural shift that educators must learn to accept and adapt to.

Deborah Brandt, a professor of English at the University of Wisconsin at Madison who studies the recent history of reading and writing, says the growth of writing online should be seen as part of a broader cultural shift toward mass authorship. Some of the resistance to a more writing-centered curriculum, she says, is based on the view that writing without reading can be dangerous because students will be untethered to previous thought, and reading levels will decline.   36

Really, people are not shaped by what they read?

But that view, she says, is "being challenged by the literacy of young people, which is being developed   37

primarily by their writing. They're going to be reading, but they're going to be reading to write, and not
to be shaped by what they read."

■ Make Connections Among Different Texts

The texts by Thompson, Haven, and Keller all deal with the emergence
of new electronic media and their effects on students' development as
writers. These texts are very much in conversation with one another, as
each author focuses on what research tells us are the benefits of the new
media and the potential ways that electronic media can limit young writers' growth:

- Thompson uses the Stanford study to emphasize the ways that students'
  participation on blogs and the like helps students learn to adapt their
  writing for specific audiences and to write fairly complex texts to affect
  the ways readers think and act.

- Haven provides a more elaborate analysis of the Stanford study to argue
  that we are witnessing a revolution in literacy, the likes of which we have
  not experienced since the development of classical rhetoric.

- Keller offers converging pieces of evidence to support the findings from
  the Stanford study that Thompson and Haven discuss, but additionally he provides a more detailed counterargument that is also based on
  research.

All three authors seem to agree that the introduction of new electronic
media has contributed to a paradigm shift in the uses of writing—to create agency and community—but they seem to vary in the concessions they
make to counterarguments.

Notice how our annotations call out connections. "Keller uses the
same student example as Haven to make the same point about college writing assignments." "Keller adds the voices of scholars of writing to comment on the value of new media." "Unlike Thompson and Haven, Keller
provides the counterarguments of scholars who dispute the findings of the
Stanford study."

With these annotations, we are starting to think critically about the
ideas in the essays. Notice, however, that not all of the annotations make
connections. Some note examples that support the argument that electronic media benefit writers, while others point to examples that provide
compelling evidence for the counterargument. Still other annotations raise
questions about the basis on which researchers and teachers reached their
conclusions. In the end, you should not expect that every annotation will
contribute to your synthesis. Instead, use them to record your responses
and also to spur your thinking.

■ Decide What Those Connections Mean

Having annotated the selections, we filled out the worksheet in Figure 7.2, making notes in the grid to help us see the three texts in relation to one another. Our worksheet included columns for

- author and source information
- the gist of each author's arguments
- supporting examples and illustrations
- counterarguments
- our own thoughts

A worksheet like this one can help you concentrate on similarities and differences in the texts to determine what the connections among texts mean. (You can download a template for this worksheet at bedfordstmartins .com/frominquiry.) Of course, you can design your own worksheet as well, tailoring it to your needs and preferences. If you want to take very detailed notes about your authors and sources, for example, you may want to have separate columns for each.

   Once you start making connections, including points of agreement and disagreement, you can start identifying counterarguments in the read-ing—for example, Keller quotes a scholar who cites a national study, the National Assessment of Education Progress, to dampen enthusiasm for the claims that Thompson and Haven give so much attention to. Identify-ing counterarguments gives you a sense of what is at issue for each author. And determining what authors think in relation to one another can help you realize what is at issue for you. Suppose you are struck by Haven's implicit argument that a revolution in literacy is occurring and that insti-tutions of higher education, not students, need to respond to changes in the nature of literacy and communication. But you also recognize in Keller's analysis that questions persist about studies conducted to assess the development of students' growth and development as writers. How persuasive are the studies conducted at Stanford, Michigan State, and George Mason? What do we really know? And how can we further test the claims experts make about electronic media and paradigm shifts? Turning these ideas and questions over in your mind, you may be able to decide on a topic you want to explore and develop.

■ Formulate the Gist of What You've Read

Remember that your gist should bring into focus the relationship among different ideas in multiple texts. Looking at the information juxtaposed on the worksheet, you can begin to construct the gist of your synthesis:

- Clive Thompson cites research conducted at Stanford to challenge pre-vailing arguments about electronic media's effects on students' literacy.

Author and Source	Gist of Argument	Examples/ Illustrations	Counterarguments	What I Think
Clive Thompson, "On the New Literacy," *Wired* (2009)	Research challenges prevailing arguments about electronic media's effects on students' literacy, suggesting they may be more literate than in the past.	The Stanford study, with its sample of more than 14,000 pieces of writing and randomized sample of student participants. One case example.	Student writing is full of "texting-speak."	The Stanford study is persuasive, especially given the size of the study. Not much counter-evidence.
Cynthia Haven, "The New Literacy: Stanford Study Finds Richness and Complexity in Students' Writing," *Stanford Report* (2009)	A study indicates a possible revolution in literacy. Using online social networks to create change, students now write more, more persuasively, and more adaptively than ever before.	Stanford study and case example of one student.	Students who spend most of their time writing on electronic networks do not attend to the technical aspects of communication and have a limited sense of their audience.	This is a more thorough review of the Stanford study. It emphasizes how much more meaningful writing is outside of the classroom.
Josh Keller, "Studies Explore Whether the Internet Makes Students Better Writers," *Chronicle of Higher Education* (2009)	Two studies suggest that electronic media, in giving students more opportunities to write and honing their sense of audience, have made them better writers than previous generations. But an emerging body of evidence challenges these recent claims, which force educators to consider what they consider good writing.	Studies at Stanford, Michigan State, and George Mason. Expert opinion from faculty at Florida State and the University of Wisconsin.	Critics like Professor Bauerlein at Emory University argue that literacy is not progressing steadily, as some have observed, at least not based on standardized tests. He suggests that writing solely to one's peers online encourages spontaneous but unfocused thought and a limited vocabulary.	The three studies together are quite powerful. I am not sure that standardized tests developed a generation ago are the best way to measure increases in literacy. And Bauerlein relies on anecdotal evidence to make his argument: that writing in electronic media limits thinking or writing quality. I should check if any studies exist to support Baeurlein.

FIGURE 7.2   Worksheet for Writing a Synthesis

Indeed, despite pundits' complaints, students may be more literate than in the past.

- Cynthia Haven also analyzes the Stanford study, which indicates that we may very well be experiencing a revolution in literacy. Students use electronic media to sustain social networks and create change. As Thompson also points out, students are writing more than ever before and are more adept at applying principles of rhetoric than were students in previous generations. Those in higher education may have to change in order to respond to students' uses of electronic media, not the other way around.

- Josh Keller points to two additional studies of writing to suggest that students are developing literate practices that are more impressive than those of previous generations. This can be attributed to the fact that current students have more opportunities to write and they know what it means to write for an audience. But he also observes that an emerging body of evidence challenges these recent claims, forcing educators to consider what constitutes good writing.

How do you formulate this information into a gist? You can use a transition word such as *although* or *however* to connect ideas that different authors bring together while conveying their differences. Thus, a gist of these essays might read:

GIST OF A SYNTHESIS

Although Clive Thompson and Cynthia Haven suggest that new electronic media have created a paradigm shift in the ways educators think about writing, journalists such as Josh Keller have also cited evidence that dampens enthusiasm for the benefits of writing on blogs without students' having instruction in formal, academic writing.

Having drafted the gist, we returned to our notes on the worksheet to complete the synthesis, presenting examples and using transitions to signal the relationships among the texts and their ideas. Here is our brief synthesis of the three texts:

The gist of our synthesis. "Although" signals that Thompson's and Haven's arguments are qualified.

Although Clive Thompson and Cynthia Haven suggest that new electronic media have created a paradigm shift in the ways educators think about writing, journalists such as Josh Keller have also cited evidence that dampens enthusiasm for the benefits of writing on blogs without students' having instruction in formal, academic writing. In particular,

Specific example of a key piece of evidence that has sparked debate.

Thompson cites research conducted at Stanford University to challenge prevailing arguments about electronic media's effects on students' literacy. The Stanford study, with its sample of more than 14,000 pieces of writing and randomized sample of student participants, seems very persuasive.

Indeed, despite pundits' complaints, students may be more literate than in the past.

Cynthia Haven also analyzes the Stanford study, indicating that we may very well be experiencing a revolution in literacy. Students use electronic media to sustain social networks and create change. As Thompson also points out, students are writing more than ever before and are more adept at applying principles of rhetoric than were students in previous generations. Those in higher education may have to change in order to respond to students' uses of electronic media, not the other way around.

Finally, Josh Keller points to two additional studies of writing to suggest that students are developing literate practices that are more impressive than those of previous generations. This can be attributed to the fact that current students have more opportunities to write and they know what it means to write for an audience. However, Keller, more than Thompson and Haven, observes that an emerging body of evidence challenges these recent claims, forcing educators to consider what constitutes good writing. Keller's analysis reveals that questions persist about studies conducted to assess the development of students' growth and development as writers. How persuasive are the studies conducted at Stanford, Michigan State, and George Mason? What do we really know, and what do we need to know? Further, how can we test the claims experts make about electronic media and paradigm shifts?

Transition: Both Thompson and Haven give less attention to the counterargument than they should.

Questions set up direction of what is to follow.

Writing a synthesis, like writing a summary, is principally a strategy for framing your own argument. In writing a synthesis, you are conveying to your readers how various points of view in a conversation intersect and diverge. The larger point of this exercise is to find your own issue—your own position in the conversation—and make your argument for it.

Steps to Writing a Synthesis

1 **Make connections between and among different texts.** Annotate the texts you are working with, with an eye to comparing them. As you would for a summary, note major points in the texts, choose relevant examples, and formulate the gist of each text.

2 **Decide what those connections mean.** Fill out a worksheet to compare your notes on the different texts, track counterarguments, and record your thoughts. Decide what the similarities and differences mean to you and what they might mean to your readers.

3 **Formulate the gist of what you've read.** Identify an overarching idea that brings together the ideas you've noted, and write a synthesis that forges connections and makes use of the examples you've noted. Use transitions to signal the direction of your synthesis.

A Practice Sequence: Writing a Synthesis

1 To practice the strategies for synthesizing that we describe in this chapter, read the following three essays, which focus on the role that electronic media play in conveying information to diverse groups of readers or viewers. As you discuss the strategies the authors use to develop their arguments, consider these questions:

- How would you explain the popularity of blogs, Twitter, and YouTube?
- What themes have the writers focused on as they have sought to enter the conversation surrounding the use of electronic media?
- To what extent do you think the criticisms of new media presented by the authors are legitimate?
- Do blogs, Twitter, and YouTube pose a threat to traditional journalism?
- Do you think that blogs, Twitter, and YouTube add anything to print journalism? If so, what?

2 To stimulate a conversation, or a debate, we suggest that you break up into four different groups:

Group 1: Print journalism

Group 2: Blogs

Group 3: Twitter

Group 4: YouTube

Students in each group should prepare an argument indicating the strengths and limitations of the particular mode of communication that they represent. In preparing the argument, be sure to acknowledge what other modes of communication might add to the ways we learn about news and opinions. One student from each group will present this argument to the other groups.

3 Based on the discussion you have had in exercise 1 and/or exercise 2, write a synthesis of the three essays using the steps we have outlined in this chapter:

- Summarize each essay.

- Explain the ways in which the authors' arguments are similar or different, using examples and illustrations to demonstrate the similarities and differences.

- Formulate an overall gist that synthesizes the points each author makes.

DAN KENNEDY

Political Blogs: Teaching Us Lessons About Community

Dan Kennedy, an assistant professor of journalism at Northeastern University, writes on media issues for *The Guardian* and for *CommonWealth* magazine. His blog, Media Nation, is online at medianation.blogspot.com.

■ ■ ■

The rise of blogging as both a supplement and a challenge to traditional journalism has coincided with an explosion of opinion mongering. Blogs—and the role they play in how Americans consume and respond to information—are increasingly visible during our political season, when our ideological divide is most apparent. From nakedly partisan sites such as Daily Kos on the left and Little Green Footballs on the right, to more nuanced but nevertheless ideological enterprises such as Talking Points Memo, it sometimes seems there is no room in blogworld for straight, neutral journalism.

The usual reasons given for this are that reporting is difficult and expensive and that few bloggers know how to research a story, develop and interview sources, and assemble the pieces into a coherent, factual narrative. Far easier, so this line of thinking goes, for bloggers to sit in their pajamas and blast their semi-informed opinions out to the world.

There is some truth to this, although embracing this view wholeheartedly requires us to overlook the many journalists who are now writing blogs, as well as the many bloggers who are producing journalism to a greater or lesser degree. But we make a mistake when we look at the opinion-oriented nature of blogs and ask whether bloggers are capable of being "objective," to use a hoary and now all but meaningless word. The better question to ask is why opinion-oriented blogs are so popular—and what lessons the traditional media can learn from them without giving up their journalistic souls.

Perhaps what's happening is that the best and more popular blogs pro-   *4*
vide a sense of community that used to be the lifeblood of traditional news organizations and, especially, of newspapers. Recently I reread part of Jay Rosen's book, *What Are Journalists For?*, his 1999 postmortem on the public journalism movement. What struck me was Rosen's description of public journalism's origins, which were grounded in an attempt to recreate a sense of community so that people might discover a reason to read newspapers. "Eventually I came to the conclusion . . . that journalism's purpose was to see the public into fuller existence," Rosen writes. "Informing people followed that."

Rosen's thesis—that journalism could only be revived by reawakening   *5*
the civic impulse—is paralleled by Robert Putnam's 2000 book, *Bowling Alone*, in which he found that people who sign petitions, attend public meetings, and participate in religious and social organizations are more likely to be newspaper readers than those who do not. "Newspaper readers are older, more educated, and more rooted in their communities than is the average American," Putnam writes.

Unfortunately for the newspaper business, the traditional idea of com-   *6*
munity, based mainly on geography, remains as moribund today as it was when Rosen and Putnam were analyzing its pathologies. But if old-fashioned communities are on the decline, the human impulse to form communities is not. And the Internet, as it turns out, is an ideal medium for fostering a new type of community in which people have never met, and may not even know each other's real names, but share certain views and opinions about the way the world works. It's interesting that Rosen has become a leading exponent of journalism tied to these communities, both through his PressThink blog and through NewAssignment.net, which fosters collaborations between professional and citizen journalists.

Attitude First, Facts Second

This trend toward online community-building has given us a mediascape   *7*
in which many people—especially those most interested in politics and public affairs—want the news delivered to them in the context of their attitudes and beliefs. That doesn't mean they want to be fed a diet of self-reinforcing agit-prop (although some do). It does mean they see their news consumption as something that takes place within their community, to be fit into a pre-existing framework of ideas that may be challenged but that must be acknowledged.

Earlier this year John Lloyd, a contributing editor for the *Financial* *8*
Times, talked about the decline of just-the-facts journalism on *Open
Source*, a Web-based radio program hosted by the veteran journalist
Christopher Lydon. It has become increasingly difficult, Lloyd said, to
report facts that are not tied to an ideological point of view. The emerging
paradigm, he explained, may be "that you can only get facts through by
attaching them to a very strong left-wing, right-wing, Christian, atheist
position. Only then, only if you establish your bona fides within this particular community, will they be open to facts."

No less a blogging enthusiast than Markos Moulitsas, founder of Daily *9*
Kos, has observed that political blogs are a nonentity in Britain, where
the newspapers themselves cater to a wide range of different opinions.
"You look at the media in Britain, it's vibrant and it's exciting and it's fun,
because they're all ideologically tinged," Moulitsas said at an appearance
in Boston last fall. "And that's a good thing, because people buy them and
understand that their viewpoints are going to be represented."

The notion that journalism must be tied to an ideological community *10*
may seem disheartening to traditionalists. In practice, though, journalism based on communities of shared interests and beliefs can be every bit
as valuable as the old model of objectivity, if approached with rigor and
respect for the truth.

Last year, for instance, Talking Points Memo (TPM) and its related *11*
blogs helped break the story of how the U.S. Department of Justice had
fired eight U.S. attorneys for what appeared to be politically motivated
reasons, a scandal that led to the resignation of Attorney General Alberto
Gonzales. TPM's reporting was based in part on information dug up and
passed along by its liberal readership. The founder and editor, Joshua
Micah Marshall, received a George Polk Award, but it belonged as much
to the community he had assembled as it did to him personally.

Of course, we still need neutral, non-opinionated journalism to help us *12*
make sense of the world around us. TPM's coverage of the U.S. attorneys
scandal was outstanding, but it was also dismissive of arguments that it
was much ado about nothing, or that previous administrations had done
the same or worse. Liberals or conservatives who get all of their news
from ideologically friendly sources don't have much incentive to change
their minds.

Connecting to Communities of Shared Interests

Even news outlets that excel at traditional, "objective" journalism do so *13*
within the context of a community. Some might not find liberal bias in
the news pages of the *New York Times*, as the paper's conservative critics

would contend, but there's little doubt that the *Times* serves a community of well educated, affluent, culturally liberal readers whose preferences and tastes must be taken into account. Not to be a journalistic relativist, but all news needs to be evaluated within the context in which it was produced, even an old-fashioned, inverted-pyramid-style dispatch from the wires. Who was interviewed? Who wasn't? Why? These are questions that must be asked regardless of the source.

We might now be coming full circle as placeblogs—chatty, conversational blogs that serve a particular geographic community—become more prevalent. Lisa Williams, founder of H2otown, a blog that serves her community of Watertown, Massachusetts, believes that such forums could help foster the sense of community that is a necessary precondition to newspaper readership. Williams also runs a project called Placeblogger.com, which tracks local blogs around the world.   *14*

"The news creates a shared pool of stories that gives us a way to talk to people who aren't family or close friends or people who we will never meet—in short, our fellow citizens," Williams says by e-mail. "The truth is, people still want those neighbor-to-neighbor contacts, but the traditional ways of doing it don't fit into the lives that people are actually living today. Your core audience is tired, sitting on the couch with their laptop, and watching *Lost* with one eye. Give them someone to sit with."   *15*

Critics of blogs have been looking at the wrong thing. While traditionalists disparage bloggers for their indulgence of opinion and hyperbole, they overlook the sense of community and conversation that blogs have fostered around the news. What bloggers do well, and what news organizations do poorly or not at all, is give their readers someone to sit with. News consumers—the public, citizens, us—still want the truth. But we also want to share it and talk about it with our like-minded neighbors and friends. The challenge for journalism is not that we'll lose our objectivity; it's that we won't find a way to rebuild a sense of community.   *16*

JOHN DICKERSON

Don't Fear Twitter

John Dickerson is *Slate* magazine's chief political correspondent and a political analyst for CBS News. Before joining *Slate*, Dickerson covered politics for *Time* magazine, including four years as the magazine's White House correspondent. Dickerson has also written for the *New York Times* and *Washington Post* and is a regular panelist on *Washington Week in Review*. This essay first appeared in the Summer 2008 issue of *Nieman Reports*.

■ ■ ■

If I were cleverer, this piece on Twitter and journalism would fit in Twitter's 140-character limitation. The beauty of Twitter when properly used—by both the reader and the writer—is that everyone knows what it is. No reader expects more from Twitter than it offers, and no one writing tries to shove more than necessary into a Twitter entry, which is sometimes called a Tweet, but not by me, thank you.

Not many people know what Twitter is, though, so I'm going to go on for a few hundred words. Twitter is a Web site that allows you to share your thoughts instantly and on any topic with other people in the Twitter network as long as you do so in tight little entries of 140 characters or less. If you're wondering how much you can write with that space limitation, this sentence that you're reading right now hits that mark perfectly.

For some, journalism is already getting smaller. Newspapers are shrinking. Serious news is being pushed aside in favor of entertainment and fluff stories. To many journalists and guardians of the trade, the idea that any journalist would willingly embrace a smaller space is horrifying and dumb. One journalism professor drew himself up to his full height and denounced Twitter journalism—or microjournalism, as someone unfortunately called it—as the ultimate absurd reduction of journalism. (I think he may have dislodged his monocle, he was waving his quill pen so violently.) Venerable CBS newsman Roger Mudd had a far lighter touch when he joked to me that he could barely say the word "texting" when he and I were talking about the idea of delivering a couple of sentences and calling it journalism.

We can all agree that journalism shouldn't get any smaller, but Twitter doesn't threaten the traditions of our craft. It adds, rather than subtracts, from what we do.

As I spend nearly all of my time on the road these days reporting on the presidential campaigns, Twitter is the perfect place for all of those asides I've scribbled in the hundreds of notebooks I have in my garage from the campaigns and stories I've covered over the years. Inside each of those notebooks are little pieces of color I've picked up along the way. Sometimes these snippets are too off-topic or too inconsequential to work into a story. Sometimes they are the little notions or sideways thoughts that become the lead of a piece or the kicker. All of them now have found a home on Twitter.

As journalists we take people places they can't go. Twitter offers a little snapshot way to do this. It's informal and approachable and great for conveying a little moment from an event. Here's an entry from a McCain rally during the Republican primaries: "Weare, NH: Audience man to McCain: 'I heard that Hershey is moving plants to Mexico and I'll be damned if I'm going to eat Mexican chocolate.'" In Scranton covering Barack Obama I sent this: "Obama: 'What's John McCain's problem?' Audience member: 'He's too old.' Obama: 'No, no that's not the problem. There are a lot of wise people. . . .'" With so many Democrats making an issue of McCain's age, here was the candidate in the moment seeming to suggest that critique was unfair.

Occasionally, just occasionally, reporters can convey a piece of news that fits into 140 characters without context. If Twitter had been around when the planes hit the World Trade Center, it would have been a perfect way for anyone who witnessed it to convey at that moment what they'd seen or heard. With Twitter, we can also pull back the curtain on our lives a little and show readers what it's like to cover a campaign. ("Wanna be a reporter? On long bus rides learn to sleep in your own hand.")   7

The risk for journalism, of course, is that people spend all day Twittering and reading other people's Twitter entries and don't engage with the news in any other way. This seems a pretty small worry. If written the right way, Twitter entries build a community of readers who find their way to longer articles because they are lured by these moment-by-moment observations. As a reader, I've found that I'm exposed to a wider variety of news because I read articles suggested to me by the wide variety of people I follow on Twitter. I'm also exposed to some keen political observers and sharp writers who have never practiced journalism.   8

Twitter is not the next great thing in journalism. No one should try to make Twitter do more than it can and no reader should expect too much from a 140-character entry. As for the critics, their worries about Twitter and journalism seem like the kind of obtuse behavior that would make a perfect observational Twitter entry: "A man at the front of the restaurant is screaming at a waiter and gesticulating wildly. The snacks on the bar aren't a four-course meal!"   9

STEVE GROVE

YouTube: The Flattening of Politics

Steve Grove directs all news, political programming, and citizen journalism for YouTube. He has been quoted as saying that he regards himself less as an editor than as a curator of the Web site's "chaotic sea of content." A native of Northfield, Minnesota, he worked as a journalist at the *Boston Globe* and ABC News before moving to YouTube.

■ ■ ■

For a little over a year, I've served as YouTube's news and political director—perhaps a perplexing title in the eyes of many journalists. Such wonderment might be expected since YouTube gained its early notoriety as a place with videos of dogs on skateboards or kids falling off of trampolines. But these days, in the 10 hours of video uploaded to   1

YouTube every minute of every day (yes—every minute of every day), an increasing amount of the content is news and political video. And with YouTube's global reach and ease of use, it's changing the way that politics—and its coverage—is happening.

Each of the 16 one-time presidential candidates had YouTube channels; seven announced their candidacies on YouTube. Their staffs uploaded thousands of videos that were viewed tens of millions of times. By early March of this year, the Obama campaign was uploading two to three videos to YouTube every day. And thousands of advocacy groups and nonprofit organizations use YouTube to get their election messages into the conversation. For us, the most exciting aspect is that ordinary people continue to use YouTube to distribute their own political content; these range from "gotcha" videos they've taken at campaign rallies to questions for the candidates, from homemade political commercials to video mash-ups of mainstream media coverage.

What this means is that average citizens are able to fuel a new meritocracy for political coverage, one unburdened by the gatekeeping "middleman." Another way of putting it is that YouTube is now the world's largest town hall for political discussion, where voters connect with candidates—and the news media—in ways that were never before possible.

In this new media environment, politics is no longer bound by traditional barriers of time and space. It doesn't matter what time it is, or where someone is located—as long as they have the means to connect through the Web, they can engage in the discussion. This was highlighted in a pair of presidential debates we produced with CNN during this election cycle during which voters asked questions of the candidates via YouTube videos they'd submitted online. In many ways, those events simply brought to the attention of a wider audience the sort of exchanges that take place on YouTube all the time. . . .

News Organizations and YouTube

Just because candidates and voters find all sorts of ways to connect directly on YouTube does not mean there isn't room for the mainstream media, too. In fact, many news organizations have launched YouTube channels, including the Associated Press, the *New York Times*, the BBC, CBS, and the *Wall Street Journal*.

Why would a mainstream media company upload their news content to YouTube?

Simply put, it's where eyeballs are going. Research from the Pew Internet & American Life project found that 37 percent of adult Internet users have watched online video news, and well over half of online adults have used the Internet to watch video of any kind. Each day on YouTube hundreds of millions of videos are viewed at the same time that television viewership is decreasing in many markets. If a mainstream news organization wants its political reporting seen, YouTube offers visibility without a cost. The ones that have been doing this for a while rely on a strategy of building audiences on YouTube and then trying to drive viewers back to their Web sites for a deeper dive into the content. And these organizations can earn revenue as well by running ads against their video content on YouTube.

In many ways, YouTube's news ecosystem has the potential to offer   *8*
much more to a traditional media outlet. Here are some examples:

1. **Interactivity:** YouTube provides an automatic focus group for news content. How? YouTube wasn't built as merely a "series of tubes" to distribute online video. It is also an interactive platform. Users comment on, reply to, rank, and share videos with one another and form communities around content that they like. If news organizations want to see how a particular piece of content will resonate with audiences, they have an automatic focus group waiting on YouTube. And that focus group isn't just young people: 20 percent of YouTube users are over age 55—which is the same percentage that is under 18. This means the YouTube audience roughly mirrors the national population.

2. **Partner with Audiences:** YouTube provides news media organizations new ways to engage with audiences and involve them in the programming. Modeled on the presidential debates we cohosted last year, YouTube has created similar partnerships, such as one with the BBC around the mayoral election in London and with a large public broadcaster in Spain for their recent presidential election. Also on the campaign trail, we worked along with Hearst affiliate WMUR-TV in New Hampshire to solicit videos from voters during that primary. Hundreds of videos flooded in from across the state. The best were broadcast on that TV station, which highlighted this symbiotic relationship: On the Web, online video bubbles the more interesting content to the top and then TV amplifies it on a new scale. We did similar arrangements with news organizations in Iowa, Pennsylvania, and on Super Tuesday, as news organizations leveraged the power of voter-generated content. What the news organizations discover is that they gain audience share by offering a level of audience engagement—with opportunities for active as well as passive experiences.

For news media organizations, audience engagement is much easier   *9*
to achieve by using platforms like YouTube than it is to do on their own. And we just made it easier: Our open API (application programming interface), nicknamed "YouTube Everywhere"—just launched a few months ago—allows other companies to integrate our upload functionality into their online platforms. It's like having a mini YouTube on your

Web site and, once it's there, news organizations can encourage—and publish—video responses and comments on the reporting they do.

Finally, reporters use YouTube as source material for their stories. With hundreds of thousands of video cameras in use today, there is a much greater chance than ever before that events will be captured—by someone—as they unfold. No need for driving the satellite truck to the scene if someone is already there and sending in video of the event via their cell phone. It's at such intersections of new and old media that YouTube demonstrates its value. It could be argued, in fact, that the YouTube platform is the new frontier in newsgathering. On the election trail, virtually every appearance by every candidate is captured on video—by someone—and that means the issues being talked about are covered more robustly by more people who can steer the public discussion in new ways. The phenomenon is, of course, global, as we witnessed last fall in Burma (Myanmar) after the government shut down news media outlets during waves of civic protests. In time, YouTube was the only way to track the violence being exercised by the government on monks who'd taken to the streets. Videos of this were seen worldwide on YouTube, creating global awareness of this situation—even in the absence of journalists on the scene. *10*

Citizen journalism on YouTube—and other Internet sources—is often criticized because it is produced by amateurs and therefore lacks a degree of trustworthiness. Critics add that because platforms like YouTube are fragmenting today's media environment, traditional newsrooms are being depleted of journalists, and thus the denominator for quality news coverage is getting lower and lower. I share this concern about what is happening in the news media today, but I think there are a couple of things worth remembering when it comes to news content on YouTube. *11*

Trusting What We See

When it comes to determining the trustworthiness of news content on YouTube, it's important to have some context. People tend to know what they're getting on YouTube, since content is clearly labeled by username as to where it originated. A viewer knows if the video they're watching is coming from "jellybean109" or "thenewyorktimes." Users also know that YouTube is an open platform and that no one verifies the truth of content better than the consumer. The wisdom of the crowd on YouTube is far more likely to pick apart a shoddy piece of "journalism" than it is to elevate something that is simply untrue. In fact, because video is ubiquitous and so much more revealing and compelling than text, YouTube can provide a critical fact-checking platform in today's media environment. And in some ways, it offers a backstop for accuracy since a journalist *12* can't afford to get the story wrong; if they do, it's likely that someone else who was there got it right—and posted it to YouTube.

Scrutiny cuts both ways. Journalists are needed today for the work they do as much as they ever have been. While the wisdom of crowds might provide a new form of fact checking, and the ubiquity of technology might provide a more robust view of the news, citizens desperately need the Fourth Estate to provide depth, context, and analysis that only comes with experience and the sharpening of the craft. Without the work of journalists, the citizens—the electorate—lose a critical voice in the process of civic decision-making. *13*

This is the media ecosystem in which we live in this election cycle. Candidates and voters speak directly to one another, unfiltered. News organizations use the Internet to connect with and leverage audiences in new ways. Activists, issue groups, campaigns, and voters all advocate for, learn about, and discuss issues on the same level platform. YouTube has become a major force in this new media environment by offering new opportunities and new challenges. For those who have embraced them—and their numbers grow rapidly every day—the opportunity to influence the discussion is great. For those who haven't, they ignore the opportunity at their own peril. *14*

AVOIDING PLAGIARISM

Whether you paraphrase, summarize, or synthesize, it is essential that you acknowledge your sources. Academic writing requires you to use and document sources appropriately, making clear to readers the boundaries between your words and ideas and those of other writers. Setting boundaries can be a challenge because so much of academic writing involves interweaving the ideas of others into your own argument. Still, no matter how difficult, you must acknowledge your sources. It's only fair. Imagine how you would feel if you were reading a text and discovered that the writer had incorporated a passage from one of your papers, something you slaved over, without giving you credit. You would see yourself as a victim of plagiarism, and you would be justified in feeling very angry indeed.

In fact, **plagiarism**—the unacknowledged use of another's work, passed off as one's own—is a most serious breach of academic integrity, and colleges and universities deal with it severely. If you are caught plagiarizing in your work for a class, you can expect to fail that class and may even be expelled from your college or university. Furthermore, although a failing grade on a paper or in a course, honestly come by, is unlikely to deter an employer from hiring you, the stigma of plagiarism can come back to haunt you when you apply for a job. Any violation of the principles set forth in Table 7.1 could have serious consequences for your academic and professional career.

TABLE 7.1   Principles Governing Plagiarism

1. All written work submitted for any purpose is accepted as your own work. This means it must not have been written even in part by another person.

2. The wording of any written work you submit is assumed to be your own. This means you must not submit work that has been copied, wholly or partially, from a book, an article, an essay, a newspaper, another student's paper or notebook, or any other source. Another writer's phrases, sentences, or paragraphs can be included only if they are presented as quotations and the source acknowledged.

3. The ideas expressed in a paper or report are assumed to originate with you, the writer. Written work that paraphrases a source without acknowledgment must not be submitted for credit. Ideas from the work of others can be incorporated in your work as starting points, governing issues, illustrations, and the like, but in every instance the source must be cited.

4. Remember that any online materials you use to gather information for a paper are also governed by the rules for avoiding plagiarism. You need to learn to cite electronic sources as well as printed and other sources.

5. You may correct and revise your writing with the aid of reference books. You also may discuss your writing with your peers in a writing group or with peer tutors at your campus writing center. However, you may not submit writing that has been revised substantially by another person.

Even if you know what plagiarism is and wouldn't think about doing it, you can still plagiarize unintentionally. Again, paraphrasing can be especially tricky: Attempting to restate a passage without using the original words and sentence structure is, to a certain extent, an invitation to plagiarism. If you remember that your paper is *your* argument, and understand that any paraphrasing, summarizing, or synthesizing should reflect *your* voice and style, you will be less likely to have problems with plagiarism. Your paper should sound like you. And, again, the surest way to protect yourself is to cite your sources.

Steps to Avoiding Plagiarism

1 Always cite the source. Signal that you are paraphrasing, summarizing, or synthesizing by identifying your source at the outset — "According to James Gunn," "Clive Thompson argues," "Cynthia Haven and Josh Keller . . . point out." And if possible, indicate the end of the paraphrase, summary, or synthesis with relevant page references to the source. If you cite a source several times in your paper, don't assume that your first citation has you covered; acknowledge the source as often as you use it.

2 Provide a full citation in your bibliography. It's not enough to cite a source in your paper; you must also provide a full citation for every source you use in the list of sources at the end of your paper.

INTEGRATING QUOTATIONS INTO YOUR WRITING

When you integrate quotations into your writing, bear in mind a piece of advice we've given you about writing the rest of your paper: Take your readers by the hand and lead them step-by-step. When you quote other authors to develop your argument—using their words to support your thinking or to address a counterargument—discuss and analyze the words you quote, showing readers how the specific language of each quotation contributes to the larger point you are making in your essay. When you integrate quotations, then, there are three basic things you want to do: (1) Take an active stance, (2) explain the quotations, and (3) attach short quotations to your own sentences.

■ Take an Active Stance

Critical reading requires that you adopt an active stance toward what you read—that you raise questions in response to a text. You should be no less active when you are using other authors' texts to develop your own argument.

Taking an active stance when you are quoting means knowing when to quote. Don't quote when a paraphrase or summary will convey the information from a source more effectively. More important, you have to make fair and wise decisions about what and how much you should quote to make your argument.

- It's not fair (or wise) to quote selectively—choosing only passages that support your argument—when you know you are distorting the argument of the writer you are quoting. You want to show that you understand the writer's argument, and you want to make evenhanded use of it in your own argument.

- It's not wise (or fair to yourself) to flesh out your paper with an overwhelming number of quotations that could make readers think that you do not know your topic well or do not have your own ideas. Don't allow quotations to take over your paragraphs. Remember that your ideas and argument—your thesis—are what is most important to the readers and what justifies a quotation's being included at all.

Above all, taking an active stance when you quote means taking control of your writing. You want to establish your own argument and guide your readers through it, allowing sources to contribute to but not dictate its direction. You are responsible for plotting and pacing your essay. Always keep in mind that your thesis is the skewer that runs through every paragraph, holding all of the ideas together. When you use quotations, then, you must organize them to enrich, substantiate, illustrate, and help support your central claim or thesis.

■ Explain the Quotations

When you quote an author to support or advance your argument, make sure that readers know exactly what they should learn from the quotation.

Read the excerpt below from one student's early draft of an argument that focuses on the value of service learning in high schools. The student reviews several relevant studies—but then simply drops in a quotation, expecting readers to know what they should pay attention to in it.

> Other research emphasizes community service as an integral and integrated part of moral identity. In this understanding, community service activities are not isolated events but are woven into the context of students' everyday lives (Yates, 1995); the personal, the moral, and the civic become "inseparable" (Colby, Ehrlich, Beaumont, & Stephens, 2003, p. 15). In their study of minority high schoolers at an urban Catholic school who volunteered at a soup kitchen for the homeless as part of a class assignment, Youniss and Yates (1999) found that the students underwent significant identity changes, coming to perceive themselves as lifelong activists. The researchers' findings are worth quoting at length here because they depict the dramatic nature of the students' changed viewpoints. Youniss and Yates wrote:
>
>> Many students abandoned an initially negative view of homeless people and a disinterest in homelessness by gaining appreciation of the humanity of homeless people and by showing concern for homelessness in relation to poverty, job training, low-cost housing, prison reform, drug and alcohol rehabilitation, care for the mentally ill, quality urban education, and welfare policy. Several students also altered perceptions of themselves from politically impotent teenagers to involved citizens who now and in the future could use their talent and power to correct social problems. They projected articulated pictures of themselves as adult citizens who could affect housing policies, education for minorities, and government programs within a clear framework of social justice. (p. 362)

The student's introduction to the quoted passage provided a rationale for quoting Youniss and Yates at length, but it did not help her readers see how the research related to her argument. The student needed to frame the quotation for her readers. Instead of introducing the quotation by saying "Youniss and Yates wrote," she should have made clear that the study supports the argument that community service can create change. A more appropriate frame for the quotation might have been a summary like this one:

Frames the quotations, explaining it in the context of the student's argument.

One particular study underscores my argument that service can motivate change, particularly when that change begins within the students who are involved in service. Youniss and Yates (1999) wrote that over the course of their research, the students developed both an "appreciation of the humanity of homeless people" and a sense that they would someday be able to "use their talent and power to correct social problems" (p. 362).

In the following example, notice that the student writer uses Derrick Bell's text to say something about how the effects of desegregation have been muted by political manipulation.* The writer shapes what he wants readers to focus on, leaving nothing to chance.

The effectiveness with which the meaning of *Brown v. Board of Education* has been manipulated, Derrick Bell argued, is also evidenced by the way in which such thinking has actually been embraced by minority groups. Bell claimed that a black school board member's asking "But of what value is it to teach black children to read in all-black schools?" indicates this unthinking acceptance that whiteness is an essential ingredient to effective schooling for blacks. Bell continued:

The assumption that even the attaining of academic skills is worthless unless those skills are acquired in the presence of white students illustrates dramatically how a legal precedent, namely the Supreme Court's decision in *Brown v. Board of Education*, has been so constricted even by advocates that its goal — equal educational opportunity — is rendered inaccessible, even unwanted, unless it can be obtained through racial balancing of the school population. (p. 255)

Bell's argument is extremely compelling, particularly when one considers the extent to which "racial balancing" has come to be defined in terms of large white majority populations and small nonwhite minority populations.

Notice that the student's last sentence helps readers understand what the quoted material suggests and why it's important by embedding and extending Bell's notion of racial balancing into his explanation.

In sum, you should always explain the information that you quote so that your readers can see how the quotation relates to your own argument. ("Take your readers by the hand . . .") As you read other people's writing, keep an eye open to the ways writers introduce and explain the sources they use to build their arguments.

■ Attach Short Quotations to Your Sentences

The quotations we discussed above are **block quotations**, lengthy quotations of more than five lines that are set off from the text of a paper with

---

*This quotation is from Derrick Bell's *Silent Covenants: Brown v. Board of Education and the Unfulfilled Hopes for Racial Reform* (New York: Oxford UP, 2005).

indention. Make shorter quotations part of your own sentences so that your readers can understand how the quotations connect to your argument and can follow along easily. How do you make a quotation part of your own sentences? There are two main methods:

- Integrate quotations within the grammar of your writing.
- Attach quotations with punctuation.

If possible, use both to make your integration of quotations more interesting and varied.

Integrate quotations within the grammar of a sentence.   When you integrate a quotation into a sentence, the quotation must make grammatical sense and read as if it is part of the sentence:

> Fine, Weiss, and Powell (1998) expanded upon what others call "equal status contact theory" by using a "framework that draws on three traditionally independent literatures — those on community, difference, and democracy" (p. 37).

If you add words to the quotation, use square brackets around them to let readers know that the words are not original to the quotation:

> Smith and Wellner (2002) asserted that they "are not alone [in believing] that the facts have been incorrectly interpreted by Mancini" (p. 24).

If you omit any words in the middle of a quotation, use an **ellipsis**, three periods with spaces between them, to indicate the omission:

> Riquelme argues that "Eliot tries . . . to provide a definition by negations, which he also turns into positive terms that are meant to correct misconceptions" (156).

If you omit a sentence or more, make sure to put a period before the ellipsis points:

> Eagleton writes, "What Eliot was in fact assaulting was the whole ideology of middle-class liberalism. . . . Eliot's own solution is an extreme right-wing authoritarianism: men and women must sacrifice their petty 'personalities' and opinions to an impersonal order" (39).

Whatever you add (using square brackets) or omit (using ellipses), the sentence must read grammatically. And, of course, your additions and omissions must not distort the author's meaning.

Attach quotations with punctuation.   You also can attach a quotation to a sentence by using punctuation. For example, this passage attaches the run-in quotation with a colon:

> For these researchers, there needs to be recognition of differences in a way that will include and accept all students. Specifically, they asked: "Within multiracial settings, when are young people invited to discuss, voice, critique, and re-view the

very notions of race that feel so fixed, so hierarchical, so damaging, and so accepted in the broader culture?" (p. 132).

In conclusion, if you don't connect quotations to your argument, your readers may not understand why you've included them. You need to explain a significant point that each quotation reveals as you introduce or end it. This strategy helps readers know what to pay attention to in a quotation, particularly if the quotation is lengthy.

Steps to Integrating Quotations into Your Writing

1 **Take an active stance.** Your sources should contribute to your argument, not dictate its direction.

2 **Explain the quotations.** Explain what you quote so your readers understand how each quotation relates to your argument.

3 **Attach short quotations to your sentences.** Integrate short quotations within the grammar of your own sentences, or attach them with appropriate punctuation.

A Practice Sequence: Integrating Quotations

1 Using several of the sources you are working with in developing your paper, try integrating quotations into your essay. Be sure you are controlling your sources. Carefully read the paragraphs where you've used quotations. Will your readers clearly understand why the quotations are there — the points the quotations support? Do the sentences with quotations read smoothly? Are they grammatically correct?

2 Working in a small group, agree on a substantial paragraph or passage (from this book or some other source) to write about. Each member should read the passage and take a position on the ideas, and then draft a page that quotes the passage using both strategies for integrating these quotations. Compare what you've written, examining similarities and differences in the use of quotations.

AN ANNOTATED STUDENT RESEARCHED ARGUMENT: SYNTHESIZING SOURCES

The student who wrote the essay "A Greener Approach to Groceries: Community-Based Agriculture in LaSalle Square" did so in a first-year writing class that gave students the opportunity to do service in the local community. For this assignment, students were asked to explore debates about community and citizenship in contemporary America and to focus their research and writing on a social justice–related issue of their choice. The context of the course guided their inquiry as all the students in the course explored community service as a way to engage meaningfully and to develop relationships in the community.

We have annotated her essay to show the ways that she summarized and paraphrased research to show the urgency of the problem of food insecurity that exists around the world and to offer possible solutions. Notice how she synthesizes her sources, taking an active stance in using what she has read to advance her own argument.

Nancy Paul   Paul 1
Professor McLaughlin
English 2102
May 11, 20—

A Greener Approach to Groceries:
Community-Based Agriculture in LaSalle Square

In our post-9/11 society, there is incessant concern for   *1*
the security of our future. Billions of dollars are spent tighten-
ing borders, installing nuclear detectors, and adjudicating safety
measures so that the citizens of the United States can grow and
prosper without fear. Unfortunately, for some urban poor, the
threat from terrorism is minuscule compared to the cruelty of
their immediate environment. Far from the sands of the Afghan
plains and encapsulated in the midst of inner-city deterioration,
many find themselves in gray-lot deserts devoid of vegetation

The student's thesis and reliable food sources. Abandoned by corporate supermarkets, millions of Americans are maimed by a "food insecurity" —
the nutritional poverty that cripples them developmentally,
physically, and psychologically.

The midwestern city that surrounds our university has   *2*
a food-desert sitting just west of the famously lush campus.
Known as LaSalle Square, it was once home to the lucrative Ben-
dix plant and has featured both a Target and a Kroger supermar-

She calls attention ket in recent years. But previous economic development
to both the imme- decisions have driven both stores to the outskirts of town, and
diacy and urgency of without a local supplier, the only food available in the neighbor-
the problem hood is prepackaged and sold at the few small convenience
stores. This available food is virtually devoid of nutrition and

Paul 2

inhibits the ability of the poor to prosper and thrive. Thus, an aging strip mall, industrial site, and approximately three acres of an empty grass lot between the buildings anchor — and unfortunately define — the neighborhood.

She proposes a possible solution.

While there are multiple ways of providing food to the destitute, I am proposing a co-op of community gardens built on the grassy space in LaSalle Square and on smaller sites within the neighborhood, supplemented by extra crops from Michiana farmers, which would supply fresh fruit and vegetables to be sold or distributed to the poor. Together the co-op could meet the nutritional needs of the people, provide plenty of nutritious food, not cost South Bend any additional money, and contribute to neighborhood revitalization, yielding concrete increases in property values. Far from being a pipe dream, LaSalle Square already hosted an Urban Garden Market this fall, so a co-op would simply build upon the already recognized need and desire for healthy food in the area. Similar coalitions around the world are harnessing the power of community to remedy food insecurity without the aid of corporate enterprise, and South Bend is perfectly situated to reproduce and possibly exceed their successes.

She places her solution in a larger context to indicate its viability.

3

Many, myself previously included, believe that the large-volume, cheap industrialization of food and the welfare system have obliterated hunger in the United States. Supermarkets like Wal-Mart and Kroger seem ubiquitous in our communities, and it is difficult to imagine anyone being beyond their influence. However, profit-driven corporate business plans do not mix well with low-income, high-crime populations, and the gap between the two is growing wider. This polarization, combined with the vitamin deficiency of our high-fructose corn syrup society, has created food deserts in already struggling communities where malnutrition is the enemy *inconnu* of the urban poor.

4

More context

LaSalle Square's food insecurity is typical of many urban areas. The grocery stores that used to serve the neighborhood have relocated to more attractive real estate on the outskirts of the city, and only local convenience stores, stocking basic necessary items and tobacco products, remain profitable. Linda Wolfson, a member of the steering committee for the LaSalle

5

Paul 3

Square Redevelopment Plan, notes that if the community was fiscally healthy, it would be reasonable to expect the inhabitants to simply drive the six miles to the strip mall district, but unfortunately many are marginally employed and do not have access to cars. For them, it is economically irresponsible to spend the extra money to get to the supermarket, and so they feed their families on the cheap soda, chips, and processed food that are readily available at the convenience store. Especially since high-calorie, low-nutrient, packaged food tends to be denser, urban mothers find that it helps their children feel full (Garnett). Sadly, a health investigation released in 2006 concluded that by the age of three, more than one-third of urban children are obese, due in large part to the consumption of low-quality food obtained from corner stores (Smith). A recent analysis of urban stores in Detroit found that only 19% offer the healthy food array suggested by the FDA food pyramid (Brown and Carter 5). The food that is offered contains 25% less nutrient density, and consequently, underprivileged socioeconomic populations consume significantly lower levels of the micronutrients that form the foundation for proper protein and brain development. In a recent study of poor households, it was found that two-thirds of children were nutritionally poor and that more than 25% of women were deficient in iron, vitamin A, vitamin C, vitamin B6, thiamin, and riboflavin (Garnett). Of course, some may challenge the relevance of these vitamins and nutrients since they are not something the average person consciously incorporates into his or her diet on a daily basis. Yet modern research, examining the severely homogenous diets of the poor, has found severe developmental consequences associated with the lack of nutritional substance. For those afflicted, these deficiencies are not simply inconvenient, but actually exacerbate their plight and hinder their progress toward a sustainable lifestyle.

The human body is a complex system that cannot be sustained merely on the simple sugars and processed carbohydrates that comprise most cheap and filling foodstuffs, and research shows a relationship between nutritional deficiencies and a host of cognitive and developmental impairments that are prevalent

Synthesizing helps illustrate the extent of the problem and bolster her view that the poor suffer the most from the problem she identifies (Garnett; Smith; Brown and Carter).

Here she paraphrases findings.

6

Paul 4

Again she both sum-marizes and cites a relevant study to advance her argument.

in the undernourished families from urban America. Standard-ized tests of impoverished siblings, one of whom received nutri-tional supplements and the other who did not, showed cognitive gains in the well-nourished child as well as increased motor skills and greater interest in social interactions when compared to the other child. In the highly formative toddler years, under-nutrition can inhibit the myelination of nerve fibers, which is responsible for neurotransmitting and proper brain function. Collaborators Emily Tanner from the University of Oxford and Matia Finn-Stevenson from Yale University published a compre-hensive analysis of the link between nutrition and brain development in 2002. Their analysis, which they linked to social policy, indicated that a shortage of legumes and leafy green vegetables, which are nearly impossible to find in corner stores, is the leading cause of the iron-deficiency anemia afflicting 25% of urban children. This extreme form of anemia is characterized by impaired neurotransmission, weaker memory, and reduced attention span (Tanner and Finn-Stevenson 186). For those who do not have access to the vitamins, minerals, and micronutrients found in fruits and vegetables, these maladies are not distant risks, but constant, inescapable threats.

In light of these severe consequences of undernutrition, the term "food insecurity" encapsulates the condition wherein the economically disadvantaged are vulnerable simply because their bodies are unable to receive adequate fuel for optimal functioning. Just as one cannot expect a dry, parched plant to bloom and pollinate a garden, by constraining the development of individuals, food insecurity also constrains the development of the neighborhoods in which the individuals contribute. For the health of a city and its communities, all roadblocks to prog-ress must be removed, and food insecurity must be cut out at its roots so that individuals have the resources for advancement.

As socially conscious citizens and local governments have recognized the prevalence and danger of food insecurity in inner cities, there have been attempts at a remedy. Obviously, the easiest solution is simply to introduce a grocery store that would provide a variety of quality, healthful foods. However, for big-box supermarkets driven by the bottom line, urban areas are

Paul 5

less than desirable business locales from a standpoint of both profitability and maintenance. It is simply irrational for a supermarket to invest in an urban area with less revenue potential, size constraints, an unattractive locale, and an increased threat of theft and defacement when it is so easy to turn a profit in spacious and peaceful suburbia (Eisenhauer 131). Supermarkets must have significant incentive, beyond humanitarian ends, if they are to take the financial risk of entering a poor, urban marketplace.

She takes an active stance in citing initiatives that could be applied more effectively to alleviate the problem of food insecurity.

Certain cities are using the power of Tax Increment Financing (TIF) districts to encourage supermarkets to invest in urban centers. Under these redevelopment laws, tax revenues from retail development or other commercial enterprises are devoted, for a specified number of years, to infrastructural improvement of the district ("TIF Reform"). This approach has been effective in enticing new businesses; in fact, the exterior growth around South Bend is the result of a TIF district established in the late 1980s. LaSalle Square is currently part of a TIF district, but there is discussion as to how the TIF monies should best be applied (Wolfson). It may be possible to use the power of the TIF to encourage another large retailer such as Kroger to establish a presence in the square, but a smaller enterprise may be a better option. Experts indicate that for the destitute and food-insecure, reliance on a corporate entity is not optimal. Elizabeth Eisenhauer, a researcher from the State University of New York, investigated the interplay between supermarkets and

She paraphrases a researcher's findings.

the urban poor; she concluded that large big-box stores lack a commitment to the communities they serve and can be relied on only when it is clear they will make a profit, which may or may not happen when TIF benefits expire (131). Even when a portion of proceeds is used in the community, the majority of the cash flow from a supermarket is going to a corporate headquarters elsewhere, not directly supporting the surrounding neighborhood. Likewise, while some employees may be local, the highest-salary management positions are generally given to outsiders, making the stores and their employees set apart, rather than integrated into the neighborhood (Eisenhauer 130). Certainly a supermarket in an urban area will greatly contribute

Paul 6

to the reduction of food insecurity, but it is not the only available option, and the city of South Bend is ripe for alternative
solutions. The city is primed for a cooperative effort that could
shift the paradigm for urban renewal from a quick, corporate
solution, to a long-term enterprise built on community contributions and under local control.

Around the globe, many destitute urban areas have   10
found the means to reverse nutritional poverty through a literal
and figurative grassroots effort. In an effort to avoid packaged,
convenience store food, neighbors in the Bronx, San Francisco,
Los Angeles, London, and most successfully in Philadelphia,
have been planting their own crops right in the heart of the city
(Brown and Carter 3-4). Truly farming the food desert, coalitions that link community gardens, local farmers, and urban
markets are providing healthy, sustainable food sources without
a supermarket. Interestingly, in the process, such coalitions are
generating jobs, increasing property value, and, in some cases,
actually reversing the effects of poverty. The city of South Bend,
uniquely situated in the breadbasket of the United States, is
in the perfect position to launch a "greening" effort, modeled
after the successes in other parts of the world, which would
both solve the problem of food insecurity of LaSalle Square and
invigorate the local economy.

While modern Americans have the tendency to think that   11
food production should be, and always has been, industrialized,
countries around the world, especially economically disadvantaged nations, are exemplifying the possibilities of local gardening efforts. Far removed from industrial farms, Cubans grow half
their vegetables within the city; vacant land in Russian cities
produces 80% of the nation's vegetables, and specifically in
Moscow, 65% of families contribute to food production. Singapore has 10,000 urban farmers, and nearly half of the residents
of Vancouver grow food in their gardens (Brown and Carter 10).
These habits are not simply a novelty; rather, populations that
garden tend to be healthier, eating six out of the fourteen veg-
etable categories more regularly than non-gardeners and also
consuming fewer sweet and sugary foods per capita (Brown and
Carter 13). These data, compiled by the North American Urban

*She cites a num-
ber of examples as
evidence to demon-
strate the viability
of the solution she
offers.*

*The use of multiple
sources would make
her case even stron-
ger than using just
one source of infor-
mation, in this case
Brown and Carter.*

Paul 7

Agriculture Committee, were synthesized from the *Journal of Public Health Policy* and the *Journal of Nutrition Education* and show the interrelatedness of nutritional access and availability to healthy personal choices. While these trends toward health-ful lifestyles and gardening have been gaining ground slowly in the United States, when food insecurity and poverty take their toll, cities are finding that urban agriculture is an increasingly attractive and profitable alternative.

American communities have shown that creativity and collaboration can be quite effective at reversing food insecurity. The Garden Project of the Greater Lansing Food Bank has suc-cessfully combined gardening and Midwest access to local farms to bring food security to urban residents and senior citizens. Their eighteen community gardens and volunteers provide fresh fruits and vegetables year-round to low-income families, food pantries, the elderly, and social service organizations. Com-pletely bypassing the commercial market, the Garden Project has trained 500 families to grow their own food in backyard plots so that they can always have healthy food in the midst of the city (Brown and Carter 1). The gardens are supplemented by a process known as "gleaning," in which volunteers harvest extra crops from local farmers that would otherwise go to waste, and deliver it to residents of subsidized housing ("Gleaning"). In 2008 alone, the Garden Project actively involved 2,500 individ-ual gardeners and was able to provide over 250,000 pounds of produce from gleaning alone, plus the yields of the commu-nity plots that were used directly by the gardeners ("GLFB Facts"). This Lansing coalition serves over 5,000 individuals per month, yet only 4,400 reside under the poverty line in the LaSalle Square area (*City-Data.com*). If half of the inhabitants of LaSalle Square became engaged in the gardening effort, a similar collaboration could meet the needs of the region, and greater participation could yield an excess.

Similar efforts have demonstrated not only that inner-city food production is achievable but also that it can be cost-effective and self-sufficient, unlike a food bank. Frustrated by the inner-city downturn she describes as "an overgrown dog toilet," industrious London entrepreneur Julie Brown created a

She synthesizes sources to make her point.

12

13

Paul 8

community gardening company aimed at providing unmechanized, local, sustainable food. The company, Growing Communities, uses organic box gardens and small farms to supply more than 400 homes with weekly deliveries of organic fruits and vegetables. After a ten-year investment in local farmers and mini-gardens within the city, Growing Communities is now financially independent and generates over $400,000 per year (Willis 53). Compelled by both capitalism and social concern, Brown's efforts have shown that community-supported agriculture not only is possible but can be profitable as well! Our own community agriculture program should not be an entrepreneurial endeavor, but Brown's work in London indicates that it need not be a financial burden to the city either. Rather, the co-op would be financially self-sufficient, with the potential to generate revenues and fiscal growth in the city.

There are environmental factors that make South Bend an even better place to launch a profitable community agriculture program than London. Chiefly, South Bend has many more farms in the immediate vicinity than Ms. Brown could ever have dreamed of in the U.K. While Brown was limited to 25 local farms within 100 miles of the city, South Bend has over 50 farms within 25 miles of LaSalle Square (*Local Harvest*). Offering a broader production base creates more potential for profits by decreasing transportation time and increasing product, thereby making it easier for a coalition to become financially self-sufficient in a shorter time frame than Ms. Brown's ten-year plan.

14

Urban Philadelphia has led the way in demonstrating the profitability of community solutions to food insecurity through an offshoot of the Pennsylvania Horticultural Society (PHS) known as Philadelphia Greens. Since the 1970s, this coalition has reclaimed parks, planted trees, and created community gardens, both to revitalize the neighborhood and to serve the nutritionally and economically poor. Through a process that plants trees, builds wooden fences, and gardens the more than 1,000 vacant lots of Philadelphia, PHS combines housing projects and reclaimed space to "green" and reinvigorate the neighborhood ("The Effects"). Since LaSalle Square is essentially a large empty grassy area at the moment, a community agricul-

15

Paul 9

tural co-op should turn this vacant lot and others in the neighborhood into community gardens, which would work in tandem
with the gleaning from local farms. Similar to the Philadelphia
project, these gardens would simultaneously yield produce and
improve the appearance of the neighborhood.

One PHS project, in the New Kensington neighborhood of
north Philadelphia, was the subject of a recent socioeconomic
study conducted by the University of Pennsylvania's renowned
Wharton School of Business. In the New Kensington area,
PHS recently planted 480 new trees, cleaned 145 side yards,
developed 217 vacant lots, and established 15 new community
gardens. The effort was a model of the collaborative strategy
between PHS and the local community development corporation,
making it the ideal subject of the Wharton study. The findings,
published in 2004, showed significant increases in property values around the PHS greening projects and were the first step in
quantifying the fiscal returns of neighborhood greening beyond
the qualitative benefits of remedying food insecurity. After analyzing the sales records of thousands of New Kensington homes
between 1980 and 2003, the study reported that PHS greening
had led to a $4 million gain in property value from tree plant-
ings alone and a $12 million gain from vacant lot improvements.
Simply greening a vacant lot increased nearby property values
by as much as 30% ("Seeing Green"). While a supermarket might
modestly improve property values for those immediately near
the store, community greening involves multiple plots across an
area, benefiting many more people and properties. The Wharton
study showed that community greening would provide increases
in the value of any property near a green space, up to multiple
millions of dollars. The New Kensington neighborhood covers
1.4 square miles, which is approximately the size of LaSalle
Square, so while the overall property values are lower simply
because South Bend is a smaller city, the gains might be proportional (*City-Data.com*). It is reasonable to believe that cleaning
up LaSalle Square and planting gardens would quantitatively
benefit the fiscal situation of the city and increase assets of the
homeowners while subsequently improving the quality of life
over many acres.

16

She summarizes a study and then para-phrases.

Paul 10

Certainly there are challenges to the sort of dynami-
cal, community-based solution that I am proposing. Such an
agricultural co-op hinges on the participation of the people it
serves and cannot be successful without the dedicated support
of the neighborhood. It could be noted that lower-income economic groups are less socially involved than their higher-income
counterparts, and some might believe that they are unlikely to
contribute to, or care about, a greening effort. Yet I believe
that there is a distinction between political involvement and
neighborhood interaction. Middle-class Americans are conscious
of gas prices and the fluctuations of the stock market that affect
their job security and ability to provide for their families; yet
the unemployed poor without cars must rely on their neighborhoods to eke out a living. Their sustenance comes not from a
salary, but from odd jobs, welfare, and the munificence of fate.
The battle to put food on the table is more familiar to the poor
than foreign conflict and is one that they fight every day. Therefore, while the poor are less inclined to vote or worry about governmental affairs because of the difficulties associated simply
with daily living, they are acutely aware of their immediate surroundings and how those surroundings challenge or contribute
to their success. This position makes them uniquely inclined to
invest in the betterment of their surroundings since it can have
a dramatic effect on their personal lives. The real success of
the sustainable food movement may come from harnessing the
power of urban communities that can derive great, immediate,
and lasting benefit from neighborhood revitalization.

17

*In this paragraph,
she takes an active
stance in using
research to alleviate
fears that the local
community would
have to start from
scratch with limited
expertise.*

It has been argued that urban growers, especially from
lower socioeconomic classes, do not have the expertise or
knowledge base to generate successful yields that will ensure
food security. Fortunately, agriculture is Indiana's fourth-largest
industry, and the state boasts over 63,000 farms ("A Look"). In
addition to the many inhabitants of LaSalle Square who have a
background in agriculture, there is a wealth of knowledge about
proper planting methods available from the farmers around the
local area. Many of these farmers have already shown a willingness to help by selling or donating their produce to the local
Urban Market. Additionally, national urban agriculture nonprofit

18

Paul 11

groups, such as Master Gardening and Cooperative Extension,
offer free public education to cities beginning community
agriculture programs, and some will even perform on-site training (Brown and Carter 16). By harnessing the assets of local,
gratuitous knowledge and supplementing that knowledge with
national support groups, South Bend has multiple resources
available to train and encourage its burgeoning urban farmers.

    The economic and nutritional gains of the people would
only be heightened by the personal well-being that is born of
interpersonal collaboration that crosses racial and social boundaries. Such an effort is ambitious; it will indeed require the time
and talents of many people who care about the health of their
community. But the local community is rich with the necessary
seeds for such a project, which may, in time, blossom and grow
to feed its people.

19

Paul 12

Works Cited

Brown, Katherine H., and Anne Carter. *Urban Agriculture and Com-
munity Food Security in the United States: Farming from the City
Center to the Urban Fringe*. Venice, CA: Community Food Security
Coalition, Oct. 2003. PDF file.

City-Data.com. Advameg, 2008. Web. 16 Apr. 20—.

"The Effects of Neighborhood Greening." *PHS*. Pennsylvania Horticultural Society, Jan. 2001. Web. 8 Apr. 20—.

Eisenhauer, Elizabeth. "In Poor Health: Supermarket Redlining and
Urban Nutrition." *GeoJournal* 53.2 (2001): 125-33. Print.

Garnett, Tara. "Farming the City." *Ecologist* 26.6 (1996): 299. *Academic Search Premier*. Web. 8 Apr. 20—.

"Gleaning." *Greater Lansing Food Bank*. Greater Lansing Food Bank,
n.d. Web. 15 Apr. 20—.

"GLFB Facts." *Greater Lansing Food Bank*. Greater Lansing Food Bank,
2005. Web. 15 Apr. 20—.

Paul 13

Local Harvest. LocalHarvest, 2008. Web. 15 Apr. 20—.

"A Look at Indiana Agriculture." *Agriculture in the Classroom*. USDA-
    CSREES, n.d. PDF file.

"Seeing Green: Study Finds Greening Is a Good Investment." *PHS*.
    Pennsylvania Horticultural Society, 2005. Web. 8 Apr. 20—.

Smith, Stephen. "Obesity Battle Starts Young for Urban Poor." *Boston
    Globe*. NY Times, 29 Dec. 2006. Web. 18 Apr. 20—.

Tanner, Emily M., and Matia Finn-Stevenson. "Nutrition and Brain
    Development: Social Policy Implications." *American Journal of
    Orthopsychiatry* 72.2 (2002): 182-93. *Academic Search Premier*.
    Web. 8 Apr. 20—.

"TIF Reform." *New Rules Project*. Institute for Local Self-Reliance,
    2008. Web. 15 Apr. 20—.

Willis, Ben. "Julie Brown of Growing Communities." *The Ecologist*
    June 2008: 52-55. Print.

Wolfson, Linda. Personal interview. 20 Apr. 20—.

From Ethos to Logos
Appealing to Your Readers

Who you believe your readers are influences how you see a particular situation, define an issue, explain the ongoing conversation surrounding that issue, and formulate a question. You may need to read widely to understand how different writers have dealt with the issue you address. And you will need to anticipate how others might respond to your argument—whether they will be sympathetic or antagonistic—and to compose your essay so that readers will "listen" whether or not they agree with you.

To achieve these goals, you will no doubt use reason in the form of evidence to sway readers. But you can also use other means of persuasion: That is, you can use your own character, by presenting yourself as someone who is knowledgeable, fair, and just; and you can appeal to your readers' emotions. Although you may believe that reason alone should provide the means for changing people's minds, people's emotions also color the way they see the world.

Your audience is more than your immediate reader, your instructor or a peer. Your audience encompasses those you cite in writing about an issue and those you anticipate responding to your argument. This is true no matter what you write about, whether it be an interpretation of the novels of a particular author, an analysis of the cultural work of horror films, the ethics of treating boys and girls differently in schools, or the moral issues surrounding homelessness in America.

In this chapter we discuss different ways of engaging your readers, centering on three kinds of appeals: **ethos**, appeals from character; **pathos**, appeals to emotion; and **logos**, appeals to reason. *Ethos*, *pathos*, and *logos*

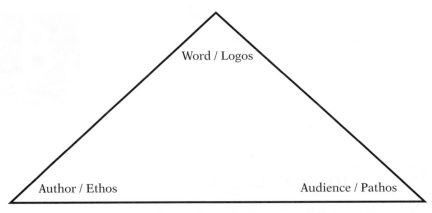

FIGURE 8.1   The Rhetorical Triangle

are terms derived from ancient Greek writers, but they are still of great value today when considering how to persuade your audience. Readers will judge your argument on whether or not you present an argument that is fair and just, one that creates a sense of goodwill. All three appeals rely on these qualities.

Figure 8.1, the **rhetorical triangle**, visually represents the interrelationship among ethos, pathos, and logos. Who we think our readers are (pathos: which of their emotions do we appeal to?) influences decisions about the ways we should represent ourselves to them (ethos: how can we come across as fair, credible, and just?). In turn, we use certain patterns of argument (logos: how do we arrange our words to make our case?) that reflect our interpretation of the situation to which we respond and that we believe will persuade readers to accept our point of view. Effective communication touches on each of the three points of the triangle. Your task as a writer is to determine the proper balance of these different appeals in your argument, based on your thesis, the circumstances, and your audience.

CONNECTING WITH READERS: A SAMPLE ARGUMENT

To see how an author connects with his audience, read the following excerpt from James W. Loewen's book *Lies My Teacher Told Me: Everything Your American History Textbook Got Wrong.* As you read the excerpt, note Loewen's main points, and select key examples that illustrate his argument. As a class, test the claims he makes: To what extent do you believe that what Loewen argues is true? This may entail recalling your own experiences in high school history classes or locating one or more of the books that Loewen mentions.

JAMES W. LOEWEN

The Land of Opportunity

In addition to *Lies My Teacher Told Me* (1995), James Loewen, who holds
a PhD in sociology, has written several other books, including *Lies Across
America: What Our Historic Sites Get Wrong* (1999) and *Sundown Towns: A
Hidden Dimension of American Racism* (2005). As the titles of these books
suggest, Loewen is a writer who questions the assumptions about history
that many people take for granted. This is especially true of the following
excerpt, from a chapter in which Loewen challenges a common American
belief—that everyone has an equal chance in what he calls the "land of
opportunity"—by arguing that we live in a class system that privileges
some people and raises barriers for others. History textbook writers, he
points out, are guilty of complicity in this class system because they leave
a great deal of history out of their textbooks.

High school students have eyes, ears, and television sets (all too many
have their own TV sets), so they know a lot about relative privilege
in America. They measure their family's social position against that of
other families, and their community's position against other communities. Middle-class students, especially, know little about how the American class structure works, however, and nothing at all about how it has
changed over time. These students do not leave high school merely ignorant of the workings of the class structure; they come out as terrible
sociologists. "Why are people poor?" I have asked first-year college students. Or, if their own class position is one of relative privilege, "Why is
your family well off?" The answers I've received, to characterize them
charitably, are half-formed and naïve. The students blame the poor for
not being successful. They have no understanding of the ways that
opportunity is not equal in America and no notion that social structure
pushes people around, influencing the ideas they hold and the lives they
fashion.

High school history textbooks can take some of the credit for this
state of affairs. Some textbooks cover certain high points of labor history,
such as the 1894 Pullman strike near Chicago that President Cleveland
broke with federal troops, or the 1911 Triangle Shirtwaist fire that killed
146 women in New York City, but the most recent event mentioned in
most books is the Taft-Hartley Act of fifty years ago. No book mentions
the Hormel meat-packers' strike in the mid-1980s or the air traffic con-
trollers' strike broken by President Reagan. Nor do textbooks describe
any continuing issues facing labor, such as the growth of multinational
corporations and their exporting of jobs overseas. With such omissions,
textbook authors can construe labor history as something that happened
long ago, like slavery, and that, like slavery, was corrected long ago. It logically follows that unions appear anachronistic. The idea that they might

be necessary in order for workers to have a voice in the workplace goes unstated.

Textbooks' treatments of events in labor history are never anchored   3
in any analysis of social class. This amounts to delivering the footnotes instead of the lecture! Six of the dozen high school American history textbooks I examined contain no index listing at all for "social class," "social stratification," "class structure," "income distribution," "inequality," or any conceivably related topic. Not one book lists "upper class," "working class," or "lower class." Two of the textbooks list "middle class," but only to assure students that America is a middle-class country. "Except for slaves, most of the colonists were members of the 'middling ranks,'" says *Land of Promise*, and nails home the point that we are a middle-class country by asking students to "Describe three 'middle-class' values that united free Americans of all classes." Several of the textbooks note the explosion of middle-class suburbs after World War II. Talking about the middle class is hardly equivalent to discussing social stratification, however; in fact, as Gregory Mantsios has pointed out, "such references appear to be acceptable precisely because they mute class differences."

Stressing how middle-class we all are is particularly problematic to-   4
day, because the proportion of households earning between 75 percent and 125 percent of the median income has fallen steadily since 1967. The Reagan-Bush administrations accelerated this shrinkage of the middle class, and most families who left its ranks fell rather than rose. This is the kind of historical trend one would think history books would take as appropriate subject matter, but only four of the twelve books in my sample provide any analysis of social stratification in the United States. Even these fragmentary analyses are set mostly in colonial America. *Land of Promise* lives up to its reassuring title by heading its discussion of social class "Social Mobility." "One great difference between colonial and European society was that the colonists had more social mobility," echoes *The American Tradition*. "In contrast with contemporary Europe, eighteenth-century America was a shining land of equality and opportunity—with the notorious exception of slavery," chimes in *The American Pageant*. Although *The Challenge of Freedom* identifies three social classes—upper, middle, and lower—among whites in colonial society, compared to Europe "there was greater *social mobility.*"

Never mind that the most violent class conflicts in American history—   5
Bacon's Rebellion and Shays's Rebellion—took place in and just after colonial times. Textbooks still say that colonial society was relatively classless and marked by upward mobility. And things have gotten rosier since. "By 1815," *The Challenge of Freedom* assures us, two classes had withered away and "America was a country of middle class people and of middle class goals." This book returns repeatedly, at intervals of every fifty years or so, to the theme of how open opportunity is in America. "In the years after 1945, *social mobility*—movement from one social class

to another—became more widespread in America," *Challenge* concludes. "This meant that people had a better chance to move upward in society." The stress on upward mobility is striking. There is almost nothing in any of these textbooks about class inequalities or barriers of any kind to social mobility. "What conditions made it possible for poor white immigrants to become richer in the colonies?" *Land of Promise* asks. "What conditions made/make it difficult?" goes unasked. Textbook authors thus present an America in which, as preachers were fond of saying in the nineteenth century, men start from "humble origins" and attain "the most elevated positions."

Social class is probably the single most important variable in society. 6 From womb to tomb, it correlates with almost all other social characteristics of people that we can measure. Affluent expectant mothers are more likely to get prenatal care, receive current medical advice, and enjoy general health, fitness, and nutrition. Many poor and working-class mothers-to-be first contact the medical profession in the last month, sometimes the last hours, of their pregnancies. Rich babies come out healthier and weighing more than poor babies. The infants go home to very different situations. Poor babies are more likely to have high levels of poisonous lead in their environments and their bodies. Rich babies get more time and verbal interaction with their parents and higher quality day care when not with their parents. When they enter kindergarten, and through the twelve years that follow, rich children benefit from suburban schools that spend two to three times as much money per student as schools in inner cities or impoverished rural areas. Poor children are taught in classes that are often 50 percent larger than the classes of affluent children. Differences such as these help account for the higher school-dropout rate among poor children.

Even when poor children are fortunate enough to attend the same 7 school as rich children, they encounter teachers who expect only children of affluent families to know the right answers. Social science research shows that teachers are often surprised and even distressed when poor children excel. Teachers and counselors believe they can predict who is "college material." Since many working-class children give off the wrong signals, even in first grade, they end up in the "general education" track in high school. "If you are the child of low-income parents, the chances are good that you will receive limited and often careless attention from adults in your high school," in the words of Theodore Sizer's best-selling study of American high schools, *Horace's Compromise*. "If you are the child of upper-middle-income parents, the chances are good that you will receive substantial and careful attention." Researcher Reba Page has provided vivid accounts of how high school American history courses use rote learning to turn off lower-class students. Thus schools have put into practice Woodrow Wilson's recommendation: "We want one class of persons to have a liberal education, and we want another class of persons, a very much larger class of necessity in every society, to forgo the privilege of a liberal education and fit themselves to perform specific difficult manual tasks."

As if this unequal home and school life were not enough, rich teenagers then enroll in the Princeton Review or other coaching sessions for the Scholastic Aptitude Test. Even without coaching, affluent children are advantaged because their background is similar to that of the testmakers, so they are comfortable with the vocabulary and subtle subcultural assumptions of the test. To no one's surprise, social class correlates strongly with SAT scores.   8

All these are among the reasons why social class predicts the rate of college attendance and the type of college chosen more effectively than does any other factor, including intellectual ability, however measured. After college, most affluent children get white-collar jobs, most workingclass children get blue-collar jobs, and the class differences continue. As adults, rich people are more likely to have hired an attorney and to be a member of formal organizations that increase their civic power. Poor people are more likely to watch TV. Because affluent families can save some money while poor families must spend what they make, wealth differences are ten times larger than income differences. Therefore most poor and working-class families cannot accumulate the down payment required to buy a house, which in turn shuts them out from our most important tax shelter, the write-off of home mortgage interest. Workingclass parents cannot afford to live in elite subdivisions or hire high-quality day care, so the process of educational inequality replicates itself in the next generation. Finally, affluent Americans also have longer life expectancies than lower- and working-class people, the largest single cause of which is better access to health care. Echoing the results of Helen Keller's study of blindness, research has determined that poor health is not distributed randomly about the social structure but is concentrated in the lower class. Social Security then becomes a huge transfer system, using monies contributed by all Americans to pay benefits disproportionately to longer-lived affluent Americans.   9

Ultimately, social class determines how people think about social class. When asked if poverty in America is the fault of the poor or the fault of the system, 57 percent of business leaders blamed the poor; just 9 percent blamed the system. Labor leaders showed sharply reversed choices: only 15 percent said the poor were at fault while 56 percent blamed the system. (Some replied "don't know" or chose a middle position.) The largest single difference between our two main political parties lies in how their members think about social class: 55 percent of Republicans blamed the poor for their poverty, while only 13 percent blamed the system for it; 68 percent of Democrats, on the other hand, blamed the system, while only 5 percent blamed the poor.   10

Few of these statements are news, I know, which is why I have not documented most of them, but the majority of high school students do not   11 know or understand these ideas. Moreover, the processes have changed over time, for the class structure in America today is not the same as it was in 1890, let alone in colonial America. Yet in *Land of Promise*, for example, social class goes unmentioned after 1670.

Reading as a Writer

1. List what you think are Loewen's main points. What appeals does he seem to draw on most when he makes those points: appeals based on his own character (ethos), on the emotions of his reader (pathos), or on the reasonableness of his evidence (logos)? Are the appeals obvious or difficult to tease out? Does he combine them? Discuss your answers with your classmates.

2. Identify what you think is the main claim of Loewen's argument, and choose key examples to support your answer. Compare your chosen claim and examples to those chosen by your classmates. Do they differ significantly? Can you agree on Loewen's gist and his key examples?

3. As a class, test the claims Loewen makes by thinking about your own experiences in high school history classes. Do you remember finding out that something you were taught from an American history textbook was not true? Did you discover on your own what you considered to be misrepresentations in or important omissions from your textbook? If so, did these misrepresentations or omissions tend to support or contradict the claims about history textbooks that Loewen makes?

APPEALING TO ETHOS

Although we like to believe that our decisions and beliefs are based on reason and logic, in fact they are often based on what amounts to character judgments. That is, if a person you trust makes a reasonable argument for one choice, and a person you distrust makes a reasonable argument for another choice, you are more likely to be swayed by the argument of the person you trust. Similarly, the audience for your argument will be more disposed to agree with you if its members believe you are a fair, just person who is knowledgeable and has good judgment. Even the most well-developed argument will fall short if you do not leave this kind of impression on your readers. Thus, it is not surprising that ethos may be the most important component of your argument.

There are three strategies for evoking a sense of ethos:

1. Establish that you have good judgment.
2. Convey to readers that you are knowledgeable.
3. Show that you understand the complexity of the issue.

These strategies are interrelated: A writer who demonstrates good judgment is more often than not someone who is both knowledgeable about an issue and who acknowledges the complexity of it by weighing the strengths *and* weaknesses of different arguments. However, keep in mind that these characteristics do not exist apart from what readers think and believe.

■ Establish That You Have Good Judgment

Most readers of academic writing expect writers to demonstrate good judgment by identifying a problem that readers agree is worth addressing. In turn, good judgment gives writers credibility.

Loewen crafts his introduction to capture the attention of educators as well as concerned citizens when he claims that students leave high school unaware of class structure and as a consequence "have no understanding of the ways that opportunity is not equal in America and no notion that social structure pushes people around, influencing the ideas they hold and the lives they may fashion" (para. 1). Loewen does not blame students, or even instructors, for this lack of awareness. Instead, he writes, "textbooks can take some of the credit for this state of affairs" (para. 2) because, among other shortcomings, they leave out important events in "labor history" and relegate issues facing labor to the past.

Whether an educator—or a general reader for that matter—will ultimately agree with Loewen's case is, at this point, up for grabs, but certainly the possibility that high schools in general, and history textbooks in particular, are failing students by leaving them vulnerable to class-based manipulation would be recognized as a problem by readers who believe America should be a society that offers equal opportunity for all. At this point, Loewen's readers are likely to agree that the problem of omission he identifies may be significant if its consequences are as serious as he believes them to be.

Writers also establish good judgment by conveying to readers that they are fair-minded and just and have the best interests of readers in mind. Loewen is particularly concerned that students understand the persistence of poverty and inequality in the United States and the historical circumstances of the poor, which they cannot do unless textbook writers take a more inclusive approach to addressing labor history, especially "the growth of multinational corporations and their exporting of jobs overseas" (para. 2). It's not fair to deny this important information to students, and it's not fair to the poor to leave them out of official histories of the United States. Loewen further demonstrates that he is fair and just when he calls attention in paragraph 6 to the inequality between rich and poor children in schools, a problem that persists despite our forebears' belief that class would not determine the fate of citizens of the United States.

■ Convey to Readers That You Are Knowledgeable

Being thoughtful about a subject goes hand in hand with being knowledgeable about the subject. Loewen demonstrates his knowledge of class issues and their absence from textbooks in a number of ways (not the least of which is his awareness that a problem exists—many people, including educators, may not be aware of this problem).

In paragraph 3, Loewen makes a bold claim: "Textbooks' treatments of events in labor history are never anchored in any analysis of social class." As readers, we cannot help wondering: How does the author know this? How will he support this claim? Loewen anticipates these questions by demonstrating that he has studied the subject through a systematic examination of American history textbooks. He observes that six of the twelve textbooks he examined "contain no index listing at all for 'social class,' 'social stratification,' 'class structure,' 'income distribution,' 'inequality,' or any conceivably related topic" and that "not one book lists 'upper class,' 'working class,' or 'lower class.'" Loewen also demonstrates his grasp of class issues in American history, from the "violent class conflicts" that "took place in and just after colonial times" (para. 5), which contradict textbook writers' assertions that class conflicts did not exist during this period, to the more recent conflicts in the 1980s and early 1990s (paras. 2 and 4).

Moreover, Loewen backs up his own study of textbooks with references to a number of studies from the social sciences to illustrate that "social class is probably the single most important variable in society" (para. 6). Witness the statistics and findings he cites in paragraphs 6 through 10. The breadth of Loewen's historical knowledge and the range of his reading should convince readers that he is knowledgeable, and his trenchant analysis contributes to the authority he brings to the issue and to his credibility.

■ Show That You Understand the Complexity of a Given Issue

Recognizing the complexity of an issue helps readers see the extent to which authors know that any issue can be understood in a number of different ways. Loewen acknowledges that most of the history he recounts is not "news" (para. 11) to his educated readers, who by implication "know" and "understand" his references to historical events and trends. What may be news to his readers, he explains, is the extent to which class structure in the United States has changed over time. With the steady erosion of middle-class households since 1967, "class inequalities" and "barriers . . . to social mobility" (para. 5) are limiting more and more Americans' access to even the most fundamental of opportunities in a democratic society—health care and education.

Still, even though Loewen has introduced new thinking about the nature of class in the United States and has demonstrated a provocative play of mind by examining an overlooked body of data (high school history textbooks) that may influence the way class is perceived in America, there are still levels of complexity he hasn't addressed explicitly. Most important, perhaps, is the question of why history textbooks continue to ignore issues of class when there is so much research that indicates its importance in shaping the events history textbooks purport to explain.

Steps to Appealing to Ethos

1 **Establish that you have good judgment.** Identify an issue your readers will agree is worth addressing, and demonstrate that you are fair-minded and have the best interests of your readers in mind when you address it.

2 **Convey to readers that you are knowledgeable.** Support your claims with credible evidence that shows you have read widely on, thought about, and understand the issue.

3 **Show that you understand the complexity of the issue.** Demonstrate that you understand the variety of viewpoints your readers may bring—or may not be able to bring—to the issue.

APPEALING TO PATHOS

An appeal to pathos recognizes that people are moved to action by their emotions as well as by reasonable arguments. In fact, pathos is a vital part of argument that can predispose readers one way or another. Do you want to arouse readers' sympathy? Anger? Passion? You can do that by knowing what readers value.

Appeals to pathos are typically indirect. You can appeal to pathos by using examples or illustrations that you believe will arouse the appropriate emotions and by presenting them using an appropriate tone.

To acknowledge that writers play on readers' emotions is not to endorse manipulative writing. Rather, it is to acknowledge that effective writers use all available means of persuasion to move readers to agree with them. After all, if your thoughtful reading and careful research have led you to believe that you must weigh in with a useful insight on an important issue, it stands to reason that you would want your argument to convince your readers to believe as strongly in what you assert as you do.

For example, if you genuinely believe that the conditions some families are living in are abysmal and unfair, you want your readers to believe it too. And an effective way to persuade them to believe as you do, in addition to convincing them of the reasonableness of your argument and of your own good character and judgment, is to establish a kind of emotional common ground in your writing—the common ground of pathos.

▪ Show That You Know What Your Readers Value

Let's consider some of the ways James Loewen signals that he knows what his readers value.

In the first place, Loewen assumes that readers feel the same way he does: Educated people should know that the United States has a class structure despite the democratic principles that the nation was founded on. He also expects readers to identify with his unwillingness to accept the injustice that results from that class structure. He believes that women living in poverty should have access to appropriate health care, that children living in poverty should have a chance to attend college, and that certain classes of people should not be written off to "perform specific difficult manual tasks" (para. 7).

Time and again, Loewen cites examples that reveal that the poor are discriminated against by the class structure in the United States not for lack of ability, lack of desire, lack of ambition, or lack of morality, but for no better reason than lack of money—and that such discrimination has been going on for a long time. He expects that his readers also will find such discrimination an unacceptable affront to their values of fair play and democracy and that they will experience the same sense of outrage that he does.

▪ Use Illustrations and Examples That Appeal to Readers' Emotions

You can appeal to readers' emotions indirectly through the illustrations and examples you use to support your argument.

For instance, in paragraph 2, Loewen contends that textbook writers share responsibility for high school students' not knowing about the continued relevance of class issues in American life. Loewen's readers— parents, educators, historians—may very well be angered by the omissions he points out. Certainly he would expect them to be angry when they read about the effects of economic class on the health care expectant mothers and then their children receive (para. 6) and on their children's access to quality education (paras. 6–8). In citing the fact that social class "correlates strongly with SAT scores" (para. 8) and so "predicts the rate of college attendance and the type of college chosen" (para. 9), Loewen forces his readers to acknowledge that the educational playing field is far from level.

Finally, he calls attention to the fact that accumulated wealth accounts for deep class divisions in our society—that their inability to save prevents the poor from hiring legal counsel, purchasing a home, or taking advantage of tax shelters. The result, Loewen observes, is that "educational inequality replicates itself in the next generation" (para. 9).

Together, these examples strengthen both Loewen's argument and what he hopes will be readers' outrage that history textbooks do not address class issues. Without that information, Americans cannot fully understand or act to change the existing class structure.

▪ Consider How Your Tone May Affect Your Audience

The **tone** of your writing is your use of language that communicates your attitude toward yourself, your material, and your readers. Of course, your tone is important in everything you write, but it is particularly crucial when you are appealing to pathos.

When you are appealing to your readers' emotions, it is tempting to use loaded, exaggerated, and even intemperate language to convey how you feel (and hope your readers will feel) about an issue. Consider these sentences: "The Republican Party has devised the most ignominious means of filling the pockets of corporations." "These wretched children suffer heartrending agonies that can barely be imagined, much less described." "The ethereal beauty of the Brandenburg concertos thrill one to the deepest core of one's being." All of these sentences express strong and probably sincere beliefs and emotions, but some readers might find them overwrought and coercive and question the writer's reasonableness.

Similarly, some writers rely on irony or sarcasm to set the tone of their work. **Irony** is the use of language to say one thing while meaning quite another. **Sarcasm** is the use of heavy-handed irony to ridicule or attack someone or something. Although irony and sarcasm can make for vivid and entertaining writing, they also can backfire and end up alienating readers. The sentence "Liberals will be pleased to hear that the new budget will be making liberal use of their hard-earned dollars" may entertain some readers with its irony and wordplay, but others may assume that the writer's attitude toward liberals is likely to result in an unfairly slanted argument. And the sentence "In my opinion, there's no reason why Christians and Muslims shouldn't rejoice together over the common ground of their both being deluded about the existence of a God" may please some readers, but it risks alienating those who are uncomfortable with breezy comments about religious beliefs. Again, think of your readers and what they value, and weigh the benefits of a clever sentence against its potential to detract from your argument or offend your audience.

You often find colorful wording and irony in op-ed and opinion pieces, where a writer may not have the space to build a compelling argument using evidence and has to resort to shortcuts to readers' emotions. However, in academic writing, where the careful accumulation and presentation of evidence and telling examples are highly valued, the frequent use of loaded language, exaggeration, and sarcasm is looked on with distrust.

Consider Loewen's excerpt. Although his outrage comes through clearly, he never resorts to hectoring. For example, in paragraph 1, he writes that students are "ignorant of the workings of the class structure" and that their opinions are "half-formed and naïve." But he does not imply that students are ignoramuses or that their opinions are foolish. What they lack, he contends, is understanding. They need to be taught something about class structure that they are not now being taught. And paragraph 1 is about as close to name-calling as Loewen comes. Even textbook writers, who are the target of his anger, are not vilified.

Loewen does occasionally make use of irony, for example in paragraph 5, where he points out inconsistencies and omissions in textbooks: "Never mind that the most violent class conflicts in American history— Bacon's Rebellion and Shays's Rebellion—took place in and just after colonial times. Textbooks still say that colonial society was relatively classless and marked by upward mobility. And things have gotten rosier since." But he doesn't resort to ridicule. Instead, he relies on examples and illustrations to connect with his readers' sense of values and appeal to their emotions.

Steps to Appealing to Pathos

1 **Show that you know what your readers value.** Start from your own values and imagine what assumptions and principles would appeal to your readers. What common ground can you imagine between your values and theirs? How will it need to be adjusted for different kinds of readers?

2 **Use illustrations and examples that appeal to readers' emotions.** Again, start from your own emotional position. What examples and illustrations resonate most with you? How can you present them to have the most emotional impact on your readers? How would you adjust them for different kinds of readers?

3 **Consider how your tone may affect your audience.** Be wary of using loaded, exaggerated, and intemperate language that may put off your readers; and be careful in your use of irony and sarcasm.

A Practice Sequence: Appealing to Ethos and Pathos

Discuss the language and strategies the writers use in the following passages to connect with their audience, in particular their appeals to both ethos and pathos. After reading each excerpt, discuss who you think the implied audience is and whether you think the strategies the writers use to connect with their readers are effective or not.

1 Almost a half century after the U.S. Supreme Court concluded that Southern school segregation was unconstitutional and "inherently unequal," new statistics from the 1998–99 school year show that segregation continued to intensify throughout the 1990s, a period in which there were three major Supreme Court decisions authorizing a return to segregated neighborhood schools and limiting the reach and duration of desegregation orders. For African American students, this trend is particularly apparent in the South, where most blacks live and where the 2000 Census shows a

continuing return from the North. From 1988 to 1998, most of the progress of the previous two decades in increasing integration in the region was lost. The South is still much more integrated than it was before the civil rights revolution, but it is moving backward at an accelerating rate.

— GARY ORFIELD, "Schools More Separate: Consequences of a Decade of Resegregation"

2 No issue has been more saturated with dishonesty than the issue of racial quotas and preferences, which is now being examined by the Supreme Court of the United States. Many defenders of affirmative action are not even honest enough to admit that they are talking about quotas and preferences, even though everyone knows that that is what affirmative action amounts to in practice.

Despite all the gushing about the mystical benefits of "diversity" in higher education, a recent study by respected academic scholars found that "college diversity programs fail to raise standards" and that "a majority of faculty members and administrators recognize this when speaking anonymously."

This study by Stanley Rothman, Seymour Martin Lipset, and Neil Nevitte found that "of those who think that preferences have some impact on academic standards those believing it negative exceed those believing it positive by 15 to 1."

Poll after poll over the years has shown that most faculty members and most students are opposed to double standards in college admissions. Yet professors who will come out publicly and say what they say privately in these polls are as rare as hens' teeth.

Such two-faced talk is pervasive in academia and elsewhere. A few years ago, in Berkeley, there was a big fight over whether a faculty vote on affirmative action would be by secret ballot or open vote. Both sides knew that the result of a secret ballot would be the direct opposite of the result in a public vote at a faculty meeting.

— THOMAS SOWELL, "The Grand Fraud: Affirmative Action for Blacks"

3 When the judgment day comes for every high school student — that day when a final transcript is issued and sent to the finest institutions, with every sin of class selection written as with a burning chisel on stone — on that day a great cry will go up throughout the land, and there will be weeping, wailing, gnashing of teeth, and considerable grumbling against guidance counselors, and the cry of a certain senior might be, "WHY did no one tell me that Introduction to Social Poker wasn't a solid academic class?" At another, perhaps less wealthy school, a frustrated and under-nurtured sculptress will wonder, "Why can't I read, and why don't I care?" The reason for both of these oversights, as they may eventually discover, is that the idea of the elective course has been seriously mauled, mistreated, and abused under the current middle-class high school system. A significant amount of the blame for producing students who are stunted, both cognitively and morally, can be traced back to this pervasive fact. Elective courses, as shoddily planned and poorly funded as they may be, constitute the only formation that many students get in their own special types of intelligences. Following the model of Howard Gardner, these may be spatial, musical, or something else. A lack of stimulation to a student's own intelligence directly causes a lack of identification with the intelligence of others. Instead of becoming moderately interested in a subject by noticing the pleasure other people receive from it, the student will be bitter, jealous, and without empathy. These are the common ingredients in many types of tragedy, violent or benign. Schools must take responsibility for speaking in some way to each of the general types of intelligences. Failure to do so will result in students who lack skills, and also the inspiration to comfort, admire, emulate, and aid their fellow humans.

"All tasks that really call upon the power of attention are interesting for the same reason and to an almost equal degree," wrote Simone Weil in her *Reflections on Love and Faith*, her editor having defined attention as "a suspension of one's own self as a center of the world and making oneself available to the reality of another being." In Parker Palmer's *The Courage to Teach*, modern scientific theorist David Bohm describes "a holistic underlying implicate order whose information unfolds into the explicate order of particular fields." Rilke's euphemism for this "holistic . . . implicate order," which Palmer borrows, is "the grace of great things." Weil's term would be "God." However, both agree that eventual perception of this singular grace, or God, is accessible through education of a specific sort, and for both it is doubtless the most necessary experience of a lifetime. Realizing that this contention is raining down from different theorists, and keeping in mind that the most necessary experience of a lifetime should not be wholly irrelevant to the school system, educators should therefore reach the conclusion that this is a matter worth looking into. I assert that the most fruitful and practical results of their attention will be a wider range of electives coupled with a new acknowledgment and handling of them, one that treats each one seriously.

—ERIN MEYERS,
"The Educational Smorgasbord as Saving Grace"

APPEALING TO LOGOS: USING REASON AND EVIDENCE TO FIT THE SITUATION

To make an argument persuasive, you need to be in dialogue with your readers, using your own character (ethos) to demonstrate that you are a reasonable, credible, fair person and appealing to your readers' emotions (pathos), particularly their sense of right and wrong. Both types of appeal go hand in hand with appeals to logos, using converging pieces of evidence—statistics, facts, observations—to advance your claim. Remember that the type of evidence you use is determined by the issue, problem, situation, and readers' expectations. As an author, you should try to anticipate and address readers' beliefs and values. Ethos and pathos are concerned with the content of your argument; logos addresses both form and content.

An argument begins with one or more premises and ends with a conclusion. A **premise** is an assumption that you expect your readers to agree with, a statement that is either true or false—for example, "Alaska is cold in the winter"—that is offered in support of a claim. That claim is the **conclusion** you want your readers to draw from your premises. The conclusion is also a sentence that is either true or false.

For instance, Loewen's major premise is that class is a key factor in Americans' access to health care, education, and wealth. Loewen also offers a second, more specific premise: that textbook writers provide little discussion of the ways class matters. Loewen crafts his argument to help readers draw the following conclusion: "We live in a class system that runs counter to the democratic principles that underlie the founding of the United States, and history textbooks must tell this story. Without this knowledge, citizens will be uninformed."

Whether readers accept this as true depends on how Loewen moves from his initial premises to reach his conclusion—that is, whether we draw the same kinds of inferences, or reasoned judgments, that he does. He must do so in a way that meets readers' expectations of what constitutes relevant and persuasive evidence and guides them one step at a time toward his conclusion.

There are two main forms of argument: deductive and inductive. A **deductive argument** is an argument in which the premises support (or appear to support) the conclusion. If you join two premises to produce a conclusion that is taken to be true, you are stating a **syllogism**. This is the classic example of deductive reasoning through a syllogism:

1. All men are mortal. (First premise)
2. Socrates is a man. (Second premise)
3. Therefore, Socrates is mortal. (Conclusion)

In a deductive argument, it is impossible for both premises to be true and the conclusion to be false. That is, the truth of the premises means that the conclusion must also be true.

By contrast, an **inductive argument** relies on evidence and observation to reach a conclusion. Although readers may accept a writer's premises as true, it is possible for them to reject the writer's conclusion.

Let's consider this for a moment in the context of Loewen's argument. Loewen introduces the premise that class matters, then offers the more specific premise that textbook writers leave class issues out of their narratives of American history, and finally draws the conclusion that citizens need to be informed of this body of knowledge in order to create change:

1. Although class is a key factor in Americans' access to health care, education, and wealth, students know very little about the social structure in the United States.

2. In their textbooks, textbook writers do not address the issue of class, an issue that people need to know about.

3. Therefore, if people had this knowledge, they would understand that poverty cannot be blamed on the poor.

Notice that Loewen's premises are not necessarily true. For example, readers could challenge the premise that "textbook writers do not address issues of class." After all, Loewen examined just twelve textbooks. What if he had examined a different set of textbooks? Would he have drawn the same conclusion? And even if Loewen's evidence convinces us that the two premises are true, we do not have to accept that the conclusion is true.

The conclusion in an inductive argument is never definitive. That is the nature of any argument that deals with human emotions and actions. Moreover, we have seen throughout history that people tend to disagree much more on the terms of an argument than on its form. Do we agree that Israel's leaders practice apartheid? (What do we mean by *apartheid* in this case?) Do we agree with the need to grant women reproductive rights? (When does life begin?) Do we agree that all people should be treated equally? (Would equality mean equal access to resources or to outcomes?)

Deductive arguments are conclusive. In a deductive argument, the premises are universal truths—laws of nature, if you will—and the conclusion must follow from those premises. That is, a^2 plus b^2 always equals c^2, and humans are always mortal.

By contrast, an inductive argument is never conclusive. The premises may or may not be true; and even if they are true, the conclusion may be false. We might accept that class matters and that high school history textbooks don't address the issue of class structure in the United States; but we still would not know that students who have studied social stratification in America will necessarily understand the nature of poverty. It may be that social class is only one reason for poverty; or it may be that textbooks are only one source of information about social stratification in the United States, that textbook omissions are simply not as serious as Loewen claims. That the premises of an argument are true only establishes that the conclusion is probably true and, perhaps, true only for some readers.

Inductive argument is the basis of academic writing; it is also the basis of any appeal to logos. The process of constructing an inductive argument involves three steps:

1. State the premises of your argument.

2. Use credible evidence to show readers that your argument has merit.

3. Demonstrate that the conclusion follows from the premises.

In following these three steps, you will want to determine the truth of your premises, help readers understand whether or not the inferences you draw are justified, and use word signals to help readers fully grasp the connections between your premises and your conclusion.

■ State the Premises of Your Argument

Stating a premise establishes what you have found to be true and what you want to persuade readers to accept as truth as well. Let's return to Loewen, who asserts his premise at the very outset of the excerpt: "Middle-class students . . . know little about how the American class structure works . . . and nothing at all about how it has changed over time." Loewen elaborates on this initial premise a few sentences later, arguing that students "have no understanding of the ways that opportunity is not equal in America and no notion that the social structure pushes people around, influencing the ideas they hold and the lives they fashion."

Implicit here is the point that class matters. Loewen makes this point explicit several paragraphs later, where he states that "social class is probably the single most important variable in society" (para. 6). He states his second, more specific premise in paragraph 2: "High school history textbooks can take some of the credit for this state of affairs." The burden of demonstrating that these premises are true is on Loewen. If readers find that either of the premises is not true, it will be difficult, if not impossible, for them to accept his conclusion that with more knowledge, people will understand that poverty is not the fault of the poor (para. 10).

■ Use Credible Evidence

The validity of your argument depends on whether the inferences you draw are justified, and whether you can expect a reasonable person to draw the same conclusion from those premises. Loewen has to demonstrate throughout (1) that students do not have much, if any, knowledge about the class structure that exists in the United States and (2) that textbook writers are in large part to blame for this lack of knowledge. He also must help readers understand how this lack of knowledge contributes to (3) his conclusion that greater knowledge would lead Americans to understand that poor people are not responsible for poverty. He can help readers with the order in which he states his premises and by choosing the type and amount of evidence that will enable readers to draw the inferences that he does.

Interestingly, Loewen seems to assume that one group of readers— educators—will accept his first premise as true. He does not elaborate on what students know or do not know. Instead, he moves right to his second premise, which involves first acknowledging what high school history textbooks typically cover, then identifying what he believes are the important events that textbook writers exclude, and ultimately asserting that "treatments of events in labor history are never anchored in any analysis of social class" (para. 3). He supports this point with his own study of twelve textbooks (paras. 3–5) before returning to his premise that "social class is probably the single most important variable in society" (para. 6). What follows is a series of observations about the rich and references to researchers' findings on inequality (paras. 7–9). Finally, he asserts that "social class determines how people think about social class" (para. 10), implying that fuller knowledge would lead business leaders and conservative voters to think differently about the source of poverty. The question to explore is whether or not Loewen supports this conclusion.

■ Demonstrate That the Conclusion Follows from the Premises

Authors signal their conclusion with words like *consequently, finally, in sum, in the end, subsequently, therefore, thus, ultimately,* and *as a result.* Here is how this looks in the structure of Loewen's argument:

1. Although class is a key factor in Americans' access to health care, education, and wealth, students know very little about the social structure in the United States.

2. In their textbooks, textbook writers do not address the issue of class, an issue that people need to know about.

3. Ultimately, if people had this knowledge, they would understand that poverty cannot be blamed on the poor.

We've reprinted much of paragraph 9 of Loewen's excerpt below. Notice how Loewen pulls together what he has been discussing. He again underscores the importance of class and achievement ("All these are among the reasons"). And he points out that access to certain types of colleges puts people in a position to accumulate and sustain wealth. Of course, this is not true of the poor "because affluent families can save some money while poor families must spend what they make." This causal relationship ("Because") heightens readers' awareness of the class structure that exists in the United States.

All these are among the reasons why social class predicts the rate of college attendance and the type of college chosen more effectively than does any other factor, including intellectual ability, however measured. After college, most affluent children get white-collar jobs, most working-class children get blue-collar jobs, and the class differences continue. As adults, rich people are more likely to have hired an attorney and to be a member of formal organizations that increase their civic power. Poor people are more likely to watch TV. Because affluent families can save some money while poor families must spend what they make, wealth differences are ten times larger than income differences. Therefore most poor and working-class families cannot accumulate the down payment required to buy a house, which in turn shuts them out from our most important tax shelter, the write-off of home mortgage interest. Working-class parents cannot afford to live in elite subdivisions or hire high-quality day care, so the process of educational inequality replicates itself in the next generation. Finally, affluent Americans also have longer life expectancies than lower- and working-class people, the largest single cause of which is better access to health care. . . .

Once Loewen establishes this causal relationship, he concludes ("Therefore," "Finally") with the argument that poverty persists from one generation to the next.

In paragraph 10, Loewen uses the transition word *ultimately* to make the point that social class matters, so much so that it limits the ways in which people see the world, that it even "determines how people think about social class." (We discuss how to write conclusions in Chapter 9.)

Steps to Appealing to Logos

1 **State the premises of your argument.** Establish what you have found to be true and what you want readers to accept as well.

2 **Use credible evidence.** Lead your readers from one premise to the next, making sure your evidence is sufficient and convincing and your inferences are logical and correct.

3 **Demonstrate that the conclusion follows from the premises.** In particular, use the right words to signal to your readers how the evidence and inferences lead to your conclusion.

RECOGNIZING LOGICAL FALLACIES

We turn now to **logical fallacies**, flaws in the chain of reasoning that lead to a conclusion that does not necessarily follow from the premises, or evidence. Logical fallacies are common in inductive arguments for two reasons: Inductive arguments rely on reasoning about probability, not certainty; and they derive from human beliefs and values, not facts or laws of nature.

Here we list fifteen logical fallacies. In examining them, think about how to guard against the sometimes-faulty logic behind statements you might hear from politicians, advertisers, and the like. That should help you examine the premises on which you base your own assumptions and the logic you use to help readers reach the same conclusions you do.

1. *Erroneous Appeal to Authority.* An authority is someone with expertise in a given subject. An *erroneous authority* is an author who claims to be an authority but is not, or someone an author cites as an authority who is not. In this type of fallacy, the claim might be true, but the fact that an unqualified person is making the claim means there is no reason for readers to accept the claim as true.

Because the issue here is the legitimacy of authority, your concern should be to prove to yourself and your readers that you or the people you are citing have expertise in the subject. An awareness of this type of fallacy has become increasingly important as celebrities offer support for candidates running for office or act as spokespeople for curbing global warming or some other cause. The candidate may be the best person for the office, and there may be very good reasons to control global warming; but we need to question the legitimacy of a nonexpert endorsement.

2. *Ad Hominem.* An ad hominem argument focuses on the person making a claim instead of on the claim itself. (*Ad hominem* is Latin for "to the person.") In most cases, an ad hominem argument does not have a bearing on the truth or the quality of a claim.

Keep in mind that it is always important to address the claim or the reasoning behind it, rather than the person making the claim. "Of course Senator Wiley supports oil drilling in Alaska—he's in the pocket of the oil companies!" is an example of an ad hominem argument. Senator Wiley may have good reasons for supporting oil drilling in Alaska that have nothing to do with his alleged attachment to the oil industry. However, if an individual's character is relevant to the argument, then an ad hominem argument can be valid. If Senator Wiley has been found guilty of accepting bribes from an oil company, it makes sense to question both his credibility and his claims.

3. *Shifting the Issue.* This type of fallacy occurs when an author draws attention away from the issue instead of offering evidence that will enable people to draw their own conclusions about the soundness of an argument. For example:

> Affirmative action proponents accuse me of opposing equal opportunity in the workforce. I think my positions on military expenditures, education, and public health speak for themselves.

The author of this statement does not provide a chain of reasoning that would enable readers to judge his or her stance on the issue of affirmative action.

4. *Either/Or Fallacy.* At times, an author will take two extreme positions to force readers to make a choice between two seemingly contradictory positions. For example:

> Either you support the war in Iraq, or you are against it.

Although the author has set up an either/or condition, in reality one position does not exclude the other. Many people support the troops in Iraq even though they do not support the reasons for starting the war.

5. *Sweeping Generalizations.* When an author attempts to draw a conclusion without providing sufficient evidence to support the conclusion or examining possible counterarguments, he or she may be making sweeping generalizations. For example:

> Despite the women's movement in the 1960s and 1970s, women still do not receive equal pay for equal work. Obviously, any attempt to change the status quo for women is doomed to failure.

As is the case with many fallacies, the author's position may be reasonable, but we cannot accept the argument at face value. Reading critically entails testing assumptions like this one—that any attempt to create change is doomed to failure because women do not receive equal pay for equal work. We could ask, for example, whether inequities persist in the public sector. And we could point to other areas where the women's movement has had measurable success. Title IX, for example, has reduced the dropout rate among teenage girls; it has also increased the rate at which women earn college and graduate degrees.

6. *Bandwagon.* When an author urges readers to accept an idea because a significant number of people support it, he or she is making a bandwagon argument. This is a fairly common mode of argument in advertising; for example, a commercial might attempt to persuade us to buy a certain product because it's popular.

> Because Harvard, Stanford, and Berkeley have all added a multicultural component to their graduation requirements, other institutions should do so as well.

The growing popularity of an idea is not sufficient reason to accept that it is true.

7. *Begging the Question.* This fallacy entails advancing a circular argument that asks readers to accept a premise that is also the conclusion readers are expected to draw:

> We could improve the undergraduate experience with coed dorms because both men and women benefit from living with members of the opposite gender.

Here readers are being asked to accept that the conclusion is true despite the fact that the premises—men benefit from living with women, and women benefit from living with men—are essentially the same as the conclusion. Without evidence that a shift in dorm policy could improve on the undergraduate experience, we cannot accept the conclusion as true. Indeed, the conclusion does not necessarily follow from the premise.

8. *False Analogy.* Authors (and others) often try to persuade us that something is true by using a comparison. This approach is not in and of itself a problem, as long as the comparison is reasonable. For example:

> It is ridiculous to have a Gay and Lesbian Program and a Department of African American Culture. We don't have a Straight Studies Program or a Department of Caucasian Culture.

Here the author is urging readers to rethink the need for two academic departments by saying that the school doesn't have two other departments. That, of course, is not a reason for or against the new departments. What's needed is an analysis that compares the costs (economic and otherwise) of starting up and operating the new departments versus the contributions (economic and otherwise) of the new departments.

9. *Technical Jargon.* If you've ever had a salesperson try to persuade you to purchase a television or an entertainment system with capabilities you absolutely *must* have—even if you didn't understand a word the salesperson was saying about alternating currents and circuit splicers—then you're familiar with this type of fallacy. We found this passage in one of our student's papers:

> You should use this drug because it has been clinically proven that it inhibits the reuptake of serotonin and enhances the dopamine levels of the body's neurotransmitters.

The student's argument may very well be true, but he hasn't presented any substantive evidence to demonstrate that the premises are true and that the conclusion follows from the premises.

10. *Confusing Cause and Effect.* It is challenging to establish that one factor causes another. For example, how can we know for certain that economic class predicts, or is a factor in, academic achievement? How do we know that a new president's policies are the cause of a country's economic well-being? Authors often assume cause and effect when two factors are simply associated with each other:

> The current recession came right after the president was elected.

This fallacy states a fact, but it does not prove that the president's election caused the recession.

11. *Appeal to Fear.* One type of logical fallacy makes an appeal to readers' irrational fears and prejudices, preventing them from dealing squarely with a given issue and often confusing cause and effect:

> We should use whatever means possible to avoid further attack.

The reasoning here is something like this: "If we are soft on defense, we will never end the threat of terrorism." But we need to consider whether there is indeed a threat, and, if so, whether the presence of a threat should lead to action, and, if so, whether that action should include "whatever means possible." (Think of companies that sell alarm systems by pointing to people's vulnerability to harm and property damage.)

12. *Fallacy of Division.* A fallacy of division suggests that what is true of the whole must also be true of its parts:

> Conservatives have always voted against raising the minimum wage, against stem cell research, and for defense spending. Therefore, we can assume that conservative Senator Harrison will vote this way.

The author is urging readers to accept the premise without providing evidence of how the senator has actually voted on the three issues.

13. *Hasty Generalization.* This fallacy is committed when a person draws a conclusion about a group based on a sample that is too small to be representative. Consider this statement:

> Seventy-five percent of the seniors surveyed at the university study just 10 hours a week. We can conclude, then, that students at the university are not studying enough.

What you need to know is how many students were actually surveyed. Seventy-five percent may seem high, but not if the researcher surveyed just 400 of the 2,400 graduating seniors. This sample of students from a total population of 9,600 students at the university is too small to draw the conclusion that students in general are not studying enough.

14. *The Straw Man Argument.* A straw man fallacy makes a generalization about what a group believes without actually citing a specific writer or work:

> Democrats are more interested in running away than in trying to win the war on terrorism.

Here the fallacy is that the author simply ignores a person's actual position and substitutes a distorted, exaggerated, or misrepresented version of that position. This kind of fallacy often goes hand in hand with assuming that what is true of the group is true of the individual, what we call the fallacy of division.

15. *Fallacy of the Middle Ground.* The fallacy of the middle ground assumes that the middle position between two extreme positions must be correct. Although the middle ground may be true, the author must justify this position with evidence.

> E. D. Hirsch argues that cultural literacy is the only sure way to increase test scores, and Jonathan Kozol believes schools will improve only if state legislators increase funding; but I would argue that school reform will occur if we change the curriculum *and* provide more funding.

This fallacy draws its power from the fact that a moderate or middle position is often the correct one. Again, however, the claim that the moderate or middle position is correct must be supported by legitimate reasoning.

ANALYZING THE APPEALS IN A RESEARCHED ARGUMENT

Now that you have studied the variety of appeals you can make to connect with your audience, we would like you to read a paper on urban health problems by Meredith Minkler and analyze her strategies for appealing to her readers. The paper is long and carefully argued, so we suggest you take detailed notes about her use of appeals to ethos, pathos, and logos as you read. You may want to refer to the Practice Sequence questions on page 236 to help focus your reading. Ideally, you should work through the text with your classmates, in groups of three or four, appointing one student to record and share each group's analysis of Minkler's argument.

MEREDITH MINKLER

Community-Based Research Partnerships: Challenges and Opportunities

Meredith Minkler is a professor of health and social behavior at the School of Public Health, University of California, Berkeley. She is an activist and researcher whose work explores community partnerships, community organizing, and community-based participatory research. With more than one hundred books and articles to her credit, she is coeditor of the influential *Community Based Participatory Research for Health* (2003). The following article appeared in *The Journal of Urban Health* in 2005.

■ ■ ■

Abstract

The complexity of many urban health problems often makes them ill suited to traditional research approaches and interventions. The resultant frustration, together with community calls for genuine partnership in the research process, has highlighted the importance of an alternative paradigm. Community-based participatory research (CBPR) is presented as a promising collaborative approach that combines systematic inquiry, participation, and action to address urban health problems. Following a brief review of its basic tenets and historical roots, key ways in which CBPR adds value to urban health research are introduced and illustrated. Case study examples from diverse international settings are used to illustrate some of the difficult ethical challenges that may arise in the course of CBPR partnership approaches. The concepts of partnership synergy and cultural humility, together with protocols such as Green et al.'s guidelines for appraising CBPR projects, are highlighted as useful tools for urban health researchers seeking to apply this collaborative approach and to deal effectively with the difficult ethical challenges it can present.

Keywords

Community-based participatory research, Ethical issues in research, Participatory action research, Partnership, Urban health.

Introduction

The complexity of urban health problems has often made them poorly   *1*
suited to traditional "outside expert"–driven research and intervention
approaches.[1] Together with community demands for authentic partnerships in research that are locally relevant and "community based" rather
than merely "community placed," this frustration has led to a burgeoning
of interest in an alternative research paradigm.[1,2] Community-based participatory research (CBPR) is an overarching term that increasingly is used
to encompass a variety of approaches to research that have as their cen-
terpiece three interrelated elements: participation, research, and action.[3]
As defined by Green et al.[4] for the Royal Society of Canada, CBPR may
concisely be described as "systematic investigation with the participation of those affected by an issue for purposes of education and action or
affecting social change." The approach further has been characterized as

> [A] collaborative process that equitably involves all partners in the research
> process and recognizes the unique strengths that each brings. CBPR begins
> with a research topic of importance to the community with the aim of com-
> bining knowledge and action for social change to improve community
> health and eliminate health disparities.[5,6]

This article briefly describes CBPR's roots and core principles and   *2*
summarizes the value added by this approach to urban health research.
Drawing on examples from a variety of urban health settings nationally
and internationally, it discusses and illustrates several of the key challenges faced in applying this partnership approach to inquiry and action.
The article concludes by suggesting that despite such challenges and
the labor-intensive nature of this approach, CBPR offers an exceptional
opportunity for partnering with communities in ways that can enhance
both the quality of research and its potential for helping address some of
our most intractable urban health problems.

Historical Roots and Core Principles

The roots of CBPR may be traced in part to the action research school de-   *3*
veloped by the social psychologist Kurt Lewin[7] in the 1940s, with its emphasis on the active involvement in the research of those affected by the
problem being studied through a cyclical process of fact finding, action,
and reflection. But CBPR is most deeply grounded in the more revolu-
tionary approaches to research that emerged, often independently from
one another, from work with oppressed communities in South America,
Asia, and Africa in the 1970s.[3,8,9] Brazilian adult educator Paulo Freire[9]
provided critical grounding for CBPR in his development of a dialogi-
cal method accenting co-learning and action based on critical reflection.

Freire,[9] Fals-Borda,[10] and other developing countries' scholars developed their alternative approaches to inquiry as a direct counter to the often "colonizing" nature of research to which oppressed communities were subjected, with feminist and postcolonialist scholars adding further conceptual richness.[11,12]

Among the tenets of participatory action approaches to research outlined by McTaggart[13] are that it is a political process, involves lay people in theory-making, is committed to improving social practice by changing it, and establishes "self-critical communities." As Israel et al.[6] adds, other core principles are that CBPR "involves systems development and local community capacity development," is "a co-learning process" to which community members and outside researchers contribute equally, and "achieves a balance between research and action." CBPR reflects a profound belief in "partnership synergy." As described by Lasker et al.[14]:

> [T]he synergy that partners seek to achieve through collaboration is more than a mere exchange of resources. By combining the individual perspectives, resources, and skills of the partners, the group creates something new and valuable together—something that is greater than the sum of its parts.

Moreover, CBPR embodies a deep commitment to what Tervalon and Murray-Garcia[15] have called cultural humility. As they point out, although we can never become truly competent in another's culture, we can demonstrate a "lifelong commitment to self evaluation and self-critique," to redress power imbalances and "develop and maintain mutually respectful and dynamic partnerships with communities."[15] Although the term *cultural humility* was coined primarily in reference to race and ethnicity, it also is of value in helping us understand and address the impacts of professional cultures (which tend to be highly influenced by white, western, patriarchal belief systems), as these help shape interactions between outside researchers and their community partners.[15]

CBPR is not a method per se but an orientation to research that may employ any of a number of qualitative and quantitative methodologies. As Cornwall and Jewkes[16] note, what is distinctive about CBPR is "the attitudes of researchers, which in turn determine how, by and for whom research is conceptualized and conducted [and] the corresponding location of power at every stage of the research process." The accent placed by CBPR on individual, organizational, and community empowerment also is a hallmark of this approach to research.

With the increasing emphasis on partnership approaches to improving urban health, CBPR is experiencing a rebirth of interest and unprecedented new opportunities for both scholarly recognition and financial support. In the United States, for example, the Institute of Medicine[17] recently named "community-based participatory research" as one of eight new areas in which all schools of public health should be offering training.

Although the renewed interest in CBPR provides a welcome contrast to   8
more traditional top-down research approaches, it also increases the dangers of co-optation as this label is loosely applied to include research and intervention efforts in search of funding that do not truly meet the criteria for this approach. The sections below illustrate some of the value added to urban research when authentic partnership approaches are taken seriously and then briefly highlight some of the ethical challenges such work may entail.

The Value Added to Urban Health Research by a CBPR Approach

CBPR can enrich and improve the quality and outcomes of urban health   9
research in a variety of ways. On the basis of the work of many scholars and institutions,[4,6,8,18] and as summarized by the National Institutes of Health (http://grants.nih.gov/grants/guide/pa-files/PAR-05-026.html), some of its primary contributions may be characterized and illustrated as follows.

CBPR Can Support the Development of Research Questions That Reflect Health Issues of Real Concern to Community Members

Ideally, CBPR begins with a research topic or question that comes from   10
the local community, as when the nongovernmental organization (NGO) Alternatives for Community and Environment (ACE) in the low-income Roxbury section of Boston, reached out to Harvard University's School of Public Health and other potential partners to study and address the high rates of asthma in their neighborhood. Collaborative studies using air-monitoring and other approaches yielded data supporting the hypothesis that Roxbury was indeed a hot spot for pollution contributing to asthma. This in turn paved the way for a variety of policy and community education actions and outcomes.[19]

Although having a community partner such as ACE identify an issue   11
and catalyze a research partnership may be the ideal, it is often the privileged outside researcher who initiates a CBPR project. In these instances too, however, a genuine commitment to high-level community involvement in issue selection, with NGOs and formal and informal community leaders engaged as equal partners, can help ensure that the research topic decided upon really is of major concern to the local population.

CBPR Can Improve Our Ability to Achieve Informed Consent, and to Address Issues of "Costs and Benefits" on the Community, and Not Simply the Individual Level[20]

With its accent on equitable community involvement in all stages of the   12
research process,[6] CBPR often finds creative means of ensuring informed consent. The "One Hand, One Heart" study in urban and rural Tibet,

which included a randomized controlled clinical trial of an indigenous medicine to prevent maternal hemorrhaging, actively involved local midwives and other community partners on the research team who played a key role in helping find locally translatable concepts to improve informed consent. Their help in early ethnographic work thus revealed that the concept of disclosing risk was highly problematic, because such disclosure was believed to disturb the wind element responsible for emotions, potentially leading to emotional upset and other adverse outcomes. By reframing risk disclosure as "safety issues," needed information could be conveyed in a far more culturally acceptable manner.[21]

CBPR also offers an important potential opening for extending the gaze of our ethical review processes such that we examine and address risks and benefits for the community. In Toronto, Travers and Flicker[20] have pioneered in developing such guidelines, pointing out the importance of having us ask such questions as "Will the methods used be sensitive and appropriate to various communities?" "What training or capacity building opportunities will you build in?" and "How will you balance scientific rigor and accessibility?" The strong philosophical fit between questions such as these and CBPR's commitments to equitable partnership and community capacity building reflect another source of value added to urban health research through this approach.

CBPR Can Improve Cultural Sensitivity and the Reliability and Validity of Measurement Tools Through High-Quality Community Participation in Designing and Testing Study Instruments

Particularly in survey research, community advisory boards (CABs) and other partnership structures can improve measurement instruments by making sure that questions are worded in ways that will elicit valid and reliable responses. In a study of urban grandparents raising grandchildren due to the crack cocaine epidemic, the author and her colleagues used validated instruments, such as those for depressive symptomatology. However, they also learned from CAB members how to word other questions about sensitive topics. Rather than asking a standard (and disliked) question about income, for example, the CAB encouraged us to rephrase the question as "How much money is available to help you in raising this child?" When this alternate wording was used, a wealth of detailed income data was obtained, which improved our understanding of the challenges faced by this population.[22]

CBPR Can Uncover Lay Knowledge Critical to Enhancing Understanding of Sensitive Urban Health Problems

Through the cultural humility and partnership synergy involved in deeply valuing lay knowledge and working in partnership with community residents, CBPR can uncover hidden contributors to health and social problems. The high rates of HIV/AIDS in India and the often sensitive nature of this subject among young men led the Deepak Charitable Trust to develop a research committee for a study in the industrial area of Nandesari, in Gujarat, comprised of several male village health workers and other young men from the area. Working closely with a medical anthropologist, the research committee planned the research, including developing a sampling plan and the phrasing of culturally sensitive questions. Their insider knowledge helped reveal that AIDS itself was not perceived as a major problem by the young men in this area. Instead, men who were engaging in high-risk behaviors wanted to find sex partners at least partly to avoid "thinning of the semen" and sexual dysfunction and fatigue, which were believed to be long-term consequences of masturbation and nocturnal emissions. These fears appeared to be contributing to high rates of unprotected intercourse with sex workers at the area's many truck stops and with other sex partners.[23] This insider knowledge both strengthened the research and led to subsequent interventions to help dispel such misinformation.

By Increasing Community Trust and Ownership, CBPR Can Improve Recruitment and Retention Efforts

In a participatory epidemiology project on diabetes in an urban Aboriginal community in Melbourne, Australia, a marked increase in recruitment was experienced following the hiring of a community codirector and the changing of the project's name to one chosen by the local community.[24] Similarly, a 69% response rate achieved in a CBPR study of the health and working conditions of the largely immigrant hotel room cleaner population (many of them undocumented) in several of San Francisco's major tourist hotels was heavily attributed to the hiring and training of a core group of 25 room cleaners as key project staff. That high response rate, together with the high quality of data collected, made a substantial contribution when results later were presented and used to help negotiate a new contract.[25]

CBPR Can Help Increase Accuracy and Cultural Sensitivity in the Interpretation of Findings

Even highly engaged community members of the research team may not wish to be involved in the labor-intensive data analysis phase of a research project,[26] nor do all methodological approaches lend themselves to such involvement. Yet when applicable and desired, community involvement in data analysis can make real contributions to our understanding of the themes and findings that emerge. In a US study of and with people with disabilities on the contentious topic of death with dignity legislation in their community, the author and an "insider/outsider" member of the research team met on alternate Saturdays with a subcommittee of the CAB to engage in joint data analysis. Using redacted transcripts, and applying lessons learned in qualitative data interpretation, the diverse CAB members came up with far richer codes and themes than outside researchers could have achieved alone.[27]

CBPR Can Increase the Relevance of Intervention Approaches and Thus the Likelihood of Success

One of the strengths of CBPR is its commitment to action as part of the research process. But without strong community input, researchers not infrequently design interventions that are ill suited to the local context in which they are applied. In the Gujarat case study mentioned above, partnership with local community members helped in the design of culturally relevant interventions, such as street theater performed by locally recruited youth at *melas* (or fairs), and the dissemination of study findings through the 15 local credit and savings groups that often provided platforms for discussing reproductive health and related issues. Both these approaches provided critical means of information dissemination on this culturally and emotionally charged topic.[23]

Ethical and Other Challenges in Community-Based Participatory Research

Engaging in urban health research with diverse community partners can indeed enrich both the quality and the outcomes of such studies. At the same time, CBPR is fraught with ethical and related challenges, several of which are now highlighted.

"Community Driven" Issue Selection

A key feature of CBPR involves its commitment to ensuring that the research topic comes from the community. Yet many such projects "paradoxically . . . would not occur without the initiative of someone outside the community who has the time, skill, and commitment, and who almost inevitably is a member of a privileged and educated group."[28] In such instances, outside researchers must pay serious attention to community understandings of what the real issue or topic of concern is.

In South Africa, for example, high rates of cervical cancer in the Black and Colored populations led Mosavel et al.[29] to propose an investigation of this problem. In response to community feedback, however, they quickly broadened their initial topic to "cervical health," a concept which "acknowledged the fact that women's health in South Africa extends well beyond the risk of developing cervical cancer, and includes HIV-AIDS and STDs, sexual violence, and multiple other social problems." In other instances, the outside researcher as an initiator of a potential CBPR project needs to determine whether the topic he or she has identified really is of concern to the local community—and whether outsider involvement is welcome. The Oakland, California–based Grandmother Caregiver Study mentioned above grew out of the interests of my colleague and me in studying the strengths of as well as the health and social problems faced by the growing number of urban African American grandmothers who were raising grandchildren in the context of a major drug epidemic. As privileged white women, however, we had to determine first whether this was a topic of local concern and, if so, whether there might be a role for us in working with the community to help study and address it. We began by enlisting the support of an older African American colleague with deep ties in the community, who engaged with us in a frank discussion with two prominent African American NGOs. It was only after getting their strong support for proceeding that we wrote a grant, with funds for these organizations, which in turn helped us pull together an outstanding CAB that was actively involved in many stages of the project.[21,26]

We were lucky in this case that a topic we as outsiders identified turned   22
out to represent a deep concern in the local community. Yet not infrequently "the community" is in fact deeply divided over an issue. Indeed, as Yoshihama and Carr[30] have argued, "communities are not places that researchers enter but are instead a set of negotiations that inherently entail multiple and often conflicting interests." In such situations, outside researchers can play a useful role in helping community partners think through who "the community" in fact is in relation to a proposed project and the pros and cons of undertaking the project to begin with. The holding of town hall meetings and other forums may then be useful in helping achieve consensus on an issue that is truly of, by, and for the community, however it is defined.[26]

Insider–Outsider Tensions

Urban health researchers in many parts of the world have written poi-   23
gnantly about the power dynamics and other sources of insider–outsider tensions and misunderstandings in CBPR and related partnership efforts. Ugalde[31] points out how in Latin America participants may be exploited as cheap sources of labor or may become alienated from their communities because of their participation. In her work with Native American and other marginalized groups in New Mexico, Wallerstein[32] further illustrates how even outsiders who pride ourselves on being trusted community friends and allies often fail to appreciate the extent of the power that is embedded in our own, often multiple sources of privilege, and how it can affect both process and outcomes in such research.

One major source of insider–outsider tensions involves the differen-   24
tial reward structures for partners in CBPR. For although a major aim of such research is to benefit the local community, the outside researchers typically stand to gain the most from such collaborations, bringing in grants, getting new publications, and so forth. The common expectation that community partners will work for little or no pay and the fact that receipt of compensation may take months if the funds are coming

through a ministry of health or a university are also sources of under-standable resentment.[6,26]

To address these and other sources of insider–outsider tensions in work with indigenous communities in both urban and rural areas, research-ers in New Zealand,[33] Australia,[34] the United States,[35] and Canada[36] have worked with their community partners to develop ethical guidelines for their collaborative work, including protocols that address

1. negotiating with political and spiritual leaders in the community to obtain their input and their approval for the proposed research,
2. ensuring equitable benefits to participants (e.g., appropriate train-ing and hiring of community members) in return for their contribu-tions and resources,
3. developing agreements about the ownership and publication of find-ings, and the early review of findings by key community leaders.

Although such protocols cannot begin to address all of the conflicts that may arise in CBPR, they can play a critical role in helping pave the way for the continued dialogue and negotiation that must be an integral part of the process.

Constraints on Community Involvement

Outside researchers committed to a CBPR approach not infrequently ex-press frustration at the difficulty moving from the goal of heavy commu-nity partner involvement in the research process to the reality. As Diaz and Simmons[37] found in their Reproductive Health Project in Brazil, de-spite a strong commitment to involving the most marginalized and vul-nerable classes (in this case, women who were users of the public sector services being studied), such individuals often "are least likely to be in a position to donate their time and energy." Further, and even when outside researchers are careful to provide child care and transportation, there are differential costs of participation by gender.[30]

Still another set of challenges may arise when community desires with respect to research design and methods clash with what outsider re-searchers consider to be "good science." In an oft-cited CBPR study with a local Mohawk community in Québec, Chataway[38] describes how com-munity members at first strongly objected to the idea of using a ques-tionnaire approach which they saw as "putting their thoughts in boxes." Through respectful listening on both sides, the value of such an approach was realized and a more qualitative methodology developed, through which community members would then be actively involved in helping analyze and interpret the quantitative findings that emerged. As such case studies illustrate, CBPR does not condone an abandonment of one's own scientific standards and knowledge base. But it does advocate a genuine co-learning process through which lay and professional ways of knowing both are valued and examined for what they can contribute.[26]

Dilemmas in the Sharing and Release of Findings
A crucial step in CBPR involves returning data to the community and   29
enabling community leaders and participants to have an authentic role in
deciding how that data will be used. As Travers and Flicker[20] suggest,
ethical research review processes that ask questions such as "Are there
built-in mechanisms for how unflattering results will be dealt with?"
should be employed at the front end of our CBPR projects. In addition
to the formal IRB process they propose, which offers a critical next step
for the field, CBPR partners can look to a variety of formal or informal
research protocols and particularly to the detailed guidelines for health
promotion research developed by Green et al.,[4,39] which help partnerships decide in advance how potentially difficult issues concerning the
sharing and release of findings and other matters will be handled.

Challenges in the Action Dimensions of CBPR
Numerous ethical challenges lastly may arise in relation to the critical   30
action component of CBPR. In some instances, community partners may
wish to move quickly into action, whereas academic and other outside research partners may want to "put the breaks on" until findings have been
published or other steps brought to fruition. In other cases, the nature
of funding (e.g., from a government body) may constrain action on the
policy level that is prohibited or discouraged by the funder. And in still
other instances, including the Brazilian Reproductive Health Project[37]
cited above, community members may not wish to be associated with a
CBPR project that appears connected to a broader political agenda.

Participation in the action phase of CBPR projects may sometimes   31
present risks to community participants, as when immigrant hotel room
cleaners in the San Francisco study took part in a Labor Day sit-in and in
some cases faced arrest.[25] And for both professionally trained researchers
and their community partners, actions that involve challenging powerful
corporate or other entrenched interests may have negative consequences
for those involved. At the same time, CBPR's fundamental commitment
to action and to redressing power imbalances makes this aspect of the
work a particularly important contributor to urban health improvement
through research.

Conclusion

Difficult ethical challenges may confront urban health researchers who   32
engage in CBPR. Yet this approach can greatly enrich the quality of our
research, helping ensure that we address issues of genuine community
concern and use methods and approaches that are culturally sensitive
and that improve the validity and reliability of our findings. Moreover,
through its commitment to action as an integral part of the research
process, CBPR can help in translating findings as we work with commu-

nity partners to help address some of our most intractable urban health problems.

Acknowledgement

Many current and former community and academic partners have con-   *33* tributed to my understanding of the advantages and pitfalls of collaborative urban health research and I am deeply grateful. Particular thanks are extended to Nina Wallerstein, Kathleen M. Roe, Barbara Israel, Lawrence W. Green, and Ronald Labonte, who have greatly stimulated my own thinking and scholarship in this area. I am grateful to former students, Rima Shaw and Caroline Bell, as well as other individuals who have shared some of the cases drawn upon in this paper. My gratitude is extended to Claire Murphy for assistance with manuscript preparation.

References

1. Minkler M, Wallerstein N. *Community Based Participatory Research for Health.* San Francisco, CA: Jossey-Bass; 2003.

2. Green LW, Mercer SL. Can public health researchers and agencies reconcile the push from funding bodies and the pull from communities? *Am J Public Health.* 2001;91:1926–1929.

3. Hall BL. From margins to center: the development and purpose of participatory action research. *Am Sociol.* 1992;23:15–28.

4. Green LW, George A, Daniel M, et al. *Study of Participatory Research in Health Promotion.* Ottawa, Ontario: Royal Society of Canada; 1995.

5. Community Health Scholars Program. *The Community Health Scholars Program: Stories of Impact.* Ann Arbor, MI; 2002.

6. Israel BA, Schulz AJ, Parker EA, Becker AB. Review of community-based research: assessing partnership approaches to improve public health. *Annu Rev Public Health.* 1998;19:173–202.

7. Lewin K. Action research and minority problems. *J Soc Issues.* 1946;2:34–46.

8. Brown LD, Tandon R. Ideology and political economy in inquiry: action research and participatory research. *J Appl Behav Sci.* 1983; 19:277–294.

9. Freire P. *Pedagogy of the Oppressed.* New York, NY: Seabury Press; 1970.

10. Fals-Borda O. The application of participatory action-research in Latin America. *Int Sociol.* 1987;2:329–347.

11. Maguire P. *Doing Participatory Research: A Feminist Approach.* Amherst, MA: Center for International Education; 1987.

12. Duran E, Duran B. *Native American Postcolonial Psychology.* Albany, NY: State University of New York Press; 1995.

13. McTaggart R. Sixteen tenets of participatory action research. In: Wadsworth Y, ed. *Everyday Evaluation on the Run.* Sydney, Australia: Allen & Unwin; 1997:79.

14. Lasker RD, Weiss ES, Miller R. Partnership synergy: a practical framework for studying and strengthening the collaborative advantage. *Milbank Q.* 2001;79:179–205, III–IV.

15. Tervalon M, Murray-Garcia J. Cultural humility vs. cultural competence: a critical distinction in defining physician training outcomes in medical education. *J Health Care Poor Underserved.* 1998; 9:117–125.

16. Cornwall A, Jewkes R. What is participatory research? *Soc Sci Med.* 1995;41:1667–1676.

17. Gebbie K, Rosenstock L, Hernandez LM. *Who Will Keep the Public Healthy? Educating Public Health Professionals for the 21st Century.* Washington, DC: Institute of Medicine; 2002.

18. O'Fallon LR, Dearry A. Community-based participatory research as a tool to advance environmental health sciences. *Environ Health Perspect.* 2002;110:155–159.

19. Loh P, Sugerman-Brozan J. Environmental justice organizing for environmental health: case study on asthma and diesel exhaust in Roxbury, Massachusetts. *Environ Health Perspect.* 2002;584: 110–124.

20. Travers R, Flicker S. Ethical issues in community based research. In: *Urban Health Community-Based Research Series Workshop.* Wellesley, MA; 2004.

21. Bell C. *One HEART (Health Education and Research in Tibet) Community Based Participatory Research on Top of the World.* Unpublished manuscript, University of California, Berkeley, School of Public Health; 2004.

22. Roe KM, Minkler M, Saunders FF. Combining research, advocacy and education: the methods of the Grandparent Caregiving Study. *Health Educ Q.* 1995;22:458–475.

23. Shah R. *A Retrospective Analysis of an HIV Prevention Program for Men in Gujarat, India.* Unpublished manuscript, University of California, Berkeley, School of Public Health; 2004.

24. Thompson SJ. Participatory epidemiology: methods of the Living With Diabetes Project. *Intl Q Community Health Educ.* 2000; 19:3–18.

25. Lee P, Krause N, Goetchius C. Participatory action research with hotel room cleaners: from collaborative study to the bargaining table. In: Minkler M, Wallerstein N, eds. *Community Based Participatory Research for Health.* San Francisco, CA: Jossey-Bass; 2003: 390–404.

26. Minkler M. Ethical challenges for the "outside" researcher in community based participatory research. *Health Educ Behav.* 2004;31: 684–701.

27. Fadem P, Minkler M, Perry M, et al. Ethical challenges in community based participatory research: a case study from the San Francisco Bay Area disability community. In: Minkler M, Wallerstein N, eds. *Community Based Participatory Research for Health.* San Francisco, CA: Jossey-Bass; 2003.

28. Reason P. *Participation in Human Inquiry.* London, UK: Sage; 1994.

29. Mosavel M, Simon C, van Stade D, Buchbinder M. *Community Based Participatory Research (CBPR) in South Africa: Engaging Multiple Constituents to Shape the Research Question.* Unpublished manuscript; 2004.

30. Yoshihama M, Carr ES. Community participation reconsidered: feminist participatory action research with Hmong women. *J Community Pract.* 2002;10:85–103.

31. Ugalde A. Ideological dimensions of community participation in Latin American health programs. *Soc Sci Med.* 1985;21:41–53.

32. Wallerstein N. Power between evaluator and community: research relationships within New Mexico's healthier communities. *Soc Sci Med.* 1999;49:39–53.

33. Cram F. Rangahau Maori: Tona tika, tona pono: The validity and integrity of Maori research. In: Tolich M, ed. *Research Ethics in Aotearoa New Zealand.* Longman, Auckland: Pearson Education; 2001:35–52.

34. Anderson I. Ethics and health research in Aboriginal communities. In: Daly J, ed. *Ethical Intersections: Health Research, Methods and Researcher Responsibility.* St. Leonards, New South Wales: Allen & Unwin; 1996:153–165.

35. Turning Point, National Association of County and City Health Officials. Thirteen policy principles for advancing collaborative activity among and between tribal communities and surrounding jurisdictions. In: Minkler M, Wallerstein N, eds. *Community Based Participatory Research for Health.* San Francisco, CA: Jossey-Bass; 2003:436, Appendix E.

36. Stuart CA. Care and concern: an ethical journey in participatory action research. *Can J Couns.* 1998;32:298–314.

37. Diaz M, Simmons R. When is research participatory? Reflections on a Reproductive Health Project in Brazil. *J Women's Health.* 1999;8:175–184.

38. Chataway CJ. Examination of the constraints of mutual inquiry in a participatory action research project. *J Soc Issues.* 1997;53: 747–765.

39. Green LW, George MA, Daniel M, et al. Guidelines for participatory research in health promotion. In: Minkler M, Wallerstein N, eds. *Community Based Participatory Research for Health.* San Francisco, CA: Jossey-Bass; 2003:419, Appendix C.

A Practice Sequence: Analyzing the Appeals in a Researched Argument

1   Make a list of the major premises that inform Minkler's argument, and examine the evidence she uses to support them. To what extent do you find her evidence credible? Do you generally agree or disagree with the conclusions she draws? Be prepared to explain your responses to your class or peer group.

2   Note instances where Minkler appeals to ethos, pathos, and logos. How would you describe the ways she makes these three types of appeals? How does she present herself? What does she seem to assume? How does she help you understand the chain of reasoning by which she moves from premises to conclusion?

3   Working in groups of three or four, compose a letter to Minkler in which you take issue with her argument. This does not mean your group has to disagree with her entire argument, although of course you may. Rather, present your group's own contribution to the conversation in which she is participating. You may want to ask her to further explain one or more of her points, or suggest what she might be leaving out, or add your own take or evidence to her argument. As a group, you will have to agree on your focus. In the letter, include a summary of Minkler's argument or the part of it on which your group is focusing. Pay close attention to your own strategies for appealing to her—how you present yourselves, how you appeal to her values and emotions, and how you present your reasons for your own premises and conclusion.

ANALYZING VISUAL RHETORIC: ADVERTISEMENTS

This section focuses on visual rhetoric; that is, how visual images communicate and create an argument designed to move a specific audience to think or act in a specific way. Every day we view films and television, read

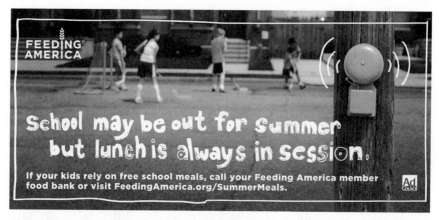

FIGURE 8.2   Feeding America Advertisement

magazines, browse the Internet, and walk the aisles of stores where signage and packaging encourage us to buy products we may not need. Everywhere we are confronted by visual images that aim to persuade us.

To examine the strategies you can use to understand how images and texts convey meaning, we would like you to analyze a public service announcement (PSA) for Feeding America, distributed by the Ad Council, a nonprofit institution founded in 1942 for the purpose of bringing attention to social issues. The long horizontal advertisement shows a blurry group of children in the background playing street hockey. In the foreground to the right is a bright red alarm bell attached to a wooden telephone pole. The text reads, "School may be out for summer but lunch is always in session." A sentence in smaller text below it reads, "If your kids rely on free school meals, call your Feeding America member food bank or visit FeedingAmerica.org/SummerMeals." Examine the advertisement (Figure 8.2) and try to answer the questions below.

1. Record what you think is the ad's overall message. What does the Ad Council want you to do or think about? What appeals does the ad seem to draw on most: appeals based on our cultural relationship to children (ethos), on the emotional reaction of potential viewers/readers (pathos), or on the ways text and image work together to convey an argument (logos)? Do you find that the appeals overlap and are difficult to tease out? Discuss with your classmates.

2. Formulate what you think is the ad's argument, and point out specific details that seem to support it. Compare your ideas with those of your classmates. Do they differ significantly? Can you agree on what the argument is?

3. As a class, test the assumption that the ad makes: When school is in session, policies are in place to insure federally funded schools feed

children in need. Less certain is the extent to which children in need receive sufficient nutrition during the summer when school is out.

Let's begin with the assumption that everything in an advertisement appears for a specific reason in a particular place to direct your attention in an exact sequence. The "economy of the genre," its constraints, dictate that the message come across quickly in a limited space.

■ Notice Where the Ad Appears

Analyzing an ad begins with noting where the ad appears. In this case, the Ad Council posted the Feeding America ad on billboards in a wide range of cities across the United States. An ad on a billboard will reach many people whose assumptions about hunger in America will vary, as will their levels of education, race, gender, and ethnicity. Therefore, it's worthwhile to consider how an ad about hunger will connect with such a wide range of possible viewers who will clearly interpret the ad in different ways and act upon its message differently. It is also worth considering the Ad Council's choice to post the ad in urban areas, as opposed to rural towns in the United States. Does the Ad Council assume there are greater hunger issues in urban areas? Is this a fair assumption? And equally important, can we assume that the people who should have access to the information on the ad will actually see it and get the support they require?

Imagine for a moment that the ad had appeared in an issue of *Time* magazine, which has the largest circulation of any news weekly in the United States. As a news magazine, not an entertainment magazine such as *People*, *Time* aims to reach a broad, educated, even affluent, readership interested in keeping up with current events. Knowing your readers' demographics is important because producers of ads always have a target audience in mind when they design and place an ad. They assume that the audience shares certain beliefs and values, and that the ad will move the audience to think and act in particular ways.

As you compare the effects of posting an ad on a billboard versus placing an ad in a widely-read magazine, you will inevitably discuss how a particular advertisement will travel from one medium to another. Certainly this Feeding America ad could appear in other weekly news magazines such as *Newsweek*. How effective would it be in a weekly tabloid? A fashion magazine? Or some place more public, such as in a bus terminal or waiting area in a public service office?

■ Identify What Draws Your Attention

The second step is to examine the main image or text that captures your attention. In the Feeding America ad, our attention is drawn to the central image of four children playing street hockey on a summer day. Their appearance suggests that they are healthy, happy, and well-cared for. The seemingly carefree scene of children playing with friends is familiar to most viewers.

■ Reflect on What Draws Your Attention

Then reflect on what draws your attention to this image or text. Is there something startling or shocking about the image or text, about the situation depicted? Something puzzling that holds your attention? Something about the use of color, the size of the image or text, or the font that catches your eye?

The Feeding America ad draws our attention to the center of the page where images of children, though blurred and in the background, catch our gaze. Evidently the ad was composed to emphasize the children's presence in our imagination. Who are these children? Where are they from? What are they like? Are they like us?

We are puzzled by the alarm bell in the foreground to the right. (In the original full-color ad, the alarm bell is bright red and demands our attention.) What does the designer want us to understand by juxtaposing children playing during the summer with an image that for many of us represents school? It's difficult to grasp the significance of these juxtapositions without further inquiry, in this case without looking at the text in the foreground of the ad. We assume that the designer expects readers to look there next, because of its size and the distinct way the letters are drawn—like children's chalk writing on the sidewalk. Finally, our eyes are drawn to the Feeding America logo. What is Feeding America and what values does it espouse?

■ Consider the Ethos of the Ad

The fourth step is to evaluate the ethos of the creator or sponsor of the ad. Ethos works in visual rhetoric just as it does in written rhetoric. Like writing, images are meant to convey how their composers or sponsors wish to be perceived. Thus, especially if you don't recognize a sponsor's logo or brand, it's important to ask: What is the sponsor's mission? What values does the sponsor embrace? What is the sponsor's track record? You need to know such things to determine how willing you are to believe what the ad promotes. In this case, you might find it helpful to go to the Feeding America Web site (listed in the ad) or to do a simple search on the Internet to see whether the organization has been discussed in blogs about hunger. Has Feeding America done significant work in the area of hunger? Is it a charity? If so, is it a reputable charity?

■ Analyze the Pathos in the Ad

The fifth step is to analyze the pathos in the ad—how images and text appeal to your emotions. An appeal to pathos is meant to evoke emotions such as empathy (which might prompt us to identify with an image) or out-rage (which might spur us to act in a certain way). In this case, the image of children playing outdoors with friends on a neighborhood street is likely to appeal to many of us, evoking as it does idyllic childhood memo-ries. Its nostalgic appeal invites us into an apparently calm, innocent world of peaceful play.

■ Understand the Logos of the Ad

The sixth and final step requires that we understand the entire composi-tion of the ad—what the cluster of images and text convey. What is the logic of the ad? How do the images and text work together to persuade us? What is the takeaway message?

The text in the Feeding America ad helps clarify the meaning of the central images of the children and the alarm bell. The alarm bell ties the image in the background to the foregrounded text—"School may be out for summer, but lunch is always in session." Food insecurity is a problem everyday for children in need. But where do these children get their food when school is not in session?

Hunger is not readily visible to most of us. Images of playfulness, even childlike innocence, can mask the deprivation that any of the people sur-rounding us may experience in their own lives. The text makes the appeal in the ad explicit. Those living in hunger are all around us.

The smaller text answers the question of where children in need can receive the nutrition they require. Children who are eligible for free lunch during the school year are also eligible to receive free meals during the summer.

Translating the discrete images and text into a coherent argument re-quires inductive reasoning, moving from specific pieces of evidence to a major premise. We would conclude that the argument in the ad goes some-thing like this:

1. Hunger in America is a reality in the lives of many children and families.

2. Food insecurity exists for children year round—whether school is in session or not.

3. Feeding America can help children and families gain access to the nu-trition they require.

There are other ways to formulate the argument, and we invite you to dis-cuss these alternatives as a class. Our main point, though, is that visual images make claims on us as viewers in much the same ways as any writ-ten text does. Having the tools of visual rhetoric can help you discern how images and text work together to produce an argument.

Steps to Visual Analysis

1 **Notice where the ad appears.** What is its target audience? To what extent does the placement of the ad in a magazine or newspaper or on a billboard determine the potential viewers of the ad?

2 **Identify what draws your attention.** Where does your eye go? To an image, some text, some odd juxtaposition?

3 **Reflect on what draws your attention.** Is there something startling or shocking about the image or text, about the situation depicted? Something puzzling that holds your attention? Something about the use of color, the size of the image or text, or the font that catches your eye?

4 **Consider the ethos of the ad.** Evaluate the legitimacy, or ethos, of the ad's sponsor. For example, what do you know about the corporation or institution sponsoring the ad? To what extent do you share its values?

5 **Analyze the pathos in the ad.** How do the images and text appeal to your emotions? What does the image or text make you feel or think about?

6 **Understand the logos of the ad.** What is the logic of the ad? Taken together, what do the cluster of images and text convey? How are the different images and text related to the claim that the ad is making?

A Practice Sequence: Analyzing the Rhetoric of an Advertisement

To practice these strategies, we would like you to choose and analyze the following ad for Microsoft (Figure 8.3). The photograph is of a girl in a robe and slippers sitting on her bed looking at a laptop. The text above the image reads, "You have your best ideas in the shower. Now you can work in the next room." Below the image the text reads, "Office and an online workspace from Microsoft let you work from almost anywhere inspiration finds you. It's easier than ever to store, view, and share all your important documents from pretty much anywhere you happen to be. That's because Microsoft Office works so easily with a free online workspace from Microsoft. So work no longer requires clothes, just Internet access. Buy it for your PC this holiday season." Text at the bottom of the ad reads, "Office2007.com Microsoft Office Real life tools." (Other advertisements for analysis appear on pages 244–246.)

First, evaluate the ethos that the ad tries to project. Do some research on the Internet to find out what Microsoft, which designs and manufactures computer software, represents as a company. In doing this research, write a brief summary of the company's values. Do you share those values? Are you confident in the company's ability to produce a good product that you want to use?

Second, reflect on and write about what the images and text make you feel about your own experiences working from home. In what ways do you identify with the message that the workplace extends into personal space?

Third, work in small groups to identify the logic of the narrative that the images and text convey. What do you see as the main premise of the ad? How did you arrive at your conclusion? Report your group's findings to the class. Be sure to present the evidence to support your claim.

FIGURE 8.3   Microsoft Advertisement

- **Further Ads for Analysis: Figures 8.4–8.6.**

FIGURE 8.4   Drinking and driving PSA   The image is of a full beer glass representing a mixture of light and dark beers. The main text heading reads: The "It's Only Another Beer" Black and Tan. A list of "ingredients" follows: 8 oz. pilsner lager. 8 oz. stout lager. 1 frosty mug. 1 icy road. 1 pick-up truck. 1 10-hour day. 1 tired worker. A few rounds with the guys. Mix ingredients. Add 1 totalled vehicle. Never underestimate 'just a few.' Buzzed driving is drunk driving. Sponsors appear at the bottom of the page: AdCouncil.org and U.S. Department of Transportation.

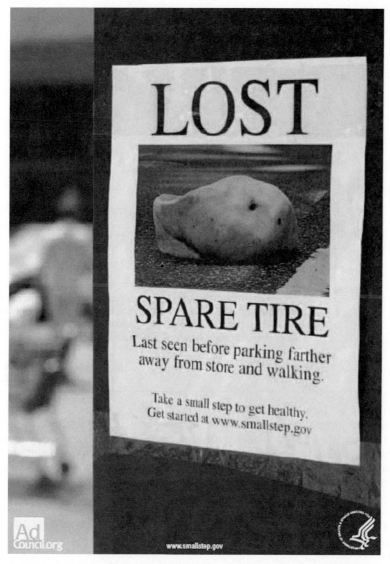

FIGURE 8.5   Exercise PSA   The image is of a poster pinned to a wall in public space, with a representation of a bulging human waistline lying on the ground. The text on the poster reads: Lost   Spare Tire   Last seen before parking farther away from store and walking. Take a small step to get healthy. Get started at www.smallstep.gov. At the bottom of the poster the sponsors are listed: AdCouncil.org, www.smallstep.gov, and the U.S. Department of Health & Human Services.

FIGURE 8.6   Health Care PSA   A tongue depressor appears against a plain white background next to a headline that reads: open up and say anything. The text underneath it reads: want better health care? start asking more questions. to your doctor. to your pharmacist. to your nurse. what are the test results? what about side effects? don't fully understand your prescriptions? don't leave confused. because the most important question is the one you should have asked. go to *www.ahrq.gov/questionsaretheanswer* or call *1-800-931-AHRQ (2477)* for the 10 questions every patient should ask. questions are the answer. The sponsors appear at the bottom of the ad: Ad Council, the U.S. Department of Health & Human Services, and AHRQ Agency for Healthcare Research and Quality.

9

From Introductions to Conclusions
Drafting an Essay

In this chapter, we describe strategies for crafting introductions that set up your argument. We then describe the characteristics of well-formulated paragraphs that will help you build your argument. Finally, we provide you with some strategies for writing conclusions that reinforce what is new about your argument, what is at stake, and what readers should do with the knowledge you convey.

DRAFTING INTRODUCTIONS

The introduction is where you set up your argument. It's where you identify a widely held assumption, challenge that assumption, and state your thesis. Writers use a number of strategies to set up their arguments. In this section we look at five of them:

- Moving from a general topic to a specific thesis (inverted-triangle introduction)
- Introducing the topic with a story (narrative introduction)
- Beginning with a question (interrogative introduction)
- Capturing readers' attention with something unexpected (paradoxical introduction)
- Identifying a gap in knowledge (minding-the-gap introduction)

Remember that an introduction need not be limited to a single paragraph. It may take several paragraphs to effectively set up your argument.

Keep in mind that you have to make these strategies your own. That is, we can suggest models, but you must make them work for your own argument. You must imagine your readers and what will engage them. What tone do you want to take? Playful? Serious? Formal? Urgent? The attitude you want to convey will depend on your purpose, your argument, and the needs of your audience.

■ The Inverted-Triangle Introduction

An **inverted-triangle introduction**, like an upside-down triangle, is broad at the top and pointed at the base. It begins with a general statement of the topic and then narrows its focus, ending with the point of the paragraph (and the triangle), the writer's thesis. We can see this strategy at work in the following introduction from a student's essay. The student writer (1) begins with a broad description of the problem she will address, (2) then focuses on a set of widely held but troublesome assumptions, and (3) finally, responding to what she sees as a pervasive problem, presents her thesis.

The student begins with a general set of assumptions about education that she believes people readily accept.

In today's world, many believe that education's sole purpose is to communicate information for students to store and draw on as necessary. By storing this information, students hope to perform well on tests. Good test scores assure good grades. Good grades eventually lead to acceptances into good colleges, which ultimately guarantee good jobs. Many teachers and students, convinced that education exists as a tool to secure good jobs,

She then cites author bell hooks, to identify an approach that makes use of these assumptions—the "banking system" of education, a term hooks borrows from educator Paulo Freire.

rely on the *banking system*. In her essay "Teaching to Transgress," bell hooks defines the *banking system* as an "approach to learning that is rooted in the notion that all students need to do is consume information fed to them by a professor and be able to memorize and store it" (185). Through the banking system, students focus solely on facts, missing the important themes and life

The student then points to the banking system as the problem. This sets up her thesis about the "true purpose" of education.

lessons available in classes and school materials. The banking system misdirects the fundamental goals of education. Education's true purpose is to prepare students for the real world by allowing them access to pertinent life knowledge available in their studies. Education should then entice students to apply this pertinent life knowledge to daily life struggles through praxis. In addition to her definition of the banking system, hooks offers the idea of praxis from the work of Paulo Freire. When incorporated into education, *praxis*, or "action and reflection upon the world in order to change it" (185), offers an advantageous educational tool that enhances the true purpose of education and overcomes the banking system.

The strategy of writing an introduction as an inverted triangle entails first identifying an idea, an argument, or a concept that people appear to accept as true; next, pointing out the problems with that idea, argument, or concept; and then, in a few sentences, setting out a thesis—how those problems can be resolved.

■ The Narrative Introduction

Opening with a short **narrative**, or story, is a strategy many writers use successfully to draw readers into a topic. A narrative introduction relates a sequence of events and can be especially effective if you think you need to coax indifferent or reluctant readers into taking an interest in the topic. Of course, a narrative introduction delays the declaration of your argument, so it's wise to choose a short story that clearly connects to your argument, and get to the thesis as quickly as possible (within a few paragraphs) before your readers start wondering "What's the point of this story?"

Notice how the student writer uses a narrative introduction to her argument in her essay titled "Throwing a Punch at Gender Roles: How Women's Boxing Empowers Women."

The student's entire first paragraph is a narrative that takes us into the world of women's boxing and foreshadows her thesis.

Glancing at my watch, I ran into the gym, noting to myself that being late to the first day of boxing practice was not the right way to make a good first impression. I flew down the stairs into the basement, to the room the boxers have lovingly dubbed "The Pit." What greeted me when I got there was more than I could ever have imagined. Picture a room filled with boxing gloves of all sizes covering an entire wall, a mirror covering another, a boxing ring in a corner, and an awesome collection of framed newspaper and magazine articles chronicling the boxers whose pictures were hanging on every wall. Now picture that room with seventy-plus girls on the floor doing push-ups, sweat dripping down their faces. I was immediately struck by the discipline this sport would take from me, but I had no idea I would take so much more from it.

With her narrative as a backdrop, the student identifies a problem, using the transition word yet to mark her challenge to the conditions she observes in the university's women's boxing program.

The university offers the only nonmilitary-based college-level women's boxing program in America, and it also offers women the chance to push their physical limits in a regulated environment. Yet the program is plagued with disappointments. I have experienced for myself the stereotypes female boxers face and have dealt with the harsh reality that boxing is still widely recognized as only a men's sport. This paper will show that the women's boxing program at Notre Dame serves as a much-needed outlet for females to come face-to-face with aspects of themselves they

The writer then states her thesis (what her paper "will show"): Despite the problems of stereotyping, women's boxing offers women significant opportunities for growth.

would not typically get a chance to explore. It will also examine how viewing this sport as a positive opportunity for women at ND indicates that there is growing hope that very soon more activities similar to women's boxing may be better received by society in general. I will accomplish these goals by analyzing scholarly journals, old *Observer* [the school newspaper] articles, and survey questions answered by the captains of the 2003 women's boxing team of ND.

The student writer uses a visually descriptive narrative to introduce us to the world of women's college boxing; then, in the second paragraph, she steers us toward the purpose of the paper and the methods she will use to develop her argument about what women's boxing offers to young women and to the changing world of sports.

■ The Interrogative Introduction

An **interrogative introduction** invites readers into the conversation of your essay by asking one or more questions, which the essay goes on to answer. You want to think of a question that will pique your readers' interest, enticing them to read on to discover how your insights shed light on the issue. Notice the question Daphne Spain, a professor of urban and environmental planning, uses to open her essay "Spatial Segregation and Gender Stratification in the Workplace."

Spain sets up her argument by asking a question and then tentatively answering it with a reference to a published study.

In the third sentence, she states her thesis — that men and women have very little contact in the workplace.

Finally, she outlines the effects that this lack of contact has on women.

To what extent do women and men who work in different occupations also work in different space? Baran and Teegarden propose that occupational segregation in the insurance industry is "tantamount to spatial segregation by gender" since managers are overwhelmingly male and clerical staff are predominantly female. This essay examines the spatial conditions of women's work and men's work and proposes that working women and men come into daily contact with one another very infrequently. Further, women's jobs can be classified as "open floor," but men's jobs are more likely to be "closed door." That is, women work in a more public environment with less control of their space than men. This lack of spatial control both reflects and contributes to women's lower occupational status by limiting opportunities for the transfer of knowledge from men to women.

By the end of this introductory paragraph, Spain has explained some of the terms she will use in her essay (*open floor* and *closed door*) and has offered in her final sentence a clear statement of her thesis.

In "Harry Potter and the Technology of Magic," literature scholar Elizabeth Teare begins by contextualizing the Harry Potter publishing phenomenon. Then she raises a question about what is fueling this success story.

In her first four sentences, Teare describes something she is curious about and she hopes readers will be curious about—the growing popularity of the Harry Potter books.

The July/August 2001 issue of *Book* lists J. K. Rowling as one of the ten most influential people in publishing. She shares space on this list with John Grisham and Oprah Winfrey, along with less famous but equally powerful insiders in the book industry. What these industry leaders have in common is an almost magical power to make books succeed in the marketplace, and this magic, in addition to that performed with wands, Rowling's novels appear to practice. Opening weekend sales charted like those of a blockbuster movie (not to mention the blockbuster movie itself), the reconstruction of the venerable *New York Times* bestseller lists, the creation of a new nation's worth of web sites in the territory of cyberspace, and of course the legendary inspiration of tens of millions of child readers—the Harry Potter books have transformed both the technologies of reading and the way we understand those technologies.

In the fifth sentence, Teare asks the question she will try to answer in the rest of the essay.

What is it that makes these books—about a lonely boy whose first act on learning he is a wizard is to go shopping for a wand—not only an international phenomenon among children and parents and teachers but also a topic of compelling interest to literary, social, and cultural critics?

Finally, in the last sentence, Teare offers a partial answer to her question—her thesis.

I will argue that the stories the books tell, as well as the stories we're telling about them, enact both our fantasies and our fears of children's literature and publishing in the context of twenty-first-century commercial and technological culture.

In the final two sentences of the introduction, Teare raises her question about the root of this "international phenomenon" and then offers her thesis. By the end of the opening paragraph, then, the reader knows exactly what question is driving Teare's essay and the answer she proposes to explain throughout the essay.

■ The Paradoxical Introduction

A **paradoxical introduction** appeals to readers' curiosity by pointing out an aspect of the topic that runs counter to their expectations. Just as an interrogative introduction draws readers in by asking a question, a paradoxical introduction draws readers in by saying, in effect, "Here's something completely surprising and unlikely about this issue, but my essay will go on to show you how it is true." In this passage from "'Holding Back': Negotiating a Glass Ceiling on Women's Muscular Strength," sociologist

Shari L. Dworkin points to a paradox in our commonsense understanding of bodies as the product of biology, not culture.

In the first sentence, Dworkin quotes from a study to identify the thinking that she is going to challenge.

Notice how Dworkin signals her own position "However" relative to commonly held assumptions.

Dworkin ends by stating her thesis, noting a paradox that will surprise readers.

Current work in gender studies points to how "when examined closely, much of what we take for granted about gender and its causes and effects either does not hold up, or can be explained differently." These arguments become especially contentious when confronting nature/culture debates on gendered *bodies*. After all, "common sense" frequently tells us that flesh and blood bodies are about biology. However, bodies are also shaped and constrained through cumulative social practices, structures of opportunity, wider cultural meanings, and more. Paradoxically, then, when we think that we are "really seeing" naturally sexed bodies, perhaps we are seeing the effect of internalizing gender ideologies—carrying out social practices—and this constructs our vision of "sexed" bodies.

Dworkin's strategy in the first three sentences is to describe common practice, the understanding that bodies are biological. Then, in the sentences beginning "However" and "Paradoxically," she advances the surprising idea that our bodies—not just the clothes we wear, for example—carry cultural gender markers. Her essay then goes on to examine women's weight lifting and the complex motives driving many women to create a body that is perceived as muscular but not masculine.

■ The Minding-the-Gap Introduction

This type of introduction takes its name from the British train system, the voice on the loudspeaker that intones "Mind the gap!" at every stop, to call riders' attention to the gap between the train car and the platform. In a **minding-the-gap introduction**, a writer calls readers' attention to a gap in the research on an issue and then uses the rest of the essay to fill in the "gap." A minding-the-gap introduction says, in effect, "Wait a minute. There's something missing from this conversation, and my research and ideas will fill in this gap."

For example, in the introductory paragraphs to their book *Men's Lives*, Michael S. Kimmel and Michael A. Messner explain how the book is different from other books that discuss men's lives, and how it serves a different purpose.

The authors begin with an assumption and then challenge it. A transition word (but) signals the challenge.

This is a book about men. But, unlike other books about men, which line countless library shelves, this is a book about men as men. It is a book in which men's experiences are not taken for granted as we explore the "real" and significant accomplishments of men, but a book in which those experiences are treated as significant and important in themselves.

The authors follow with a question that provokes readers' interest and points to the gap they summarize in the last sentence.

But what does it mean to examine men "as men"? Most courses in a college curriculum are about men, aren't they? But these courses routinely deal with men only in their public roles, so we come to know and understand men as scientists, politicians, military figures, writers, and philosophers. Rarely, if ever, are men understood through the prism of gender.

Kimmel and Messner use these opening paragraphs to highlight both what they find problematic about the existing literature on men and to introduce readers to their own approach.

Steps to Drafting Introductions: Five Strategies

1 **Use an inverted triangle.** Begin with a broad situation, concept, or idea, and narrow the focus to your thesis.

2 **Begin with a narrative.** Capture readers' imagination and interest with a story that sets the stage for your argument.

3 **Ask a question that you will answer.** Provoke readers' interest with a question, and then use your thesis to answer the question.

4 **Present a paradox.** Begin with an assumption that readers accept as true, and formulate a thesis that not only challenges that assumption but may very well seem paradoxical.

5 **Mind the gap.** Identify what readers know and then what they don't know (or what you believe they need to know).

A Practice Sequence: Drafting an Introduction

1 Write or rewrite your introduction (which, as you've seen, may involve more than one paragraph), using one of the strategies described above. Then share your introduction with one of your peers and ask the following questions:

- To what extent did the strategy compel you to want to read further?

- To what extent is my thesis clear?

- How effectively do I draw a distinction between what I believe others assume to be true and my own approach?

- Is there another way that I might have made my introduction more compelling?

After listening to the responses, try a second strategy and then ask your peer which introduction is more effective.

2 If you do not have your own introduction to work on, revise the introduction below from one of our students' essays, combining two of the strategies we describe above.

> News correspondent Pauline Frederick once commented, "When a man gets up to speak people listen then look. When a woman gets up, people look; then, if they like what they see, they listen." Ironically, the harsh reality of this statement is given life by the ongoing controversy over America's most recognizable and sometimes notorious toy, Barbie. Celebrating her 40th birthday this year, Barbie has become this nation's most beleaguered soldier (a woman no less) of idolatry who has been to the front lines and back more times than the average "Joe." This doll, a piece of plastic, a toy, incurs both criticism and praise spanning both ends of the ideological spectrum. Barbie's curvaceous and basically unrealistic body piques the ire of both liberals and conservatives, each contending that Barbie stands for the distinct view of the other. One hundred and eighty degrees south, others praise Barbie's (curves and all) ability to unlock youthful imagination and potential. M. G. Lord explains Barbie best: "To study Barbie, one sometimes has to hold seemingly contradictory ideas in one's head at the same time. . . . The doll functions like a Rorschach test: people project wildly dissimilar and often opposing meanings on it. . . . And her meaning, like her face, has not been static over time." In spite of the extreme polarity, a sole unconscious consensus manifests itself about Barbie. Barbie is "the icon" of womanhood and the twentieth century. She is the American dream. Barbie is "us." The question is always the same: What message does Barbie send? Barbie is a toy. She is the image of what we see.

DEVELOPING PARAGRAPHS

In your introduction, you set forth your thesis. Then, in subsequent paragraphs, you have to develop your argument. Remember our metaphor: If your thesis, or main claim, is the skewer that runs through each paragraph in your essay, then these paragraphs are the "meat" of your argument. The paragraphs that follow your introduction carry the burden of evidence in your argument. After all, a claim cannot stand on its own without supporting evidence. Generally speaking, each paragraph should include a topic sentence that brings the main idea of the paragraph into focus, be unified around the main idea of the topic sentence, and adequately develop the idea. At the same time, a paragraph does not stand on its own; as part of your overall argument, it can refer to what you've said earlier, gesture toward where you are heading, and connect to the larger conversation to which you are contributing.

We now ask you to read an excerpt from "Reinventing 'America': Call for a New National Identity," by Elizabeth Martínez, and answer some questions about how you think the author develops her argument, paragraph by paragraph. Then we discuss her work in the context of the three key elements of paragraphs: *topic sentences*, *unity*, and *adequate development*. As you read, pay attention to how, sentence by sentence, Martínez develops her paragraphs. We also ask that you consider how she makes her argument provocative, impassioned, and urgent for her audience.

ELIZABETH MARTÍNEZ

From Reinventing "America": Call for a New National Identity

Elizabeth Martínez is a Chicana activist who since 1960 has worked in and documented different movements for change, including the civil rights, women's, and Chicano movements. She is the author of six books and numerous articles. Her best-known work is *500 Years of Chicano History in Pictures* (1991), which became the basis of a two-part video she scripted and codirected. Her latest book is *De Colores Means All of Us: Latina Views for a Multi-Colored Century* (1998). In "Reinventing 'America,'" Martínez argues that Americans' willingness to accept a "myth" as "the basis for [the] nation's self-defined identity" has brought the country to a crisis.

■ ■ ■

For some fifteen years, starting in 1940, 85 percent of all U.S. elementary schools used the Dick and Jane series to teach children how to read. The series starred Dick, Jane, their white middle-class parents, their dog Spot, and their life together in a home with a white picket fence.

"Look, Jane, look! See Spot run!" chirped the two kids. It was a house full of glorious family values, where Mom cooked while Daddy went to work in a suit and mowed the lawn on weekends. The Dick and Jane books also taught that you should do your job and help others. All this affirmed an equation of middle-class whiteness with virtue.

In the mid-1990s, museums, libraries, and eighty Public Broadcasting Service (PBS) stations across the country had exhibits and programs commemorating the series. At one museum, an attendant commented, "When you hear someone crying, you know they are looking at the Dick and Jane books." It seems nostalgia runs rampant among many Euro-Americans: a nostalgia for the days of unchallenged White Supremacy—both moral and material—when life was "simple."

We've seen that nostalgia before in the nation's history. But today it signifies a problem reaching a new intensity. It suggests a national identity crisis that promises to bring in its wake an unprecedented nervous breakdown for the dominant society's psyche.

Nowhere is this more apparent than in California, which has long been on the cutting edge of the nation's present and future reality. Warning sirens have sounded repeatedly in the 1990s, such as the fierce battle over new history textbooks for public schools, Proposition 187's ugly denial of human rights to immigrants, the 1996 assault on affirmative action that culminated in Proposition 209, and the 1997 move to abolish bilingual education. Attempts to copycat these reactionary measures have been seen in other states.

The attack on affirmative action isn't really about affirmative action.   6
Essentially it is another tactic in today's war on the gains of the 1960s, a tactic rooted in Anglo resentment and fear. A major source of that fear: the fact that California will almost surely have a majority of people of color in 20 to 30 years at most, with the nation as a whole not far behind.

Check out the February 3, 1992, issue of *Sports Illustrated* with its   7
double-spread ad for *Time* magazine. The ad showed hundreds of new-born babies in their hospital cribs, all of them Black or brown except for a rare white face here and there. The headline says, "Hey, whitey! It's your turn at the back of the bus!" The ad then tells you, read *Time* magazine to keep up with today's hot issues. That manipulative image could have been published today; its implication of shifting power appears to be the recurrent nightmare of too many potential Anglo allies.

Euro-American anxiety often focuses on the sense of a vanishing na-   8
tional identity. Behind the attacks on immigrants, affirmative action, and multiculturalism, behind the demand for "English Only" laws and the rejection of bilingual education, lies the question: with all these new people, languages, and cultures, what will it mean to be an American? If that question once seemed, to many people, to have an obvious, universally applicable answer, today new definitions must be found. But too often Americans, with supposed scholars in the lead, refuse to face that need and instead nurse a nostalgia for some bygone clarity. They remain trapped in denial.

An array of such ostriches, heads in the sand, began flapping their   9
feathers noisily with the publication of Allan Bloom's 1987 best-selling book, *The Closing of the American Mind*. Bloom bemoaned the decline of our "common values" as a society, meaning the decline of Euro-American cultural centricity (shall we just call it cultural imperialism?). Since then we have seen constant sniping at "diversity" goals across the land. The assault has often focused on how U.S. history is taught. And with reason, for this country's identity rests on a particular narrative about the historical origins of the United States as a nation.

The Great White Origin Myth

Every society has an origin narrative that explains that society to itself   10
and the world with a set of stories and symbols. The origin myth, as scholar-activist Roxanne Dunbar Ortiz has termed it, defines how a soci-

ety understands its place in the world and its history. The myth provides the basis for a nation's self-defined identity. Most origin narratives can be called myths because they usually present only the most flattering view of a nation's history; they are not distinguished by honesty.

Ours begins with Columbus "discovering" a hemisphere where some 80 million people already lived but didn't really count (in what became the United States, they were just buffalo-chasing "savages" with no grasp of real estate values and therefore doomed to perish). It continues with the brave Pilgrims, a revolution by independence-loving colonists against a decadent English aristocracy, and the birth of an energetic young republic that promised democracy and equality (that is, to white male landowners). In the 1840s, the new nation expanded its size by almost one-third, thanks to a victory over that backward land of little brown people called Mexico. Such has been the basic account of how the nation called the United States of America came into being as presently configured. *11*

The myth's omissions are grotesque. It ignores three major pillars of our nationhood: genocide, enslavement, and imperialist expansion (such nasty words, who wants to hear them?—but that's the problem). The massive extermination of indigenous peoples provided our land base; the enslavement of African labor made our economic growth possible; and the seizure of half of Mexico by war (or threat of renewed war) extended this nation's boundaries north to the Pacific and south to the Rio Grande. Such are the foundation stones of the United States, within an economic system that made this country the first in world history to be born capitalist. . . . *12*

Racism as Linchpin of the U.S. National Identity

A crucial embellishment of the origin myth and key element of the national identity has been the myth of the frontier, analyzed in Richard Slotkin's *Gunfighter Nation*, the last volume of a fascinating trilogy. He describes Theodore Roosevelt's belief that the West was won thanks to American arms, "the means by which progress and nationality will be achieved." That success, Roosevelt continued, "depends on the heroism of men who impose on the course of events the latent virtues of their 'race.'" Roosevelt saw conflict on the frontier producing a series of virile "fighters and breeders" who would eventually generate a new leadership class. Militarism thus went hand in hand with the racialization of history's protagonists. . . . *13*

The frontier myth embodied the nineteenth-century concept of Manifest Destiny, a doctrine that served to justify expansionist violence by means of intrinsic racial superiority. Manifest Destiny was Yankee conquest as the inevitable result of a confrontation between enterprise and progress (white) versus passivity and backwardness (Indian, Mexican). *14*

"Manifest" meant "God-given," and the whole doctrine is profoundly rooted in religious conviction going back to the earliest colonial times. In his short, powerful book *Manifest Destiny: American Expansion and the Empire of Right*, Professor Anders Stephanson tells how the Puritans reinvented the Jewish notion of chosenness and applied it to this hemisphere so that territorial expansion became God's will. . . .

Manifest Destiny Dies Hard

The concept of Manifest Destiny, with its assertion of racial superiority sustained by military power, has defined U.S. identity for 150 years. . . .   15

Today's origin myth and the resulting concept of national identity make for an intellectual prison where it is dangerous to ask big questions about this society's superiority. When otherwise decent people are trapped in such a powerful desire not to feel guilty, self-deception becomes unavoidable. To cease our present falsification of collective memory should, and could, open the doors of that prison. When together we cease equating whiteness with Americanness, a new day can dawn. As David Roediger, the social historian, has said, "[Whiteness] is the empty and therefore terrifying attempt to build an identity on what one isn't, and on whom one can hold back."   16

Redefining the U.S. origin narrative, and with it this country's national identity, could prove liberating for our collective psyche. It does not mean Euro-Americans should wallow individually in guilt. It does mean accepting collective responsibility to deal with the implications of our real origin. A few apologies, for example, might be a step in the right direction. In 1997, the idea was floated in Congress to apologize for slavery; it encountered opposition from all sides. But to reject the notion because corrective action, not an apology, is needed misses the point. Having defined itself as the all-time best country in the world, the United States fiercely denies the need to make a serious official apology for anything. . . . To press for any serious, official apology does imply a new origin narrative, a new self-image, an ideological sea-change.   17

Accepting the implications of a different narrative could also shed light on today's struggles. In the affirmative-action struggle, for example, opponents have said that that policy is no longer needed because racism ended with the Civil Rights Movement. But if we look at slavery as a fundamental pillar of this nation, going back centuries, it becomes obvious that racism could not have been ended by 30 years of mild reforms. If we see how the myth of the frontier idealized the white male adventurer as the central hero of national history, with the woman as sunbonneted helpmate, then we might better understand the dehumanized ways in which women have continued to be treated. A more truthful origin narrative could also help break down divisions among peoples of color by revealing common experiences and histories of cooperation.   18

Reading as a Writer

1. To what extent does the narrative Martínez begins with make you want to read further?
2. How does she connect this narrative to the rest of her argument?
3. How does she use repetition to create unity in her essay?
4. What assumptions does Martínez challenge?
5. How does she use questions to engage her readers?

■ Use Topic Sentences to Focus Your Paragraphs

The **topic sentence** states the main point of a paragraph. It should

- provide a partial answer to the question motivating the writer.
- act as an extension of the writer's thesis and the question motivating the writer's argument.
- serve as a guidepost, telling readers what the paragraph is about.
- help create unity and coherence both within the paragraph and within the essay.

Elizabeth Martínez begins by describing how elementary schools in the 1940s and 1950s used the Dick and Jane series not only to teach reading but also to foster a particular set of values—values that she believes do not serve all children enrolled in America's schools. In paragraph 4, she states her thesis, explaining that nostalgia in the United States has created "a national identity crisis that promises to bring in its wake an unprecedented nervous breakdown for the dominant society's psyche." This is a point that builds on an observation she makes in paragraph 3: "It seems nostalgia runs rampant among many Euro-Americans: a nostalgia for the days of unchallenged White Supremacy—both moral and material—when life was 'simple.'" Martínez often returns to this notion of nostalgia for a past that seems "simple" to explain what she sees as an impending crisis.

Consider the first sentence of paragraph 5 as a topic sentence. With Martínez's key points in mind, notice how she uses the sentence to make her thesis more specific. Notice too, how she ties in the crisis and breakdown she alludes to in paragraph 4. Essentially, Martínez tells her readers that they can see these problems at play in California, an indicator of "the nation's present and future reality."

> *Nowhere is this more apparent than in California, which has long been on the cutting edge of the nation's present and future reality.* Warning sirens have sounded repeatedly in the 1990s, such as the fierce battle over new history textbooks for public schools, Proposition 187's ugly denial of human rights to immigrants, the 1996 assault on affirmative action that culminated in Proposition 209, and the 1997 move to abolish bilingual education. *Attempts to copycat these reactionary measures have been seen in other states.*

The final sentence of paragraph 5 sets up the remainder of the essay.

As readers, we expect each subsequent paragraph to respond in some way to the issue Martínez has raised. She meets that expectation by formulating a topic sentence that appears at the beginning of the paragraph. The topic sentence is what helps create unity and coherence in the essay.

■ Create Unity in Your Paragraphs

Each paragraph in an essay should focus on the subject suggested by the topic sentence. If a paragraph begins with one focus or major point of discussion, it should not end with another. Several strategies can contribute to the unity of each paragraph.

Use details that follow logically from your topic sentence and maintain a single focus — a focus that is clearly an extension of your thesis.   For example, in paragraph 5, Martínez's topic sentence ("Nowhere is this more apparent than in California, which has long been on the cutting edge of the nation's present and future reality") helps to create unity because it refers back to her thesis (*this* refers to the "national identity crisis" mentioned in paragraph 4) and limits the focus of what she includes in the paragraph to "the fierce battle over new history textbooks" and recent pieces of legislation in California that follow directly from and support the claim of the topic sentence.

Repeat key words to guide your readers.   A second strategy for creating unity is to repeat (or use synonyms for) key words within a given paragraph. You can see this at work in paragraph 12 (notice the words we've underscored), where Martínez explains that America's origin narrative omits significant details:

> The myth's omissions are grotesque. It ignores three major pillars of our nationhood: genocide, enslavement, and imperialist expansion (such nasty words, who wants to hear them? — but that's the problem). The massive extermination of indigenous peoples provided our land base; the enslavement of African labor made our economic growth possible; and the seizure of half of Mexico by war (or threat of renewed war) extended this nation's boundaries north to the Pacific and south to the Rio Grande. Such are the foundation stones of the United States, within an economic system that made this country the first in world history to be born capitalist. . . .

Specifically, Martínez tells us that the origin narrative ignores "three major pillars of our nationhood: genocide, enslavement, and imperialist expansion." She then substitutes *extermination* for "genocide," repeats *enslavement*, and substitutes *seizure* for "imperialist expansion." By connecting words in a paragraph, as Martínez does here, you help readers understand that the details you provide are all relevant to the point you want to make.

Use transition words to link ideas from different sentences.   A third strategy for creating unity within paragraphs is to establish a clear relationship among different ideas by using **transition words** or phrases. Transition words or phrases signal to your readers the direction your ideas are taking. Table 9.1 lists common transition words and phrases grouped by function—that is, for adding a new idea, presenting a contrasting idea, or drawing a conclusion about an idea.

Martínez uses transition words and phrases throughout the excerpt here. In several places, she uses the word *but* to make a contrast—to draw a distinction between an idea that many people accept as true and an alternative idea that she wants to pursue. Notice in paragraph 17 how she signals the importance of an official apology for slavery—and by implication genocide and the seizure of land from Mexico:

> . . . A few apologies, for example, might be a step in the right direction. In 1997, the idea was floated in Congress to apologize for slavery; it encountered opposition from all sides. But to reject the notion because corrective action, not an apology, is needed misses the point. Having defined itself as the all-time best country in the world, the United States fiercely denies the need to make a serious official apology for anything. . . . To press for any serious, official apology does imply a new origin narrative, a new self-image, an ideological sea-change.

Similarly, in the last paragraph, Martínez counters the argument that affirmative action is not necessary because racism no longer exists:

> . . . In the affirmative-action struggle, for example, opponents have said that that policy is no longer needed because racism ended with the Civil Rights Movement. But if we look at slavery as a fundamental pillar of this nation, going back centuries, it becomes obvious that racism could not have been ended by 30 years of mild reforms. . . .

There are a number of ways to rephrase what Martínez is saying in paragraph 18. We could substitute *however* for "but." Or we could combine the two sentences into one to point to the relationship between the two competing ideas: *Although some people oppose affirmative action, believing that racism no longer exists, I would argue that racism remains a fundamental pillar of this nation.* Or we could pull together Martínez's different points to draw a logical conclusion using a transition word like *therefore.* Martínez observes that our country is in crisis as a result of increased immigration. *Therefore, we need to reassess our conceptions of national*

TABLE 9.1   Common Transition Words and Phrases

ADDING AN IDEA	PRESENTING A CONTRASTING IDEA	DRAWING A LOGICAL CONCLUSION
also, and, further, moreover, in addition to, in support of, similarly	although, alternatively, as an alternative, but, by way of contrast, despite, even though, however, in contrast to, nevertheless, nonetheless, rather than, yet	as a result, because of, consequently, finally, in sum, in the end, subsequently, therefore, thus

identity to account for the diversity that increased immigration has created. We can substitute any of the transition words in Table 9.1 for drawing a logical conclusion.

The list of transition words and phrases in Table 9.1 is hardly exhaustive, but it gives you a sense of the ways to connect ideas so that readers understand how your ideas are related. Are they similar ideas? Do they build on or support one another? Are you challenging accepted ideas? Or are you drawing a logical connection from a number of different ideas?

■ Use Critical Strategies to Develop Your Paragraphs

To develop a paragraph, you can use a range of strategies, depending on what you want to accomplish and what you believe your readers will need in order to be persuaded by what you argue. Among these strategies are using examples and illustrations; citing data (facts, statistics, evidence, details); analyzing texts; telling a story or an anecdote; defining terms; making comparisons; and examining causes and evaluating consequences.

Use examples and illustrations.   Examples make abstract ideas concrete through illustration. Using examples is probably the most common way to develop a piece of writing. Of course, Martínez's essay is full of examples. In fact, she begins with an example of a series of books—the Dick and Jane books—to show how a generation of schoolchildren were exposed to white middle-class values. She also uses examples in paragraph 5, where she lists several pieces of legislation (Propositions 187 and 209) to develop the claim in her topic sentence.

Cite data.   **Data** are factual pieces of information. They function in an essay as the bases of propositions. In the first few paragraphs of the excerpt, Martínez cites statistics ("85 percent of all U.S. elementary schools used the Dick and Jane series to teach children how to read") and facts ("In the mid-1990s, museums, libraries, and eighty Public Broadcasting Service . . . stations across the country had exhibits and programs commemorating the series") to back up her claim about the popularity of the Dick and Jane series and the nostalgia the books evoke.

Analyze texts.   Analysis is the process of breaking something down into its elements to understand how they work together. When you analyze a text, you point out parts of the text that have particular significance to your argument and explain what they mean. By *texts*, we mean both verbal and visual texts. In paragraph 7, Martínez analyzes a visual text, an advertisement that appeared in *Sports Illustrated*, to reveal "its implication of shifting power"—a demographic power shift from Anglos to people of color.

Tell narratives or anecdotes.   Put simply, a narrative is an account of something that happened. More technically, a narrative relates a sequence of events that are connected in time; and an **anecdote** is a short narrative that recounts a particular incident. An anecdote, like an example, can bring an abstraction into focus. Consider Martínez's third paragraph, where the anecdote about the museum attendant brings her point about racially charged nostalgia among white Americans into memorable focus: The tears of the museum-goers indicate just how profound their nostalgia is.

By contrast, a longer narrative, in setting out its sequence of events, often opens up possibilities for analysis. Why did these events occur? Why did they occur in this sequence? What might they lead to? What are the implications? What is missing?

In paragraph 11, for example, Martínez relates several key events in the origin myth of America. Then, in the next paragraph, she explains what is omitted from the myth, or narrative, and builds her argument about the implications and consequences of those omissions.

Define terms.   A definition is an explanation of what something is and, by implication, what it is not. The simplest kind of definition is a synonym, but for the purpose of developing your argument, a one-word definition is rarely enough.

When you define your terms, you are setting forth meanings that you want your readers to agree on, so that you can continue to build your argument on the foundation of that agreement. You may have to stipulate that your definition is part of a larger whole to develop your argument. For example: "Nostalgia is a bittersweet longing for things of the past; but for the purposes of my essay, I focus on white middle-class nostalgia, which combines a longing for a past that never existed with a hostile anxiety about the present."

In paragraph 10, Martínez defines the term *origin narrative*—a myth that explains "how a society understands its place in the world and its history . . . the basis for a nation's self-defined identity." The "Great White Origin Myth" is an important concept in her developing argument about a national crisis of identity.

Make comparisons.   Technically, a **comparison** shows the similarities between two or more things, and a **contrast** shows the differences. In practice, however, it is very difficult, if not impossible, to develop a comparison that does not make use of contrast. Therefore, we use the term *comparison* to describe the strategy of comparing *and* contrasting.

Doubtless you have written paragraphs or even whole essays that take as a starting point a version of this sentence: "X and Y are similar in some respects and different in others." This neutral formulation is seldom helpful when you are developing an argument. Usually, in making your comparison—in setting forth the points of similarity and difference—you have to take an evaluative or argumentative stance.

Note the comparison in this passage:

> Although there are similarities between the current nostalgias for Dick and Jane
> books and for rhythm and blues music of the same era — in both cases, the object
> of nostalgia can move people to tears — the nostalgias spring from emotional
> responses that are quite different and even contradictory. I will argue that the Dick
> and Jane books evoke a longing for a past that is colored by a fear of the present, a
> longing for a time when white middle-class values were dominant and unquestioned.
> By contrast, the nostalgia for R&B music may indicate a yearning for a past when
> multicultural musicians provided white folks with a sweaty release on the dance
> floor from those very same white-bread values of the time.

The writer does more than list similarities and differences; he offers an analysis of what they mean and is prepared to argue for his interpretation.

Certainly Elizabeth Martínez takes an evaluative stance when she compares versions of American history in paragraphs 11 and 12. In paragraph 11, she angrily relates the sanitized story of American history, setting up a contrast in paragraph 12 with the story that does not appear in history textbooks, a story of "genocide, enslavement, and imperialist expansion." Her evaluative stance comes through clearly: She finds the first version repugnant and harmful, its omissions "grotesque."

Examine causes and evaluate consequences. In any academic discipline, questions of cause and consequence are central. Whether you are analyzing the latest election results in a political science course, reading about the causes of the Vietnam War in a history course, or speculating about the long-term consequences of global warming in a science course, questions of why things happened, happen, or will happen are inescapable.

Examining causes and consequences usually involves identifying a phenomenon and asking questions about it until you gather enough information to begin analyzing the relationships among its parts and deciding which are most significant. You can then begin to set forth your own analysis of what happened and why.

Of course, this kind of analysis is rarely straightforward, and any phenomenon worthy of academic study is bound to generate a variety of conversations about its causes and consequences. In your own thinking and research, avoid jumping to conclusions and continue to sift evidence until plausible connections present themselves. Be prepared to revise your thinking—perhaps several times—in light of new evidence.

In your writing, you also want to avoid oversimplifying. A claim like this—"The answer to curbing unemployment in the United States is to restrict immigration"—does not take into account corporate outsourcing of jobs overseas or the many other possible causes of unemployment. At the very least, you may need to explain the basis and specifics of your analysis and qualify your claim: "Recent studies of patterns of immigration and unemployment in the United States suggest that unrestricted immigration is a major factor in the loss of blue-collar job opportunities in the South-west." Certainly this sentence is less forceful and provocative than the other one, but it does suggest that you have done significant and focused research and respect the complexity of the issue.

Throughout her essay, Martínez analyzes causes and consequences. In paragraph 8, for example, she speculates that the *cause* of "attacks on immigrants, affirmative action, and multiculturalism" is "Euro-American anxiety," "the sense of a vanishing national identity." In paragraph 13, she concludes that a *consequence* of Theodore Roosevelt's beliefs about race and war was a "militarism [that] went hand in hand with the racialization of history's protagonists." In paragraph 16, the topic sentence itself is a statement about causes and consequences: "Today's origin myth and the resulting concept of national identity make for an intellectual prison where it is dangerous to ask big questions about this society's superiority."

Having shown where and how Martínez uses critical strategies to develop her paragraphs, we must hasten to add that these critical strategies usually work in combination. Although you can easily develop an entire paragraph (or even an entire essay) using comparison, it is almost impossible to do so without relying on one or more of the other strategies. What if you need to tell an anecdote about the two authors you are comparing? What if you have to cite data about different rates of economic growth to clarify the main claim of your comparison? What if you are comparing different causes and consequences?

Our point is that the strategies described here are methods for exploring your issue in writing. How you make use of them, individually or in combination, depends on which can help you best communicate your argument to your readers.

Steps to Developing Paragraphs

1 **Use topic sentences to focus your paragraphs.** Remember that a topic sentence partially answers the question motivating you to write; acts as an extension of your thesis; indicates to your readers what the paragraph is about; and helps create unity both within the paragraph and within the essay.

2 **Create unity in your paragraphs.** The details in your paragraph should follow logically from your topic sentence and maintain a single focus, one tied clearly to your thesis. Repetition and transition words also help create unity in paragraphs.

3 **Use critical strategies to develop your paragraphs.** Use examples and illustrations; cite data; analyze texts; tell stories or anecdotes; define terms; make comparisons; and examine causes and evaluate consequences.

A Practice Sequence: Working with Paragraphs

We would like you to work in pairs on paragraphing. The objective of this exercise is to gauge the effectiveness of your topic sentences and the degree to which your paragraphs are unified and fully developed.

Make a copy of your essay and cut it up into paragraphs. Shuffle the paragraphs to be sure they are no longer in the original order, and then exchange cut-up drafts with your partner. The challenge is to put your partner's essay back together again. When you both have finished, compare your reorderings with the original drafts. Were you able to reproduce the original organization exactly? If not, do the variations make sense? If one or the other of you had trouble putting the essay back together, talk about the adequacy of your topic sentences, ways to revise topic sentences in keeping with the details in a given paragraph, and strategies for making paragraphs more unified and coherent.

DRAFTING CONCLUSIONS

In writing a conclusion to your essay, you are making a final appeal to your audience. You want to convince readers that what you have written is a relevant, meaningful interpretation of a shared issue. You also want to remind them that your argument is reasonable. Rather than summarize all of the points you've made in the essay—assume your readers have carefully read what you've written—pull together the key components of your argument in the service of answering the question "So what?" Establish why your argument is important: What will happen if things stay the same? What will happen if things change? How effective your conclusion is depends on whether or not readers feel that you have adequately addressed "So what?"—that you have made clear what is significant and of value.

In building on the specific details of your argument, you can also place what you have written in a broader context. (What are the sociological implications of your argument? How far-reaching are they? Are there political implications? Economic implications?) Finally, explain again how your ideas contribute something new to the conversation by building on, extending, or even challenging what others have argued.

In her concluding paragraph, Elizabeth Martínez brings together her main points, puts her essay in a broader context, indicates what's new in her argument, and answers the question "So what?":

> Accepting the implications of a different narrative could also shed light on today's struggles. In the affirmative-action struggle, for example, opponents have said that that policy is no longer needed because racism ended with the

Civil Rights Movement. But if we look at slavery as a fundamental pillar of this nation, going back centuries, it becomes obvious that racism could not have been ended by 30 years of mild reforms. If we see how the myth of the frontier idealized the white male adventurer as the central hero of national history, with the woman as sunbonneted helpmate, then we might better understand the dehumanized ways in which women have continued to be treated. A more truthful origin narrative could also help break down divisions among peoples of color by revealing common experiences and histories of cooperation.

Let's examine this concluding paragraph:

1. Although Martínez refers back to important events and ideas she has discussed, she does not merely summarize. Instead, she suggests the implications of those important events and ideas in her first sentence (the topic sentence), which crystallizes the main point of her essay: Americans need a different origin narrative.

2. Then she puts those implications in the broader context of contemporary racial and gender issues.

3. She signals what's new in her argument with the word *if* (if we look at slavery in a new way, if we look at the frontier myth in a new way).

4. Finally, her answers to why this issue matters culminate in the last sentence. This last sentence connects and extends the claim of her topic sentence, by asserting that a "more truthful origin narrative" could help heal divisions among peoples of color who have been misrepresented by the old origin myth. Clearly, she believes the implications of her argument matter: A new national identity has the potential to heal a country in crisis, a country on the verge of a "nervous breakdown" (para. 4).

Martínez also does something else in the last sentence of the concluding paragraph: She looks to the future, suggesting what the future implications of her argument could be. Looking to the future is one of five strategies for shaping a conclusion. The others we discuss are echoing the introduction, challenging the reader, posing questions, and concluding with a quotation. Each of these strategies appeals to readers in different ways; therefore, we suggest you try them all out in writing your own conclusions. Also, remember that some of these strategies can be combined. For example, you can write a conclusion that challenges readers, poses a question, looks to the future, and ends with a quotation.

■ Echo the Introduction

Echoing the introduction in your conclusion helps readers come full circle. It helps them see how you have developed your idea from beginning to end. In the following example, the student writer begins with a voice speaking from behind an Islamic veil, revealing the ways that Western culture misunderstands the symbolic value of wearing the veil. The writer repeats this visual image in her conclusion, quoting from the Koran: "Speak to them from behind a curtain."

Notice that the author begins with "a voice from behind the shrouds of an Islamic veil" and then echoes this quotation in her conclusion: "Speak to them from behind a curtain."

Introduction: A voice from behind the shrouds of an Islamic veil exclaims: "I often wonder whether people see me as a radical, fundamentalist Muslim terrorist packing an AK-47 assault rifle inside my jean jacket. Or maybe they see me as the poster girl for oppressed womanhood everywhere." In American culture where shameless public exposure, particularly of females, epitomizes ultimate freedom, the head-to-toe covering of a Muslim woman seems inherently oppressive. Driven by an autonomous national attitude, the inhabitants of the "land of the free" are quick to equate the veil with indisputable persecution. Yet Muslim women reveal the enslaving hijab as a symbolic display of the Islamic ideals — honor, modesty, and stability. Because of an unfair American assessment, the aura of hijab mystery cannot be removed until the customs and ethics of Muslim culture are genuinely explored. It is this form of enigmatic seclusion that forms the feminist controversy between Western liberals, who perceive the veil as an inhibiting factor against free will, and Islamic disciples, who conceptualize the veil as a sacred symbol of utmost morality.

Conclusion: By improperly judging an alien religion, the veil becomes a symbol of oppression and devastation, instead of a representation of pride and piety. Despite Western images, the hijab is a daily revitalization and reminder of the Islamic societal and religious ideals, thereby upholding the conduct and attitudes of the Muslim community. Americans share these ideals yet fail to recognize them in the context of a different culture. By sincerely exploring the custom of Islamic veiling, one will realize the vital role the hijab plays in shaping Muslim culture by sheltering women, and consequently society, from the perils that erupt from indecency. The principles implored in the Koran of modesty, honor, and stability construct a unifying and moral view of the Islamic Middle Eastern society when properly investigated. As it was transcribed from Allah, "Speak to them from behind a curtain. This is purer for your hearts and their hearts."

Notice how the conclusion echoes the introduction in its reference to a voice speaking from behind a curtain.

■ Challenge the Reader

By issuing a challenge to your readers, you create a sense of urgency, provoking them to act to change the status quo. In this example, the student writer explains the unacceptable consequences of preventing young women from educating themselves about AIDS and the spread of a disease that has already reached epidemic proportions.

Here the author cites a final piece of research to emphasize the extent of the problem.

Here she begins her explicit challenge to readers about what they have to do to protect themselves or their students from infection.

The changes in AIDS education that I am suggesting are necessary and relatively simple to make. Although the current curriculum in high school health classes is helpful and informative, it simply does not pertain to young women as much as it should. AIDS is killing women at an alarming rate, and many people do not realize this. According to Daniel DeNoon, AIDS is one of the six leading causes of death among women aged 18–45, and women "bear the brunt of the worldwide AIDS epidemic." For this reason, DeNoon argues, women are one of the most important new populations that are contracting HIV at a high rate. I challenge young women to be more well-informed about AIDS and their link to the disease; otherwise, many new cases may develop. As the epidemic continues to spread, women need to realize that they can stop the spread of the disease and protect themselves from infection and a number of related complications. It is the responsibility of health educators to present this to young women and inform them of the powerful choices that they can make.

■ Look to the Future

Looking to the future is particularly relevant when you are asking readers to take action. To move readers to action, you must establish the persistence of a problem and the consequences of letting a situation continue unchanged. In the concluding paragraph below, the student author points out a number of things that teachers need to do to involve parents in their children's education. She identifies a range of options before identifying what she believes is perhaps the most important action teachers can take.

The second through fifth sentences present an array of options.

First and foremost, teachers must recognize the ways in which some parents are positively contributing to their children's academic endeavors. Teachers must recognize nontraditional methods of participation as legitimate and work toward supporting parents in these tasks. For instance, teachers might send home suggestions for local after-school tutoring programs. Teachers must also try to make urban parents feel welcome and respected in their school. Teachers might call parents to ask their opinion about a certain difficulty their child is having, or invite them to talk about something of interest to them. One parent, for instance, spoke highly of the previous superintendent who had let him use his work as a film producer to help with a show for students during homeroom. If teachers can develop innovative ways to utilize parents' talents and interests rather than just inviting them to be passively involved in an already-in-place curriculum, more parents might respond. Perhaps, most importantly, if teachers want parents to be involved in their students' educations, they

In the last two sentences, the writer looks to the future with her recommendations.

must make the parents feel as though their opinions and concerns have real weight. When parents such as those interviewed for this study voice concerns and questions over their child's progress, it is imperative that teachers acknowledge and answer them.

▪ Pose Questions

Posing questions stimulates readers to think about the implications of your argument and to apply what you argue to other situations. This is the case in the following paragraph, in which the student writer focuses on immigration and then shifts readers' attention to racism and the possibility of hate crimes. It's useful to extrapolate from your argument, to raise questions that test whether what you write can be applied to different situations. These questions can help readers understand what is at issue.

Also, my research may apply to a broader spectrum of sociological topics. There has been recent discussion about the increasing trend of immigration. Much of this discussion has involved the

The first question.

distribution of resources to immigrants. Should immigrants have equal access to certain economic and educational resources in America? The decision is split. But it will be interesting to see how this debate will play out. If immigrants are granted more

Other speculative questions follow from possible responses to the writer's first question.

resources, will certain Americans mobilize against the distribution of these resources? Will we see another rise in racist groups such as the Ku Klux Klan in order to prevent immigrants from obtaining more resources? My research can also be used to understand global conflict or war. In general, groups mobilize when their established resources are threatened by an external force. Moreover, groups use framing processes to justify their collective action to others.

▪ Conclude with a Quotation

A quotation can add authority to your argument, indicating that others in positions of power and prestige support your stance. A quotation also can add poignancy to your argument, as it does in the following excerpt, in which the quotation amplifies the idea that people use Barbie to advance their own interests.

> The question still remains, what does Barbie mean? Is she the spokeswoman for the empowerment of women, or rather is she performing the dirty work of conservative patriarchy? I do not think we will ever know the answer. Rather, Barbie is the undeniable "American Icon." She is a toy, and she is what we want her to be. A test performed by Albert M. Magro at Fairmont State College titled "Why Barbie Is Perceived as Beautiful" shows that Barbie is the epitome of what we as humans find beautiful. The test sought to find human preferences on evolutionary changes in the human body. Subjects were shown a series of photos comparing different human body parts, such as the size and shape of the eyes, and asked to decide which feature they preferred: the primitive or derived (more evolved traits). The test revealed that the subjects preferred the derived body traits. Ironically, it is these preferred evolutionary features that are utilized on the body of Barbie. Barbie is truly an extension of what we are and what we perceive. Juel Best concludes his discourse on Barbie with these words: "Toys do not embody violence or sexism or occult meanings. People must assign toys their meanings." Barbie is whoever we make her out to be. Barbie grabs hold of our imaginations and lets us go wild.

The writer quotes an authority to amplify the idea that individually and collectively, we project significance on toys.

Steps to Drafting Conclusions: Five Strategies

1. **Pull together the main claims of your essay.** Don't simply repeat points you make in the paper. Instead, show readers how the points you make fit together.

2. **Answer the question "So what?"** Show your readers why your stand on the issue is significant.

3. **Place your argument in a larger context.** Discuss the specifics of your argument, but also indicate its broader implications.

4. **Show readers what is new.** As you synthesize the key points of your argument, explain how what you argue builds on, extends, or challenges the thinking of others.

5. **Decide on the best strategy for writing your conclusion.** Will you echo the introduction? Challenge the reader? Look to the future? Pose questions? Conclude with a quotation? Choose the best strategy or strategies to appeal to your readers.

A Practice Sequence: Drafting a Conclusion

1 Write your conclusion, using one of the strategies described in this section. Then share your conclusion with a classmate. Ask this person to address the following questions:

   - Did I pull together the key points of the argument?
   - Did I answer "So what?" adequately?
   - Are the implications I want readers to draw from the essay clear?

   After listening to the responses, try a second strategy, and then ask your classmate which conclusion is more effective.

2 If you do not have a conclusion of your own, analyze each example conclusion above to see how well each appears to (1) pull together the main claim of the essay, (2) answer "So what?" (3) place the argument in a larger context, and (4) show readers what is new.

From Revising to Editing
Working with Peer Groups

Academic writing is a collaborative enterprise. By reading and commenting on your drafts, your peers can support your work as a writer. And you can support the work of your peers by reading their drafts with a critical but constructive eye.

In this chapter, we set out the differences between revising and editing, discuss the peer editing process in terms of the composition pyramid, present a model peer editing session, and then explain the writer's and reader's responsibilities through early drafts, later drafts, and final drafts, providing opportunities for you to practice peer response on three drafts of a student paper.

REVISING VERSUS EDITING

We make a distinction between revising and editing. By **revising**, we mean making changes to a paper to reflect new thinking or conceptualizing. If a reader finds that the real focus of your essay comes at the end of your draft, you need to revise the paper with this new focus in mind. Revising differs from **editing**, which involves minor changes to what will be the final draft of a paper—replacing a word here and there, correcting misspellings, or substituting dashes for commas to create emphasis, for example.

When you're reading a first or second draft, the niceties of style, spelling, and punctuation are not priorities. After all, if the writer had to change the focus of his or her argument, significant changes to words, phrases, and punctuation would be inevitable. Concentrating on editing errors early on, when the writer is still trying to develop an argument with evidence, organize information logically, and anticipate counterarguments, is inefficient and even counterproductive.

Here are some characteristics of revising and editing that can guide how you read your own writing and the comments you offer to other writers:

REVISING	EDITING
Treats writing as a work in progress	Treats writing as an almost-finished product
Focuses on new possibilities both within and beyond the text	Addresses obvious errors and deficiencies
	Focuses on the text alone
Focuses on new questions or goals	Considers grammar, punctuation, spelling, and style
Considers both purpose and readers' needs	Polishes up the essay
Encourages further discovery	

Again, writing is a process, and revising is an integral part of that process. Your best writing will happen in the context of real readers' responding to your drafts. Look at the acknowledgments in any academic book, and you will see many people credited with having improved the book through their comments on drafts and ideas. All academic writers rely on conversations with others to strengthen their work.

THE PEER EDITING PROCESS

We emphasize that the different stages of writing—early, later, and final—call for different work from both readers and writers because writers' needs vary with each successive draft. These stages correspond to what has been called the composition pyramid (Figure 10.1).* The composition pyramid represents elements of writing that can help you decide what to pay attention to at different stages of writing.

1. The top of this inverted pyramid corresponds to the early stages of writing. At this point, members of the writing group should identify the situation the writer is responding to (for example, homelessness, inequality, or air pollution), the issue the writer has defined (for example, the economic versus the social costs of homelessness), the

*We thank Susannah Brietz-Monta and Anthony Monta for this idea.

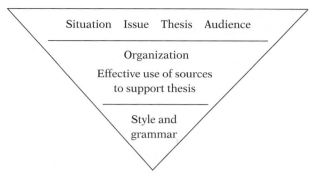

FIGURE 10.1   The Composition Pyramid

thesis or argument the writer advances, and the extent to which the writer addresses a given audience appropriately.

2. The middle portion of the pyramid corresponds to a later stage of the writing process, the point at which members of the group should move on to discuss the extent to which the writer has organized the argument logically and used sources effectively to support the thesis. Has the writer integrated quotations smoothly into the paper? Is the evidence relevant, recent, and credible?

Steps in the Peer Editing Process

1 The writer distributes copies of the draft to each member of the writing group. (Ideally, the group should not exceed four students.)

2 The writer distributes a cover letter, setting an agenda for each member of the group.

3 The members read the cover letter.

4 The writer then reads the draft aloud, while members follow along, underlining passages and making notes to prepare themselves to discuss the draft.

5 Members ask questions that help the writer identify concepts that need further elaboration or clarification.

6 Discussion focuses on the strengths and weaknesses of the draft appropriate to the stage of writing and the writer's concerns. (Even in the early stage, readers and the writer should sustain discussion for at least ten minutes before the next student takes a turn as writer.)

3. Finally, the bottom of the pyramid corresponds to the final stages of drafting. As the writer's focus shifts to grammar and style, so should the group's. Questions to ask: Is this specific language appropriate to the intended audience? Has the writer presented the argument in ways that will compel readers—even those who disagree—to listen?

PEER GROUPS IN ACTION: A SAMPLE SESSION

Let's take a look at one writing group in action to see the potential of this approach to writing. One student, Brett Preacher, worked collaboratively with three other students, Caitlin, Meghan, and Daimon, on a paper about whether the movie *Million Dollar Baby* portrays poverty accurately. Brett explained to his group that he had struggled to find ways to advance his argument at the same time that he was trying to synthesize different authors' points of view. Moreover, he was worried that he didn't do the assignment:

> BRETT: That was the assignment, to argue whether the movie portrays poverty justly or unjustly. That was the assignment, what we were supposed to do, and I didn't do that at all.
>
> CAITLIN: Well, I didn't do that either, but I used hooks's "Seeing and Making Culture: Representing the Poor" and Freedman's *From Cradle to Grave: The Human Face of Poverty in America*.
>
> BRETT: Yeah, well, I kind of quit. I strayed off the movie at the end. I basically quit talking about the movie about halfway through the paper, so basically the whole second half of my paper is the weak part. I just kind of quit talking about *Million Dollar Baby*.

Brett restated his understanding of the assignment before reading his draft aloud. This is a valuable starting point because a writer's interpretation of the assignment—the task, the purpose, the audience—helps the peer readers understand why the writer is taking a particular approach. If the readers disagree with the writer's interpretation, they should discuss their differences before the writer shares the draft, to determine an appropriate response to the assignment.

AN ANNOTATED STUDENT DRAFT

Here we reprint Brett's draft, with annotations on passages that elicited comments from his peer editors. Following the draft, we present their discussion in more detail.

Preacher 1

Brett Preacher
Professor Tindall
English 200
October 10, 20—

Representing Poverty in *Million Dollar Baby*

In "Seeing and Making Culture: Representing the Poor," bell hooks discusses the extent to which the media describe the poor as all nihilistic and longing for material worth. This image is slightly expressed in the movie *Million Dollar Baby* through Maggie's family. In the only scenes where her family makes an appearance, they present themselves as white trash by worrying that their welfare will be taken away and trying to make an easy dollar off a crippled Maggie. Jonathan Friedman, however, seems to capture the essence of the movie much more accurately in a chapter out of his book *Cradle to the Grave*, called "The Human Face of Poverty in America." In this chapter, Friedman presents many stories that support his argument that perseverance can help people rise from a life of poverty. This argument is portrayed perfectly by Maggie throughout the movie.

In the movie, Maggie strives to become a professional boxer to support herself rather than succumb to a life of poverty as her family did. Through drive and determination, Maggie strives to rise out of poverty despite all the doubt and negativity directed toward her. With nothing more than her wages and tips from her waitressing job, she saves her money, sacrificing much along the way to pay for her trainer. Her family, however, represents the other side of the spectrum and looks for nothing more than an easy way out of their welfare-sustained lifestyle. Rather than working to better themselves, they depend on welfare, and after putting Maggie down repeatedly about her career, they try to sign her savings over to themselves when she gets injured. Through her hard work and determination, Maggie achieves her dream in the end, helping to support the argument Friedman makes. Jonathan Friedman catches the face of poverty precisely by arguing that perseverance can put anyone out of a life of poverty. Most people, however, cannot fathom this idea until they have witnessed something similar.

In her essay, hooks describes the generalizations that the media have of the poor, which convey stereotypes.

Brett's point is not clear. His group member Caitlin wonders if he is saying the film does, or does not, support hooks's argument.

Brett introduces some examples related to the character Maggie, and he could include more; but he needs to decide what point he wants to make. Is he saying that the film portrays poverty in a realistic way?

Brett no longer focuses on the film

1

2

3

Preacher 2

at the end, a problem that even he recognizes. Daimon points out that Brett doesn't talk enough about the film throughout the paper.

Friedman observes that it takes money, organization, and laws to maintain a social structure, but none of it works if there are not opportunities for people to meet and help each other along the way. For example, he tells the story about Nitza, a young homeless mother with four children. She is forced to put her children into foster care for three years until she works her way out of poverty and can support her family. Friedman's point is that there is not enough opportunity to maintain the social structure that we desire. At the same time, we see that Nitza succeeds because she is motivated to change her circumstances.

Unable to identify Brett's key claim, his writing group members asked a number of questions that they hoped would guide Brett toward making an explicit claim about whether the film *Million Dollar Baby* represents poverty in a fair way:

CAITLIN: So what you are saying is that the film does and doesn't support hooks's argument that the media misrepresent the poor?

MEGHAN: You give a lot of examples here, like about Maggie. You could expand those into a paper. But what point do you want to make?

BRETT: Yeah, each example could be in a different paragraph.

CAITLIN: Those could be your main points, you know?

Caitlin believed that Brett's point may have been more implicit than explicit, that the film *Million Dollar Baby* "does and doesn't support hooks's argument that the media misrepresent the poor." Caitlin's suggestion underscores the complexity of what Brett was trying to argue—that the film does and doesn't represent poverty in a fair way—and poses a challenge that Meghan appeared to understand. Meghan suggested to Brett that he formulate different paragraphs to advance the point that *Million Dollar Baby* offers a contradictory image of poverty that is at once realistic and unrealistic. Caitlin agreed when she said that "those could be your main points." (Actually, that's just one key claim.)

However, Daimon recognized that Brett would have to develop his discussion of the film to clarify whether it offers two conflicting images of poverty:

DAIMON: It's just you don't talk about *Million Dollar Baby* enough, and I think that's what the essay is supposed to be about. Not so much about the other two. You can use the other two, but not so much as you did.

BRETT: Just tie in *Million Dollar Baby* a little more, you think?

CAITLIN: Well, because you talk a lot, it does fit with your paper, but it doesn't . . . it's supposed to be about *Million Dollar Baby*. . . . Do you think the film portrays poverty in a realistic way?

MEGHAN: Yeah, give examples of the way the film describes Maggie's family. It's like they depend on her to get themselves out of poverty.

And then Caitlin steered Brett back to the point she made earlier—that Brett could revise his paper to address the complicated way the film represents poverty:

CAITLIN: That could be the issue. There are contradictory images of poverty and how people deal.
BRETT: Yeah, well, I don't know. I'm going to have to think about that.

Brett's draft reflects his first attempt to get his ideas down. It's fine for a first draft to be exploratory. When writers formulate a working thesis or when they fail to formulate a thesis, readers in a peer group can offer support, noting strengths or pointing to places of greatest interest in an effort to sustain the writer's energy for writing. Caitlin helped Brett generate a plan for taking the next step by pointing out how he could define the issue—"There are contradictory images of poverty and how people deal."

A peer group can also ask questions to help a writer set new goals. A good strategy is to paraphrase particular parts of the draft so that the writer can hear how you, the reader, have understood what he or she is trying to say. This is what Caitlin did when she said, "So what you are saying is that the film does and doesn't support hooks's argument that the media misrepresent the poor?"

WORKING WITH EARLY DRAFTS

■ Understand the Writer's Responsibilities

When you present an early draft of your essay to your writing group, you want the group to focus on top-level pyramid concerns—situation, issue, thesis, and audience. You should explain this and any other concerns you have in a cover letter. Use the template in Figure 10.2 as a model for what needs explaining in the letter to your readers.

1. What is your question (or assignment)?
2. What is the issue motivating you to write?
3. How have published writers addressed the issue about which you are writing?
4. What is your working thesis?
5. Who is your audience, and what kind of response do you want from your readers?
6. What do you think is working best?
7. What specific aspect of the essay are you least satisfied with at this time?
8. What kind of feedback do you especially want today?

FIGURE 10.2   The Writer's Cover Letter: Early Drafts

During the session, it's important to be open to suggestions. Although you don't have to incorporate every suggestion your group makes when you revise your draft, be sure you at least understand the members' comments and concerns. If you don't understand what the members are saying about your draft, ask them to clarify or give you an example.

Finally, if you decide not to take someone's suggestion, have a good reason for doing so. If a suggested change means you won't be addressing the terms of the assignment or that you would no longer be interested in the issue, it's fine to say no.

■ Understand the Reader's Responsibilities

Your task as a reader is to follow along as the early draft is read, paying special attention to the concerns the writer has explained in the cover letter and focusing on the top of the pyramid: situation, issue, thesis, and audience. Take notes directly on the draft copy, circling or underlining sections you find confusing or have questions about, so that you can refer to them specifically in the discussion.

When it's your turn to talk, have a conversation about your reactions to the draft—where the draft amused, confused, or persuaded you, for example. Don't just jump in and start telling the writer what he or she should be doing in the paper. Your role as a reader is to give the writer a live audience: Your responses can help the writer decide what parts of the paper are working and what parts need serious revision. There are times, however, when you should play the role of *deferring reader*, putting off certain comments. You don't want to overwhelm the writer with problems no matter how many questions the essay raises.

Offer both positive and negative remarks. Start by pointing out what is working well in the paper, so the writer knows where he or she is on the right track. This also leaves the writer more open to constructive criticism. But don't shy away from telling the writer what should be working better. It's your job as a reader to offer honest and specific responses to the draft, so the writer can develop it into an effective piece of writing. Figure 10.3 lists key questions you should ask as a reader of an early draft.

---

1. Are the questions and issues that motivate the writer clear?
2. Has the writer effectively related the conversation that published writers are engaged in?
3. What is at issue?
4. What is the writer's thesis?
5. Is the writer addressing the audience's concerns effectively?
6. What passages of the draft are most effective?
7. What passages of the draft are least effective?

FIGURE 10.3   A Reader's Questions: Early Drafts

■ Analyze an Early Draft

Keep these questions in mind as you read the following excerpt from a student's early draft. After reading a number of scholarly articles on the civil rights movement, Tasha Taylor decided to address what she sees as the difference between scholars' understanding of the movement and more popular treatments in textbooks and photographs. She also tries to tie in the larger question of historical memory to her analysis of southern blacks' struggle for equality—what people remember about the past and what they forget. In fact, she begins her essay with a quotation she believes summarizes what she wants to argue ("The struggle of man against power is the struggle of memory against forgetting").

As you read Taylor's essay, take detailed notes, and underline passages that concern you. Then write a paragraph or two explaining what she could do to strengthen the draft. Keep in mind that this is an early draft, so focus on the top level of the pyramid: the situation or assignment; the issue; the thesis; and the audience.

Taylor 1

Tasha Taylor
Professor Winters
English 111
October 23, 20—
                Memory Through Photography

         The struggle of man against power is the struggle of
         memory against forgetting.
                                    —Milan Kundera

        Ask the average American what the key components of the
civil rights movement are, and most people will probably recall
Martin Luther King Jr. speaking of a dream in front of the Lincoln
Memorial, Rosa Parks riding a bus, a few court decisions, and perhaps
a photograph of Elizabeth Eckford cowering before an angry mob
in front of Central High School in Little Rock. Few people are aware
A. Philip Randolph planned the march on Washington. Few could
describe Rosa Parks's connection to the civil rights movement
(for example, the fact that she had been a member of the NAACP
since 1943) before her legendary refusal to give up her seat in
December 1955, which led to the Montgomery Bus Boycott. Few recognize the years of struggle that existed between the *Brown v. Board*

Taylor 2

of Education decision and the actual desegregation of schools. Few consider the fate of Elizabeth Eckford after the federal troops were sent to protect her and the other members of the Little Rock Nine had left Central High or the months of abuse (physical and emotional) that they endured in the name of integration. What most people know is limited to textbooks they read in school or the captions under photographs that describe where a particular event occurred.

Why is it that textbooks exclusively feature the stories of larger than life figures like Martin Luther King? Why is it that we remember things the way we do? Historical events "have little meaning without human interpretation, without our speaking about them within the contexts of our lives and our culture, without giving them names and meanings" (Kolker xix). Each person experiencing the exact same event will carry a different memory from that event. Trying to decipher what memories reveal about each person is a fascinating yet difficult endeavor, because each retelling of a memory and each additional memory alters existing ones.

The story that photographs and textbooks tell us does not even begin to describe the depth of the movement or the thousands who risked their lives and the lives of their families to make equality a reality. Embracing this selective memory as a nation prevents understanding and acknowledgment of the harsh reality of other images from the civil rights movement (demonstrators being plowed down by fire hoses, beatings, and the charred bodies of bombing victims) which are key aspects of understanding who we are as a society. The question therefore is why. Why is it that textbook writers and publishers have allowed so much of this history to be skewed and forgotten? How can it be that barely 50 years after these events so many have been forgotten or diluted?

2

3

Reading as a Writer

1. What is working well in Taylor's draft?
2. What is Taylor's thesis or argument?
3. To what extent does she connect her analysis of the civil rights movement and historical memory?

4. What parts of her analysis could Taylor explain further? (What do you still need to know?)

5. What would you suggest Taylor do next?

WORKING WITH LATER DRAFTS

■ Understand the Writer's Responsibilities

At a later stage, after you've had the opportunity to take readers' suggestions and do further research, you should be able to state your thesis more definitively than you did in your earlier draft. You also should be able to support your thesis with evidence, anticipating possible counterarguments. Ideally, your readers will still provide constructive criticism, offering their support, as in the first draft, but they will also question and challenge more than before.

Here, too, you want to help readers focus on your main concerns, which you should explain in a cover letter. You may still need to work on one or two top-level pyramid concerns, but your focus will likely be midlevel concerns—organization and the effective use of sources. Use the list of questions in Figure 10.4 to help you write your cover letter.

■ Understand the Reader's Responsibilities

In a later draft, your focus as a reader should be on midlevel concerns in the composition pyramid: places in the writer's text that are confusing,

---

1. What is your research question?

2. What is the issue motivating you to write?

3. What is your thesis?

4. How do you go about identifying a gap in readers' knowledge, modifying others' ideas, or trying to correct readers' misunderstandings?

5. To what extent do you distinguish your argument from the information you quote, summarize, or paraphrase from the sources you have read?

6. To what extent have you organized your ideas in ways that will help readers follow the logic of your argument?

7. To what extent have you anticipated potential counterarguments to your thesis?

8. What do you think is working best?

9. What specific aspect of the essay are you least satisfied with at this time?

FIGURE 10.4   The Writer's Cover Letter: Later Drafts

1. To what extent is it clear what questions and issues motivate the writer?

2. What is the writer's thesis?

3. How effectively does the writer establish the conversation — identify a gap in people's knowledge, attempt to modify an existing argument, or try to correct some misunderstanding?

4. How effectively does the writer distinguish between his or her ideas and the ideas he or she summarizes, paraphrases, or quotes?

5. How well does the writer help you follow the logic of his or her argument?

6. To what extent are you persuaded by the writer's argument?

7. To what extent does the writer anticipate possible counterarguments?

8. To what extent does the writer make clear how he or she wants readers to respond?

9. What do you think is working best? Explain by pointing to specific passages in the writer's draft.

10. What specific aspect of the draft is least effective? Explain by pointing to a specific passage in the writer's draft.

FIGURE 10.5 A Reader's Questions: Later Drafts

that require better transitions, or that could use sources more effectively. You can challenge writers at this stage of the composing process, perhaps playing the role of *naive reader*, suggesting places in the draft where the writer has left something out or isn't clear. The naive reader's comments tend to take the form of questions: "Do you mean to suggest that everyone who learns to write well succeeds in life? What kind of success are you talking about?" Closely related to the naive reader is the *devil's advocate reader*. This reader's comments also challenge the writer, often taking the form of a question like this: "But why couldn't this be attributed to the effects of socialization rather than heredity?" Figure 10.5 offers questions for reading later drafts.

■ Analyze a Later Draft

Now read the following excerpt from Taylor's second draft. You will see that she begins with her discussion of historical memory. She also has included an analysis of a book of photographs that Nobel Prize–winning author Toni Morrison compiled. Take notes as you read the draft and write a paragraph in which you describe what you see as some of the strengths of what Taylor has written and what she can do to make other elements stronger. In particular, focus on the middle level of the composition pyramid—on organization and the effective use of sources and evidence to support her thesis.

Taylor 1

Tasha Taylor
Professor Winters
English 111
November 14, 20—

Memory Through Photography

The struggle of man against power is the struggle of
memory against forgetting.

—Milan Kundera

Memory is such an integral part of what it is to be human, yet
is something so often taken for granted: people assume that their
memories are accurate to protect themselves from the harsh realities
of the atrocities committed by ordinary people. Even the pictures
used to represent the much-celebrated civil rights movement give
us a false sense of security and innocence. For example, the Ku Klux
Klan is most often depicted by covered faces and burning crosses; the
masks allow us to remove ourselves from responsibility. Few could
describe Rosa Parks's connection to the civil rights movement (for
example, the fact that she had been a member of the NAACP since
1943) before her legendary refusal to give up her seat in December
1955, which led to the Montgomery Bus Boycott. Few recognize the
years of struggle that existed between the *Brown v. Board of Education* decision and the actual desegregation of schools. Few consider
the fate of Elizabeth Eckford after the federal troops were sent to
protect her and the other members of the Little Rock Nine had left
Central High or the months of abuse (physical and emotional) that
they endured in the name of integration. What most people know is
limited to textbooks they read in school or the captions under photographs that describe where a particular event occurred.

It is important, therefore, to analyze what is remembered and
even more importantly to recognize what it is forgotten: to question
why it is that it is forgotten, what that says about society today,
how far it has come and how much it has unwittingly fallen back
into old patterns such as prejudice and ignorance. The discrepancies
in cultural memory are due more to a society's desire to remember
itself in the best light and protect itself from the reality of its brutality and responsibility. Such selective memory only temporarily heals

Taylor 2

the wounds of society; lack of awareness does not cause healing. Although there have been many recent moves to increase awareness, they are tainted by unavoidable biases and therefore continue to perpetuate a distorted memory.

Images play a central role in the formation of cultural memory because people can point to photographs and claim them as concrete evidence: "Images entrance us because they provide a powerful illusion of owning reality. If we can photograph reality or paint or copy it, we have exercised an important kind of power" (Kolker 3). A picture of black and white children sitting at a table together is used to reinforce the cultural perception that the problems of racism are over, that it has all been fixed.

In her book *Remember*, Toni Morrison strives to revitalize the memory of school integration through photographs. The book is dedicated to Denise McNair, Carole Robertson, Addie Mae Collins, and Cynthia Wesley, the four girls killed in the 16th Street Baptist Church bombing in 1963. Morrison writes, "Things are better now. Much, much better. But remember why and please remember us" (Morrison 72). The pictures are of black and white children happily eating together, solemnly saluting the flag together, and holding hands. The photographs of the four murdered girls show them peacefully and innocently smiling as if everything really is better now. In reality, according to the United States Bureau of Alcohol, Tobacco and Firearms, between 1995 and 1997 there were 162 incidents of arson or bombing in African American houses of worship. There are a few images of people protesting integration, but they are also consistent with the cultural memory (protesters are shown simply holding signs and yelling, not beating and killing innocent children). Finally, the captions are written in a child's voice. Yet it is not a child's voice at all it is merely a top down view of children that serves to perpetuate a distorted cultural memory.

The photographs used to suggest how things are much, much better now are misleading. For example, the last photograph is of a black girl and a white girl holding hands through a bus window, which was transporting them to an integrated school. The caption reads: "Anything can happen. Anything at all. See?" (71). It is a very powerful image of how the evil of Jim Crow and segregation exists in a distant past and the nation has come together and healed.

Taylor 3

However, Morrison neglects to point out that the picture was taken in Boston, Massachusetts, not the deep south, the heart of racism. Children holding hands in Boston is much less significant than if they were in Birmingham where that action would be concrete evidence of how far we as a nation have come.

Morrison also glorifies of Martin Luther King, Jr. and Rosa Parks pointing to them as epitomizing the movement. Unfortunately, she perpetuates the story that one needs to be special or somehow larger than life to affect change. Paul Rogat Loeb writes in *Soul of a Citizen*:

> Once we enshrine our heroes, it becomes hard for mere mortals to measure up in our eyes . . . in our collective amnesia we lose the mechanisms through which grassroots social movements of the past successfully shifted public sentiment and challenged entrenched institutional power. Equally lost are the means by which their participants managed to keep on, sustaining their hope and eventually prevailing in circumstances at least as difficult as those we face today. (Loeb 36, 38)

Placing a select few on pedestals and claiming them as next to divine heroes of the movement does society a disservice; people fail to realize that ordinary people can serve as agents of change.

Morrison's book ignores the thousand of ordinary people who risked their lives for the cause to bring about equality. The caption besides the picture of Rosa Parks in *Remember* reads "because if I ever feel helpless or lonely I just have to remember that all it takes is one person" (Morrison 62). Ironically, Morrison gives credit for the Montgomery Bus Boycott to one person, ignoring the months of planning and involved dozens of planners. Even the photograph presents Rosa Parks in a position of power. It is a low-angle shot up at Parks that makes her appear larger than life and authoritative. The photographs of Martin Luther King, Jr. also further the impression of power with a close up shot of his face as he stands above thousands of participants in the March on Washington. Although these photographs were selected to perpetuate the hero illusion, it is more inspiring to remember the ordinary people who took a stand and were able to accomplish extraordinary feats because of their dedication and persistence rather than glorify extraordinary people who were destined for greatness.

Reading as a Writer

1. What is Taylor's thesis or argument?

2. How well does she help you follow the logic of her argument with transitions?

3. How effectively does she distinguish between her ideas and the ideas she summarizes, paraphrases, or quotes?

4. To what extent are you persuaded by her argument?

5. What should Taylor do next?

WORKING WITH FINAL DRAFTS

■ Understand the Writer's Responsibilities

Your final draft should require editing, not revising. At this stage, readers should focus on errors in style and grammar in the text, not on the substance of your work. Here, too, indicate your main concerns in a cover letter (Figure 10.6).

■ Understand the Reader's Responsibilities

Once a writer's ideas are developed and in place, readers should turn their attention to the bottom level of the composition pyramid, to matters of style and grammar. At this stage, details are important: Is this the best word to use? Would this sentence be easier to follow if it was broken into two sentences? Which spelling is correct—*Freedman* or *Friedman*? Are citations handled consistently? Should this question mark precede or follow the quotation mark? The *grammatically correct reader* evaluates and makes judgments about the writer's work. This reader may simply indicate with a mark of some sort that there's a problem in a sentence or paragraph, or may even correct the writer's work. Figure 10.7 is a list of questions a reader should ask of a final draft.

■ Analyze a Near-Final Draft

Now read Taylor's near-final draft and write a paragraph detailing what she can do to strengthen it. Again, you will see that Taylor has made sub-

---

1. What is your unique perspective on your issue?

2. To what extent do the words and phrases you use reflect who you believe your readers are?

3. Does your style of citation reflect accepted conventions for academic writing?

4. What do you think is working best?

5. What specific aspect of the essay are you least satisfied with at this time?

FIGURE 10.6   The Writer's Cover Letter: Final Drafts

1. How does the writer go about contributing a unique perspective on the issue?
2. To what extent does the writer use words and phrases that are appropriate for the intended audience?
3. To what extent does the style of citation reflect accepted conventions for academic writing?
4. What do you think is working best?
5. What specific aspect of the essay are you least satisfied with at this time?

FIGURE 10.7   A Reader's Questions: Final Drafts

stantial changes. She compares Morrison's book of photographs to a Spike Lee documentary that she watched with her class. As you read the essay, focus on the bottom level of the composition pyramid: Does the writer use appropriate language? Does she adhere to appropriate conventions for using and citing sources? (See the Appendix for information on MLA and APA formats.)

Taylor 1

Tasha Taylor
Professor Winters
English 111
December 5, 20—

Memory Through Photography

Memory is such an integral part of what it is to be human, yet it is something so often taken for granted: people assume that their memories are accurate to protect themselves from the harsh realities of the atrocities committed by ordinary people. Even the pictures used to represent the much-celebrated civil rights movement give us a false sense of security and innocence. For example, the Ku Klux Klan is most often depicted by covered faces and burning crosses; the masks allow us to remove ourselves from responsibility. Few could describe Rosa Parks's connection to the civil rights movement before her legendary refusal to give up her seat in December 1955, which led to the Montgomery Bus Boycott (for example, the fact that she had been a member of the NAACP since 1943). Few recognize the years of struggle that existed between the 1954 *Brown v. Board of Education* decision and the actual desegregation of schools. Few consider the fate of Elizabeth Eckford after the federal troops sent to protect her and the other members of the Little Rock Nine had left

Taylor 2

Central High or the months of abuse (physical and emotional) that they endured in the name of integration. What most people know is limited to the textbooks they read in school or the captions under photographs that describe where a particular event occurred.

It is important, then, to analyze what is remembered, and even more important to recognize what is forgotten: to question why it is that it is forgotten, what that says about society today, how far it has come and how much it has unwittingly fallen back into old patterns of prejudice and ignorance. The discrepancies in cultural memory are due more to society's desire to remember itself in the best light and protect itself from the reality of its brutality and responsibility. Such selective memory only temporarily heals the wounds of society; lack of awareness does not cause healing. Although there have been many recent moves to increase awareness, they are tainted by unavoidable biases and therefore continue to perpetuate a distorted memory.

2

Images play a central role in the formation of cultural memory because people can point to photographs and claim them as concrete evidence: "Images entrance us because they provide a powerful illusion of owning reality. If we can photograph reality or paint or copy it, we have exercised an important kind of power" (Kolker 3). A picture of black and white children sitting at a table together is used to reinforce the cultural perception that the problems of racism are over, that they have all been fixed.

3

In her book *Remember*, Toni Morrison strives to revitalize the memory of school integration through photographs. The book is dedicated to Denise McNair, Carole Robertson, Addie Mae Collins, and Cynthia Wesley, the four girls killed in the 16th Street Baptist Church bombing in 1963. Morrison writes: "Things are better now. Much, much better. But remember why and please remember us" (72). The pictures are of black and white children happily eating together, solemnly saluting the flag together, and holding hands. The photographs of the four murdered girls show them peacefully and innocently smiling as if everything really is better now. In reality, according to the United States Bureau of Alcohol, Tobacco and Firearms, between 1995 and 1997 there were 162 incidents of arson or bombing in African American houses of worship. There are a few images of people protesting integration, but they are also consistent

4

Taylor 3

with the cultural memory (protesters are shown simply holding signs and yelling, not beating and killing innocent children). Finally, the captions are written in a child's voice. Yet it is not a child's voice at all; it is merely a top-down view of children that serves to perpetuate a distorted cultural memory.

The photographs used to suggest how things are much, much better now are misleading. For example, the last photograph, taken through a bus window, is of a black girl and a white girl holding hands; the bus was transporting them to an integrated school. The caption reads: "Anything can happen. Anything at all. See?" (Morrison 71). It is a very powerful image of how the evil of Jim Crow and segregation exists in a distant past and the nation has come together and healed. However, Morrison neglects to point out that the picture was taken in Boston, not in the Deep South, the heart of racism. Children holding hands in Boston is much less significant than if they were in Birmingham, where that action would be concrete evidence of how far we as a nation have come.

Morrison also glorifies Martin Luther King Jr. and Rosa Parks, pointing to them as epitomizing the movement. Unfortunately, she perpetuates the story that one needs to be special or somehow larger than life to effect change. Paul Rogat Loeb writes in *Soul of a Citizen*:

> Once we enshrine our heroes, it becomes hard for mere mortals to measure up in our eyes. . . . In our collective amnesia we lose the mechanisms through which grassroots social movements of the past successfully shifted public sentiment and challenged entrenched institutional power. Equally lost are the means by which their participants managed to keep on, sustaining their hope and eventually prevailing in circumstances at least as difficult as those we face today. (36, 38)

Placing a select few on pedestals and claiming them as next-to-divine heroes of the movement does society a disservice; people fail to realize that ordinary people can serve as agents of change.

Morrison's book ignores the thousands of ordinary people who risked their lives for the cause to bring about equality. The caption beside the picture of Rosa Parks in *Remember* reads "Because if I ever feel helpless or lonely I just have to remember that all it takes is one person" (Morrison 62). Ironically, Morrison gives credit for the Montgomery Bus Boycott to one person, ignoring the months

Taylor 4

of planning that involved dozens of planners. Even the photograph presents Rosa Parks in a position of power. It is a low-angle shot up at Parks that makes her appear larger than life and authoritative. The photographs of Martin Luther King Jr. also further the impression of power with a close-up shot of his face as he stands above thousands of participants in the March on Washington. Although these photographs were selected to perpetuate the hero illusion, it is more inspiring to remember the ordinary people who took a stand and were able to accomplish extraordinary feats because of their dedication and persistence rather than to glorify extraordinary people who were destined for greatness.

In contrast, Spike Lee's 1998 documentary titled *4 Little Girls*   8
is a stirring depiction of the lives and deaths of the girls who died in the 1963 16th Street Baptist Church bombing. In his film, Spike Lee looks behind what some would call "societal amnesia" to disclose the harsh realities of the civil rights movement. Lee interviews family members and friends of the murdered girls, revealing the pain and anger that they grapple with more than forty years after the tragedy. Lee includes not only images of the bombed church but also the charred and nearly unrecognizable bodies of the murdered girls. These disturbing images underscore the reality of their deaths without appearing sensationalist. The film does an exceptional job of reminding the viewer of the suffering and mindless hate that were prevalent during the civil rights movement.

However, the documentary is also biased. For instance, the   9
girls were not little; they were fourteen, not really little girls. Lee chose to describe them as little to elicit emotion and sympathy for their tragic deaths. They were victims. They had not marched through the streets demanding equality; instead, Denise McNair, Carole Robertson, Addie Mae Collins, and Cynthia Wesley were simply attending Sunday school and were ruthlessly murdered. Victimizing Denise, Carole, Addie Mae, and Cynthia is not detrimental to the cultural memory in and of itself. The problem is that the victimization of the four girls is expanded to encompass the entire black community, undermining the power and achievement of the average black citizen. We need to remember the people who struggled to gain employment for blacks in the labor movement of the 1940s and 1950s that initiated the civil rights movement.

Taylor 5

One can argue that despite the presence of misleading images *10* in Spike Lee's film and Toni Morrison's book, at least some of the story is preserved. Still, it is easy to fall victim to the cliché: those who do not remember history are doomed to repeat it. Just because a portion of the story is remembered, it does not mean that society is immune to falling back into its old habits. This cultural amnesia not only perpetuates the injustices of the time but leaves open the possibility that these atrocities can occur again. If people believe the government can simply grant black equality, then they may believe that it can also take it away. In essence memory is about power: "The struggle of man against power is the struggle of memory against forgetting" (Kundera). Those who are remembered hold power over the forgotten. Their legacy is lost and so is their ability to inspire future generations through their memory.

Taylor 6

Works Cited

4 Little Girls. Dir. Spike Lee. 40 Acres & A Mule Filmworks, 1997. Film.

Kolker, Robert. *Film, Form, and Culture*. New York: McGraw Hill, 1998. Print.

Kundera, Milan. *QuotationsBook*. QuotationsBook, 2007. Web. 22 Nov. 20—.

Loeb, Paul Rogat. *Soul of a Citizen: Living with Conviction in a Cynical Time*. New York: St. Martin's/Griffin, 1999. Print.

Morrison, Toni. *Remember*. Boston: Houghton Mifflin, 2004. Print.

United States. Dept. of the Treasury. Bureau of Alcohol, Tobacco and Firearms. "Arson and Explosives: Incidents Report 1994." *ATF.gov*. US Dept. of Justice, 1995. Web. 15 Nov. 20—.

Reading as a Writer

1. What would you say is Taylor's argument?
2. To what extent does she provide transitions to help you understand how her analysis supports her argument?

3. To what extent does she integrate quotations appropriately into the text of her argument?

4. To what extent does the style of citation reflect accepted conventions for academic writing?

5. If Taylor had more time to revise, what would you suggest she do?

FURTHER SUGGESTIONS FOR PEER EDITING GROUPS

Monitoring your own writing group can help ensure that the group is both providing and receiving the kinds of responses the members need. Here is a list of questions you might ask of one another after a session:

- What topics were discussed?
- Were most questions and comments directed at the level of ideas? Structure? Language?
- Were topics always brought up with a question or a comment?
- Who initiated talk more frequently—the writer or the readers?
- What roles did different group members play?
- Did each author open with specific questions or concerns?
- Did the readers begin by giving specific reactions?

After answering these questions, identify two things that are working well in your group. Then identify two things that you could improve. How would you go about making those improvements?

When we asked our students what they thought contributed to effective conversation in their writing groups, here is what they told us:

- Honest and spontaneous expression
- Free interaction among members
- High levels of personal involvement
- Members' commitment to insight and change
- The sense that self-disclosure is safe and highly valued
- Members' willingness to take responsibility for the group's effectiveness
- Members' belief that the group is important
- Members' belief that they are primary agents of help for one another
- Members' focus on communication within the group over other discussions

Other Methods of Inquiry
Interviews and Focus Groups

Sometimes to advance your argument you may need to do original research. By **original research**, we mean using primary sources of evidence you gather yourself. (Another common term for this type of investigation is *field research*.) Remember that primary sources of evidence include firsthand or eyewitness accounts like those found in letters or newspapers, or in research reports in which the researcher explains his or her impressions of a particular phenomenon—for example, gender relations in classroom interactions. (In contrast, a secondary source is an analysis of information contained in primary sources.)

The type of original research we discuss in this chapter relies on people—interviewees and members of focus groups—as primary sources of information. To inquire into gender dynamics in college science classrooms, then, you might conduct interviews with young women to understand their perceptions of how gender affects teaching. Or you might convene a focus group to put a variety of perspectives into play on questions about gendered teaching practices. The pages that follow present strategies for conducting interviews and setting up focus groups that can generate multiple responses to your research questions.

When you conduct research, keep in mind that you are not setting out to prove anything; instead, the process of inquiry will enable you to answer the questions *you* ask, address problems, and move readers to rethink their positions. Good critical readers know that the arguments they produce as writers are influenced by what they choose to discuss and how they construe the evidence they provide.

Although there is really no way to avoid the limitations of writing from one point of view, writers can provide readers with multiple sources of information so that they can make their own judgments about what to believe or not believe. In fact, this is the argument we make above in studying inequities in education. Relying on a single source of data will inevitably limit your field of vision. Multiple sources of information add complexity and texture to your analysis, conveying to readers the thoroughness of your approach.

WHY DO ORIGINAL RESEARCH?

We can think of four reasons (all of which overlap to some extent) why you might do original research for a writing class.

To Increase Your Ability to Read Critically.   When you do original research, you learn, at a basic and pragmatic level, how the studies you consult in a researched argument come into being. You're on the ground floor of knowledge making.

As a critical reader, you know it's important to ask questions like these: What is the source of the author's claim? Why should I believe the author? What is the source of the author's authority? What are the possible counterarguments? When you are doing original research, you are in the position of that author, with a real stake in establishing your own authority. By coming to understand what it takes to establish your own authority, you are in a better position to evaluate how effectively other researchers establish theirs.

Let's say your research question concerns gender differences in math education. You might read a study that asserts that girls and young women are being shortchanged in math classes, impeding their ability to go into math-related fields. You would want to ask about the nature of the data used to support this claim. If the author of the study states that 56 percent of the female students interviewed said they were discouraged from going into math-related fields, you might wonder where the figure of 56 percent came from. How many girls and young women were interviewed? How was this sample selected? What were the students asked? Questions like these inform your own use of interviews and focus groups.

To Increase Your Own Research Skills.   Doing original research broadens your own range of research methods. By developing a repertoire of research methods, you will be better able to explore questions that may be too complex to answer by examining texts alone. One scholar put it this way: "I couldn't see what a text was doing without looking at the worlds in which these texts served as significant activities."* After all, it is one thing to

---

*C. Bazerman, *Shaping Written Knowledge: The Genre and Activity of the Scientific Article in Science* (Madison: University of Wisconsin Press, 1988), p. 4.

read a research report and understand its purpose, its intended audience, the nature of its claims, and the like. But it is quite another to watch scientists at work and begin to understand how they have come to know what they know. The discovery of DNA, for example, was the result of an arduous process that involved much risk, collaboration, chance, error, and competition. The neat structure of a scientific report could mislead you into thinking that science is a linear process that begins with a question, moves on to an experiment, and ends with an answer. Real research is messier than that. Original research takes us behind the words we read, introducing levels of complexity.

To Broaden Your Scope of Inquiry.   Doing original research may also broaden the scope of your inquiry. First, it is useful to use different research methods than the ones you are accustomed to using. Learning to interview and run focus groups, at the very least, can give you insight and practice for nonacademic applications—market research, for example. Second, it can make you aware of how people outside your field address the questions you raise. Consider, for example, the different perspectives an educator, a sociologist, and an economist would bring to the question of educational inequities. An educator might study educational inequities as a curricular problem and therefore analyze the content of different curricula within and across schools. A sociologist might visit students' homes, noting the presence or absence of books or asking parents how they go about preparing their children for school. An economist might examine income levels in both wealthy and impoverished neighborhoods. The point is that each field brings its own perspective to a problem, adding complexity and richness to your own discussion of that problem.

To Make a Unique Contribution to a Conversation of Ideas.   Finally, doing original research affords you the opportunity to make a unique contribution to a conversation of ideas. Instead of relying exclusively on texts others have written as evidence for your claims, you can offer your own data to address a question or problem, data that others do not have available. For instance, if you wanted to examine claims that primary school teachers pay more attention to boys in class than to girls, you could review the relevant literature and then add to that literature a study that systematically analyzes the ways in which teachers in different classrooms treat boys and girls.

GETTING STARTED: WRITING A PROPOSAL

A **proposal** is a formal plan that outlines your objectives for conducting a research project, specifies the methods you intend to use, and describes what you expect the implications of the work to be. The proposal is a tool that helps guide you through various stages of the project. The most immediate benefit of writing a proposal is that through the act of writing—by setting forth an outline of your project—your thinking will become more focused and precise.

At a minimum, a research proposal should include three sections: purpose, method, and discussion and implications. You may also want to include additional sections with materials that provide concrete support for your proposal—some of the tools that will help you get the job done. You should arrange your plan and use headings so that readers can find information quickly.

■ Describe Your Purpose

In the purpose section of your proposal, formulate the question that is motivating your study. Inquiry begins with a good question.

- A good question can help you think through the issue you want to write about.
- It is specific enough to guide your inquiry and to be answered with the tools and resources you have available and have decided to use.
- It does not limit the answer to yes, no, or either/or.
- It asks how, why, should, or the extent to which.
- It conveys a clear idea of who you are answering the question for—your audience.

In your purpose section (usually the introduction), you should summarize the issue and explain how it has led to the question driving your research. You also should explain why you are interested in this issue area, why it is important, and what is at stake. Ask yourself why others should be interested in your effort to answer the question.

■ Define Your Method

In the method section, you list and describe the tools and strategies you will use to conduct your research. Some of the tools and strategies of original research are

- conducting interviews or focus groups
- taking notes
- recording on audio- or videotape a particular activity or activities
- doing background, historical, or archival work
- observing and coming to terms with your own impressions

In addition to identifying your method, you need to discuss the appropriateness of your tools and strategies, why they are the best means for answering your research question. Given the objectives you have set for yourself and the constraints of doing the research, are some methods better than others?

■ Discuss Your Implications

It may seem a little premature to talk about what you hope to find in your study, but it is important to address "So what?"—to explain what you believe is the significance of your study. Place your argument in the context of the conversation you want to join, and explain how your study can contribute to that conversation. Write about how your study will build on, challenge, or extend other studies in your area of research. And, finally, identify what you believe is going to be new about your findings.

■ Include Additional Materials That Support Your Research

Depending on your instructor and the level of formality of your proposal, you may be asked to include additional materials that reveal other dimensions of your research. Those materials may include (1) an annotated bibliography, (2) scripts of the questions you are planning to ask in interviews and focus groups, and (3) the consent forms you will ask interviewees or participants in your focus groups to sign.

Annotated Bibliography. An **annotated bibliography** is a list of sources (arranged alphabetically by author) that you plan to consult and make use of in your research paper. Typically you provide a citation (author, date, title of source, and publication information) and a short summary of the source. You can present all your sources in one long list or organize them by type of source (books, journals, and so forth). An excerpt from a student's annotated bibliography in APA style is shown in Figure 11.1.

Questions You Plan to Ask. Including a list (or lists) of the questions you expect to ask those you plan to interview or survey will help you focus your thinking. What personal information do you need to know? What information about your issue? What opinions and recommendations would be helpful? Each list should include at least five good questions but can include many more. A sample set of questions to ask the parents of homeless children appears in Figure 11.2.

Consent Forms. Whenever you plan to solicit information in an interview or focus group, you need to get the interviewee's or participants' permission to make use of that information in your research paper. We have included a sample consent form for an interview in Figure 11.3.

Bibliography

Books

Dupper, D. R. (2003). *School social work: Skills and interventions for effective practice.* Hoboken, NJ: John Wiley & Sons.

    This book provides a general overview of the duties and responsibilities of school social workers. It explains various social problems that many students encounter, and evaluates intervention and prevention programs.

Kryder-Coe, J. H., Salamon, L. H., & Molnar, J. M. (Eds.). (1991). *Homeless children and youth: A new American dilemma.* New Brunswick, NJ: Transaction.

    This book examines the impact of child homelessness on society, the causes of child homelessness, and society's response to child homelessness. Part of the book focuses on the developmental and educational consequences of homelessness on children.

Vostanis, P., & Cumella, S. (Eds.). (1999). *Homeless children: Problems and needs.* London, England: Jessica Kingsley.

    This book is a collection of articles examining the various aspects of life for homeless children. One article focuses specifically on problems surrounding education for homeless youth.

Journal Articles

All of the following journal articles focus on the educational and developmental needs of homeless youth. They relate this issue to the effectiveness of the McKinney-Vento Homeless Assistance Act (1987), to the current and future work of school counselors and social workers, and to the development of community programs.

Markward, M. J., & Biros, E. (2001). McKinney revisited: Implications for school social work. *Children & Schools, 23*(3), 182-187. Retrieved from http://puck.naswpressonline.org/v1=933544/cl=17/nw=1/rpsv/journal/journal4_home.htm.

    This article examines the extent to which the McKinney-Vento Act has affected homeless children and youth. It discusses the implications the act has had for school social work.

FIGURE 11.1   An Excerpt from a Student's Annotated Bibliography

Moroz, K. J., & Segal, E. A. (1990). Homeless children: Intervention strategies for school social workers. *Social Work in Education, 12*(2), 134-143.
This article investigates the various effects of homelessness on children. The authors propose a model for intervention for school social workers that would connect them with community services.

FIGURE 11.1 (*continued*)

■ Establish a Timeline

To write a proposal, you'll need to draw up a schedule for your research. This timeline should include the dates when you expect to finish the proposal, when you will conduct interviews and focus groups, when you hope to have a draft, and when you will complete the project. As you develop your timeline, you need to be realistic about when you can actually complete the different stages of collecting your data and writing. You can anticipate that events will prevent everything from going as planned.

Parent(s)

1. a. Describe your current living and family situation (parents, siblings, how long homeless, where living, where child attends school).
   b. Describe your child.
   c. Describe your relationship with your child.

2. a. Do you think homelessness is affecting your child's schooling?
   b. If so, tell me how (grades, friends, attendance, transportation).

3. Tell me about enrolling your child in school. What was the process like? Were there any problems? Conditions? Challenges?

4. a. Do you feel that your child's right to an education has been recognized?
   b. Why or why not? What experiences can you point to to support your answer?

5. Describe the relationship between your child and his or her teachers.

6. a. What types of support services is your child currently being offered in school and in the community?
   b. How effective are those services?
   c. How supportive of your child's educational and developmental growth do you feel your child's school has been?
   d. What about the Center for the Homeless?
   e. Do you have any recommendations for these sources of help or requests for other types of help or services for your child that are not currently offered?

7. How do you envision your child's future?

FIGURE 11.2   Sample Interview Questions

You are invited to participate in a study of homelessness and education conducted by Mary Ronan, an undergraduate at the University of Notre Dame, during the next few months. If you decide to participate, you will

1. provide up to two interviews with the researcher,
2. allow the researcher to use excerpts from the interviews in publications about research with the understanding that your identity will not be revealed at any time.

   Participation is completely voluntary. You may choose to stop participating at any time prior to completion of the project. Should you have any questions at any time, you are welcome to contact the researcher by phone or e-mail. Your decision to participate will have no effect on or prejudice your future relationship with the University of Notre Dame. One possible benefit of participating in the study is that you will have the opportunity to learn about the implications of homelessness on education.

   If you are willing to participate in this research, please read and sign the consent form below. You will be given a copy of this form to keep.

CONSENT FORM

I agree to participate in all of the procedures above. I understand that my identity will be protected during the study and that others will not have access to the interviews I provide. I also understand that my name will not be revealed when data from the research are presented in publications. I have read the above and give the researcher, Mary Ronan, permission to use excerpts from transcripts of tapes without identifying me as the writer or speaker.

_____

Date   Signature

                                   _____

                                   Signature of Researcher
                                   [Telephone number]/[E-mail address]

FIGURE 11.3   Sample Interview Consent Form

People cannot always meet you when you would like them to, and you may have to change your own schedule. Therefore, be sure to contact participants well in advance of the time you would like to speak with them in interviews or focus groups.

Steps to Writing a Proposal

1 **Describe your purpose.** Summarize your issue, describing how it has led you to the question motivating your research.

2 **Define your method.** What tools and strategies are you planning to use? Why are they appropriate and sufficient for your purposes?

> **3** **Discuss your implications.** What is the context of the conversation you are entering? What significant information do you expect your study to uncover?
>
> **4** **Include additional materials that support your research.** These may include an annotated bibliography, a series of interview questions, and blank consent forms.

AN ANNOTATED STUDENT PROPOSAL

Our student Mary Ronan submitted a formal proposal for a study of the education of a homeless child. Ronan's proposal was exceptionally well prepared, thorough, and thoughtful, and she included a number of additional materials: an annotated bibliography; sample questions for the teachers, students, and parents she planned to interview; and sample consent forms. We reprint only the main part of her proposal, the part that includes her purpose, methods, and discussion and implications sections, for you to consider as a model for proposal writing. Notice how Ronan summarizes her issue and explains how it led to her research, and how she makes her readers understand why her research is important.

CASE STUDY OF ONE HOMELESS CHILD   1

Research Paper Proposal:
A Case Study of One Homeless Child's Education and Lifestyle
Mary Ronan

Identifies a pressing concern that readers should be aware of.

In 2000, the Urban Institute estimated that 1.35 million children experience homelessness over the course of a year (Urban Institute, 2000). The U.S. Department of Education estimated that the number of children and youth in homeless situations increased from approximately 841,700 to 930,000 in 2000 (U.S. Department of Education, 2000). It also determined that preschool and elementary-aged children make up the largest numbers of children experiencing homelessness (U.S. Department of Education, 2000). Homelessness as experienced by school-aged children is clearly increasing.   *1*

Provides a definition of a key concept to clarify the focus of research.

Homeless children and youth are defined as "those individuals who lack a fixed, regular, and adequate nighttime residence" (McKinney-Vento Homeless Assistance Act, 1987).   *2*

CASE STUDY OF ONE HOMELESS CHILD   2

This includes children who live in shelters, cars, motels, and numerous other inadequate housing situations. The McKinney-Vento Act states that each child of a homeless individual and each homeless youth must have equal access to the same free, appropriate public education as provided to other children. It states specifically that homelessness alone is not a sufficient reason to separate these students from the mainstream school environment.

Explains why the increase in home-lessness is such a pressing problem for educators and reviews research to determine what we know.

Homelessness has serious implications for children's developmental and academic growth. Developmental problems include withdrawal, aggression, short attention span, sleep disorders, speech delays, regressive behaviors, immature motor behavior, immature peer interaction, and inappropriate social interaction with adults (Baumohl, 1996; Pawlas, 1994). These developmental problems lead to academic problems, which are especially evident in reading and math. The majority of home-less students read below grade level and score below grade level in mathematics (Pawlas, 1994; Stormont-Spurgin & De Reus, 1995; Walsh & Buckley, 1994; Ziesemer & Marcoux, 1992). Homeless students have higher rates of school transfer, special education services, and grade retention (Baumohl, 1996; Walsh & Buckley, 1994). Homeless students face barriers to school enrollment and attendance. These students often do not have the documents required for school enrollment; as a result, many children are turned away from attending school until this issue is resolved (U.S. Department of Education, 2000). Transporta-tion to and from school is the biggest problem for homeless youth (U.S. Department of Education, 2000). These barriers directly and negatively affect the success of homeless students in school.

A stable lifestyle for these children is crucial to their mental, emotional, physical, and social well-being. "Stability is central to children's growth and development, and times of tran-sition are times of risk" (Baumohl, 1996, p. 118). Homelessness creates great risks for the developmental and academic growth of youth; these risks need to be confronted. "Children who have lost their homes live the experience of having, as they describe it, 'nowhere to go'" (Walsh & Buckley, 1994, p. 2).

CASE STUDY OF ONE HOMELESS CHILD   3

Identifies a gap: what we still need to know that research has not focused on.

Communities need to examine how they are reacting and responding to the struggles and needs of homeless students. Despite the obstacles that homeless students face, schools are an ideal setting for developing and organizing the educational and social services they need (Wall, 1996). Comprehensive services including both educators and social workers can be done both within and outside the school system (Wall, 1996). If these homeless children's lives are to improve, they will require the help of schools and social agencies, both working as parts of a community that is sensitive and responsive to these students' needs. It is clear that society understands the importance of caring for homeless students, but to what extent have schools and social service agencies carried out their suggestions or plans?

Formulates the question motivating the writer's research.

The McKinney-Vento Homeless Assistance Act defines homeless youth and explains the rights of students facing homelessness. It provides specific guidelines for how schools and social service agencies are to care for homeless students' educational needs. Yet Congress has not adequately funded state or local efforts to implement this legislation. In 2003, Congress appropriated $55 million for educational programs under the McKinney-Vento Act. However, this appropriation is $15 million less than the authorized amount of $70 million (National Coalition for the Homeless, 2004). Is the country doing everything it can to ensure the rights of homeless children as stated in the McKinney-Vento Homeless Assistance Act?

Further defines the gap in what is necessary to address the problem the writer identifies.

Purpose

Provides a more specific version of the question motivating this research. Develops a rationale for conducting further research and answers the question "What's at stake?"

The question this research is attempting to answer is "To what extent are schools and social service agencies, working as parts of larger communities, creating a stable lifestyle that will improve homeless students' developmental and educational growth?" There has not been much research examining how effectively schools and social service agencies are creating stability in homeless students' lives. In order to better the lives of these children, research must be done investigating and evaluating the current services offered.

5

6

7

CASE STUDY OF ONE HOMELESS CHILD   4

The developmental and academic lives of students are   *8*
threatened by the lack of stability resulting from homelessness.
This issue is a very important one as the numbers of homeless
children continue to increase each year. Answering this question will provide valuable information to both schools and social
agencies about how to better care for the specific needs and
rights of homeless students. Moreover, this research will lead to
a greater sense of community caring for those who live in poverty. It may inspire future research and the creation of programs
that better aid homeless students.

Methods

Describes the
approach to answer-
ing the research
question.

I will take a case study approach in order to better   *9*
understand this issue and attempt to answer my research question. My case study will focus on one child from the South Bend
Center for the Homeless. I will interview the child, his or her
parents, teacher, school social worker, and others who play a
role in creating stability in this child's life. I will take notes as

Explains what the
approach will help
uncover and how she
will build on others'
work to offer a per-
spective that others
have neglected.

well as audio-record the interviews. These interviews will allow
me to explore the connections between homelessness and education as explained by the voices of those who witness or are
affected by homelessness every day.

I will also be using archival information, including both   *10*
journal articles and books, from the library. I will explore what
other researchers have contributed to this issue and what they
are currently saying about it. I will also examine present-day
statistics involving homelessness, youth, and education and will
study the plans of various government and community programs
and policies, particularly the McKinney-Vento Homeless Assistance Act. This will help me to further develop and answer my
own questions about homelessness and education.

Utilizing these various methods will provide me with a   *11*
broad range of information and resources that will aid me in
completing my research. Directly discussing this education issue
with participants will lead to an honest and realistic perspective. It is the true stories of those who are faced with the issue
of homelessness on a daily basis that will bring this important
issue to the surface.

CASE STUDY OF ONE HOMELESS CHILD   5

Discussion and Implications

Elaborates on what
we can learn from
the study and why it
matters.
In America, over 800,000 children are homeless. In
South Bend, over 300 children live in one of three homeless
shelters. It is believed that 50% of these local children will grow
up to be homeless. Many homeless children do not attend school
regularly. Studies have found that those who do attend school
do not perform as well as their peers and have difficulties socializing with others. A school should be a permanent safe-haven
for these students. A school should be one place that these students might be able to consider their home. Why then do problems involving homeless youth and education continue to exist? *12*

Homelessness traps the young in a vicious cycle from
which they may never be able to escape. If they are continuously moving from shelter to shelter, they are continuously
moving from school to school. As a result, their attendance may
drop; their performance may not be at grade level; they may be
stereotyped and labeled by others based on their temporary lifestyle. Without the psychological, social, and mental benefits a
strong formal education imparts, the homeless child seems to be
left to the fate of his or her parents. The cycle of homelessness
continues for another generation. *13*

Further explains the
positive changes the
research can bring
about.
Perhaps as a result of this study, there will be more community and school action and involvement to support homeless students. Perhaps there will be better busing systems so
that these students can remain enrolled in the same school for
longer periods. Perhaps school social workers can work toward
finding more permanent living arrangements for their homeless
students. Perhaps more mentoring and tutoring programs can be
formed to aid homeless students. Much can be done and should
be done to better the lives of these students. *14*

INTERVIEWING

An **interview** is a face-to-face conversation in which you ask questions to
collect information or opinions that relate to your research question. It's
certainly possible to conduct an interview by phone, especially if the interviewee is not local, but a face-to-face conversation, in which you can note
physical details and body language, is preferable.

The ways writers incorporate interviews into their writing appears almost seamless; but keep in mind that a finished text hides the process involved in conducting a successful interview. What you don't see is the planning that occurs. Writers have to make appointments with each of the people they interview; they have to develop a script, or list of questions, before actually conducting the interview; and they have to test the questions to be sure that they work—that is, that the answers give them the information they are looking for. In other words, the key to a successful interview is preparation. The following information should help you plan for your interview and prepare you for writing down your results.

■ Plan the Interview

You'll want to do some preliminary research to identify people who can help you understand more about your subject: What kind of expertise or experience do they have? Then you have to contact them to find out if they are willing to be interviewed. Begin by explaining your project and why you want to interview them (you may want to send them a copy of your proposal). Let them know how much of their time you are requesting: Half an hour? An hour? (More than an hour is probably excessive.) If you are planning to record the interview—always a wise idea—make sure the person consents to being recorded. Then make the necessary arrangements. For example, you may need to reserve a room where you can conduct your interview without being disturbed.

Obviously it is crucial to find out in your first contact whether your candidates actually have expertise in an area relevant to your study. If they lack that expertise, consider asking if they can recommend someone who has it.

It's important to set up appointments with people early on. To keep on schedule, list the names of people who have agreed to be interviewed:

Interviewee 1: _____ Contacted? _____(y/n)

Interviewee 2: _____ Contacted? _____(y/n)

■ Prepare Your Script

You should now begin to work on your script in earnest. If you submitted a series of questions with your proposal, you may have received some response to them from your instructor or classmates. Perhaps they suggested refinements or proposed additional questions. If you agree with their suggestions, now is the time to incorporate them. As you work on your script, keep the following points in mind.

Try to establish common ground.   In any conversation, you want to establish common ground, and an interview is no different. Do you have any interests in common with the person that may ease you into the interview?

Order your questions so that you begin by establishing common ground and then move on to the issues you want to learn more about.

Start with nonthreatening questions.   For example, "How long have you been working at the homeless shelter?" "What prompted you to work at a homeless shelter?" "What role do you play with the children at the homeless shelter?"

Ask filter questions.   Filter questions help you determine what the person you are interviewing knows or has experienced. For instance, you might ask a worker at a homeless shelter if he or she works with children. If not, does he or she work with parents? Of course, if you've done your homework, you will know where to start the interview.

Beware of yes/no questions.   Try not to ask questions that encourage simple yes or no responses. Work on rephrasing yes/no questions in your script so that you're more likely to get an enlightening answer. For example, don't ask "Do you think that the children at the homeless shelter can overcome the obstacles they face?" Instead, ask something like this: "How do you think children at the homeless shelter can overcome the obstacles they face?"

Try funneling.   *Funneling* means moving from more-general questions — "What challenges have you faced as an educator in the homeless shelter?" — to more-specific ones — "How did you respond to those challenges?"

Rehearse and then revise the script.   After you've reworked your script, rehearse it with your writing group or some friends to see how it works. You want to develop a sense of how an interviewee is going to respond to your questions. Is the wording clear? Are you getting the information you need? If not, what other questions should you ask? How did the order and pacing of the questions make your stand-in interviewees feel? How long did the interview take? After the rehearsal, revise the script to improve the content, order, and pacing of your questions.

▪ Conduct the Interview

On the day of an interview, contact your interviewee again to make sure he or she remembers the time of the interview and knows how to find the location where it will take place. See to it that your tape recorder or video camera is charged and functioning and has sufficient recording capacity for the interview. Be on time. Start by having the person sign a simple consent form (see Figure 11.3). It should specify how you will use the material and should indicate that the interviewee knows you will be recording the interview and agrees to let you use quotes from the interview in your paper.

Once you begin asking questions, if at all possible, take notes and record the conversation. Be flexible with the script as you go. Pursue new questions that are raised by what the interviewee tells you. If the interviewee's answers are vague, evasive, or misdirected, try rephrasing your questions to be more specific about the information you need. If you think the interviewee is implying something that is of special interest to you, ask for clarification. This kind of reflective query may shake loose some interesting new material.

Toward the end of the interview, check your script for important questions you may have forgotten to ask. If there are several, try to ask only the most important ones in the time remaining.

■ Make Sense of the Interview

Conducting an interview is only part of the challenge; you then have to make sense of what was said. That process involves four steps:

1. *Familiarize yourself with the conversation.* If you recorded the interview, listen to or watch it a couple of times to become really familiar with what was said. Read through your notes several times too.

2. *Transcribe the interview.* Being familiar with the conversation will make it easier to transcribe. Keep in mind that transcription takes more time than you think, so plan accordingly. An hour-long interview usually takes about three hours to transcribe.

3. *Analyze the interview.* Read through the interview again. Look for answers to the questions motivating your research, and look for recurring patterns or themes. Make a list of those ideas relevant to the issues you intend to focus on, especially evidence that might support your argument.

4. *Find one good source.* Using the themes you identify in your analysis as a guide, find one good source that relates to your interview in some way. Maybe your subject's story fits into an educational debate (for example, public versus private education). Or maybe your subject's story counters a common conception about education (that inner-city schools are hopelessly inadequate). You're looking for a source you can link to your interview in an interesting and effective way.

■ Turn Your Interview into an Essay

Try to lay out on paper, in paragraphs, the material you've collected that pertains to the focus of your paper. In a first draft, you might take these steps:

1. State your argument, or the purpose of your essay. What do you want to teach your readers?

2. Begin writing your supporting evidence for your thesis. What examples from your reading, observations, or interviews do you want to offer your readers? How do those examples illuminate your claim?

3. Place quotations from more than one source in as many paragraphs as you can, so that you can play the quotations off against one another. What is significant about the ways you see specific quotations "in conversation" with one another? How do these conversations between quotations help you build your own point?

4. Consider possible counterarguments to the point you want to make.

5. Help readers understand what is at stake in adopting your position.

Steps to Interviewing

1 Plan the interview. After you've identified candidates through research, contact them to explain your project and set up appointments if they are willing to participate.

2 Prepare your script. Draft your questions, rehearse them with your classmates or friends, and then make revisions based on their responses.

3 Conduct the interview. Be flexible with your script as you go, making sure to take good notes even if you are recording the interview.

4 Make sense of the interview. Review the recording and your notes of the interview, transcribe the interview, analyze the transcript, and connect the conversation to at least one good source.

5 Turn your interview into an essay. State your argument, organize your evidence, use quotes to make your point, consider counterarguments, and help your readers understand what's at stake.

USING FOCUS GROUPS

Focus groups can provide you with an original source of evidence to complement (or complicate, contradict, or extend) the evidence you find in books and articles. Conducting a focus group is much like conducting an interview. According to Bruce L. Berg, in *Qualitative Research Methods for the Social Sciences*, a **focus group** "may be defined as an interview style designed for small groups . . . addressing a particular topic of interest or relevance to the group and the researcher." College administrators often speak with groups of students to understand the nature of a problem—for instance, whether writing instruction is as effective as it should be beyond a first-year writing course, or whether technology is used to best effect in classes across the curriculum. One advantage of a focus group, as opposed to an interview, is that once one person starts talking, others join in. It is generally easier to get a conversation going in a focus group than to get an interview started with a single person.

A typical focus group session is guided by a facilitator, or moderator. The moderator's job is much like the interviewer's: to draw out information from the participants on topics of importance to a given investigation. The informal atmosphere of the focus group is intended to encourage participants to speak freely and completely about their behaviors, attitudes, and opinions. Interaction among group members often takes the form of brainstorming, generating a larger number of ideas, issues, topics, and even solutions to problems than could be produced through individual conversations.

The following are several basic tasks necessary to orchestrating a focus group.

■ Select Participants for the Focus Group

Focus groups should consist of five to seven participants, in addition to you, the moderator. Think carefully about the range of participants you'll need in order to gather the information you're hoping to find. Depending on your issue, you might choose participants based on gender, ethnicity, major, year in school, living situation, or some other factor. Do you want a wide range of participants? Or do you want to control the focus of the conversation by looking at just one particular group of people? For instance, if you wanted to find out if technology is serving students' needs, would you talk only to people in the sciences? Or would you want a cross section of disciplines represented? Or if your question is whether colleges and universities should take race and ethnicity into consideration when selecting students from the applicant pool, would you limit participation to the admissions staff? Where should you look for input on the purpose of giving preference to minority students or the advantages of a diverse campus?

■ Plan the Focus Group

Planning is as important for a focus group as it is for an interview. Make specific arrangements with participants about the time and place of the focus group session, and be clear about how much time it will take, usually thirty minutes. You should tape-record or videotape the session, in addition to any notes you take. Jot down important information during the session, and allow yourself time to make more extensive notes as soon as it is over. You will need to get permission from respondents to use the information they give you and ensure their anonymity. (In your essay, you can refer to participants by letter, number, or some other designation.) Make a sheet with your signature that spells this out clearly, and make sure all your participants sign it before the session. You should include a state-

You are invited to participate in a study of academic writing at the university over the next four years. You were selected from a random sample of all first-year students. If you decide to participate, you will

1. provide the researcher with copies of the writing you complete for every class and the assignment, when available.
2. attend up to four focus group sessions during a given academic year.
3. allow the researcher to use excerpts from the writing you complete and the focus group sessions in publications about research with the understanding that your identity will not be revealed at any time.

In all, out-of-class participation will take no more than four hours during an academic year.

Participation is completely voluntary; you may stop participating at any time prior to completion of the project. Should you have any questions at any time, you are welcome to contact the researcher at the address below or via e-mail. Your decision to participate or not will have no effect on your grade in any course or prejudice your future relationship with the university. One benefit of participating in the study is that you will have the opportunity to learn important information about writing.

If you are willing to participate in this research, please read and sign the consent form below. You will be given a copy of this form to keep.

CONSENT FORM

I agree to participate in all of the procedures above. I understand that my identity will be protected during the study and that instructors will not have access to the statements I make in focus group sessions. I also understand that my name will not be revealed when data from the research are presented in publications. (Tapes from this study will be kept for five years and then destroyed.) I have read the above and give the researcher, Stuart Greene, and his coauthors permission to use excerpts from what I write or transcripts of tapes without identifying me as the writer or speaker.

_____   _____

Date   *Signature*

                                               _____
                                               Signature of Researcher
                                               [Telephone number]/[E-mail address]

FIGURE 11.4   Sample Consent Form for a Focus Group

ment pointing out that people have the right not to participate. We have included sample consent forms in Figures 11.4 and 11.5.

■ Prepare Your Script

Many of the guidelines for designing interview questions (see pp. 308–09) apply equally well to focus group questions. So, for example, you might start by establishing common ground or with a couple of nonthreatening

Should colleges and universities take race and ethnicity into consideration when selecting new freshmen from the applicant pool? What is the purpose of giving preference to minority status in admissions? What does a diverse campus offer its students? These are some of the issues I want to discuss in today's focus group. But before we start, let me tell you about the assignment and your involvement.

The focus group is an interview style designed for small groups of five to seven participants. Focus group interviews are guided discussions that address a particular topic of interest or relevance to the group and the researcher. The informality of the focus group structure is intended to encourage participants to speak freely about their behaviors, attitudes, and opinions. For the purposes of my research, focus groups are a way to include multiple perspectives in my paper.

This session will be recorded so that I can prove my research. No names will be used in any drafts or in my final paper; instead, I will use letters (A, B, C) to identify different speakers. Two focus groups — one for minority students at Notre Dame and another for nonminority students — are being held so that I can obtain opinions and viewpoints from both sides of the issue and discuss their similarities and differences in my report. Some things to keep in mind during the session:

- Because I need to transcribe the dialogue, try not to talk over another person.
- Feel free to agree or disagree with a question, statement, or another person's answer.
- Focus on the discussion, not the question.
- Avoid going off on tangents.
- Be open and honest in all your responses.

Thank you for taking the time to be involved in my research. By signing below you give me permission to use the comments you provide for my paper. You understand that in no way will your identity be revealed, except by your minority or nonminority status. If you would like a copy of the results of the focus groups, please include your e-mail address, and the documents will be sent to you.

Name _____   Male Female (circle one)

Ethnicity _____   Class of _____

E-mail address _____

FIGURE 11.5   Sample Consent Form for a Focus Group

questions. For variety, and to keep the discussion moving, use both open-ended and closed-ended (yes/no answer) questions. Consider asking participants for definitions, impressions, examples, their ideas of others' perceptions, and the like. Also, you might quote from key passages in the scholarly research you will be using and ask for the group's responses to these "expert" theories. Not only will this be interesting; it also will help you organize and integrate your focus group evidence with evidence from library sources in your essay. Ask a wider range of questions than you think you might need so that you can explore side issues if they arise.

▪ Conduct the Focus Group

On the day you conduct the focus group, contact those who have agreed to participate to remind them of when and where it will happen. Show up ahead of time to make sure that your tape recorder or video camera is in good working order and that the room has sufficient seating for the participants. And don't forget your script. Here are three other guidelines.

Ask questions that draw people out.   During the focus group, be ready to draw out participants with follow-up questions ("Can you offer an example?" "Where do you think this impression comes from?"). Encourage all participants to speak; don't allow one member to dominate the discussion. (You may need to ask a facilitating question like "Do the rest of you agree with X's statement?" or "How would you extend what X has said?" or "Has anyone had a different experience?")

Limit the time of a focus group session.   It's a good idea to limit the session to twenty to thirty minutes. When deciding how long the session should last, remember that it will take approximately three times longer to transcribe it. You must transcribe the session so that you can read through the participants' comments and quote them accurately.

Notice nonverbal interactions.   The tape recorder or video camera will give you a record of what was said, but be sure to notice nonverbal interactions and responses in your session, taking notes of body language, reluctance or eagerness to speak, and dynamics among group members that either open up or shut down conversation. These responses should be part of the data you analyze.

▪ Interpret the Data from the Focus Group

Once you transcribe your focus group session, decide how you will refer anonymously to your participants. You then need to interpret the significance of the way participants talk about issues, as well as the information they relate. Interpret the nonverbal communication in the group as well as the verbal communication.

In making claims based on focus group data, remember that data from focus group interviews are not the same as data from individual interviews. They reflect collective thinking, ideas shared and negotiated by the group. Also, although you might speculate that data from a focus group are indicative of larger trends, be careful about the kinds of claims you make. One first-year student's idea is not necessarily every first-year student's idea.

The principal aim of doing original research is to make a contribution to a conversation using primary material as evidence to support your argument. For instance, when you conduct interviews or focus group discussions, you are collecting information (or data) that can offer a unique perspective. And doing original research also can enable you to test others' claims or assumptions and broaden your scope of inquiry beyond secondary materials. An effective piece of original research still relies on secondary materials, particularly as you find ways to locate what you discover in the context of what other authors have observed and argued. Moreover, there is the value of using multiple sources of information to support your claims—using your observations and the findings of others to say something about your subject. Also important, the research methods you choose depend on the question you ask. A focus on the types of educational opportunities available to the homeless lends itself more to close observation, interviews, and perhaps focus groups.

Finally, we want to end with an ethical reminder: *Be fair to your sources.* Throughout this chapter, we have included a number of forms on which you can base your own consent forms when you conduct interviews and focus groups. When people give you their consent to use their words, it is incumbent on you—really it is essential—that you represent as faithfully as possible what people have said. As a researcher, you are given a kind of power over the people you interview and write about, using what they tell you for your own purposes. You cannot abuse the trust they place in you when they consent to be part of your research. It is important that they understand why you're doing the research and how your theories and assumptions will likely figure into your interpretation of the information you gather. You must also be aware of how their words will be construed by those who read what you write.

Steps for Conducting a Focus Group

1 **Select participants for the focus group.** Identify the range of your five to seven participants. Are you looking for diverse perspectives or a more specialized group?

2 **Plan the focus group.** Make sure that you have a specified time and place and that your participants are willing to sign consent forms.

3 **Prepare your script.** Prepare a variety of open-ended and closed-ended questions; consider quoting research you are interested in using in your paper to get participants' responses; and try to rehearse and revise.

4 **Conduct the focus group.** Record the session; ask questions that draw people out; limit the time of the session; and notice nonverbal interactions. And don't forget the consent forms.

5 **Interpret the data from the focus group.** Transcribe and analyze the data, including nonverbal communications; draw conclusions, but be careful not to overgeneralize from your small sample.

APPENDIX:
Citing and Documenting Sources

You must provide a brief citation in the text of your paper for every quotation or an idea taken from another writer, and you must list complete information at the end of your paper for the sources you use. This information is essential for readers who want to read the source to understand a quotation or an idea in its original context. How you cite sources in the body of your paper and document them at the end of your paper varies from discipline to discipline, so it is important to ask your instructor what documentation style he or she prefers.

Even within academic disciplines, documentation styles can vary. Specific academic journals within disciplines will sometimes have their own set of style guidelines. The important thing is to adhere faithfully to your chosen (or assigned) style throughout your paper, observing all the niceties of form prescribed by the style. You may have noticed small differences in the citation styles in the examples throughout Chapter 7. That's because the examples are taken from the work of a variety of writers, both professionals and students, who had to conform to the documentation requirements of their publication venues or of their teachers.

Here we briefly introduce two common documentation styles that may be useful in your college career: the Modern Language Association (MLA) style for listing bibliographic information in the humanities, and the American Psychological Association (APA) style, in the social sciences. The information is basic, for use when you begin drafting your paper. In the final stages of writing, you should consult either the *MLA Handbook for Writers of Research Papers* (7th ed.) or the *Publication Manual of the American Psychological Association* (6th ed.).

Although you'll need the manuals for complete style information, both the MLA (http://www.mla.org/style_faq/) and the APA (http://www.apastyle .org/learn/faqs/) maintain Web sites for frequently asked questions. Again, before you start your research, check with your instructor to find out whether you should use either of these styles or if there's another style he or she prefers.

MLA and APA styles have many similarities—for example, both require short citations in the body of an essay linked to a list of sources at the end of the essay. But it is their differences, though subtle, that are crucial. To a great extent, these differences reflect the assumptions writers in the humanities and in the social sciences bring to working with sources. In particular, you should understand each style's treatment of the source's author, publication date, and page numbers in in-text citations, and verb use in referring to sources.

Author.   MLA style requires that you give the author's full name on first mention in your paper; APA style uses last names throughout. The humanities emphasize "the human element"—the individual as creative force—so MLA style uses the complete name at first mention to imply the author's importance. Because the social sciences emphasize the primacy of data in studies of human activity, in APA style last names are deemed sufficient.

Publication Date.   In-text citations using MLA style leave out the date of publication. The assumption is that the insights of the past may be as useful as those of the present. By contrast, APA style gives the date of the study after the author's name, reflecting a belief in the progress of research, that recent findings may supersede earlier ones.

Page Numbers.   MLA style requires that page numbers be included with paraphrases and summaries as well as quotations (the written text is so important that a reader may want to check the exact language of the original). By contrast, APA style requires attribution but not page numbers for paraphrases and summaries (it is the findings, not how they are described, that are most important).

Verb Use.   MLA style uses the present tense of verbs ("Writer X claims") to introduce cited material, assuming the cited text's timelessness, whether written last week or centuries ago. By contrast, the verbs introducing citations in APA style acknowledge the "pastness" of research ("Writer X claimed" or "Writer Y has claimed") on the assumption that new data may emerge to challenge older research.

Although it is useful to understand that different citation styles reflect different attitudes toward inquiry and research in different disciplines, for the purposes of your writing it is mainly important to know the style you have to follow in your paper, and to stick to it scrupulously. Whenever you

TABLE A.1   Basic Information Needed for Citing Sources

BOOKS	CHAPTERS IN BOOKS	JOURNAL ARTICLES	ONLINE SOURCES
Author(s) or editor(s)	Author(s)	Author(s)	Author(s)
Title and subtitle	Chapter title and subtitle	Article title and subtitle	Document title and subtitle
Edition information	Book editor(s)	Journal title	Print publication information, if any
Place of publication	Book title	Volume and issue number	Site sponsor
Publisher	Edition information	Date of publication	Site title
Year of publication	Place of publication	Page numbers	Year of publication
Medium of publication	Publisher	Medium of publication	Medium of publication
	Year of publication		Date accessed
	Page numbers		
	Medium of publication		

consult a source—even if you don't end up using it in your paper—write down complete citation information so that you can cite it fully and accurately if you need to. Table A.1 shows the basic information needed to cite books, chapters in books, journal articles, and online sources. You also should note any other information that could be relevant—a translator's name, for example, or a series title and editor. Ideally, you want to be able to cite a source fully without having to go back to it to get more information.

THE BASICS OF MLA STYLE

In-Text Citations.   In MLA style, you must provide a brief citation in the body of your essay (1) when you quote directly from a source, (2) when you paraphrase or summarize what someone else has written, and (3) even when you use an idea or a concept that originated with someone else.

In the excerpt below, the citation tells readers that the student writer's argument about the evolution of Ebonics is rooted in a well-established source of information. Because the writer does not mention the author in the paraphrase of her source in the text, she gives the author's name in the citation:

> The evolution of US Ebonics can be traced from the year 1557 to the present day. In times of great oppression, such as the beginning of the slave codes in 1661, the language of the black community was at its most "ebonified" levels, whereas in times of racial progress, for example during the abolitionist movement, the language as a source of community identity was forsaken for greater assimilation (Smitherman 119).

The parenthetical citation refers to page 119 of Geneva Smitherman's book *Talkin and Testifyin: The Language of Black America* (1977). Smitherman is a recognized authority on Ebonics. Had the student mentioned Smither-man's name in her introduction to the paraphrase, she would not have had to repeat it in the citation. Notice that there is no punctuation within the parentheses and no *p.* before the page number. Also notice that the citation is considered part of the sentence in which it appears, so the period ending the sentence follows the closing parenthesis.

By contrast, in the example that follows, the student quotes directly from Richard Rodriguez's book *Hunger of Memory: The Education of Richard Rodriguez* (1982):

> Many minority cultures in today's society feel that it is more important to maintain cultural bonds than to extend themselves into the larger community. People who do not speak English may feel a similar sense of community and consequently lose some of the individuality and cultural ties that come with speaking their native or home language. This shared language within a home or community also adds to the unity of the community. Richard Rodriguez attests to this fact in his essay "Aria." He then goes on to say that "it is not healthy to distinguish public words from private sounds so easily" (183).

Because the student mentions Rodriguez in her text right before the quotation ("Richard Rodriguez attests"), she does not need to include his name in the citation; the page number is sufficient.

Works Cited.   At the end of your researched essay, and starting on a new page, you must provide a list of works cited, a list of all the sources you have used (leaving out sources you consulted but did not cite). Entries should be listed alphabetically by author's last name or by title if no author is identified. Figure A.1 is a sample works cited page in MLA style that illustrates a few (very few) of the basic types of documentation.

Steps to Compiling an MLA List of Works Cited

1 Begin your list of works cited on a new page at the end of your paper.

2 Put your last name and page number in the upper-right corner.

3 Double-space throughout.

4 Center the heading ("Works Cited") on the page.

5 Arrange the list of sources alphabetically by author's last name or by title if no author is identified.

6 Begin the first line of each source flush left; second and subsequent lines should be indented ½ inch.

7 Invert the author's name, last name first. In the case of multiple authors, only the first author's name is inverted.

8 Italicize the titles of books, journals, magazines, and newspapers. Put the titles of book chapters and articles in quotation marks. Capitalize each word in all titles except for articles, short prepositions, and coordinating conjunctions.

9 For books, list the place of publication, the name of the publisher, and the year of publication. For chapters, list the editors of the book, the book title, and the publication information. For articles, list the journal title, volume and issue numbers, and the date of publication.

10 List the relevant page numbers for articles and selections from longer works.

11 Give the medium of publication, such as Print, Web, CD, DVD, Film, Lecture, Performance, Radio, Television, PDF file, MP3 file, or E-mail.

The steps outlined here for compiling a list of works cited apply to printed sources. MLA formats for citing online sources vary, but this is an example of the basic format:

Author. "Document Title." *Name of Site*. Site Sponsor, date posted/revised. Medium. Date you accessed the site.

Things to remember:

- Invert the author's name or the first author's name.
- Italicize the name of the site.
- If the site sponsor—usually an institution or organization—isn't clear, check the copyright notice at the bottom of the Web page.
- MLA style uses the day-month-year format for dates in the works-cited list.
- Notice that there's a comma between the sponsor and the publication date.
- In general, the medium of publication for online sources is "Web."
- Notice that you do not need to include a URL after the date of access.

In addition to online sources, you will likely use other nonprint sources in researching your papers. Our students, for example, regularly analyze films, recordings, television and radio programs, paintings, and photographs. For details on how to format these sources, consult the *MLA Handbook* or go to Purdue University's Online Writing Lab (OWL) site (http://owl.english.purdue.edu/owl/section/2/11).

Eck 10

Works Cited

Gutiérrez, Kris D., Patricia Baquedano-López, and Jolynn Asato. "English for the Children: The New Literacy of the Old World Order." *Bilingual Review Journal* 24.1&2 (2000): 87-112. Print.

Online scholarly journal/article, no author

"History of Bilingual Education." *Rethinking Schools* 12.3 (1998): n. pag. Web. 15 Feb. 2008.

Lanehart, Sonja L. "African American Vernacular English and

Article in a scholarly journal

Education." *Journal of English Linguistics* 26.2 (1998): 122-36. Print.

Article in a magazine

Pompa, Delia. "Bilingual Success: Why Two-Language Education Is Critical for Latinos." *Hispanic* Oct. 1996: 96. Print.

Rawls, John. *Political Liberalism*. New York: Columbia UP, 1993. Print.

Essay in an edited collection; second source by same writer

---. "Social Unity and Primary Goods." *Utilitarianism and Beyond*. Ed. Amartya Sen and Bernard Williams. Cambridge, Eng.: Cambridge UP, 1982. 159-85. Print.

Rodriguez, Richard. "Aria." *Hunger of Memory: The Education of Richard Rodriguez*. New York: Bantam, 1982. 11-40. Print.

Schrag, Peter. "Language Barrier." *New Republic* 9 Mar. 1998: 14-15. Print.

A book

Smitherman, Geneva. *Talkin and Testifyin: The Language of Black America*. Detroit: Wayne State UP, 1977. Print.

Willis, Arlette. "Reading the World of School Literacy: Contextualizing the Experience of a Young American Male." *Harvard Educational Review* 65.1 (1995): 30-49. Print.

FIGURE A.1   Sample List of Works Cited, MLA Format

THE BASICS OF APA STYLE

In-Text Citations.   In APA style, in-text citations identify the author or authors of a source and the publication date. If the author or authors are mentioned in the text, only the publication date is needed:

> Feingold (1992) documented the fact that males perform much better than females in math and science and other "masculine" areas.

Notice that the in-text citation does not include a page number. Because Feingold is only cited, not quoted, no page reference is necessary. If the source is quoted directly, a page number is added in parentheses following the quote:

> Feingold (1992) argued that "men scored significantly higher than women in situations designed to test aptitude in mathematics and hard sciences" (p. 92).

APA style uses the abbreviation *p.* or *pp.* before page numbers, which MLA style does not. If the author is not identified with a signal phrase, the name, year, and page number would be noted parenthetically after the quotation:

> One study found that "men scored significantly higher than women in situations designed to test aptitude in mathematics and hard sciences" (Feingold, 1992, p. 92).

Many studies in the social sciences have multiple authors. In a work with two authors, cite both authors every time:

> Dlugos and Friedlander (2000) wrote that "sustaining passionate commitment to work as a psychotherapist reflects passionate commitment in other areas of life" (p. 298).

Here, too, if you do not identify the authors in a signal phrase, include their names, the year the source was published, and the relevant page number parenthetically after the quotation—but use an ampersand (&) instead of the word *and* between the authors' names:

> Some believe that "sustaining passionate commitment to work as a psychotherapist reflects passionate commitment in other areas of life" (Dlugos & Friedlander, 2000, p. 298).

Use the same principles the first time you cite a work with three to five authors:

> Booth-Butterfield, Anderson, and Williams (2000) tested . . .
> (Booth-Butterfield, Anderson, & Williams, 2000, p. 5)

Thereafter, you can use the name of the first author followed by the abbreviation *et al.* (Latin for "and others") in roman type:

Booth-Butterfield et al. (2000) tested . . .
(Booth-Butterfield et al., 2000, p. 5)

For a work with six or more authors, use *et al.* from the first mention.

These are only some of the most basic examples of APA in-text citation. Consult the APA manual for other guidelines.

References.   APA style, like MLA style, requires a separate list of sources at the end of a research paper. This list is called "References," not "Works Cited." The list of references starts on a new page at the end of your paper and lists sources alphabetically by author (or title if no author is identified). Figure A.2 shows a sample list of references with sources cited in APA style.

Steps to Compiling an APA List of References

1 Begin your list of references on a new page at the end of your paper.

2 Put a shortened version of the paper's title (not your last name) in all caps in the upper-left corner; put the page number in the upper-right corner.

3 Double-space throughout.

4 Center the heading ("References") on the page.

5 Arrange the list of sources alphabetically by author's last name or by title if no author is identified.

6 Begin the first line of each source flush left; second and subsequent lines should be indented ½ inch.

7 Invert all authors' names. If a source has more than one author, use an ampersand (not *and*) before the last name.

8 Insert the date in parentheses after the last author's name.

9 Italicize the titles of books, capitalizing only the first letter of the title and subtitle and proper nouns.

10 Follow the same capitalization for the titles of book chapters and articles. Do not use quotation marks around chapter and article titles.

11 Italicize the titles of journals, magazines, and newspapers, capitalizing the initial letters of all key words.

12 For books, list the place of publication and the name of the publisher. For chapters, list the book editor(s), the book title, the relevant page numbers, and the place of publication and the name of the publisher. For articles, list the journal title, the volume number, the issue number if each issue of the volume begins on page 1, the relevant pages, and the DOI (digital object identifier) number if available. If you retrieve a journal article online and there is no DOI, include the URL of the journal's home page.

GENDER AND TEACHING   15

References

Journal article with no DOI

Campbell, R. J. (1969). Co-education: Attitudes and self-concepts of girls at three schools. *British Journal of Educational Psychology, 39*, 87.

Report, seven authors

Coleman, J., Campbell, E., Hobson, C., McPartland, J., Mood, A., Weinfeld, F., & York, R. (1966). *Equality of educational opportunity (The Coleman report)*. Washington, DC: U.S. Government Printing Office.

Journal article with a DOI

Feingold, A. (1992). Sex differences in variability in intellectual abilities: A new look at an old controversy. *Review of Educational Research, 62*, 61-84. doi:10.3102/00346543062001061

Online source

Haag, P. (2003). *K-12 single-sex education: What does the research say?* Retrieved from http://www.ericdigests.org/2001-2/sex.html

Journal article retrieved online with no DOI

Hallinan, M. T. (1994). Tracking: From theory to practice. *Sociology of Education, 67*, 79-84. Retrieved from http://www.asanet.org/journals/soe/

Hanson, S. L. (1994). Lost talent: Unrealized educational aspirations and expectations among U.S. youth. *Sociology of Education, 67*, 159-183. Retrieved from http://www.asanet.org/journals/soe/

Jovanovic, J., & King, S. S. (1998). Boys and girls in the performance-based science classroom: Who's doing the performing? *American Educational Research Journal, 35*, 477-496. doi:10.3102/00028312035003477

FIGURE A.2   Sample List of References, APA Format

Lee, V. E., & Marks, H. M. (1990). Sustained effects of the single-sex secondary school experience on attitudes, behaviors, and values in college. *Journal of Educational Psychology, 82*, 578-592.

Mickelson, R. A. (1989). Why does Jane read and write so well? The anomaly of women's achievement. *Sociology of Education, 62*, 47-63. Retrieved from http://www.asanet.org/journals/soe/

Scholarly book   Rosenberg, M. (1965). *Society and the adolescent self-image.* Princeton, NJ: Princeton University Press.

Schneider, F. W., & Coutts, L. M. (1982). The high school environment: A comparison of coeducational and single-sex schools. *Journal of Educational Psychology, 74*, 898-906.

Essay in edited collection   Spade, J. Z. (2001). Gender education in the United States. In J. H. Ballantine & J. Z. Spade (Eds.), *Schools and society: A sociological approach to education* (pp. 270-278). Belmont, CA: Wadsworth/Thomson Learning.

Streitmatter, J. L. (1999). *For girls ONLY: Making a case for single-sex schooling.* Albany, NY: State University of New York Press.

Dissertation from a database   Winslow, M. A. (1995). *Where the boys are: The educational aspirations and future expectations of working-class girls in an all-female high school* (Doctoral dissertation). Available from ProQuest Dissertations and Theses database. (AAT 9622975)

FIGURE A.2   Sample List of References, APA Format (*continued*)

The *APA Manual* is your best resource for formatting online sources, but here is an example of a basic reference to an online source:

Author. (Date posted/revised). *Document title.* Retrieved from URL

- If no author is identified, alphabetize the entry under the title.
- Capitalize an online document title like an article title, and italicize it; don't enclose it in quotes.
- Include a retrieval date after the word "Retrieved" only if the content is likely to change.
- Notice that there is no end punctuation after the DOI or URL.

- APA style asks you to break lengthy DOIs or URLs after a slash or before a period, being sure that your program doesn't insert a hyphen at the line break.

The *APA Manual* is also your best resource for formatting references to other nonprint sources. You should know that certain nonprint sources you are likely to rely on in your research in the social sciences—interviews and focus groups, for example—do not have to be included in your list of references. Instead, you would cite the person you interviewed or the focus group you conducted in the text of your paper. For example:

(J. Long, interview, April 7, 2007)

A NOTE ON THE COUNCIL OF WRITING PROGRAM ADMINISTRATORS' (WPA) OUTCOMES

From Inquiry to Academic Writing: A Practical Guide is coauthored by a former Writing Program Administrator, and the WPA outcomes are espoused and reinforced throughout the book's pedagogy and readings. Below, the outcomes are listed, and *italic* references link specific outcomes to particular chapters.

Rhetorical Knowledge: By the end of first-year composition, students should

- Focus on a purpose. *See especially Chapter 2.*
- Respond to the needs of different audiences. *Throughout; see especially Chapter 8.*
- Respond appropriately to different kinds of rhetorical situations. *Throughout; see especially Chapter 4.*
- Use conventions of format and structure appropriate to the rhetorical situation. *Throughout; see especially Chapter 1 and Chapter 7.*
- Adopt appropriate voice, tone, and level of formality. *See especially Chapter 8.*
- Understand how genres shape reading and writing. *Discussions of audience, especially in Chapters 2, 4, and 8, bear on genres.*
- Write in several genres. *Throughout.*

Critical Thinking, Reading, and Writing: By the end of first-year composition, students should

- Use writing and reading for inquiry, learning, thinking, and communicating. *See especially Chapters 1, 2, and 3 for coverage of inquiry and critical thinking and reading.*
- Understand a writing assignment as a series of tasks, including finding, evaluating, analyzing, and synthesizing appropriate primary and secondary sources. *See especially Chapters 6 and 7.*
- Integrate their own ideas with those of others. *See especially Chapters 5 and 7.*
- Understand the relationships among language, knowledge, and power. *Readings throughout the text address issues of language, knowledge, and power.*

Processes: By the end of first-year composition, students should

- Be aware that it usually takes multiple drafts to create and complete a successful text. *See especially Chapter 1 and Chapter 10.*

- Develop flexible strategies for generating, revising, editing, and proof-reading. *See especially Chapters 4, 5, and 10.*

- Understand writing as an open process that permits writers to use later invention and re-thinking to revise their work. *See especially Chapters 4, 5, and 10.*

- Understand the collaborative and social aspects of writing processes. *See especially Chapter 1 and Chapter 10.*

- Learn to critique their own and others' works. *See Chapter 10.*

- Learn to balance the advantages of relying on others with the responsibility of doing their part. *See Chapter 10.*

- Use a variety of technologies to address a range of audiences. *Readings in Chapters 3, 4, 5, and 7 explore different cultural and cognitive impacts of new technologies.*

Knowledge of Conventions: By the end of first-year composition, students should

- Learn common formats for different kinds of texts. *See documented readings throughout and Appendix on documentation.*

- Develop knowledge of genre conventions ranging from structure and paragraphing to tone and mechanics. *See especially Chapter 7 and Chapter 9.*

- Practice appropriate means of documenting their work. *See Chapter 7 and documented readings in different disciplines.*

- Control such surface features as syntax, grammar, punctuation, and spelling. *Chapters 9 and 10 touch on these features.*

Composing in Electronic Environments: By the end of first-year composition, students should

- Use electronic environments for drafting, reviewing, editing, and sharing texts. *The book's Web site and related Bedford/St. Martin's resources facilitate such work.*

- Locate, evaluate, organize, and use research material collected from electronic sources, including scholarly library databases; other official databases (e.g. federal government databases); and informal electronic networks and Internet sources. *See especially Chapter 6.*

- Understand and exploit the differences in the rhetorical strategies and in the affordances available for both print and electronic texts. *Readings in Chapters 3, 4, 5, and 7 raise issues of strategies in print and electronic communication.*

ACKNOWLEDGMENTS

William Deresiewicz. "The End of Solitude." *The Chronicle of Higher Education*. The Chronicle Review, January 30, 2009. Copyright © 2009. All rights reserved.

John Dickerson. "Don't Fear Twitter." *Nieman Reports*, Summer 2008. Nieman Foundation for Journalism at Harvard. Reprinted by permission.

Barbara Ehrenreich. "Cultural Baggage." From *The New York Times Magazine*, April 5, 1992. Reprinted by permission of International Creative Management, Inc. Copyright © 1992 by Barbara Ehrenreich.

Gerald Graff. "Hidden Meaning, or Disliking Books at an Early Age," from *Beyond the Culture Wars: How Teaching the Conflicts Can Revitalize American Education*. Copyright © 1992 by Gerald Graff. Used by permission of W. W. Norton & Company, Inc.

Steve Grove. "YouTube: The Flattening of Politics." *Nieman Reports*. Nieman Foundation for Journalism at Harvard University. Summer 2008. Reprinted by permission.

Cynthia Haven. "The New Literacy: Stanford Study Finds Richness and Complexity in Student Writing." *Stanford University News*, Stanford Report, October 12, 2009.

Shirley Brice Heath. Excerpt from "Protean Shapes in Literacy Events: Ever-Shifting Oral and Literate Traditions." Reprinted by permission.

E. D Hirsch, Jr. "Preface to Cultural Literacy." From *Cultural Literacy* by E. D. Hirsch, Jr. Copyright © 1987 by Houghton Mifflin Company. Reprinted by permission of Houghton Mifflin Company. All rights reserved.

Josh Keller. "Studies Explore Whether Internet Makes Students Better Writers." *The Chronicle of Higher Education*, June 11, 2009.

Dan Kennedy. "Political Blogs: Teaching Us Lessons About Community." *Nieman Reports*, Summer 2008.

James W. Loewen. "The Land of Opportunity." From *Lies My Teacher Told Me: Everything Your American History Textbook Got Wrong* by James W. Loewen. Copyright © 1996 by James W. Loewen. Reprinted by permission of The New Press.

Elizabeth Martínez. "Reinventing 'America': Call for a New National Identity." From *De Colores Means All of Us: Latina Views for a Multi-Colored Century* by Elizabeth Martínez. Copyright © 1998 by Elizabeth Martínez. Reprinted by permission of South End Press.

Meredith Minkler. "Community-Based Research Partnerships: Challenges and Opportunities." *Journal of Urban Health: Bulletin of the New York Academy of Medicine*, vol. 82, no. 2, supplement 2. Copyright © 2005 by Meredith Minkler. Published by Oxford University Press on behalf of the New York Academy of Medicine. All rights reserved. Reprinted by permission.

Phil Primack. "Doesn't Anybody Get a C Anymore?" The *Boston Globe*, October 5, 2008. Reprinted by permission.

Eugene F. Provenzo, Jr. "Hirsch's Desire for a National Curriculum." This essay previously appeared in Eugene F. Provenzo, Jr., *Critical Literacy: What Every American Ought to Know*. Boulder, CO: © Paradigm Publishers 2005, pp. 53–55.

Anna Quindlen. "Doing Nothing Is Something." *Newsweek*, May 13, 2002.

Richard Rodriguez. From *Hunger of Memory: The Education of Richard Rodriguez*. Reprinted by permission of David R. Godine, Publisher, Inc. Copyright © 1982 by Richard Rodriguez.

Stuart Rojstaczer. "Grade Inflation Gone Wild." *Christian Science Monitor*, March 24, 2009. Reprinted by permission.

Myra Sadker and David Sadker. "Hidden Lessons." Reprinted with the permission of Scribner, a Division of Simon & Schuster, Inc., from *Failing at Fairness: How Our Schools Cheat Girls* by Myra Sadker and David Sadker. Copyright © 1994 by Myra M. Sadker and David Sadker. All rights reserved.

Sidonie Smith and Julia Watson. "Agency" from *Reading Autobiography: A Guide to Interpreting Life Narratives*. University of Minnesota Press, 2001, pp. 42–45.

Clive Thompson. "The New Literacy." *Wired Magazine* August 24, 2009. Reprinted by permission of the author.

Images

Lost—Spare Tire. www.smallstep.gov

Open Up and Say Anything. Agency for Healthcare Research and Quality. Reprinted by permission.

Photo illustration for "Internet Market Considers Microsoft Bid for Yahoo." Chris Jackson / Getty Images.

School may be out for summer, but lunch is always in session. Courtesy of Feeding America.

The "It's Only Another Beer" Black and Tan. US Department of Transportation.

You Have Your Best Ideas in the Shower. Used with permission from Microsoft.

Index of Authors, Titles, and Key Terms

RESOURCES FOR TEACHING

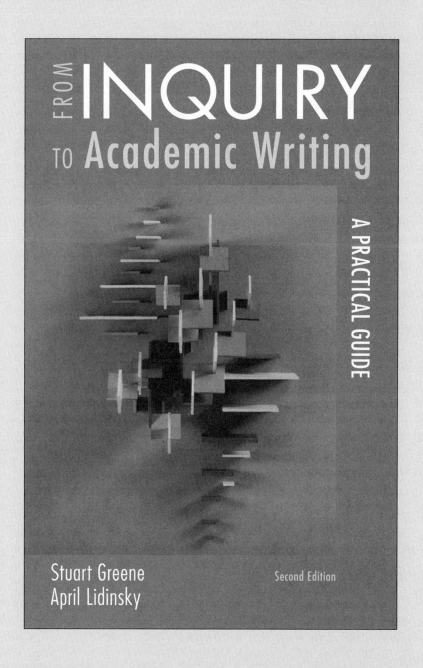

FROM **INQUIRY** TO **Academic Writing**

A PRACTICAL GUIDE

Stuart Greene
April Lidinsky

Second Edition

Stuart Greene   April Lidinsky   WITH Joanna Mangeney

Resources for Teaching
FROM INQUIRY
TO ACADEMIC
WRITING
A Practical Guide

Second Edition

Resources for Teaching
FROM INQUIRY
TO ACADEMIC
WRITING
A Practical Guide

Stuart Greene
University of Notre Dame

April Lidinsky
Indiana University South Bend

with **Joanna Mangeney**
University of Notre Dame

Bedford/St. Martin's   BOSTON ■ NEW YORK

For information, write: Bedford/St. Martin's, 75 Arlington Street, Boston, MA
02116 (617-399-4000)

ISBN-13: 978-0-312-55830-7

Preface

This manual is designed to be an introductory (or a quick-refresher) course in using *From Inquiry to Academic Writing: A Practical Guide*, Second Edition. We distill the main points of each chapter, comment on each reading, and discuss each exercise we provide in the practice sequences. Additionally, we offer some suggestions for further reading and research, include numerous teaching tips coming out of our own experiences using these materials with our students, and provide exercises to supplement those in the book. If you misplace or want an extra copy of this manual, you can download one from the companion site, **bedfordstmartins.com/frominquiry.** Additional resources on the Web site include downloadable templates, worksheets, and summary boxes for students; AuthorLinks that supplement the readings in the book; and connections to the suite of online resources offered by Bedford/ St. Martin's, including *Re:Writing*.

Contents

Planning a Syllabus

All instructors will have their own ideas about how to make use of *From Inquiry to Academic Writing: A Practical Guide,* Second Edition, in their composition courses. We ourselves tend to focus on a particular theme or topic over the course of a semester, and assign outside readings that fit the particular theme or topic. In a broad sense, all the readings in *From Inquiry to Academic Writing: A Practical Guide* deal with issues of social justice and equality, which may give some direction to your course. Still, it's easy enough to focus on the readings as models of academic writing and take your course in an entirely different thematic or topical direction. For example, while we hope your students will wrestle with E. D. Hirsch's ideas about cultural literacy in Chapter 2, our main intent is that they come away from reading "Preface to *Cultural Literacy*" with a sense of how to perform a rhetorical analysis. We want them to look beyond what Hirsch says and analyze how and why he says it. These skills will help students work with whatever readings you decide to build your course around.

Still, we do think the arrangement of chapters represents a logical sequence. We initially describe the habits of mind and core skills of academic writers, and all the subsequent chapters follow a well-marked path from reading to writing. We think the title of Chapter 2—"From Reading as a Writer to Writing as a Reader"—conveys the interconnected and recursive nature of the process, which is reflected in the rest of the chapters. In Chapters 2 through 6, the emphasis falls more on the "Reading as a Writer" side of the equation, while in Chapters 7 through 10 it falls on the "Writing as a Reader" side. Assigning Chapter 1 ("Starting with Inquiry: Habits of Mind of Academic Writers") in the first week of class may be a useful way to introduce your students to the "academic thinking and writing" framework of the book, but if time is short you can probably summarize its key points from the front of the room, or ask a selected group of students to make the presentation. However, we do believe that in the first week of classes, your students should read Chapter 2, as it is (in our view) the most important preview and treatment of the critical and rhetorical habits of mind and core skills we emphasize in our courses.

If you plan to emphasize collaborative learning and peer group work, you may want to have your students read Chapter 10 ("From Revising to Editing: Working with Peer Groups") very early in the semester as well. Although much of the chapter presents practical advice about revision, and thus can readily be assigned later in the course, it also reinforces, from the writing side, the "conversational" nature of the academic writing enterprise, and the multistage process of developing and writing academic arguments. Although it may be several weeks before your students are in a position to revise and edit their writing, if they read Chapter 10 they will have been introduced to important concepts of working with their peers to develop their writing—a habit of mind that should firmly be implanted early on.

Although we address the notion of academic writing as argument right from the beginning of the book, if your composition program places a heavy emphasis on argumentation as a set of rhetorical skills, you may want to assign Chapter 3, "From Identifying Claims to Analyzing Arguments" and Chapter 8, "From Ethos to Logos: Appealing to Your Readers" as a unit early in the semester. These chapters present the concepts and vocabulary of Toulmin argument, Rogerian argument, and classical argument. Again, as with Chapter 1, you could spare your students the reading and present this material from the front of the room, or have a group of students present it. Alternatively, Chapter 8 can be assigned later in the semester, in conjunction with a first or second draft of your students' papers.

It makes sense to assign Chapters 4 ("From Identifying Issues to Forming Questions") and 5 ("From Formulating to Developing a Thesis") as a unit. If you prefer not to inject a strong argument component in the early stages of your course, then these might be the chapters to assign right after students have Chapter 2 under their belts. Once students have a sense from Chapter 2 of what is involved in a rhetorical reading (understanding situation, purpose, claim, audience), Chapters 4 and 5 will help them sharpen their critical reading skills and begin to find in their reading what they need to help them write their own papers: an issue to explore and a thesis to argue.

Chapter 6 ("From Finding to Evaluating Sources"), Chapter 7 ("From Summary to Synthesis: Using Sources to Build an Argument"), and Chapter 11 ("Other Methods of Inquiry: Interviews and Focus Groups") represent the research component of *From Inquiry to Academic Writing*. Of the three, Chapter 7 may be the most important to assign. Often students are given some kind of training—often through the campus library—in finding and evaluating sources (the subject of Chapter 6), and often "field research" (the subject of Chapter 11) is not encouraged or required in a composition course. But we cannot imagine a course in academic writing in which students will not be required to learn and practice the skills of paraphrasing, summarizing, synthesizing, and quoting. If research is a heavy component of your course, we suspect you may want to assign Chapter 7 within the first few weeks—possibly as early as the second week of the course. (In fact, we can imagine a course—possibly at a school that has a quarter rather than a semester calendar—in which only five chapters of our book would be assigned: Chapters 2, 4, 5, 7, and 9, in that order.)

Speaking of Chapter 9 ("From Introductions to Conclusions: Drafting an Essay"): We expect that you would assign this chapter just prior to your students writing the first draft of their full-blown academic argument. The templates we present in the chapter—of introductions and conclusions—have proven extremely useful to our own students as a way of organizing their thoughts and staking out their own positions in writing when the prospect of a draft looms. Moreover, the templates are very useful for breaking students of the "five-paragraph essay" mindset that they so often carry with them into their college composition courses. In fact, if your first writing assignment makes clear that many of your students are in thrall to this mindset, you may want to assign Chapter 9 early on and ask them to try to revise their five-paragraph essays using these heuristics.

1

Starting with Inquiry
Habits of Mind of Academic Writers

This chapter introduces students to four key habits of mind that we believe are important to the process of academic writing: inquiring, seeking and valuing complexity, understanding that academic writing is a conversation, and understanding that writing is a process. The ideas we develop about these habits of mind grow out of years of teaching writing and doing research in different academic contexts. Although your students probably already use these habits of mind in their everyday lives, they may be unfamiliar with how they should apply them to academic writing. Moreover, they have not thought about writing as a process of inquiry in large part because the writing they have done has been limited to what they may already know, not what they need to know. Thus, during the first few weeks of a new semester, you may find yourself addressing what may very well be a new orientation to writing for students.

Students are especially surprised when introduced to the idea that writing is a form of conversation. To address students' concerns, it is helpful to begin with where they are, encouraging them to write about and discuss how they approach composing a paper in school, the assignments they have done recently, the challenges they faced as writers, and how others responded to what they had written. In turn, it is useful to discuss how writing may differ in an academic context and why it is necessary for them to reorient themselves to a new approach, given the added challenges of writing in this new context.

Students making the transition from high school to college are more accustomed to writing based on their experiences. When they have based their essays on information they have found through reading or research, they typically ended up writing summaries rather than analyses or arguments. Writing for a college course requires them to learn how to transform information rather than simply recount or summarize it. Transforming information entails gathering it from different and often conflicting sources and adapting it for their own purposes as writers who are expected to contribute something new to an academic conversation, often in the service of changing readers' points of view. Such writing must use evidence to persuade readers that something holds true (or does not).

The differences between writing in high school and college are not immediately apparent to students. Sometimes it takes an assignment or two in their first college classes (for example, in philosophy or sociology courses) to help them to see that their well-learned strategies for writing may not apply to what they are now being asked to do. To draw their attention to these differences, you can ask students to keep a log documenting the kinds of assignments and examples of papers they receive in other classes. In turn, they can share with their classmates what they are learning through such an exercise about writing across disciplines. What students learn from each other can be more powerful than anything we try to tell them about differences between what they have been accustomed to writing and what they are now required to write. (For example, see Stuart Greene,"Exploring the Relationship between Authorship and Reading" in *Hearing Ourselves Think: Process Research in the Classroom*, eds. A. Penrose and B. Sitko. [New York: Oxford University Press, 1993] 33–51.)

Similarly, we find it necessary to work with students on their conceptions of argument. Arguments represented in the media tend to be combative, often hostile. But writing in an academic argument, students will find, involves a respectful engagement with the ideas of other writers whose points of view may conflict with their own. Again, it is useful to begin with where students are and why they have the conceptions of argument that they believe hold true. Although we address these concerns in our introduction, **"What Is Academic Writing?"** (p. 1), we expect that you will need to work patiently with students as you introduce a new terminology for writing that embodies a new way of thinking about how writing works in the transaction between reader and writer. We hope that the examples we provide will support you in your efforts to aid students in their transition from a familiar to a new context for writing and expressing ideas. These are examples we have used in our own classes to build on what students already know (on p. 3, for instance, we use an example about analyzing the issues in an election to help students decide how they will vote).

The first key habit of mind is **inquiry** (p. 4). Every piece of academic writing begins with a question that someone has asked about the way the world works. We call attention to this questioning frame of mind to contrast it with the topically oriented way that writing and research are often taught in high schools. Teachers ask students to generate a list of topics for a paper, which assumes that students already have in their grasp the information they will need to write a paper. For us, inquiry of any kind begins with *observations* about what others have written. In turn, these observations will lead writers to *ask questions* in order to *examine alternatives* to explore how things could be different. Underlying such a conception of inquiry is our view that academic readers and writers examine unquestioningly accepted ideas.

The **Practice Sequence** (p. 6) that we include in our discussion of inquiry is typical of how we ask students to enact the strategies we have discussed. After all, it is one thing to tell students what they need to do and think about but quite another for students to actually try out a set of strategies or activities with which they may not be altogether familiar. Thus, they should practice the habit of making observations, writing down questions that puzzle them, and addressing alternatives even when the answers to a question appear simple.

Students are familiar with analyzing advertisements, our first activity, but we push them in the second activity (p. 8) to examine issues on campus, which are often presented in the school newspaper. The example about majors is derived from conversations on our campus, where students appear to choose majors based on their career aspirations. (For example, students major in history and political science because they believe it is necessary to do so to get into law school.) At issue for faculty is that students should make the best use of a liberal arts education by exploring areas of study that can challenge what students know and help them add to their depth of knowledge in a given subject.

The next key habit of mind we identify is **seeking and valuing complexity** (p. 6). Here we address the concern that students often experience issues as having just two sides. Examples of this kind of *binary thinking* abound in the media, especially on television, where split screens show two people who represent two conflicting points of view. Because every issue has more than two sides, we want students to learn to see the limits of binary thinking—to look at issues from many different perspectives. Moreover, academic writers are expected to examine every issue from multiple perspectives. The **Practice Sequence** (p. 8) builds on the previous set of activities (p. 6), in which we encouraged students to identify issues and raise questions in response to advertisements and their study of preferred college majors. We challenge students to imagine a world of beliefs and values beyond their own and to seek alternative views. This is often quite difficult for them, and it is worth devoting a fair amount of time to this activity. After all, much of their writing will need to anticipate and grasp the worldviews that others hold. An alternative assignment is to ask students to interview different people on campus (for example, their roommates or professors in various disciplines) about this or any other issue to see how different people's perspectives differ. A further exercise to help students respect other views and increase their willingness to revise their own ideas would be to have them write a short paragraph supporting a claim that is opposite to their own position or preference.

The next key habit of mind is **understanding that writing is a conversation** (p. 8). Like oral conversations or e-mail chains, academic writing builds on what has come before and grows stronger from the multiple perspectives of others involved in the conversation. A student used to writing rote summaries on a text may have some difficulty with the idea that academic writing is a more complex transaction that has to demonstrate what others have discussed and what they believe is at issue. Using Martin Marty's discussion of hospitality in his book *When Faiths Collide* (p. 8), we illustrate that meaning is always tied to context. In the Marty example, the word *hospitality* has many different meanings in contemporary culture, history, and religion. Thus, not all people agree on the meaning of a word that to some might seem a well-defined term whose definition is widely accepted. Academic writers know that they must be aware of how terms, issues, and ideas have been discussed and debated in the past; in turn, they must be aware that how they choose to approach a given issue or idea will be judged relative to how others have done so. The lesson we try to bring home for students is that their writing is a transaction between the past and the present that will undoubtedly become part of future conversational transactions.

In the **Practice Sequence** (p. 10) the short passage from Thomas Patterson's *The Vanishing Voter* introduces students to some of the problems associated with a democracy in which a relatively small proportion of citizens vote. For example, a sudden crisis could cause millions more citizens to vote, resulting in an explosive situation. Furthermore, voting has been shown to strengthen citizenship by giving citizens a sense of participation and encouraging volunteerism. However, the trend in the United States has been a diminished sense of commitment to the political process. This exercise asks students to reflect on Patterson's argument in order to look at different perspectives and points of view.

Alternatively, you could try any of the following exercises to help students think about writing as a conversation:

1. Choose, or have the class choose, a controversial issue or issues. Ask students to form pairs, with one student for the issue and one student against. Have each student state his or her case, making sure to respect the views of the other side. Afterward, have students talk about what they see as the strong points of the other's argument. Are the students willing to revise their views at all?

2. Choose, or have the class choose, a controversial issue. Divide the class and set up a debate in which each side has a few minutes to state its case and the other side has a chance for rebuttal. You can easily find resources for conducting classroom debates online if you would like more instructions.

3. Divide students into pairs or small groups. Give them time to have a conversation on an issue or a topic. What did they gain from the conversation? Did the conversation give them any ideas they could use if they were to write on this topic?

The final key habit of mind discussed in this chapter is **understanding that writing is a process** (p. 12). Writing in general, and academic writing in particular, does not depend on inspiration and should not occur at the last minute; it is a process of defining issues, formulating questions, and developing sound arguments. If students' writing assignments prior to college have been mainly brief summaries of what they have read or personal-experience essays, then they may not see the benefits of looking at writing as a process. But when they begin to see the complexity of what we are asking them to do, they begin to realize the value of rehearsing their ideas—their arguments— in drafts. Moreover, once they see that writing is relational—that it is designed to affect what real readers think and how they may act—then students also begin to see the value of revising their ideas to accommodate others' perspectives.

BECOMING ACADEMIC

We end this chapter with two literacy narratives to help students see that learning to read and write in an academic sense is a lifelong process. For example, in **"Scholarship Boy"** (p. 15), an excerpt from "The Achievement of Desire," **Richard Rodriguez** reflects upon his desire to assimilate into a dominant American culture by erasing his Mexican accent and acquiring knowledge of this dominant culture by reading classic literature. However, he also describes a key turning point in his life well after he began this process of assimilation. Specifically, he was struck by Richard Hoggart's description of what Hoggart calls the habits of the "scholarship boy."

The notion of a "scholarship boy" is pejorative in the sense that good students, like Rodriguez, tend to read and take in knowledge without really reflecting upon information or thinking critically. The result means that the scholarship boy, with whom Rodriguez readily identifies, is ill equipped to apply the knowledge he has acquired or to make informed critical judgments about the worlds he inhabits.

Rodriguez's revelations are very much in keeping with what we try to impart throughout this book—that academic reading and writing require critical judgment. We encourage students to suspend judgments about what they read and write until they have sufficiently examined the claims that writers make and the evidence that writers use to support those claims.

Rodriguez also enacts a strategy that demonstrates the ways academic writing is a kind of conversation. Very much in conversation with Hoggart's ideas about the scholarship boy, Rodriguez applies what he learns from Hoggart for his own purposes. In turn, he aspires to make a contribution to this conversation by building upon and extending Hoggart's ideas.

In **"Disliking Books"** (p. 22), an excerpt from *Beyond the Culture Wars: How Teaching the Conflict Can Revitalize American Education,* English professor **Gerald Graff** reveals that he has not always loved reading. He outlines his background: middle class, Jewish, part of an environment that viewed bookworms as "sissies." Though his father tried to force him to read, Graff couldn't get interested in anything besides comic books and sports magazines. However, he went to college, as was expected of all young men of his background. Because of his lack of interest in other areas, he majored in English, and read to avoid flunking out of school. Though he read widely, his enjoyment of reading did not increase, and he did not see anything resembling his experience in the novels he had to read.

Another problem for Graff was that he did not know how to talk about literature, and when he was able to produce the rare bit of analysis, it sounded strange in his mouth. This was when Graff was first exposed to critical debates, particularly a debate on Mark Twain's *Adventures of Huckleberry Finn.* Critics had judged that the book's ending trivialized Jim's struggle to be free, and Graff found himself interested in this controversy. He was fascinated by the idea that famous authors might make amateurish mistakes. After reading the criticism surrounding this debate, he found himself reading the novel with excitement. Having something to look for while reading had made him feel personally engaged with the novel.

Graff then compares his story of reading with the standard one, in which a future teacher is inspired by a primary experience with a book, and then learns the secondary critical skills of reading. In this model, the future teacher's reading experience is intentionally free of critical discourse, which according to Graff is traditionally portrayed as ruining the innocence of reading. Based on this idea of literacy, Graff says, he was corrupted before he was innocent. He needed the critical discourse before he could truly engage with the text.

Graff disputes the idea that one should be left completely alone with the text, which for him is a boring and impersonal experience. His view is that we should not attempt to protect ourselves from critical discourse, but rather embrace it, because our ability to read well depends more on that critical discourse than we think. Graff ends by writing that he believes that his own experience in learning to love reading makes him a better teacher.

In the **Practice Sequence: Composing a Literacy Narrative** (p. 27), we encourage students to reflect on their experiences as readers and writers. We invite them to discuss the similarities and differences in their experiences, the extent to which Hoggart's notion of the "scholarship boy" might resonate for them, and whether or not they believe that school explicitly cultivates the kind of learning that Hoggart and Rodriguez are so critical of.

Similarly, students can assess their own experiences in light of Graff's and the extent to which it makes sense to maintain the kind of innocence about literature that Graff describes as so central to teaching. Does it make sense to avoid reading about the debates surrounding works of literature? Does reading about critical debates enhance the literary experience for students, as Graff argues it did for him?

We have found that sharing literacy narratives in class can be very enlightening for students. Many of our own students have taken their opportunities for granted, particularly their access to resources such as excellent teachers, libraries, bookstores, and enrichment activities, and the ability to attend cultural events and even travel on vacations. They learn quickly that not all of their peers have had similar experiences.

Connecting their experiences to those of Rodriguez and Graff can be equally enlightening. After all, Rodriguez and Graff grew and developed as a result of much outside support. Neither had to go it alone as they progressed through school and made the discoveries they did.

Thus, the broader question may be this: Under what circumstances can we say that any of us can flourish as readers and writers? What do we need? For that matter, what factors can impede our ability to flourish? In turn, how do any of us overcome these impediments or help others gain access to the many resources we can take for granted?

2

From Reading as a Writer to Writing as a Reader

In this chapter, we discuss the role that reading plays in academic writing. In our view, reading is actually the first step in the writing process. Reading requires that students comprehend the content of what they read, but reading as a writer also entails identifying issues that writers believe they might like to address, forming questions that can guide inquiry, and developing an argument.

Reading actively is a general term that we use to describe the process of engaging with the ideas of others, questioning and testing those ideas, and inquiring into their significance. To encourage our students to read actively, we ask them to enter into a conversation with the author by bringing their own knowledge, experiences, and interests to a text and using them to respond to what they read. *Reading strategically* is a form of analysis that involves separating out the parts of a text to better understand how the argument works as a whole. *Reading rhetorically* is a more specific kind of strategic reading that involves identifying the situation that a writer responds to, the writer's purpose, the writer's claims, and the audience for whom the text is written. We then ask students to consider how these components contribute to the writer's argument as a whole. Reading rhetorically will not only help students better understand how a text works as a piece of writing, but it will also help them develop their own writing because they can make use of the strategies they have identified as they begin to develop their own argument.

We have been struck over the years with how deferentially our students read. They read to gather information without questioning its validity or appropriateness; if it appears in a book or an article, it must be true, and if they've taken the time to read it, they feel obliged to use it in their papers. Moreover, our students typically do not make notes in their books. Instead, they simply underline information without a clear set of criteria for doing so. Therefore, if your students are like ours, you will find it important to encourage them to read critically and to annotate what they read with questions and some initial responses. (See our discussion of these practices on pp. 139–71 and in Chapter 2.) The jottings that students make in their books represent the first steps toward writing by reading in the role of writers who respond to what they are reading. While a few students may be familiar with annotating and rhetorically analyzing texts, most will be learning these skills for the first time. For this reason, it is important that students practice the skills of annotating and rhetorically analyzing, even if these techniques seem straightforward.

We asked one of our students to read a brief excerpt from Massey and Denton's *American Apartheid: Segregation and the Making of the Underclass* (p. 31) and to "mark it up in a way that she would normally take notes in her book in preparing for a class discussion." Her annotation represents one of many approaches that students can take to writing in their books. The passage we chose discusses the history of the residential segregation of black Americans. This residential segregation first came about due to racist attitudes, private behaviors, and institutional practices that denied black Americans access to urban housing markets. In theory, a series of court decisions and federal legislation during the 1960s banned discrimination and eliminated residential segregation, but the practice has remained for several decades — a point that is often new information for our students and that sets them up to read E. D. Hirsch (p. 33), who ignores this context in addressing literacy in low-income minority neighborhoods. We include the Denton and Massey excerpt not only because we want students to take Hirsch's argument seriously but also because it will give them a perspective that will enable them to read Hirsch's argument critically.

On pages 33–36 we reprint **E. D. Hirsch's Preface to *Cultural Literacy.*** Although Hirsch wrote his influential book decades ago, the ideas about which he writes resonate quite powerfully in public schools across the United States. We find that most of our students are drawn to his argument because they believe that success in school (possibly their own success) follows from simply learning important facts in history, science, and literature and being able to report them on a test. But we want students to understand how an author uses specific strategies to move an audience to agree. Whatever you may feel about the stance that he takes, Hirsch lays out his argument in a clear, instructive way. We use this reading to illustrate a rhetorical analysis in which an author identifies the situation he wishes to respond to, defines his purpose, makes a claim, and writes with an audience in mind. We also chose Hirsch's preface because it is part of an ongoing conversation in our book that focuses on education, access to opportunity, social justice, and race. In class, we always ask students to draw examples from their own reading and experiences.

Hirsch begins by introducing the idea of "cultural literacy," explaining that "to be culturally literate is to possess the basic information needed to thrive in the modern world." Hirsch takes his concept one step further, claiming that cultural literacy is the only sure way for disadvantaged children to succeed and that schools must alter curricula to incorporate cultural literacy if they wish to promote equality. Specifically, cultural literacy entails knowledge that literate Americans possess; Hirsch gives the example of *Das Kapital*, which few citizens have actually read but which many have read about.

In later paragraphs, Hirsch explains his theory of cultural literacy in the context of other educational theories. He closely relates cultural literacy to the anthropological view that all human communities are founded on specific knowledge, implying that this specific knowledge (cultural literacy) should be the main goal of schools. He places his view somewhere in between those of Rousseau and Dewey on the one hand, who advocated content-neutral natural development, and Plato on the other, who believed that the specific content taught to children was by far the most important aspect of education.

In the context of analyzing Hirsch's argument, we introduce students to the importance of writing to an audience (p. 38), an idea that will occur throughout the text. To familiarize students with the concept of *audience*, divide them into small groups. Give each group the same idea to articulate, but ask each group to write to a different audience (for example, to a friend on instant messenger, to a class listserv, to grandparents in a letter, to a professor in conversation). Have each group share its version. As a class, you can talk about the ways writers' perceptions of an audience influence what and how they write.

We include **Eugene F. Provenzo Jr.'s** essay, **"Hirsch's Desire for a National Curriculum"** (p. 39), to illustrate the continued relevance of E. D. Hirsch's ideas, even though Hirsch first published his ideas about cultural literacy over twenty years ago. Hirsch's essay serves as a significant intellectual touchstone that many scholars reference in their work, but it also warrants the kind of critical analysis that Provenzo offers contemporary readers.

In the excerpt we provide, Provenzo claims that E. D. Hirsch's advocacy for a national curriculum is deceptive, since the nation already has a standard curriculum in the form of standards decided upon by both local communities and national accreditation groups. There is uniformity across the nation on what first graders learn, for example, or the order in which to learn certain skills, or what grade in which to teach algebra.

Provenzo characterizes creating a curriculum as a political act, and argues that Hirsch's desire to create a new curriculum is an attempt to replace the existing one with one that serves Hirsch's ideological purposes. Hirsch's argument, that the sheer number of schools in the United States with separate policies is causing the loss of national literacy, is apparently counter to the typical conservative view, that local schools should have more control.

Besides this point, Provenzo questions whether Hirsch has a valid curriculum as described in his book *Cultural Literacy*. Critics of this book have pointed out that the fragmentation of curriculum, according to Hirsch, can be solved by more fragmentation and that the organization of Hirsch's knowledge that people need is arbitrary.

One of our favorite exercises is to ask students to write a one-page rhetorical analysis based on their reading of a single paragraph. This encourages students to write a focused analysis of a portion of an essay that interests them, to connect their reading to other essays they have read, and to relate what they have read to what they are writing (or thinking of writing). In turn, students share their analyses in class. We begin with an excerpt from **Sidonie Smith and Julia Watson's** book, ***Reading Autobiography: A Guide for Interpreting Life Narratives*** (p. 42).

Smith and Watson review the ways different theorists have treated agency—a notion that seeks to account for the ways individuals interact within culture and society. Much of literary history has demonstrated a distinct emphasis on the individual who is able to fashion a self apart from the influence of others. But such a notion has been challenged, and yet Smith and Watson identify a scholarly conversation revealing the extent to which the notion of agency is still a disputed concept. Scholars have not agreed upon what agency means, and the authors show that this is a complex issue that is indeed unresolved.

Smith and Watson begin with the theory of agency put forward by Louis Althusser disputing the idea of free will. Althusser argues that the notion of free will is nothing but a misunderstanding of an ideological concept as something natural. Instead, he argues that our sense of who we are is socially constructed, created by the dominant class's beliefs and values. Institutions within this class draw subjects into their discourse and define what the subject becomes. In addition, the individual cannot see the ideology that has influenced them, and therefore concludes that individuals are free to fashion their own identities.

French sociologist Michel de Certeau sees agency as a series of acts by one system to counteract or combine with another system—for example, the workplace or the housing project. Another French theorist, Jean-Francois Lyotard, sees language as an uncontrollable and flexible network through which people construct their worlds.

The postcolonial theorist Arjun Appadurai is concerned with agency as it pertains to social practices. He states that we participate in imaginary communities, and this is particularly true in the global system of capitalism. In this case, imagination becomes a fact with which to navigate global networks.

Judith Butler's theories center around the idea that identity is enacted in our daily lives, and that identity is informed by social norms. Because there are many norms, our identities are constantly being reinvented.

In the end, we want students to understand the nature of the debate here, so it's fine to let them discuss how they perceive the issue of freedom of the will and identity. But we want students to fully grasp how writers develop their ideas, examining *how* writers like Smith and Watson engage others' ideas in offering their own perspectives. The *how* is as important as the *what* as students learn to read in the role of writers and aspire to make their own contribution to ongoing scholarly debates.

We ask students to read and analyze an excerpt from Smith and Watson's book, which describes the major theories concerning the idea of agency, particularly as it pertains to autobiography. As we mention in the text, the authors begin by stating the premise that agency is not as simple as the subject acting on his or her own behalf, but rather comes from a complex set of cultural and discursive influences.

In the example we annotate, the student has chosen to do an analysis of paragraph 3 from the excerpt from Smith and Watson's book. She is deliberate in stating what she believes is the purpose motivating Smith and Watson's own analysis, the audience the authors have in mind in discussing the concept of agency, and the style of their analysis. Specifically, she mentions the ways they engage others' ideas as a means for supporting the argument they develop and the methodology they present.

Next, the student considers aspects of Smith and Watson's writing that she would like to incorporate into her own essay, a point we want students to consider as they read in the role of writers. For example, we often ask students if they would use a strategy they have seen another writer use. If so, why? If not, why not? By answering these questions, students can develop a meta-awareness of what works in an effective piece of writing, why it works, and when it might work in their own writing. It's worth discussing with students that in reality, not all strategies work all of the time.

We end the chapter by giving students an occasion to practice their skills by writing a rhetorical analysis of **Barbara Ehrenreich's "Cultural Baggage"** (p. 46). Ehrenreich provides a humorous account of her ethnicity, or lack thereof. She introduces the essay with an anecdote in which an acquaintance asks her what her ethnicity is. Her answer is automatic. "None," she says. This event triggers a reflection on ethnicity that follows Ehrenreich as she deals with the guilt of rejecting her Irish/English/neutral heritage, the memories of growing up "none," and her longing for an ethnic heritage. In the end, she comes to, what for her, is the satisfying realization that she is of the "kind of people who do *not* believe, who do not carry on traditions, who do not do things just because someone has done them before," the kind of people who think for themselves. Ehrenreich's essay is an excellent complement to the selection on identity written by Elizabeth Martínez in Chapter 9.

The first part of the **Practice Sequence** (p. 49) offers an opportunity for each student to write a rhetorical analysis of Ehrenreich's essay, but the second part, the group option, may offer a more lively way to get students to reflect on how an essay works to exert a rhetorical effect on readers. By asking students to imagine themselves in conversation with Ehrenreich, it should bring home to them how important it is to write with a certain audience in mind.

3

From Identifying Claims to Analyzing Arguments

Our experience tells us that students are uncertain about what we mean by *argument* because it is used in so many different ways. For example, when philosophy professors ask their students to compose an argument, they mean something quite different than the English professor who asks students to develop an argument about a literary text. To complicate matters further, students read arguments in the newspaper and watch debates (often highly scripted and relying on either/or oppositions) between political adversaries on television. Thus it is helpful to acknowledge the different ways people use the term *argument* — as a single claim, as a claim that runs throughout an entire essay — so that students can accurately interpret what it means to identify and actually produce an argument.

In this chapter, we break down the notion of argument into its constituent parts — the main and minor claims, the reasons provided to support claims, the writer's concessions, and the writer's attempts to handle possible counter-arguments — in order to help students better understand how these parts interact to form an effective argument. In a researched argument, a writer uses evidence in the interest of advancing an argument that contributes to the ongoing conversation about an issue that is open to dispute. If students can build a kind of map of an argument, they will be able to comprehend the complexities of what a writer argues; conversely, with a map of their own arguments, students can lay out their positions clearly for readers in ways that anticipate counterarguments. (You might be interested in reading Stuart Greene's essay "Argument as Conversation: The Role of Inquiry in Writing a Researched Argument," which appeared in *The Subject Is Research*, eds. W. Bishop and Pavel Zemliansky [Portsmouth, NH: Boynton/Cook Heinemann, 2001], 145–64, 240–41).

To illustrate how arguments work, we ask students to read **Myra Sadker and David Sadker's "Hidden Lessons"** (p. 52). The Sadkers' research introduces readers to the hidden sexism that exists in American schools and serves as still another perspective on American education that educators often ignore in their discussions of reform. The Sadkers' perspective differs significantly from E. D. Hirsch's (p. 33).

In their essay, the Sadkers claim that boys and girls in the United States receive very different educations and that girls are more likely to be "invisible members of the classroom." Specifically, they claim that teachers, regardless of sex and race, interact more with boys, challenge them with better questions, and give them better feedback. The possible consequences for girls include low self-esteem, decreased achievement, and diminished career opportunities.

Sadker and Sadker acknowledge that most people, including teachers and students, cannot identify sexism in the classroom until it is pointed out to them. In fact, the authors do not blame teachers, calling them "skillful, well-intentioned professionals who inadvertently teach boys better than girls." To illustrate the elusiveness of sexism in schools, the authors offer an example in which the producers of the television news show *Dateline*, while working on a story about the Sadkers' findings, watched a video over and over but did not notice anything unfair about the instructor's teaching. Then the Sadkers pointed out several instances of sexism, including an entire math lesson during which the teacher faced the male students with her back to the female students.

In our analysis of the Sadkers' essay and its claims that begins on page 55, we draw on Stephen Toulmin's theory of argument as well as our own study of over one thousand student essays written across the disciplines as part of a four-year research project. The research we conducted was designed to understand the relationship between the writing students produce in first-year composition and across disciplines.

On pages 55–57, our discussion focuses on **identifying claims.** An argument usually contains both a *main claim* (or *thesis*) and *minor claims*. The thesis summarizes the writer's position on the situation to which he or she responds and encompasses all the minor claims of the argument as well. A writer can make three types of claims: a claim of fact, which makes assertions that a condition existed, exists, or will exist; a claim of value, in which a writer expresses his or her evaluation of a condition that has existed, exists, or will exist; and a claim of policy, which advances a call for change and is directed at some future action—what should exist. An argument need only contain one type of claim, but some writers incorporate all three types. We have found that students typically write arguments based on claims of fact and that they rarely have opportunities to evaluate or develop policy as undergraduates. Still, students should be able to identify these types of arguments and we can give them opportunities to write such essays in the composition classroom. The **Practice Sequence** on page 57 provides a list of claims that we ask students to identify by type. Students tend to like this exercise, and you may want to tap into their enthusiasm and give the exercise more currency by bringing the day's newspaper into class and reading aloud some claims for your students to identify.

A claim must be backed up with evidence, and it is the reader's job to evaluate the extent to which the writer has provided good reasons to support his or her position. In the section **"Analyzing Arguments"** (p. 58), we explain that strong evidence is *recent, relevant, accurate,* and *reliable* and discuss these points (pp. 58–61) as we show how the Sadkers make use of evidence in their essay. We indicate that students need to evaluate the extent to which a writer has provided *good reasons* to support his or her position. In turn, they will need to decide whether the support for a claim is *recent, relevant, accurate,* and *reliable*. These are new ideas for students and are more complicated than we might indicate. For example, while suggesting that evidence should be recent, we explain that there are exceptions. Similarly, readers do not always agree on what constitutes "relevant" evidence. Further discussions of these points is well worth it. As we suggested earlier, it can be useful to ask students to keep a log about their writing in other courses. In such a log, they can write about how these terms—*recent, relevant, accurate, reliable*—apply in other disciplines.

Just as the notion of argument varies across disciplines, so does the idea of what people mean by effective evidence. Thus, it is important to show students examples of different types of evidence and to talk with them about what kind of evidence is appropriate within a given context. We cannot emphasize enough the value of helping students develop a meta-awareness of writing that can inform the choices they make as writers.

The next two parts of an argument—the author's concessions and the author's attempt to address counterarguments—are important to the conversational nature of academic writing, and we discuss them in the context of the Sadkers' argument on pages 61–63. *Concessions*, which acknowledge that others may see an issue differently than the writer does, and *counterarguments*, which anticipate the readers' objections to the writer's argument and respond to them, show that the writer values the complexity of having multiple perspectives and is willing to consider different and conflicting opinions.

This conversational, rather than confrontational, approach to argument is what composition scholars have called the *Rogerian* approach, based on the theories of psychologist Carl Rogers. (Douglas Brent provides an excellent overview in his essay, "Rogerian Rhetoric: An Alternative to Traditional Rhetoric," which can be found in *Argument Revisited, Argument Redefined: Negotiating Meaning in the Composition Classroom*, eds. Barbara Emmel, Paula Resch, and Deborah Tenny [Sage, 1996], 73–96.) However, in our discussion of Rogerian argument (p. 63), we do not adhere to a strict definition of *Rogerian rhetoric* or precisely to the ways that others have described the structure of a Rogerian argument. Instead, we encourage students to develop an empathic imagination to enable them to understand the worldviews that others have adopted in writing their arguments. By doing so, students can understand where in laying out their own positions they might make a concession to certain groups of readers ("I can see why you might not agree") and anticipate possible counterarguments.

The idea of Rogerian or conversational argument is new to students and we often divide our classes into two groups to clarify the differences between a Toulmin argument (a claim and support) and a Rogerian argument (a claim, concessions, counterarguments). Each group prepares its stand on a given issue and then individual members contribute to advancing the argument. As one group presents its argument, the other students take notes and we ask them to evaluate the extent to which they believe the group they observe made an "effective" argument. In the end, we encourage students to talk about what constitutes an effective argument that they can translate into strategies for writing. The difference between telling students about arguments and showing them can be dramatic and goes a long way toward helping students understand what we mean. This may be especially so when we talk to students about the difference between a concession and a counterargument, as well as what constitutes persuasive evidence.

On page 64, we provide a student essay that we have annotated to illustrate ways students in your class might approach their own analysis of a written argument. In **"The End of the World May Be Nigh, and It's the Kindle's Fault," Marques Camp** argues that the Kindle, in its form and function, will cancel out the benefits that books offer as social and material objects. Note how Camp identifies the problem by linking the Kindle to the overall shift from printed paper to the digitalization of information, beginning with newspapers being taken over by blogs, with TV replaced by On-Demand, and finally, with the Kindle taking over the book.

Camp then offers a challenge to accepted ideas, arguing that if the Kindle means access to the world of literature, it is still not the case that everyone has equal access to this world. Traditionally, books have been passed from person to person in an act symbolic of the passing of knowledge. For the poor, the book often represents a source of hope and in this way acts as an equalizing force. The intellectual value of the book outweighs the financial value.

Ultimately, Camp argues that the Kindle will widen both the intellectual and the financial gap between the elite and the non-elite, by depriving the non-elite of access to literacy and ideas. While a single book is an affordable item for a poor person, Camp argues, the Kindle's high cost makes even that single book unattainable. Because of its price tag, the Kindle becomes a tool of illiteracy, not greater literacy.

Camp emphasizes the e-book's ability to transform the reading experience from a process of inspiration and personal growth to viewing words on a screen. As Camp characterizes it, an e-book is devoid of personality and without any uniqueness, separated from other books only by a title.

In addition, the social process that leads books from one hand to another is destroyed with the Kindle, because of the restrictions on selling and reselling e-books. The reading process has thus gone from being communal to being highly individualistic. Camp argues that the experience of reading as a communal activity is often more important than the actual words on a page.

Extending and enlarging this argument, Camp highlights the importance of libraries, because of the power they have to symbolize intellectual achievement. With the Kindle, the connection between the intellectual world and the physical one is threatened. The progress made on the literal plane will be replaced by a virtual database, available only to those with the money to spare.

A Practice Sequence: Analyzing and Comparing Arguments

After Camp's piece, we include a pair of recently published articles on grade inflation that seem to capture the debate preoccupying so many academics. The debate that academics have waged over the years is as relevant as ever, especially since current research has begun to reveal that students are studying less than ever and yet their grades continue to rise.

It would be worthwhile comparing with students the styles of argument that Stuart Rojstaczer and Phil Primack use to develop their arguments and the impressions that their respective styles leave on students. Would students adopt specific strategies that Rojstaczer and Primack use? Do they find the authors' appeals to personal experience persuasive? For that matter, to what extent are students persuaded that grade inflation is an issue?

In **"Grade Inflation Gone Wild"** (p. 67), which appeared in the *Christian Science Monitor*, **Stuart Rojstaczer** begins with a personal story about how he came to the realization that grade inflation was a serious problem while teaching at a small liberal arts college. Curious, he investigated the data of over eighty universities, and found that in the last thirty years, grades have gone way up. Inflation began in the 1960s, slowed somewhat in the 1970s, and then began rising again in the 1980s. Private schools are more prone to grade inflation than public schools.

Rojstaczer then links grade inflation to the quality of education. If a 3.6 is the average GPA at a private school, students know that they do not have to work as hard to earn a B+. The hours the average student spends studying will go down, thanks to grade inflation. Rojstaczer estimates that students now spend less than half the hours studying than they did forty years ago. Overall, this leads to an education that is increasingly expensive, yet increasingly without substance.

Adding to this argument, Rojstaczer connects the fewer hours spent studying to a prevalent college student activity, drinking. Surveys show that nearly half of first-year college students spend more time drinking than studying. Rostaczer argues that this will lead to students graduating with a poor education and an addiction to alcohol.

Rojstaczer then turns to solutions for this problem. Princeton University has limited the number of As given out, which has worked to bring more rigor to academics. Other universities are trying out their own policies in this vein, but not many, because these policies are difficult to implement. Rojstaczer argues that this hard work is necessary in order for real learning to take place.

In **"Doesn't Anybody Get a C Anymore?"** (p. 69) which appeared in the *Boston Globe*, **Phil Primack** also begins with a personal story; in this case, it is about one of his own grading mishaps: After giving his student what he thought was a generous B, the student complained about his low grade. Primack argues that this is a result of grade inflation, which has led to a steady rise in GPAs since 1960. Whereas B used to mean "good," it now means bad; and a C is no longer average, but a disaster.

According to Primack's sources in the education field, grade inflation is a huge problem because it makes it impossible to distinguish an outstanding job from a good one, leading to laziness. If students come to expect good grades for low effort, professors will feel pressured to give out high grades in order to attract students.

Primack cites Harvard as a perfect example of grade inflation. From 1950 to 2007, the percentage of students earning B+ or better went from 15 to over 50. At the University of Massachusetts in Amherst, the GPA has gone up in the last decade to 3.19. UMass representatives claim that this is simply because students are better and better, which Primack notes is a common response to the accusation of grade inflation.

The response in nonpublic forums, however, is different. Administrators and faculty members claim that colleges are unwilling to confront the problem of grade inflation because of a fear of losing tuition-paying parents. Some schools, such as Princeton and Wellesley, have implemented policies that limit the number of top grades given; however, such policies are not the norm. Many university employees are privately upset about grade inflation, and yet feel they have no choice but to deny its existence in public.

We offer a number of questions that help guide students' discussion of the authors' style of argument, especially their use of evidence to support their respective arguments. We also encourage students to reflect upon their experiences in college classes as a measure of how to judge the relevance of the issue and what is at stake for students and faculty alike.

Students might conduct a modest study of their own by interviewing students and faculty on campus to gather additional viewpoints, or even conducting focus groups with administrators to understand still another perspective. We offer suggestions for conducting interviews and focus groups in Chapter 11.

Further Activities for Analyzing Arguments

Below we offer some sample exercises that go beyond those we include in the book, to help students understand each part individually and then to understand the interaction of the parts in the formation of an argument.

Main and Minor Claims

1. Give students a series of introductions or full essays written by other authors, students, or scholars. Ask students to identify the authors' major and minor claims. Are they claims of fact, value, or policy?

2. Give students in small groups a full essay to look at. What claims does the author make in the introduction? How do these claims act as signposts? What does the author want the reader to pay attention to? Next, have students read the essay in its entirety. Were they correct about the author's signals?

3. Play a video clip of an argument in a movie or television show (e.g., a reality show, a political debate on network news, a talk show). Ask students to identify the claims made by one of the characters/individuals. Are they claims of fact, policy, or value?

4. Try the above exercise with two opposing editorials.

Support for Claims

5. Have students look at introductions or full essays. What kinds of evidence do the authors provide to support their claims?

6. Give students a research-based essay to read. Ask students to work in groups to decide whether or not the author's support for his or her claims is recent, relevant, accurate, and reliable.

7. As a class, brainstorm different ways an author can provide support for a sample claim. Students should come up with recent, relevant, accurate, and reliable evidence. Would qualitative or quantitative evidence better suit this claim? Would both?

Identifying a Writer's Concessions

8. Give students a claim to analyze. Either as a class or in small groups, have students come up with possible concessions a supporter of this argument might make to someone opposed to this claim.

Identifying an Author's Counterarguments

9. Using the same claim as in the "Identifying a Writer's Concessions" exercise, either as a class or in small groups, have students come up with possible counterarguments a supporter of this argument might need to address. How are the counterarguments different from the concessions students came up with earlier? Help them to distinguish between these two elements of an argument by looking at the author's use of each in an argument.

4

From Identifying Issues to Forming Questions

Many of your students may know a three-stage model of the writing process (prewriting, drafting, revising). In this chapter, we break the process down much further and connect it to reading. Specifically, we describe multiple steps to identifying issues and to formulating questions as a way of getting students started on their writing. It's useful to think of these steps and the questions we include in this chapter as heuristics for prompting different types of actions. Identifying issues and formulating questions help students discover fundamental tensions that are worth writing about and guide inquiry as students enter a conversation of ideas.

We want students to think about their writing as responding to issues, not topics. It is important for students to remember that an issue does not simply exist in the world already well formed. Rather, writers construct and develop issues out of what they observe, think, and value. Again, we try to break down the process into things your students can do and think about in order to identify an issue: (1) draw on their personal experience as a starting point; (2) begin to identify what is open to dispute in an area that interests them; (3) in doing so, resist binary thinking in order to examine an issue from multiple perspectives; (4) build on and extend others' ideas, which, at this point, will mean that students should go beyond their own experiences as points of reference; (5) read to discover possible ways to frame arguments about a given issue; and (6) consider the constraints of the situation—the type of writing they are asked to produce and for whom.

The researched writing we describe requires that students read widely to get a broad perspective on the issue that motivates them to write. Personal experience is a valuable starting point, but academic writing builds on what others have written. In turn, once students begin to grasp what is at issue for them in what they read, they will be in a better position to ask a question. Writing will be more purposeful for students if they have a question to guide them rather than a topic. (We often know when we have answered a question, but trying to write about a topic can seem to go on without end.) Issue-based questions should be specific enough to guide inquiry into what others have written.

Students can begin to formulate an issue-based question as they address the following in short pieces of writing or in discussing their ideas in small groups: (1) refining their topics by articulating what about the topic interests them; (2) explaining why they are interested in the topic; (3) identifying their issue; (4) formulating their topics as questions; and (5) addressing who will be interested in reading about this issue.

While these steps can be very useful for guiding students toward doing research and writing, the approach we describe can be daunting for inexperienced students. Therefore, we give students plenty of time in class to write, share their ideas, and receive responses from us and their peers. We also spend time helping students understand the meaning of such concepts as "situation," "topic," "issue," and "questions." It would be worth having students explain what they see are differences in Table 4.1 (p. 74) in this chapter. Still, we have found that students' first drafts are often motivated by their interest in a topic as opposed to an issue. This is not altogether surprising given students' well-learned habits of mind for writing topic-driven essays.

Below we touch on the various sections of the chapter and suggest some activities to help students hone their skills in each of the six steps involved in identifying issues. Then we have provided broader exercises to help students practice formulating issue-based questions.

In the **"Draw on Your Personal Experience"** section (p. 75), we cite E. D. Hirsch to make the point that academic writers often use personal experience to advance their arguments. The trick is to avoid simply telling stories. Students struggle with this as they are used to thinking of personal-experience essays as entirely separate from more formal writing for which they may have been warned never to use the first-person *I*.

Activities

1. Because students may be unsure of how to effectively incorporate personal experience into their arguments, we suggest that you ask them to identify an issue that comes out of personal experience. Ask students to come up with anecdotal evidence that advances their argument. How might they incorporate this anecdotal evidence into a full essay?

2. Have students read two essays on a similar topic: one that includes personal evidence and one that does not. What effect does personal experience have on the argument? Are students more or less sympathetic to the author who uses personal experience?

In **"Identify What Is Open to Dispute"** (p. 75), we refer to the arguments of E. D. Hirsch and Jonathan Kozol to tease out an exemplary issue, using the idea that a fundamental tension exists between their positions and that at that point lies an issue. This sets the stage for later in the chapter where we discuss formulating issue-based questions (p. 85).

Activity

1. Give students opposing editorials from a campus or local newspaper. Ask them to identify what is open to dispute between the two writers and then develop some criteria for what constitutes an effective statement of an issue. Students can always use a model, but they should be able to articulate some principle to guide their work, especially when they begin to work independently.

In **"Resist Binary Thinking"** (p. 76), we cite the arguments of Hirsch, Kozol, and a student author to illustrate that an issue can have more than two sides. The student describes her school experience in racial terms. Her perspective adds something important to the debate on education reform that Hirsch and Kozol do not address. While Hirsch blames the curriculum and Kozol unequal resources, this student suggests that poor treatment of minority students may be a cause for the achievement gap. Having moved from Colorado Springs to Tallahassee, this student found herself the victim of educationally detrimental racial abuse, such as belittlement and nonacceptance.

Activities

1. Using the same opposing editorials as in the "Identify What Is Open to Dispute" exercise, ask students to identify other points of view in this debate.

2. Ask students to come up with even more possible causes based on their experiences in school. What evidence can they offer? We include other related examples in the sample exercises about seeking and valuing complexity in Chapter 1.

In the section **"Build on and Extend the Ideas of Others"** (p. 77), we include a student example to show how the student used his reading to build on his own experience with homelessness. Specifically, he refers to Melissa Stormont-Spurgin's description of homelessness, in which she explains the unfortunate and saddening conditions in which homeless children live and their effect on these children's readiness to learn in school. Greatly affected by Stormont-Spurgin, the student extended the ideas he read about to include issues of democracy, fairness, and education. This is the kind of broad perspective that brings richness and complexity to any piece of writing.

Activity

1. Ask students to keep a log in which they identify an issue that they discover through reading another writer's work. After students have read several articles or essays about their topic/issue, how has the issue changed for them? Finally, ask students to briefly trace the development of their issues. How did they extend previous writers' ideas? How did they extend their own?

Of the strategies we discuss in this chapter, **"Read to Discover a Writer's Frame"** (p. 78) is perhaps the most challenging new idea for students. Yet, writers often begin their essays by explaining the frame they use to understand a given issue. We include an excerpt from Richard Rodriguez's "Hunger of Memory" in which he uses the frame of "scholarship boy" to examine his experiences as a nonnative English speaker struggling to fit in with mainstream culture. He borrows this framing concept from Richard Hoggart, who describes a boy caught between the warm, spontaneous nature of his family and home life on the one hand and the reflective, mental calm of a wealthy school on the other. Early on, the boy is subject to the diversity of the different cultures of his day, and he must retreat from his family more and more if he is to succeed at his new school. Rodriguez responds to this piece in his work, explaining how he identifies with the scholarship boy and through him was able to frame the meaning, and costs, of his academic success.

Activities

1. You may want to have students examine the ways that Barbara Ehren-reich (p. 46), in Chapter 2, and Elizabeth Martínez (p. 255), in Chapter 9, take up the notion of ethnicity and ethnic identity.

2. Ask students to find another example of writing in which the writer uses a frame to bring his ideas into perspective. How does this frame affect the writer's argument?

3. Have students write a short sample essay in which they create a frame to bring their ideas regarding an issue into perspective. Have students share their frames in small groups and invite peers to offer alternative framing concepts.

In **"Consider the Constraints of the Situation"** (p. 80), we take up the idea that an essay's audience (often partially dictated by where the essay will appear) constrains a writer's options.

Activities

1. To help students recognize what constraints they may face in their own writing and how to address these constraints, give them sample essays to look at in small groups. Have the groups explain what constraints the author faced and how he or she addressed them through the structuring of ideas, the evidence used, or the language employed. Have each group present its findings to the class. Distribute a range of writing types to each group so that a variety of constraints will be discussed.

2. Continuing with the above exercises, ask students to identify alternative ways in which the authors could have dealt with a given constraint. Why did the author choose the method that he or she used?

3. Divide the class into several groups and give each group writing on the same issue a different set of constraints. Ask students to regroup in order to talk about how their writings differed given their different constraints.

We include **Anna Quindlen's "Doing Nothing Is Something"** (p. 82) to illustrate the ways students can use their experiences to shape a problem that may appeal to others. Using personal experience is a legitimate strategy for defining issues and problems that students take up in their writing, but Quindlen also demonstrates the importance of placing one's personal issues within a broader context.

In her essay, Quindlen laments that children no longer have enough free time to be bored during the summer. She claims that the downtime she had as a child led to her own self-development and made her a better writer. Quindlen characterizes modern American children as being overscheduled, going from one activity to another to the point that even downtime has to be scheduled. She cites psychological research, which supports her main claim that doing nothing actually leads to creativity. Children whose time is controlled wholly by schedules may be missing out on the ability to think outside the box.

Quindlen mentions efforts by several groups to reinstate playtime for children. However, for the most part, adults don't trust children to have free time any longer, because they assume that a child not going to summer camp will turn to crime or drugs. In addition, many adults believe that no time should be lost in preparing their children for a prestigious college or a successful career. A third factor is that parents themselves are too busy, and often rely on these activities to give themselves more time.

Quindlen's conclusion contrasts the busy lives of most families with the idleness that she enjoyed in childhood. In the end, she poses the implicit question of whether it is truly better to keep children constantly busy or to give them the gift of boredom. Is this how your students view the question Quindlen seems to ask? What are some other ways to formulate an issue-based question in light of Quindlen's concerns?

The **Practice Sequence** (p. 84) asks students to work alone and with their peers to try out the various steps we have discussed so far in the chapter, a process that begins with their personal experience and culminates in their writing a brief editorial for the campus newspaper. We provide some model sentences that make concrete our notions of building on the ideas of others and using a writer's frame.

In the section **"Formulating Issue-Based Questions"** (p. 85), we follow the process a student takes to refine her *topic* — a concept that students tend to be familiar with — into an *issue-based question*. The student defines her issue in response to E. D. Hirsch's ideas in *Cultural Literacy*. The **Practice Sequence** at the end of the chapter (p. 89) asks students to work through a five-step process that mirrors the student's process. Again, we provide model sentences and questions that students can adapt to help them through the process, as well as sample topics that they can use to help their thinking. Below are some additional activities that you can use or adapt to help students on the way to formulating issue-based questions.

1. Help students to read in the role of writer. Using a campus or local newspaper, have students choose an article for which they will summarize the situation, identify the issue, and formulate a question similar to the example on page 88 of this chapter.

2. Next, ask students to identify their own situations, issues, and issue-based questions, which they have uncovered through reading and researching. Ask students to explain how their question identifies their audience.

3. If students are having difficulty developing a situation into an issue, and in turn an issue into a question, have them follow the brief steps on page 89 in order to clarify the process.

We end the chapter with **William Deresiewicz's "The End of Solitude"** (p. 91), as an opportunity to give students some practice identifying and formulating issue-based questions. To guide students through this complex essay, you can ask students to consider what they see as at issue and the extent to which they see the problems that Deresiewicz identifies, especially when he speaks to the isolation of the current generation:

- What problem or problems does Deresiewicz identify in "The End of Solitude"?

- Do you agree with his view that "loneliness is the great emotion of the Web generation"?
- To what extent do you think Deresiewicz is right in his view that suburbia isolates people and creates loneliness?

In "The End of Solitude," Deresiewicz begins by defining the contemporary self as wanting constant visibility, either through celebrity or connectivity. With this constant search for visibility comes the loss of solitude, a theme that is similar to Quindlen's. As many young people are accustomed to sending a stream of text messages throughout the day, they are never alone, and can't understand why a person would want to be.

To illustrate the appeal of solitude, Deresiewicz uses the examples of known cultural figures, such as the saint, the prophet, and the hermit. These visionaries use solitude to cultivate a relationship with divinity, which then rejuvenates a society. This changed when solitude became a resource available to all with the Reformation. Any faithful self could access God, and characters in literature became more inwardly focused. As the printing press made reading as ubiquitous as TV and the Internet are for us today, Deresiewicz argues, the souls of everyday people turned more inward and reflective.

Deresiewicz provides a historical overview of his subject, pointing to the changing idea of self in the Romantic, modern, and postmodern ages, and speculates on whether the current self is one incompatible with solitude, thanks to the connectivity of technology. Romanticism, according to Deresiewicz, pushed hardest toward solitude. Figures such as Rousseau and Wordsworth made solitude a physical rather than figurative state of being, accomplished by venturing out into Nature.

With the advent of modernism, Freud's theories of narcissism exemplify the extent to which the self became inaccessible and closed-in. The world, meanwhile, became an assault on this self. This was due in part to the emergence of cities, which tend to isolate individuals from one another.

Deresiewicz then turns to the suburbs, which he sees as also pushing people farther apart while offering them better forms of transportation and communication. The effect of this is loneliness, which Deresiewicz also sees as characteristic of the suburbs. With the arrival of televisions in every home and the fear of crime rising, children began staying in instead of playing with friends on the streets.

Deresiewicz portrays the Internet as a boon to the suburbs, allowing people to communicate with each other and find people with whom to identify. But Deresiewicz sees the current Internet as too much of a good thing, with too many forms of communication and contact with complete strangers. The point is no longer contact, but rather gaining self-esteem through acquiring more followers, more visitors to one's Web site, more friends on social networks. As a result, solitude has completely disappeared.

Deresiewicz argues that young people seem to want to stave off solitude, in fact, and the Internet is geared exactly toward that. As long as there is an imaginary presence of others, we do not have to deal with solitude, which has become a more and more terrifying possibility.

Drawing a distinction between loneliness and boredom, Deresiewicz portrays both as modern, but associates television with boredom, and the Internet with loneliness. Whereas television took away the public's ability to know how to spend free time, and thus manufactured boredom, the Internet takes away its users' ability to be alone, and thus manufactures loneliness. Deresiewicz claims that loneliness is the great emotion of the Web generation.

With the loss of solitude comes the loss of ability for introspection, for wisdom, as demonstrated by the Puritans and Romantics. The Internet has greatly shortened our attention spans, leaving us unable to engage with our own thoughts. The idea of a solitary mind has disappeared, and been replaced by a social or networked mind. Deresiewicz points out that a large number of scientists currently stress the extent to which the human brain is dependent on social input to grow. By defining themselves on Web and social media sites, the Internet users of today deny the existence of a self that is not social, and cannot be known. The self has become shallow.

Deresiewicz then explores the benefits of having the kind of self that can be secure without others, illustrating his points with passages from Virginia Woolf's *Mrs. Dalloway* and quotes by Emerson and Thoreau. The self that is untouchable by society has a dignity that the social self doesn't, and according to Deresiewicz, can achieve excellence where the social self can't. Solitude isn't for everyone, and can seem impolite. Deresiewicz argues that a figure like Thoreau, who lived a very solitary life, may have seemed unfriendly, but possessed a more valuable quality, that of being sure of himself.

In addition to the guiding questions we suggest above, you might ask students to compare and contrast Deresiewicz's approach to writing with Anna Quindlen's. The comparison seems appropriate since both authors suggest that the current generation is not very introspective and they have lost sight of the value that solitude—and even a bit of boredom—holds.

5

From Formulating
to Developing a Thesis

In many ways, a writer's thesis is the most important part of the work. The thesis is the main claim and pervades every aspect of the writing. Therefore, it is very important that students fully understand how to construct one and provide a context for stating that thesis. It is equally important for them to see that constructing a thesis is the result of an ongoing process of reading, identifying issues, and raising questions. In fact, as our students are in the initial stages of writing, we continually ask them, "What's the issue you are focusing on?"; "What's your question?"; and "What's at stake?" We don't expect them to have a thesis until they are well into the writing process.

Our emphasis on issues and questions is different from what students are accustomed to. In high school, many of our students are simply given a thesis and asked to develop an essay that includes three examples and a conclusion. But in college, students are engaged in a more complicated process of identifying what is at issue and grappling with answers to complex questions. Thus, we begin on page 100 by distinguishing between two different types of theses: a working thesis—a writer's first attempt at an assertion that represents his or her position—and a more definitive thesis—a writer's assertion that advances an argument. Students should be prepared to change and develop their theses, understanding that a working thesis is a tool that helps a writer read selectively and eventually develop a definitive thesis. We use the metaphor of a shish kebab to describe the way a thesis encompasses all of the information a writer uses to further his or her argument. The thesis is the skewer that penetrates and holds together every paragraph, just as a skewer penetrates and holds together the ingredients of a shish kebab.

Students are often startled to discover that writers sometimes state their theses in more than one sentence. (You will see that we include numerous examples that present a thesis using more than one sentence.) It's up to you as the instructor to set the ground rules about whether or not students can use one or more sentences to state a thesis. We ourselves give students a great deal of latitude in their writing. That is, we don't limit them to writing a single sentence if it is reasonable to write more than one. You will also see that we take it for granted that students will include their theses in the first paragraph of their essays. Again, in working with students on their drafts, you may see that this does not need to be the case.

To help students organize the information they acquire in response to their issue-based questions, we provide them with three strategies in the section **"Developing a Working Thesis: Three Models"** (p. 101). In thinking about these strategies, we were influenced by studies of writing conducted by Charles Bazerman and John Swales in the sciences and social sciences and Marie Secor and Jeanne Fahnestock in literary studies. We were also influenced by David Bartholomae's approach to helping students distinguish between their ideas and others' arguments by identifying different *topoi* ("Although author X believes that _____, we might begin to see that the problem is more complicated"). For a study of student writing in the discipline of history, see Stuart Greene's "Students as Authors in the Study of History," which appeared in *Teaching and Learning in History*, eds. G. Leinhardt, I. Beck, and K. Stainton (Hillsdale, NJ: Lawrence Erlbaum, 1994), 133–68.

We present the three model strategies for drafting a thesis statement. First, we describe the *misinterpretation model* (p. 101), in which the writer seeks to correct a position that people have unquestioningly accepted. Second, the *gap model* (p. 102) indicates what other writers or researchers may have overlooked or ignored in discussing a given issue. Finally, the *modification model* (p. 103) builds on and expands the ideas of other writers. In our own teaching, we introduce all three models fairly early in the writing process, when, for example, students begin to formulate issues and questions. At this early stage, we ask students to address whether or not they see their work as correcting some misconception, filling a gap, or modifying what others have written about. This helps them think about the question they are answering and the claim that they can imagine making. By the time they begin to formulate a working thesis, they will have begun to organize their ideas accordingly. Still, we want students to know that the approach they take can change. That is, they may have sought to fill a gap, but end up modifying an accepted position with new information. You can show your students the example of how one writer revises her thesis across three drafts in Chapter 10, pages 281–93.

The **Practice Sequence** (p. 103) provides a selection of thesis statements (several of them more than one sentence long) that we ask students to identify using the models we discussed. Below we offer some additional exercises that can help students identify types of thesis statements, which they can then use in their own writing, and provide the context for stating a thesis, a vital skill for strong writing.

1. Provide students with a list of thesis statements or ask them to identify thesis statements in the articles and essays they read. As a class or in small groups, ask students to identify the theses as correcting misinterpretations, filling a gap, or modifying what others have said.

2. Give students an issue that you have been discussing in class. In small groups, ask students to come up with a sample thesis statement of each type regarding the issue.

3. Try the exercise above (Question 2) in small groups. Have students choose a topic with which everyone is familiar.

4. Have students look for signpost words in sample introductory sections. How do these words function? What effects do they have?

5. Ask students to read the introductory section of an article or essay. What do they predict the author will write in the remainder of the paper? What makes them think this?

Based on the research of others and our own study of over one thousand student and professional essays, we discuss **"Establishing a Context for a Thesis"** (p. 104) — the idea that students need to contextualize their theses by making four rhetorical moves. They should (1) establish that the issue is current and relevant — that it is on people's minds, or should be (otherwise, why are they talking about this issue?); (2) summarize briefly what others have said in order to show that they are familiar with how others have addressed the issue; (3) explain what they see as a misinterpretation, gap, or misconception in how others have addressed the topic or issue; and (4) state their thesis, suggesting that their view adds something new to the conversation of ideas. (You might be interested in reading Stuart Greene and Amy Orr's "First Year Students Writing Across the Disciplines," which appeared in *Blurring Boundaries: Developing Writers, Researchers and Teachers, a Tribute to William L. Smith*, ed. P. O'Neill [Chicago: Hampton Press, 2007], 123–56; Stuart Greene's "'Making Sense of My Own Ideas': Problems of Authorship in a Beginning Writing Classroom," which appeared in *Written Communication* [1995]: 186–218; or Stuart Greene's "The Question of Authenticity: Teaching Writing in a First-Year College History of Science Class," which appeared in *Research in the Teaching of English* [May 2001]: 525–69.)

It is useful to keep in mind that researchers have found that these moves can vary from discipline to discipline. At times, writers use three of these moves; at others, they use up to seven different moves. And the moves they make may not appear in the order we describe. However, sufficient research exists to show that these four moves are fairly typical. Finally, as the examples in this chapter show, writers do not always limit themselves to one introductory paragraph to set forth the context for their theses.

We include a student example to illustrate how this works — an excerpt from **Jennifer Eck's *"Nuestra Clase:* Making the Classroom a Welcoming Place for English Language Learners"** (p. 105) — in which the author challenges the English-only movement. Eck establishes that her issue — the extent to which the American educational system meets the needs of those whose primary language is not English — is current and relevant. Specifically, Eck notes that the Hispanic population in the United States is rapidly growing and calls attention to California's Proposition 227, which prohibits bilingual instruction in schools. Eck summarizes both sides of the Proposition 227 debate and also introduces the frame of sociocultural theory as a way of understanding the importance of incorporating students' language and culture into learning. This is a variation on the four moves we describe that reflects Eck's reading of Guadalupe Valdes's *Learning and Not Learning English*. Next, Eck explains that she sees the lack of knowledge about the significance of sociocultural factors as a gap in understanding, which led to the passage of Proposition 227. Finally, she states her thesis, which asserts that failure of schools to include sociocultural factors in instruction has failed to create classrooms that embrace cultural differences and so has failed to create optimal conditions for teaching and learning.

Providing the context for a thesis is an essential skill for strong academic writing, but one which many students will find difficult, at least initially. Thus we want students to practice identifying how writers establish this context. We assume that with practice students will begin to internalize the strategies they observe other writers using. It is equally important for them not only to articulate what these strategies are but also why they might be effective in reaching an audience.

We ask students to analyze an introductory section of **Shirley Brice Heath's "Protean Shapes in Literacy Events: Ever-Shifting Oral and Literate Traditions"** (p. 110) because it offers a model of the kind of highly academic thesis development that we describe in this chapter. Heath's excerpt is by far the most "academic" in the book up until now. Because she is truly addressing her peers, students who haven't been prepped on the kinds of moves they should look for would be daunted by this passage. Therefore, we provide analytical notes in the margins of this text that should help students answer subsequent questions (p. 113) about Heath's issue, specific word use, and thesis.

If you are teaching a writing class on the topic of education or literacy, Heath's excerpt can be quite useful because her description of literacy as an "event" is an interesting frame for thinking about Hirsch's conception of cultural literacy. Heath points out that, since the mid-1970s, scholars have turned to a variety of new tools of analysis in the study of oral and literate societies. Much of the research sees societies along a continuum in which oral traditions develop into literate traditions. However, a close reading of the previous scholarship leaves room for questions. In particular, Heath cites Goody, who mentions a number of societal and cultural factors, such as lack of access and limited social mobility, which could have restricted literacy in the past. Next, Heath introduces what she sees as a gap: that the media focus on the loss of literacy in school settings without paying much attention to literacy in everyday contexts such as work and family settings. To help fill the gap, Heath borrows from Goody who emphasizes the concrete context of written communication. Among other questions, she asks, "Where, when, how, for whom, and with what results are individuals in different social groups of today's highly industrialized society using reading and writing skills?"

We include an annotated student essay at the end of this chapter, so that students can see the ways a writer might use different sets of claims in order to advance an argument. Our annotations point out the various moves the writer makes to put forth, develop, and support her thesis. To guide students, you might review our discussion of how to make different types of claims in Chapter 3. You should also discuss the nature of causal claims ("if . . . then") since the student below links the phenomenon of texting to declines in literacy. In particular, you might define causal arguments and discuss the criteria one might use to judge the extent to which a causal argument is legitimate. In this case, does texting lead to declines in literacy?

In student **Veronica Stafford's "Texting and Literacy"** (p. 115), she formulates a causal argument, making a direct link between text messaging and a decline in literacy. Specifically, she points out the negative effects that text messaging has on academic ability, enjoyment of reading, and personal relationships. Again, this is a common theme in many of the readings thus far, including in Chapter 4 Anna Quindlen's and William Deresiewicz's essays focusing on the isolating effects of the Web.

Stafford initially supports her claim by citing statistics on the widespread use of text messaging. Many young people who own mobile phones spend more time text messaging than reading. While over half the population sends text messages daily, less than half have read a book in the last year. The author considers these statistics to be linked, and argues that as text messaging increases, reading decreases. Of concern for Stafford is that reading is declining fastest in eighteen- to twenty-four-year-olds. This is the same group that sends the most text messages.

Stafford introduces another causal claim when she underscores the connection between reading ability and academic success. She anticipates the claim that text messaging develops quicker thinking and response times by citing a study in which students were given a chance to write responses to open-ended questions. The students who owned mobile phones wrote much less and made more grammatical errors. Stafford then gives examples of how writing for school has become polluted with the kind of writing done in text messaging, with words abbreviated and letters replaced by numbers or other shortcuts. This gives teachers even more work in teaching students to overcome these habits. Though some argue that text messaging increases literacy because a student must have knowledge of a word before she can abbreviate it, Stafford claims that, on the contrary, writers who text have decreased creativity and are unable to compose something as complex as a poem.

Addressing the negative effect of text messaging on personal relationships, Stafford again supports her claim with statistics. Many teens now argue and end relationships through text message, because they prefer this over calling or meeting face-to-face. Though text messaging is more convenient, it lacks an important component of communication: body language. Personal interaction relies on body language and vocal inflection with the actual verbiage making up only a tiny portion of the entire message. Losing most of the message leads to lower quality relationships.

Stafford makes one final causal argument when she links the decrease in enjoyment of reading to a deterioration of literacy. Text messaging detracts from such important activities as reading for fun, keeping informed on important topics, and having conversations about great literature.

Given the importance of literacy in today's society, Stafford argues that it is those with a genuine love for reading who will score better on tests, get into better universities, and ultimately secure the most competitive jobs. Reading instead of text messaging thus gives a student an advantage over his peers. To bring home her point, Stafford imagines a learning environment in which students are not looking at their phones, but writing letters and conversing with those around them.

From Finding to Evaluating Sources

Few college courses provide students with opportunities to learn how to do research and to develop adequate strategies for accessing information. Our students are familiar enough with Google and Wikipedia, but without knowing how to find "good" sources that contain scholarly information, students may waste time reading inappropriate material that will not contribute anything worthwhile to their essays. For this reason, Chapter 6 looks at strategies for expanding the base of sources students work with as they investigate their issue-based questions to form arguments.

We draw the distinction between a researched argument and a research paper to emphasize that students must use research to advance their purposes as writers, not simply retrieve information and report it as they may have done for their high school research papers. Initially, they may do research to find out what is at issue, to see how current the issue is, to discover who has addressed this issue, and the like, but ultimately they will need to do research to support the working thesis they have formulated. As they progress and share their writing with their classmates, their peers may ask that they include additional information or evidence to support their argument or students may find that what they thought they wanted to write about has changed.

Regardless of the stage of their research, students need to be strategic as they identify sources, evaluate library sources, and evaluate Internet sources. With the proliferation of information on Web sites, students need to be vigilant in determining the value and legitimacy of what they find. Finding information is not the challenge; the challenge is to learn how to evaluate information in terms of its relevance, accuracy, and authority. Thus we loop back to some of the strategies for reading critically that we introduced in Chapter 2.

We encourage you to work with a librarian to tailor library instruction to the specific needs of your students and the course you are teaching. All of our students attend at least three hours of instruction in the library where, using laptops provided by the library, they can practice the strategies the librarian has introduced them to. On their first visits to the library, they learn to navigate the online catalog and even find full text articles. Their time in the library is all the more purposeful because we ask students to prepare research questions beforehand and we give the librarians a list of these questions — some of which they use to help students search for information. Because technology changes and disciplinary conventions for inquiry vary, it is important to encourage students to seek help from a librarian during their four years in college.

In the section **"Identifying Sources"** (p. 121) we present four possible steps that students can take to identify sources. First, students can consult experts who can help them in their research—including their writing instructor, librarians, and local experts in fields related to their topic—and the work of experts, such as research manuals (p. 121). Next, students should develop a working knowledge of standard types of sources along with the information they provide and their purposes (p. 122). We include a table on page 123 that will help students develop a basic working knowledge of different types of sources. As final steps, students can distinguish between primary and secondary sources (p. 122) and popular and scholarly sources (p. 125) and discern which types of sources are best for their individual arguments. However, it is not enough for students to understand these differences; they should also grasp the reasons *why* they should use certain types of sources and not others. This will depend on the readers whom they are trying to reach and their expectations of what constitutes a persuasive argument.

After students have identified the types of sources relevant to the question they are answering, they will need to develop search strategies to locate useful information. Thus we provide step-by-step guides for three types of searches within a library catalog: performing keyword searches (p. 129), browsing (p. 130), and conducting journal/newspaper title searches (p. 131).

Finding the right information in a library and online can be overwhelming for even our best students. Often this anguish occurs because students have never been thoroughly or properly taught how to use the resources readily available to them. In addition to the **Practice Sequences** on research in the chapter (pp. 127, 132), we suggest some hands-on exercises to help students become comfortable and confident researchers:

1. See if your campus or local library offers a research tutorial. Sometimes these tutorials allow students to follow along on individual computers as a librarian shows them how to look up resources relevant to the course. If your campus or local library does not offer a research tutorial, you might consider writing your own. Even if you only follow the steps given in the textbook, allowing students to watch you complete the steps or follow along on their own personal computers will make the task of research seem less daunting. You will need to familiarize students with approaches to "keyword" searches and strategies for "browsing" subject headings in the library.

2. Students need to pick the types of sources that will best support their argument. Usually, a variety of sources can be used in combination to provide well-rounded support for an argument. Give students a passage that uses multiple types of sources (scholarly/popular, primary/secondary, number of types of information). Ask students to evaluate what type of sources are used and how each type affects the writer's argument.

3. Ask students to share their research tricks. Students, who may have taken previous research-intensive courses, may have developed additional, less traditional but still beneficial methods of research. For example, one of our students used Google Books to search books for the exact pages that related to her research question. She searched for keywords or phrases, such as "Catholic social teaching and democracy," and Google Books returned a list of books that contained those words or phrases on the same page. She could then find the book in the library and turn directly to the pages she needed.

4. To help students learn to evaluate library sources (see discussion on pp. 132–35), have them find three sources in the library related to an issue of interest. Have them follow the steps on page 135 of this chapter to evaluate whether or not these sources are valuable and should be given further consideration.

5. To help students learn to evaluate Internet sources (see discussion on pages 136–38), have students find three sources on the Internet related to the same issue as in the above "library sources" exercise. Have them follow the steps on p. 138 of this chapter to evaluate whether or not these sources are valuable and should be given further consideration.

6. Ask students to develop their own criteria for evaluating the extent to which the library and Internet sources they found are authoritative.

From Summary to Synthesis

Using Sources to Build an Argument

In this chapter, we build on our discussion of finding sources by focusing on how to work closely with the sources students find. Specifically, we focus on the skills of summary, paraphrase, synthesis, and quotation that students are often asked to use in writing a wide range of papers, including response papers, reviews, arguments, and research papers across disciplines. Summarizing a text may seem pretty straightforward, but such a task can actually be quite difficult for students, depending on the length and complexity of the text they are asked to summarize. Summarizing also encompasses analysis, which requires that students understand how ideas and examples contribute to the overall meaning of a given text.

More often than not, students are asked to synthesize information in the academic essays they write. Unfortunately, students are accustomed to writing about single sources of information. Because synthesizing different and competing points of view can be quite challenging for them, we devote a great deal of time to helping students use their synthesis of ideas in advancing their own arguments. We find that students will often provide summaries of what they have read in a listlike fashion in their initial drafts of an argument. As an alternative, we show them how to construct topic sentences that relate to their thesis and help readers understand how that information supports their argument.

We also describe ways that students can integrate quotations from others' work in their writing. This is especially important as students need to distinguish between their ideas and the ideas of authors whose work they have read. Still, students may choose to paraphrase information rather than quote directly. We provide distinctions between these two approaches and the reasons why one approach may be more effective than another in a given context. More than helping students learn the distinctions, we want them to articulate the reasons why one approach may be more appropriate or effective in a given context.

Finally, we also provide a brief introduction to MLA and APA formats and their similarities and differences. Students can find additional resources on the MLA and APA Web sites. As students enter their majors, they should understand the discipline-specific sources that exist in each discipline and subdiscipline. They need to become accustomed to using a specific approach to documenting sources and formulating bibliographies.

We begin (p. 140) by briefly describing what paraphrases, summaries, and quotations are, providing some rules of thumb for when to use each strategy. We give some examples of paraphrases and summaries to illustrate the distinctions between them, and we go into some detail about the distinctions in our discussion. Early in the chapter we give steps for **writing a paraphrase** (p. 143) and include a **Practice Sequence** (p. 144) for students to try out the steps to writing a paraphrase. We have found, however, that students are far more likely to make use of summary and synthesis, so we pay much more attention to these skills later in the chapter.

As we note at the beginning of this chapter, academic writing requires students to compose accurate summaries of what they have read. To guide students' writing of summaries, we provide specific strategies for reading a text: identifying the gist of what students have read, focusing on key words that help them understand the author's point of view (e.g., *however, therefore*), and illustrations that a given author uses to elaborate upon the gist.

On pages 146–51, we show how these strategies work in the context of analyzing **Clive Thompson's "On the New Literacy."** Thompson considers the debate focusing on technology and writing skills, in particular the pervasive but unsubstantiated claims that new forms of communicating are detrimental to literacy. However, while the argument that kids can't write because of technology is commonplace, Thompson cites a study at Stanford, which has suggested that this claim is not accurate. Thompson points out that researchers at Stanford collected over 14,000 pieces of student writing samples, from academic essays to e-mails, blogs, and chat sessions. The results show that students now write far more than any previous generation, and that over a third of their writing is done outside of class.

Thompson compares this current golden age of writing to the recent past, when Americans would often leave school and, if their job did not require it, never write again. The team conducting the Stanford study finds that modern writers are more adept at assessing their audiences and adapting their tone, a technique that hails back to the Greek traditions of argument. This too was far less prevalent in earlier generations of writing.

Because of this focus on audience, researchers at Stanford explain that students today define good writing as something which has an effect on other people and which persuades or advances debate. They are less enthusiastic about academic writing, whose only audience is the professor and whose only purpose is a grade.

Thompson doesn't deny that teaching precision in writing is still important. Nonetheless, he argues that online writing has pushed the form into interesting directions that build key skills, such as audience awareness, concision, and the ability to write at great length.

On page 150, we include a worksheet that we filled out with information from the reading to write our summary, and we encourage students to use such a worksheet themselves in the **Practice Sequence** (p. 151). As students internalize and get used to the steps to writing a summary, they doubtless will not need such a worksheet, but in the early stages of their practice it may be useful to have such a heuristic tool.

To help students practice these steps, we almost always have them work in groups at first. This is because we agree with Lev Vygotsky and others who argue that our students can accomplish more in groups than by themselves when learning something new. With practice in groups, they can develop confidence that will inform the work they begin to do on their own. Here is a group exercise in summarizing:

1. After showing students an example of a summary and discussing the decisions made in constructing it, divide students into small groups and give each a brief sample article or essay to read. As a group, have students follow the four steps to write a summary of the article. After they have written the summary, ask students to explain how they accomplished each step.

On page 152, we make distinctions between summarizing and synthesizing. We emphasize that a summary is a way for students to demonstrate their knowledge of a source, while a synthesis uses sources to lay the groundwork for students to stake out their own positions in a conversation of ideas.

"Writing a Synthesis" (p. 153) involves identifying broad similarities and differences in articles. Students are adept at ignoring differences in order to create consistency among the articles they read. Therefore, it's useful to encourage them to bring out the complexities in what they have read. Having them annotate the articles as they work through them (we briefly discuss and illustrate annotation in Chapter 2) is a good way to get them to slow down — slower, more careful reading makes it harder for them to ignore complexities. The steps we describe in synthesizing — (1) making connections between texts, (2) deciding what those connections mean, and (3) formulating the gist of what has been read — are quite complex tasks, which is why we spend so much time in this chapter unpacking those steps.

After discussing strategies for writing summaries, we include two additional essays to illustrate how students can go about writing a synthesis in which they use what they have read to develop an argument. This kind of writing is a challenging but critical genre of academic writing. Again, we set out to break down writing a synthesis of this kind as systematically as possible.

As in the case of showing students how to write a summary, we introduce the idea of using a template to organize the ideas that students find in what they have read. The template for writing a synthesis prompts students to identify the argument of each piece they read, the evidence the author provides to support the argument, possible counterarguments, and what students think about the issue or issues raised by a given author. Completing the template also gives students a visual representation of where the gaps are — what each author focuses on and what a given author might not consider. Identifying gaps is an important habit of mind in academic writing and gives students a way to identify how they might contribute to a scholarly conversation.

To exemplify how to write a synthesis, we add to the conversation about literacy **Cynthia Haven's "The New Literacy: Stanford Study Finds Richness and Complexity in Students' Writing"** (p. 153). Like Thompson, Haven cites the Stanford study to support her claim that literacy is flourishing in an age of new media. But she adds to her very positive analysis of the Stanford study the case of an alum from Stanford to further support the ways students can use the new media to be creative and succeed academically. In this case, the student, Mark Otuteye, once a participant in the Stanford study, was a Marshall Scholar and has earned two advanced degrees, one in Modern Thought and the other in Artificial Intelligence.

One might ask what this example adds to the conversation and whether or not a case of one student is sufficient to support the argument that Haven (or Thompson) makes. This is where comparing Thompson's and Haven's articles becomes useful and where students in your class should begin to formulate their own ideas about this issue—that is, whether or not writing on electronic media is a "good" thing or is detrimental to students' growth and development as writers, as some would claim.

Haven also introduces Andrea Lunsford's observation that the current landscape for writing is simply different than it was in the not-so-distant past. Lunsford points out that writing is not limited to communicating information, but exploring one's ideas in different forms, such as journals, letters, and blogs. Instead of lamenting what some critics believe is the loss of writing skills, Lunsford argues that we should celebrate the new literacy, which has enabled young and old alike to take on a sense of authorship and agency.

Haven does provide some balance to the argument that electronic media have enhanced literacy when she mentions some of the specific criticisms leveled at student writing. Still, Haven quickly returns to Lunsford's argument, which underscores the playfulness of language.

The third article in this sequence is **Josh Keller's "Studies Explore Whether the Internet Makes Students Better Writers"** (p. 158). The article itself is a wonderful illustration of a synthesis of different and conflicting ideas, although Keller resists developing an argument reflecting what he thinks. Instead, Keller details the growing number of studies concerning student writing quality, both inside and outside of school.

Like Thompson and Haven, Keller cites the Stanford study, and like Haven, he describes Mark Otuteye's experiences to support the view that new electronic media are supporting the flourishing of literacy. Keller reiterates the point that students with more access to media often write far more outside of school, in the form of blog posts, Facebook messages, and e-mails. Again, scholars such as Lunsford indicate that this new kind of writing is more connected to an audience, which offers lessons to students.

Keller points out that studies examining students' writing habits over time are becoming more and more common. Not all are on the scale of the study conducted at Stanford, but this is an added detail that builds upon and extends the conversation readers find in Thompson and Haven. In these additional studies, students submit all of their writing in a given period, or write diaries detailing the writing they have done. Educators have found that the total amount of writing done is rising, while the percentage of writing done for school was surprisingly small.

Because writing is required to interact on the Web, some professors see this as a writing-heavy age, with more people composing with words than ever. The kind of writing done for media, however, is far more social than academic writing is.

There is debate as to whether simply writing more means greater writing ability, especially considering that, as one professor points out, there have not been gains in reading and writing scores. Keller cites Mark Bauerlein, a professor of English at Emory University, who is critical of studies like the one conducted at Stanford and cited extensively by Clive Thompson and Cynthia Haven above. This is also a significant part of the conversation that both Thompson and Haven leave out in their discussions.

Specifically, Bauerlein points out that studies of student writing are difficult to control and to draw conclusions from. The difficulty of drawing sound conclusions stems from the huge amount of writing that researchers have collected from in-class writing and students' self-sponsored writing outside of class, the variety of forms that different kinds of writing take, and whether or not the researchers use agreed-upon methods to analyze the data. That is, Bauerlein wonders how researchers draw conclusions about whether or not a student has a clear, explicit purpose or has considered his or her audience in the ways researchers at Stanford claim.

Keller points out that for many, it remains unclear whether the information from studies like the one at Stanford should be used to change curriculum. Some professors believe that writing courses should improve both forms of writing—academic writing and out-of-class writing—since the two often have opposing aims. Out-of-class writing usually attempts to solve real-world problems, whereas in-class writing is done to achieve an academic goal. These professors believe that out-of-class writing can be used in the classroom to draw connections between different types of writing, and that it is important not to create a barrier between the two.

However, Bauerlein is among a growing number of academics who frown on out-of-class writing. After all, he argues that out-of-class writing is generally directed at one's peers, rather than for teachers. Therefore, it often leads to bad writing habits, which teachers then have to spend time correcting. Other professors therefore have curbed their enthusiasm for the new media.

In the end, Keller cites scholars who are strident in their claim that new forms of out-of-class writing are part of a larger cultural trend, in which all citizens are authors. They are not necessarily all readers, a fact that has concerned some. The new literacy is being developed by out-of-class writing rather than traditional academic reading.

We believe the synthesis worksheet on page 167 of this chapter is an excellent tool for helping students develop their skills. Ask students to create their own synthesis table from three sources they have been using to write their essays.

A Practice Sequence: Writing a Synthesis

To give students an opportunity to practice the strategies of writing a summary and synthesis, the **Practice Sequence** (p. 170) includes three essays, each providing some commentary on the new electronic media and its effects on students' literacy and involvement in communities. At issue is the extent to which the new media, including blogging and tweeting, contribute to students' developing writing skills, facilitate critical thinking, or foster social relationships. These are themes that relate directly to **Marque Camp's** essay in Chapter 3, **"The End of the World May Be Nigh, and It's the Kindle's Fault,"** and **Veronica Stafford's "Texting and Literacy,"** which appears in Chapter 5.

The authors in this practice sequence also prompt students to think about journalism in new ways and whether or not new forms of journalism such as "place-blogs" are legitimate forms of journalism. Questions about legitimacy give way to questions about authority and democracy. Indeed, who has the authority to publish, and how do we determine what is accurate?

The questions guiding students earlier in this chapter can help students as they construct a summary or synthesis in pairs or in small groups. We also encourage students to use the templates we include in this chapter for constructing a summary and/or synthesis as a way to help them organize their ideas.

Supporting students as they compose a synthesis requires that students use what they have read to formulate what they see as at issue, to summarize different and conflicting points of view, and to write an argument that foregrounds what they think. Our students typically end up summarizing the articles they have read and leave their own perspective for the conclusion. This is despite our efforts to explain that we want them to establish their arguments early in the essay and to use what they have read as evidence to support their argument, possible arguments and concessions, and as points of departure.

Thus it is important to give students time to write and rewrite their synthesis essays to ensure that they foreground their arguments. Equally important, students need explicit instruction in ways to organize their essays around their arguments, construct paragraphs with topic sentences that make students' arguments clear, and use others' writing in the service of the claim(s) students make.

In the first of three essays in this practice sequence, **Dan Kennedy** begins his piece **"Political Blogs: Teaching Us Lessons About Community"** (p. 171) by introducing the short history of blogging and its relationship to traditional journalism. As blogs that skew far to either the left or the right become more prominent, it appears that neutral journalism is no longer the norm. Unlike reporters who research, develop, and assemble interviews into a story, the typical blogger is supposedly sitting in his pajamas, broadcasting opinions. Kennedy takes issue with this depiction and argues that it is more important to ask what such opinion-oriented blogs offer, rather than how they might be more objective.

Raising this question leads Kennedy to reexamine the purpose of journalism in the first place. As authorities on the topic have written, journalism's purpose is to enforce the idea of a public that needs to stay informed—a community. This community of newspaper readers is more likely to participate in political, religious, and social events.

The traditional idea of community bound by geography is slowly being replaced with newer models. The Internet can be used to forge new communities, in this case ones between people who may not know each other's real names, but who share the same views and opinions. This leads Kennedy to the conclusion that blogging offers something besides objectivity: a sense of community.

The dominant characteristic of these new online communities is that they want the news delivered in the context of their views and beliefs. This does not mean that they want propaganda, but rather that they view the news as an activity that takes place within their community. It is becoming more and more expected that the news is reported with an ideological slant in order for it to be accepted by these online communities.

Traditional journalists might be dismayed by this, but Kennedy argues that this type of journalism is just as valuable as the old model of objectivity as long as standards are upheld. Kennedy gives the example of a story that was broken by a prominent liberal news Web site, in part because of information that had been dug up by the site's readership.

Kennedy is not arguing, however, that this kind of journalism can replace all the non-biased journalism that we rely on to understand the world. A reader who gets all of his information from liberal or conservative news sites is unlikely to consider the opposing point of view.

Even supposedly traditional, objective journalism is often part of a community, such as the *New York Times*, perceived by conservative critics as biased toward liberals. The context of any journalism is important, and questions such as "Who was interviewed? Who wasn't?" are always relevant. Kennedy also writes that place-blogs—blogs that serve geographical communities—can be another tool to foster a sense of community, one that can overcome the decrease of direct neighbor-to-neighbor contact.

Kennedy concludes by arguing that critics of blogs are missing out on the sense of community that blogs provide by focusing on their supposed lack of objectivity. Traditional journalism, according to Kennedy, must find a way to offer a sense of community like blogs do.

In the second essay, **"Don't Fear Twitter," John Dickerson** (p. 174) argues in favor of Twitter as a supplement to journalism, and not a threat. Twitter is a real-time information network that allows users to write entries of 140 characters or less, which is far shorter than the ideal article length for journalists, leading many journalists to denounce it as reductive.

Dickerson goes on to argue that Twitter does not threaten the craft of journalism. He uses personal examples of his own use of Twitter during his time on the road, traveling with presidential campaigns. After accumulating many short asides in notebooks, Dickerson then posted them to Twitter. These notes serve to give stories more color or points of interest and can even be the thought that eventually becomes the main idea of a piece.

Dickerson presents Twitter as informal and approachable, often giving readers inside views of important events that they otherwise would have no access to. It can also become vital in the rare event of breaking cultural news, such as the 2011 demonstrations in Egypt. In addition, Twitter allows a more intimate look at the everyday lives of its users.

The worry that Twitter will distract readers from other forms of news is not a major worry for Dickerson. Instead, Dickerson sees Twitter as a community, which leads its readers to other, longer articles through suggestions from other members. He concludes that Twitter is limited, but that it does add to the tradition rather than ruining it.

Finally, in **"YouTube: The Flattening of Politics," Steve Grove** (p. 176) makes the case that YouTube is an innovative and reliable vehicle for journalism, especially in the recent election cycle. As director of YouTube's news and political division, Grove emphasizes the huge number of videos added to YouTube every day by everyone from presidential candidates to ordinary people. Because of this widespread opportunity for anyone to contribute directly and without a middleman to select or choose content, Grove argues, YouTube has become the world's biggest town hall for political discussion. The site offers a direct connection between candidates and voters, in a political environment no longer defined by barriers of time and space.

Grove points out that mainstream media has a place on YouTube, as many major news organizations have channels on the site. This provides them with more exposure, since a high percentage of adults have used the Internet to watch video. There is no cost associated with creating content on YouTube, and media organizations can make money from ads run beside their videos. YouTube's high level of interactivity provides media organizations with an instant, focused audience who rank content and recommend it to one another. Grove then illustrates how news media organizations have used YouTube to allow their audiences to engage with content by asking for videos from voters to broadcast during elections and political events. As videos on the Internet rise to the top in popularity, their exposure is amplified through the second medium of TV.

Another way that media organizations use YouTube is for source material. Because content can be captured by anyone, anywhere, it can be easier to get footage of important events through YouTube. Grove argues that YouTube might represent a new method of gathering news, because journalists don't necessarily have to be present at an event for the world to know of it.

Journalism produced by citizens, Grove acknowledges, is subject to criticism, because it is produced by amateurs without credentials. However, he adds that there are two factors mitigating this: One, that users of YouTube can discern from the information on the Web site whether a video is from an official news media outlet or a single user. Two, the high level of user involvement and evaluation of each video ensures that those videos that deserve to be discredited will be. Grove argues that YouTube presents a new method of fact checking for journalism as well as motivation for journalists to get the story right, lest someone on YouTube outdoes them.

Grove ends by saying that despite all these new measures of the quality of news content contributed by normal citizens, professional journalists are still needed to provide the depth and quality of analysis they learn through their craft. What YouTube provides is a new relationship between candidates and voters, and news organizations and their audiences. Grove portrays this new media force as an opportunity to be ignored at one's peril.

In the section **"Integrating Quotations into Your Writing"** (p. 182), we emphasize the three strategies of taking an active stance (p. 182), explaining the quotations (basically, analyzing them in context) and effectively attaching (some prefer the more general term *integrating*) shorter quotations into sentences. Many students will not realize how important it is to explain or analyze each quotation they use in their writing. In fact, our students often justify attaching without explaining quotations because they do not want to "interrupt the flow of their ideas." Therefore, it is useful to discuss the reasons why authors cite others' research to support their arguments with authority. We do provide a **Practice Sequence** on integrating quotations (p. 186), but here are some additional exercises to help students understand these practices:

Activities

1. Give students a series of excerpts from writing that uses quotations. Cover up the explanation of the quotation and ask students to interpret what the author hopes the reader will gain from this quote. Then give them the complete excerpt with the author's explanation. Were they correct?

2. Students will have to decide whether to quote or paraphrase other authors in their own writing. As a class, ask students to brainstorm about what situations might require a quote and what situations might require a paraphrase. What are the benefits and drawbacks of each?

3. Students should be able to use quotations both within the grammar of their sentences and by using a colon. Give them a series of quotations about a topic you have been covering in class. Ask them to incorporate a quotation into a sentence using both methods.

We end this chapter with a student-written essay, **Nancy Paul's "A Greener Approach to Groceries: Community-Based Agriculture in LaSalle Square"** (pp. 187–98), to illustrate different ways that authors cite sources. We have annotated the essay to direct students' attention to the strategies the author uses in writing her essay and that students can use in their own work. You will see that the author uses her research to (1) give background information to clarify a problem, (2) establish the feasibility of a given solution by showing the existence of one or more precedents, (3) make or support a claim, (4) formulate a counterargument, or (5) address a possible counterargument.

In the essay, Nancy Paul argues that food insecurity for low-income families in her local community necessitates some creative thinking to solve the problem. Based on her research, she suggests that community leaders develop a co-op of community gardens. Paul makes the case that a co-op of farms is the best solution for the area, not only because of this demonstrated need, but also because LaSalle Square's position near hundreds of farms makes it perfectly positioned to take advantage of local agriculture.

Research indicates that corporate businesses frequently abandon urban areas in favor of wealthier areas. As a result, Paul argues, urban "food deserts" have become common across the United States, not just her local community, where malnutrition is a serious problem. Residents of these areas are unlikely to be able to drive elsewhere to get food, so they shop at local convenience stores and feed their children low-quality, high-calorie food. Paul uses her research to provide evidence demonstrating increasing trends of childhood obesity in urban areas, and lack of access to essential vitamins in urban children and women. She then cites a study that has linked these deficiencies to developmental and cognitive difficulties, including problems with motor function and social interaction.

As essential as it is to eliminate food insecurity from communities in order for them to bloom, bringing in grocery stores is not always easy. Corporations are not attracted to areas with high crime and low income. Paul details legislation that is meant to funnel tax revenue from retail development into infrastructure improvement, which currently applies to LaSalle Square in her local community. However, there is debate surrounding how this money should be used. There are other reasons that reliance on corporations is not ideal: Big-box stores do not contribute to local economies but rather to corporate headquarters. Therefore, the highest paying jobs are often given to outsiders.

Paul uses her research to catalogue several examples of grassroots efforts from all over the world to promote urban farming. These projects demonstrate the feasibility of what she explains in the first part of her essay. She also uses prior studies to underscore the potential to provide sustainable food sources for those families in need, generate jobs, and actually reverse the effects of poverty. Cities in Cuba, Singapore, Russia, and Canada have all shifted a percentage of their food production to local methods, and their populations are healthier for it.

Closer to her home community, a project in Lansing has prospered on a combination of community farms and surplus produce sold to the project by local farmers. Paul emphasizes that such ventures can actually be profitable and readily applied to the LaSalle Square co-op that she has proposed.

Paul presents LaSalle Square as an area ideal for community farming projects because of its proximity to numerous local farms, which would decrease transportation time and increase product. In addition to farms, the many projects she has done research on have included other components, such as reclaiming parks and planting trees. Such a project at LaSalle Square would, Paul argues, improve the appearance of the neighborhood. Collaborations between farming projects and local community development corporations have been shown to increase local property values. This offers benefits above and beyond the revenue that corporate stores provide. The gains that might come to South Bend from a LaSalle Square neighborhood community greening project would likely be quite significant.

Paul recognizes possible counterarguments by acknowledging challenging aspects of her solution, including securing the participation of local residents. Again, she uses her research to note the extent to which low-income populations are usually less socially involved than their higher-income counterparts. Indeed, she recognizes that this can be a serious stumbling block. However, Paul uses her studies to dismiss such a counterargument. Specifically, she argues that because urban residents spend so much time in their neighborhoods and use them to eke out a living from odd jobs and welfare, they are more likely to participate in improvements of their immediate surroundings than they are to participate in national or governmental affairs.

Paul notes that some have argued that urban residents do not have sufficient knowledge of farming techniques to ensure high enough yields. The solution to this, according to Paul, lies with Indiana's significant farming industry. Farmers have already demonstrated a desire to donate and sell produce to urban farms as well as offering free public education in agriculture.

From Ethos to Logos

Appealing to Your Readers

In this chapter, we use terminology from classical rhetoric, focusing on three types of appeals that can help students connect with their readers: *ethos* (appeals from character), *pathos* (appeals to emotions), and *logos* (appeals to reason). We link all three types of appeals to their relationship to *fairness, justice,* and *goodwill.* That is, writers should present themselves as people who possess these values, and they should acknowledge that their readers also share these values. Finally, they should present an argument supported by evidence that appeals to readers' sense of these values.

For many students, this chapter will be their first introduction to ethos, pathos, and logos. It is important to show them how important these appeals can be in advancing an argument and to help them develop the skills necessary to use these appeals in their own writing. To these ends, we offer some sample exercises related to each type of appeal below.

To illustrate how these appeals work, we ask students to read **James W. Loewen's** essay, **"The Land of Opportunity"** (p. 201). In his essay, Loewen observes that many high school students are not aware of how American class structure works. That is, they have a "half-formed and naïve" understanding of why the poor are poor and the rich are rich and the extent to which wealth is not distributed equitably in the United States. Loewen blames history textbooks, which treat the labor movement and unions as phenomena of historical rather than continuing importance. Such treatment ignores differences in social class, depicting the nation as entirely middle class.

Loewen argues that in reality social class is probably the most important variable in American society, as it correlates to most forms of opportunity. Specifically, he demonstrates the increased opportunities available to upper-class individuals from prenatal care through educational opportunities and finally to longer life expectancy. Finally, Loewen describes the ironic fact that social class itself affects social class when he describes how 57 percent of business leaders blame the poor for their situation while only 15 percent of labor leaders blame the poor. With all of this documentation about the importance of social class, how can history textbooks virtually ignore its existence?

You could pair Loewen's examination of history textbooks with Sadker and Sadker's study of gender (p. 52) and ask students to compare how Loewen and the Sadkers present their research to establish ethos and support their arguments. How are their strategies similar and different? What can students learn about the use of primary research? This is a question that anticipates our discussion of research in Chapter 11.

Our discussion of **appealing to ethos** begins on page 205. Ethos appeals to a writer's character. We suggest that students can take three steps to present a positive ethos, which will engage readers. First, students should establish that they have good judgment by identifying a problem that readers will agree is worth addressing. This point is related to our discussion of model introductions in Chapter 5 (p. 104), where we indicate the importance of the relevance and currency of a given issue. Second, students should convey to readers that they are knowledgeable, which can be accomplished by showing that they have done detailed research and that they fully understand the issue. Third, students should show that they understand the complexity of a given issue by acknowledging its many angles and perspectives. Here are two other exercises to clarify ethos through group work:

Activities

1. Ask students to search the Web for a video of a recent political speech. (No doubt they can find some on YouTube.) Have students identify how the speaker uses ethos and to what end. What did they think about the speaker? Have students share their findings either as a class or in small groups. A similar exercise can be done with a recent media story.

2. As a class or in small groups, have students generate different ways an author can establish that he or she has good judgment, is knowledgeable, and understands the complexity of a given issue. How can students incorporate these ideas into their own writing?

Our discussion of **appealing to pathos** begins on page 208. Pathos appeals to readers' emotions. By using this appeal, a writer recognizes that people's emotions move them and can affect how a reader will feel toward an argument. Usually, appeals to pathos are indirect. We offer three steps (p. 211) that students should use to appeal effectively to pathos. First, students should show that they know what readers value. Second, students should use illustrations and examples that appeal to readers' emotions. Third, students should use a tone that reflects their own stance but is calibrated to appeal to and not alienate their audience. Here is a further exercise for exploring pathos:

Activity

1. Ask students to search the Web for a recent political speech or analyze the same one they used for the previous exercise. Have students identify how the speaker uses pathos and to what end. How did the speech make them feel? Have students share their findings either as a class or in small groups. A similar exercise can be done with a recent media story.

In the **Practice Sequence** (p. 211) we ask students to analyze three excerpts that are critical of some recent policies.

In the first excerpt, from "Schools More Separate," Gary Orfield explains that southern schools are regressing to the state of segregation that preceded the civil rights movement. Orfield uses such words and phrases as *segregation, intensify, moving backward, accelerating rate,* and *progress.* By doing so, he appeals to readers' sense of justice and goodwill by asserting that the progress made since the civil rights movement is being erased.

In the second excerpt, from the editorial "The Grand Fraud: Affirmative Action for Blacks," Thomas Sowell describes the differences between academics' public and private feelings toward affirmative action. Sowell cites "studies" conducted by "respected academic scholars" to create a credible ethos. However, his use of belittling language to describe what he sees as the dishonesty surrounding this topic ("saturated with dishonesty," "gushing about the mystical benefits," and "two-faced talk"), while designed to appeal to readers' sense of justice and fairness, may backfire if some readers take him to be dismissive of alternative points of view.

In the third and longest excerpt, Erin Meyers, a student, criticizes the educational system in her essay "The Educational Smorgasbord as Saving Grace." Specifically, she argues that educators do not equally recognize students' multiple intelligences. As an alternative, she advocates a broad offering of elective courses and equal treatment for these courses in order to better suit students' needs. Meyers creates an intelligent and well-informed ethos through her ability to synthesize complex information from a variety of authors. She appeals to pathos through word choice that describes the current educational system with its *stunted* students, *lack of stimulation*, and *tragedy*. These words appeal to readers' sense of fairness and goodwill to the extent that they believe all children should be able to develop through education.

Our discussion of **appealing to logos** begins on page 214. Logos appeals to reason and goes hand in hand with ethos and pathos. However, whereas the previous appeals deal only with content, logos deals with both form and content, combining as it does converging pieces of evidence to support a claim. The types of evidence students should use will depend on their issues, problems, situations, and readers' expectations. We explain some of the main terms of formal reasoning, including premises, deduction, and induction (p. 214) and present three traditional steps for appealing to logos (p. 218): stating the premise or premises, using credible evidence, and making sure the conclusion follows from the premise or premises. Here are some additional exercises to help students understand logos:

Activities

1. To help students better understand deductive and inductive arguments, give them an argument of each type to look at in small groups. Ask them to determine the benefits and drawbacks of each type of argument. Is one type better for certain types of arguments? How so?

2. Students may need practice demonstrating how a conclusion follows from a premise. Divide students into small groups. Ask each group to make a list of facts and illustrations that lead to a conclusion. Have groups switch lists. Finally, have each group add signal words to effectively demonstrate how the conclusion follows from the items in the list.

3. Another exercise to help students use signals to demonstrate how a conclusion follows from a premise is to have students read a scholarly argument. Ask them to highlight the ways in which the author has signaled the link between premises and conclusion.

As a further analytical tool, we present a list and discussions of **logical fallacies** (p. 218). Identifying logical fallacies is an exercise that students enjoy, but beware of letting them turn it into a "gotcha!" game, in which they assume a fallacy automatically invalidates an entire argument. Help them see that most arguments are complex chains of reasoning and appeals and that they have to weigh all the evidence and appeals to take fair measure of the effectiveness of an argument. Here are some exercises for teaching logical fallacies:

Activities

1. Students often enjoy learning about common fallacies and identifying them in ads and political speeches. You could share video clips of commercials or political speeches that you bring in from home. Or you could simply use the Internet if you have access to technology in your classroom and search YouTube. Students can work in groups and then present their analyses to the class.

2. You can also ask students how they might construct the arguments they observe to make them more persuasive — that is, to avoid the fallacies they identify.

We include a scholarly article, **Meredith Minkler's "Community-Based Research Partnerships: Challenges and Opportunities,"** for two reasons: (1) to expose students to the kind of academic writing they are likely to read and analyze in their college classes, and (2) to give them practice identifying the ways a given writer will make appeals to *ethos*, *pathos*, and *logos* in developing an argument. The **Practice Sequence** on page 236 asks students to note her premises and how she deploys the appeals to support them. Minkler's focus on community-based participatory research is very similar to Nancy Paul's argument about addressing local problems with solutions that draw upon local resources — not just funding, but people.

Minkler introduces the concept of community-based participatory research (CBPR) as a means of confronting urban health problems. It's likely that students will be unfamiliar with the notion of CBPR, so it will be important to make sure that they understand what Minkler means by this approach.

Minkler's focus on community and local resources contributes to building her *ethos* as a writer — someone who is motivated by doing the right thing. In this case, she conveys her concern for the health of the local community, demonstrating that she understands the need to work with the community to define and solve problems. She is less sympathetic to traditional approaches to solving problems with outside experts who come into a community and then leave community members to fend for themselves. Indeed, part of the *ethos* that Minkler projects is a just person who cares about people.

That Minkler is a just person is evident in her concern for ethics and what it means to fulfill the requirements of doing good work that is also just. For example, she recognizes that community members who participate in studies can be exploited or ostracized by their own communities. In addition, outside researchers are often rewarded differently for their research than community participants: they receive rewards in the form of publications, grants, and the like. Meanwhile, community participants may work for little or no pay and compensation might not come for months.

To solve the problem, Minkler describes ethical guidelines that have been developed by researchers and community partners in several countries to address these problems. These guidelines prescribe getting input from political and spiritual leaders in the community, ensuring equitable benefits to participants, and developing agreements on ownership and publication of findings.

Minkler details the benefits that come from intensive cooperation with communities at all stages of research. First, in posing the research topic or question, it is essential to ensure that the issue is one of real concern to the community. Normally, an outside researcher will initiate a CBPR project without consideration of the issue's relevance or importance to a local community.

Minkler argues that CBPR can provide guidelines for research that address such questions as the sensitivity and appropriateness of the methods employed, the training opportunities offered by the research, and the balance between scientific rigor and accessibility. Preliminary research, such as surveys or community advisory boards (CABs), can improve measurement instruments by carefully considering the wording of research questions and modifying them to be culturally sensitive.

CBPR's attention to lay knowledge is also important, since community-based research can uncover hidden contributors to health and social problems — breaches of ethics that Minkler wants to correct. In addition, CBPR can lead to higher recruitment of participants and community involvement in the analysis of data received. Such involvement leads to greater understanding and more informative, helpful interpretations of data, with richer themes.

However, it is important to show students that CBPR is not without challenges, and Minkler is more than aware of CBPR's limitations. Identifying issues remains an issue because outsiders frequently cannot define accurately what health issues are important to a community. Minkler points out that a community is often divided over an issue, which might require a reassessment of who "the community" actually is. Acknowledging this as a problem adds to her *ethical* stance (i.e., ethos) as someone who is able to examine an issue from multiple perspectives. Thus she avoids accepting her own position uncritically and appeals to her audience's sense of skepticism about whether CBPR is a sound approach to solving healthcare problems in local communities.

In her essay, Minkler appeals to pathos by explaining to her audience the value of community, cooperation, and mutual understanding. She appeals to their good sense and values as human beings interested in the health of others. Minkler also wants to ensure that her audience, made up of healthcare workers and scientists, understands that CBPR does not compromise the integrity they seek. CBPR does not recommend that researchers alter their scientific standards, but at the same time it does require that all stakeholders in a community contribute to the process of research. Still, she seems to concede to her audience that there is a lack of agreement between researchers and community members regarding what is "good science." Such a concession is very much a part of an appeal to pathos as a given audience recognizes the extent to which the author has thought through the issue.

Minkler's use of logos manifests itself in (1) the research she has done, (2) the evidence she provides, and (3) the reasoning she uses to establish the value of CBPR. Based on prior research, she demonstrates that outsider-based research frequently employs intervention strategies that are not suited to the local community. Through CBPR, community members can help make decisions regarding information dissemination, often a complex issue because of the emotions and customs surrounding health issues.

We follow our analysis of ethos, pathos, and logos with a set of strategies that can enable students to apply what they learned about different rhetorical appeals to visual texts. In **"Analyzing Visual Rhetoric: Advertisements"** (p. 236), our analysis of an ad focusing on hunger in America takes students through different steps for making sense of images and written texts. These steps include paying attention to the images or text that first capture their attention as readers, the ways that image and text work together, and how to use deductive reasoning to reach a reasoned conclusion about what the ad tells us. These steps focus on logos and the methods of argument that the designer of a given ad uses to appeal to readers.

In this particular case, the most prevalent image in the ad focuses on children playing carefree on a typical summer's day. So what is going on here and why is this image juxtaposed to an image of an alarm bell, which might normally be associated with school hours or sounding a warning? What cues do the written text provide that would enable us to identify the argument the designer of the ad is making?

As part of this analysis, we ask students to consider who the sponsor of the ad is as a way to understand the motives behind the ad. We ask students to do a little research to find out about the sponsor and the extent to which the sponsor is credible. What is the Ad Council and what does this corporation stand for? What sense of ethos does it project? What about Feed America, the other sponsor of this ad on hunger in America?

Finally, we explain to students that they should identify where an ad appears as a way to understand audience. It makes a difference where an ad appears since the designer of an ad will make decisions based on who the intended audience is. Does the ad appear in *Time Magazine*, on a billboard near a highway, on the side of a bus, or at a bus stop? Where an ad appears will influence the way a designer appeals to an audience's beliefs, values, and emotions—what we have referred to as *pathos*.

The **Practice Sequence** (p. 241) asks students to use what they've learned about visual analysis on a Microsoft ad, "You Have Your Best Ideas in the Shower," that we found in a December 2009 issue of *Time* magazine. We include guiding questions for reading the Microsoft ad, but let students loose to apply the strategies of analyzing the rhetoric of image and text on several public service ads at the end of the chapter. As we have suggested throughout this book, you might ask students to work in small groups as a first step in asking students to apply a new set of ideas and strategies:

Group One: Students would focus on the ethos that the ad projects through image, text, and sponsor of the ad. What ethos does the ad project? Does the ad convey a sense of what is just and reasonable?

Group Two: Students would focus on pathos and the strategies that the designer of the ad uses to both infer the audience of the ad and the strategies the designer uses to reach that audience. Who is the audience? How do we know? What can we say about the beliefs and values they hold?

Group Three: Students would focus on logos, the strategies of argument the designer uses to inform an audience, influence what that audience thinks, and perhaps move the audience to action. What is the premise of the ad? How does the design of the ad move from premise to conclusion? To what extent is there a logical progression in moving from premise to conclusion?

After students work in groups, you can ask students to share what they found in a broader discussion involving the whole class.

Next, students can apply what they have learned by analyzing one or more of the ads we include at the end of this chapter. Alternatively, you might ask that students find their own ad to analyze and share with the class.

9

From Introductions to Conclusions

Drafting an Essay

In this chapter, we discuss the major parts of an essay—introduction, paragraphs, and conclusion. The introduction brings into focus the writer's perception of what is at issue, establishes what is at stake, and sets up the writer's point of view. Students will have to make choices about what strategies to use based on their purpose, argument, and audience. The paragraphs carry the burden of an academic argument. Therefore, it is very important that paragraphs be clear and develop purposefully to advance the writer's argument. In a conclusion, writers make their final appeal to readers, reestablishing the importance of the issue and drawing out the implications of their arguments.

Our discussion of **drafting introductions** (p. 247) begins with the familiar strategy of the **inverted triangle.** The student whose essay we excerpt (p. 248) begins with a general set of assumptions about the purpose of education. She then narrows her focus by citing an author who criticizes these assumptions, calling them the "banking system." Next, the writer suggests that the "banking system" is a source of the problem; this step sets up the student's thesis that education's true purpose is to prepare students for the real world by giving them pertinent life knowledge. This is a variation on the correcting-misinterpretations model we present in Chapter 5 and is both direct and fairly conventional in academic writing.

Another familiar strategy is the **narrative introduction** (p. 249), which offers a less direct approach than an inverted triangle. In this sample introduction, the student sets up her thesis by telling a story about her first day at women's boxing practice at her university. Her narrative draws the reader into the world of women's boxing, as it describes such details as the sweat dripping from the athletes' faces. Using the narrative as backdrop, the writer moves on to identify a problem—the stereotypes female boxers face—by using a transition to mark her shift. Finally, the student states her thesis that despite stereotyping, women's boxing offers significant growth opportunities for its participants.

The introduction from an essay by Daphne Spain (p. 250) illustrates the potential value of beginning an essay with a question—the **interrogative introduction** (p. 250). Spain asks, "[T]o what extent do women and men who work in different occupations also work in different spaces?" Next she provides a tentative answer, which comes from previous scholars. (It is not sufficient to simply raise the question.) Spain then states her thesis: Men and women have very little contact in the workplace. She ends by describing the effects of this separation, further giving the reader a stake in the issue. Similarly, in her introduction Elizabeth Teare (p. 251) asks a question that she tries to answer in her essay "Harry Potter and the Technology of Magic": What is it that makes Harry Potter so interesting not only to children, parents, and teachers but also to literary, social, and cultural critics? In this introduction, she describes the situation, formulates her question, and then states her thesis—a partial response to her question.

The introduction from Shari L. Dworkin (p. 252) is an example of a **paradoxical introduction** (p. 251). Dworkin begins by identifying a situation derived from the current research in gender studies that she will challenge. Next, she sets up her own position, marking it with the signal word *however*. Finally, she states her thesis by noting a paradox—when we "see" naturally sexed bodies, we are really seeing the effect of internalizing gender ideologies that affect our idea of sexed bodies. In this way, Dworkin illustrates what we identified in Chapter 5 as the modifying-what-others-have-said model.

One more strategy for writing an introduction is **"minding the gap"** (p. 252). To illustrate this approach, we include an excerpt from Michael S. Kimmel and Michael A. Messner's book *Men's Lives*. In this brief excerpt, the authors signal that their book fills a gap in the research, claiming it is "unlike other books about men." Then they state the gap: Men are rarely understood through the lens of gender.

The **Practice Sequence** (p. 253) asks students to use one of the strategies we describe to revise an introduction they may have already drafted and to discuss the results with a classmate. The second exercise provides an excerpt on Barbie that students can use in lieu of their own writing. Other exercises you might consider include the following:

1. Give students a short essay to read in small groups. Ask them to identify the type of introduction used. Why do students think the author chose this type of introduction? What effect does this introduction have on them as readers? As writers, would students choose this approach? As a class, consider under what circumstances each type of introduction would work best. Why?

2. Writing instructors often tell students to write the body of their essays before constructing the introduction. You can play on this advice by giving students an essay without the introduction. In small groups, ask students to compose their own introduction and explain why they think it will strengthen the essay. Give students the writer's actual introduction to compare to the one they wrote.

We begin **"Developing Paragraphs"** (p. 254) with **Elizabeth Martínez's "Reinventing 'America': Call for a New National Identity"** (p. 255) to illustrate how topic sentences, guiding transitions, and examples contribute to readers' understanding of a text and give readers a sense of coherence. Martínez begins with a narrative introduction about the Dick and Jane book series, which she says appeals to white Americans' nostalgia for a time when *American* was easy to define, before there was widespread anxiety about a loss of national identity. The author puts national identity into a historical perspective by largely blaming our nation's origin myth and frontier myth for the current crisis. For Martínez, the myth defines America in positive terms, ignoring the genocide, enslavement, imperialist expansion, racism, and militarism that made this country what it is today. By reforming these myths to better match the truth of our history, the author suggests, America could begin to ignore differences of color and embrace similarities in experience and history.

We analyze the Martínez selection in terms of its topic sentences, its use of transitions to create unity, and its strategies of development ("critical strategies"). The critical strategies should be familiar ones to instructors (narration, exemplification, comparison, definition, and so forth), but we make the point that these strategies seldom work in isolation and often combine and overlap even within the short space of a single paragraph, much less an entire paper.

The **Practice Sequence** on page 266 asks students to cut up their own essays and pair up with partners who have to try to reassemble the paragraphs in the original order. This can be a fun exercise, although it's best not to have students work with essays that are especially lengthy and have many paragraphs, as the amount of paper being shuffled back and forth can get confusing. Here are some other exercises for working with paragraphs:

1. Students may have difficulty understanding how one sentence, the topic sentence, can serve so many functions. Show the class examples of good topic sentences that serve many functions. Ask students to separate into small groups to discuss how these sentences achieve so much.

2. To give students further practice, ask them to identify and analyze topic sentences in the sources they have found for their own essays. To what extent do these topic sentences provide a partial answer to the question motivating the writer? Extend the writer's thesis? Serve as signposts telling readers what the paragraph is about? Help create unity and coherence within the paragraph and the essay? Is each topic sentence effective? Would students revise any of the topic sentences? If so, how?

3. Students often have difficulty using transitions well. Ask them to use the lists on page 261 of this chapter as a guide to adding transition words to any of their previous papers in which they may have ignored transitions or used them improperly.

Our discussion of **drafting conclusions** begins on page 266. Our students commonly think of the conclusion as the point at which they restate what their essay is about. Therefore, it is useful to explain the ways that conclusions can serve other kinds of purposes, especially in writing that seeks to have an impact on readers' thinking and actions.

In this first example on **echoing the introduction** (p. 267), we provide an introduction and a conclusion from a student who writes about Western misconceptions about wearing a veil. Doing so illustrates how a conclusion can echo the introduction. Specifically, the author of this introduction begins with the phrase "a voice from behind the shrouds of an Islamic veil"; in her conclusion, she echoes this phrase with a quotation from the Koran that says, "Speak to them from behind a curtain." Such an approach creates a sense of unity and will likely force readers to reread the introduction.

To illustrate a conclusion that **challenges the reader** (p. 268) we provide a conclusion from a student essay on AIDS in women. The author challenges women to be more well-informed about AIDS and its specific effects on women and urges health educators to fulfill their responsibility of educating young women. Thus, she concludes by asking readers to act on their convictions.

As an example of a conclusion that urges readers to **look to the future** (p. 269), we also provide a conclusion from a student essay on parental involvement in schools. The writer advocates that teachers must acknowledge and answer the concerns and questions of all parents in order to improve urban parent-school relationships.

The excerpt on immigrants' rights illustrates how a conclusion can **pose questions** (p. 270). Most notably, the student uses questions to link her discussion of whether or not immigrants should have access to economic and educational resources to the possible racism and hate crimes that may arise from the distribution of these resources to immigrants.

The final excerpt in this section exemplifies **concluding with a quotation** (p. 270). This conclusion, from an essay on the meaning of Barbie, begins with a question that the author has been asking: "[W]hat does Barbie mean?" To amplify her point, she ends with a provocative quotation from a published author that indicates that we, as consumers of culture, determine what Barbie means.

Having asked students to look at models of five types of conclusions, we step back to put those models in the larger rhetorical context in the "Steps to Drafting Conclusions" box on page 271. Whatever model they might prefer to work with, they still need to pull together the main claims of their essay without simply summarizing; answer the question "So what?"; place their arguments in a larger context; and show readers what is new. The second part of the **Practice Sequence** (p. 272) asks students to look at each of the model conclusions to see how well they appear to meet those four criteria. Here are two additional activities for working with conclusions:

Activities

1. The exercises we suggested in the drafting introductions section above can all be altered to work with conclusions as well. Why do students think the author chose this type of conclusion? What effect does this conclusion have on them as readers? As writers, would students choose this approach?

2. Give students an essay without the conclusion. In small groups, ask students to compose their own conclusion and explain why they think it will strengthen the essay. Give students the writer's actual conclusion to compare to the one they wrote.

10

From Revising to Editing

Working with Peer Groups

In this chapter, we suggest some ways that readers can support students' writing at different stages. Peer readers can help student writers clarify what their questions are, refine the problems they are addressing, and prompt them to offer more evidence to support their arguments. Furthermore, the individual knowledge, experience, and interests that readers have can positively influence the conversations that have been joined by writers.

Educators in composition studies have long advocated the use of collaborative writing, making at least four assumptions about the role it can play in learning to write: (1) Students who write together understand that the purpose of writing is rhetorical, even though such understanding may not be "conscious." A rhetorical perspective on literacy research and practice calls attention to the ways in which language use crystallizes relations between readers and writers. (2) Discourse provides the catalyst and support for learning by engendering conflict and reciprocity. (3) Conversation is the result of a natural experience of cooperative, collaborative interaction through which people enact the essence of compromise. (4) Students may be able to perform tasks together that would be too difficult to accomplish individually. (For a review of research, see Stuart Greene and Erin Smith's "Teaching Talk About Writing: Student Conflict in Acquiring a New Discourse of Authorship Through Collaborative Planning," which appeared in Katherine L. Weese, Stephen L. Fox, and Stuart Greene's *Teaching Academic Literacy: The Uses of Teacher-Research in Developing a Writing Program* [Lawrence Erlbaum, 1999], 149–74. The strategies discussed in Chapter 10 are based on Greene and Smith's study.)

Understanding students' identities and cultural backgrounds is crucial to supporting students in ways that will foster success in school writing. This is especially true when we attempt to map the practices that work in one cultural context onto another when it is possible that a particular approach potentially conflicts with the values and sensibilities students bring to the classroom.

Studies show that inexperienced writers may actually abandon their own intentions or plans when challenged by their peers, that they often focus on topic knowledge rather than on rhetorical concerns in writing, and that students may settle for less demanding tasks by writing reports rather than the argumentative papers they set out to compose.

Thus, it is one thing to create conditions for learning new discourses by providing a supportive social context in which students write and share their writing. However, studies of collaborative writing reveal that it is quite another thing for students to enact the sort of strategies that will enable them to write in a mindful, principled way.

As we discuss throughout this guide, students need to be metacognitively aware. This means that they need to understand the kinds of discourse strategies that are appropriate in writing and the ways to use a repertoire of strategies for composing. This might entail employing different types of evidence, using a particular genre, and evaluating the appropriateness of students' choices in assessing how readers might respond—especially when they are not writing to readers they know.

In **"Revising Versus Editing"** (p. 273) we explain the differences between revising, or rethinking a paper, and editing, or changing and correcting word choice, misspellings, and punctuation. Students should understand that writing is a work in progress that requires them to make thoughtful changes that will increase the effectiveness of their writing. Such a view can be quite liberating as students realize that they are not expected to come up with a thesis at the very outset or write a perfect first draft. These are lessons that we hope students learned as they identified issues, developed questions, and formulated a working thesis in earlier chapters.

This is not to diminish the value of editing. Instead, by emphasizing revision, we want students to commit themselves to learning as much about a subject as they can and be willing to let their writing evolve to reflect that learning. Our approach to writing means giving students plenty of time to work on fewer papers during a semester than students in many writing classes produce. We typically ask students to write three papers for their portfolios. In addition to giving them time, we ensure that students receive plenty of response from us and their peers as they write multiple drafts.

Ultimately, students need to learn how to edit their writing to ensure that it is grammatically correct. Still, it is not worthwhile to edit writing while students are still trying to decide what they are trying to say. To help students decide what to focus on at different stages of revising, we introduce the idea of a composition pyramid. In fact, we ask students to keep the composition pyramid in front of them as they work together in groups.

Apropos of our discussion of the **peer editing process** (p. 274): As we have said, one of the challenges in having students work in writing groups is to keep them focused on the rhetorical dimension of writing, not just on the content. That is, we want students to help each other develop the key points of their essays, to provide evidence to support a claim, to make connections among different and conflicting ideas, to anticipate possible counterarguments, and to draw implications from what they find to be true.

To help students understand what they should address and the roles they can play in their group, we provide a model of what effective group talk looks like. One option that we have used to model effective peer-group talk is to show students a videotape of students working together from a previous semester. In turn, we explain the importance of helping each develop their key points and the like. A second option is to ask peer tutors from the writing center to model what they do when they assist students.

Students will need time to internalize the questions and language for talking about writing that we want them to use in helping one another. This time will be especially important as they learn to trust one another. Our students are often reluctant to criticize each other during the first few weeks of a semester. And yet they need to learn to be critical, constructive readers if they are to support one another's efforts as writers.

We present a sample peer-editing interlude under the rubric of **"Peer Groups in Action: A Sample Session"** (p. 276). To illustrate the ways students can work with one another on a draft, we include an early draft of a student's paper, **"Representing Poverty in *Million Dollar Baby"*** (p. 277). The student writer, Brett, discusses the representations of poverty in the film *Million Dollar Baby*. However, even Brett is aware that he has not decided what his paper is really about. Throughout the peer-revising sessions, Brett's peers help him generate a plan to ensure that he clearly states his position and better organizes his thoughts. Given what we suggest above, it's important to emphasize the extent to which Brett's peers keep pressing him to explain his key point and to make connections among different ideas. The annotations on the draft indicate specific comments by Brett's peers.

In the sections **"Working with Early Drafts"** (p. 279), **"Working with Later Drafts"** (p. 283), and **"Working with Final Drafts"** (p. 288), we follow one student as she revises her essay from early stages to final draft, showing the value of revision. **Tasha Taylor's "Memory Through Photography"** (p. 289) responds to an assignment that asks students to write a researched argument in considering the ways memorials can help people remember certain events but also can forget some things. In her essay, Tasha considers a number of images that represent what readers might remember about the civil rights movement, but she is concerned with the issue that public memory tends to ignore significant events and people who contributed to the fight for integration. She seems to write as much for her peers as published writers, who, Tasha argues, limit our vision of the civil rights movement.

What appears to work well in her first draft is that Taylor defines an issue. Specifically, she provides familiar examples of people and events that many of her readers will know, but she also introduces some lesser known people and events who are not a part of our collective memory. In doing so, she raises a provocative question that might very well get us all thinking about why it is we remember the things we do and why we remember larger-than-life figures like Martin Luther King; however, she has not linked her thoughts to those of any other authors, and her ideas are still broad. In her second draft, she will need to synthesize others' ideas, point out what she sees as a gap, and state her claim.

In her second draft, Taylor's introduction is much more pointed in its focus on memory and its challenge to readers: Why is it that we forget? In the first draft, she simply observes that we do forget, but now she wants readers to consider memory and identity. Does forgetting have something to do with how we want to be remembered? To place this issue in a broader context, she incorporates quotations from other authors, she provides a thorough analysis and critique of one specific example to illustrate her point, and she states her claim: "The discrepancies in cultural memory are due more to a society's desire to remember itself in the best light and protect itself from the reality of its brutality and responsibility." Finally, in stating her claim, she acknowledges a gap: that scholars have called attention to how memory works, but they have not prevented the dissemination of distorted information about the civil rights movement. She ultimately argues that elevating larger-than-life figures like Martin Luther King Jr. is important; however, she points to an unintended consequence: History has ignored the contributions of ordinary citizens in the struggle for civil rights. To make her next draft even stronger, she should connect her claim about memory in the beginning to her claim about the role that ordinary people play in history. She will also need to cite sources appropriately.

In her near-final draft, Taylor introduces the additional example of Spike Lee's film, *Four Little Girls*, to demonstrate the kind of reality that we need to be aware of, but she points out that even Lee's efforts fall short. She has made sure to properly cite her sources both within the text and with a works cited page. In the end, however, one might argue that the writer could do a better job of connecting the different parts of her essay in advancing a coherent claim.

We close with some **further suggestions for peer editing groups** (p. 294). Although students probably recognize the difference between revising and editing, they may feel uncomfortable revising other students' papers for fear of offending them. Therefore, they may very well revert to editing because it is more "objective." We also find that students use their previous teachers' approaches to commenting on their papers, approaches that tend to emphasize the etiquette and "correctness" of writing. As a consequence, their teachers' comments have typically amounted to editing.

Because peer editing is an important part of the writing process for students, we encourage you to find ways to make them comfortable and effective revisers. We offer some additional suggestions below.

Activities

1. Have students work in small groups or with partners to revise papers and do not change the groups. As students continue to work with the same student(s), they will feel more comfortable making suggestions.

2. Have students revise each other's papers anonymously. Use a coding system to identify papers.

3. Make sure students know that it is okay not to mention everything they would change about the paper. Highlighting too many problems may overwhelm the writer.

4. Moreover, have students offer both positive comments (what the writer did well) and constructive criticism (what the writer should work on). Following these steps will make both writer and reader feel more comfortable.

11

Other Methods of Inquiry

Interviews and Focus Groups

In this chapter, we describe some of the functions and challenges of doing original research. Original research uses primary sources of evidence writers gather themselves, as Myra and David Sadker did in "Hidden Lessons" (reprinted in Chapter 3). We also explain why writers might conduct original research: to increase their ability to read critically, to increase their own research skills, to broaden their scope of inquiry, and to make a contribution to a conversation of ideas.

In the rest of the chapter, we turn to the process of conducting original research. Four concerns should inform and guide students' research projects: the importance of asking good questions; the role of background, experience, and interpretation in formulating an argument; the value of using multiple sources of information; and the importance of representing other people's words faithfully. This latter point touches on the ethics of research.

As Cameron McCarthy and Warren Crichlow point out, the way we construct our research agendas, carry out these projects, and disseminate the results "directly raise questions about who has the power to define whom, and when, and how" (C. McCarthy and W. Crichlow, *Race Identity and Representation in Education* [London: Routledge, 1993], xvi). Thus, it is important to raise the following questions with students: How are you representing those you study? What is missing? How do you decide what is significant? How will you decide how to describe what is significant?

For related discussion of representation and the necessity of acquiring informed consent from participants in a study, see B. Moss and K. Walters, "Rethinking Diversity: Axes of Difference in the Writing Classroom" (in *Theory and Practice in the Teaching of Writing: Rethinking the Discipline*, ed. Lee Odell [Carbondale: Southern Illinois University Press, 1993], 132–85). See also L. Weis, M. Fine, S. Weseen, and M. Wong's "Qualitative Research, Representations, and Social Responsibilities" (in *Speed Bumps: A Student-Friendly Guide to Qualitative Research*, L. Weis and M. Fine, eds. [New York: Teachers College Press, 2000], 32–66).

To keep within the guidelines for doing research at your university and to maintain ethical standards, you should consult the office of research regarding the use of human subjects. Most universities disseminate the following information to faculty, staff, and students:

All research involving human subjects whether conducted by faculty, staff, or students must be reviewed and approved by the human subjects institutional review board (HSIRB) before human subjects can be involved. Neither the source of funds nor lack of funding for such research has any bearing on this requirement.

The HSIRB on your campus can provide the protocol for writing a proposal in order to receive consent to do a study. The proposal usually includes the following:

1. Purpose of Study: Brief statement (hypothesis)
2. Background
3. Sources of Funding
4. Type and Number of Subjects
5. Location of Study
6. Duration of Study
7. Total Amount of Time Involved for Each Subject
8. Study Methodology
9. Possible Risks
10. Possible Benefits
11. Special Precautions
12. Procedures to Maintain Confidentiality

Perhaps the most important part of the process of original research entails writing a proposal, which we discuss in **"Getting Started: Writing a Proposal"** (p. 297). The proposal is a tool that will help guide students through the various stages of their projects. It has several parts, which can be altered to meet students' needs: the major ones are a description of the purpose, a definition of the method, and a discussion of the implications of the research. But a timeline is also something you should encourage students to include (and be sure that they adhere to it!). It may also be useful for students to include in their proposal any forms or scripts that will be used in the research. In this section, we set out steps for writing a proposal and include a student example by **Mary Ronan, "A Case Study of One Homeless Child's Education and Lifestyle"** (p. 303), including an excerpt from her annotated bibliography (as a model) and some sample forms that students might adapt for their own research. We round out the chapter with sections on **interviewing** (pp. 307–11) and **using focus groups** (pp. 311–16).

For most students, conducting original research will be a completely new experience. Students may feel overwhelmed and nervous at first, but eventually they find the experience immensely valuable. Therefore, as their instructor, you can help students through the new and somewhat intimidating process of conducting research. Below we offer some exercises to help students develop the new skills of conducting original research and also to gain confidence as researchers.

Activities

1. The first step in conducting research is to decide the method that will best enable students to answer their research question. As a class, you can

describe different issues/situations that would work well with each type of research described in the chapter. Why would those methods work well? Also, ask students what other original research methods they might want to try, such as surveys. For what kinds of research would these methods be effective? Why?

2. Once students have decided on issues and have begun reading secondary sources, divide them into small groups. Have students work together to consider the benefits and drawbacks of different types of original research for each of their issues. What type is best, and why?

3. A very important step in conducting original research is finding participants for interviews and focus groups. If you are able, set up a community resource list that contains contact information for organizations willing to participate in research.

4. Successful interviews and focus groups require that students ask good questions that guide the participant(s) in the right direction. Have students draft scripts and practice their questions on other students. Are the questions clear? Can the other students suggest more or different questions? Students may also want to practice their scripts on people outside the class because their classmates are likely to know something about their issue, which will skew their interpretation of the questions.

5. It can sometimes be difficult for students to turn their research into viable elements of an argument. Give students examples of previous authors who have used similar research. In small groups, ask students to discuss the effectiveness of this author's synthesis of research into his or her essay. What tips can they take away?

6. If you are able, set up a sample interview or focus group that students can watch and take notes on. After the sample, ask the class to make observations about what worked well and what did not. How will they use this information when conducting their own interviews and focus groups? Not only will this exercise improve students' skills, it will also relieve their anxiety as they see how informal and simple focus groups can be.

7. Foster partnerships with organizations with which students can conduct their research. Encourage students to share their findings with these organizations. Students may not believe it, but their research, even at the undergraduate level, can have a positive impact on the community. Working toward such a goal can have an energizing and empowering effect on students as they conduct their research.